T0280816

Pro Azure Governance and Security

A Comprehensive Guide to Azure Policy, Blueprints, Security Center, and Sentinel

Peter De Tender
David Rendon
Samuel Erskine

Apress®

Pro Azure Governance and Security: A Comprehensive Guide to Azure Policy, Blueprints, Security Center, and Sentinel

Peter De Tender
Daknam, Belgium

David Rendon
Ags, Mexico

Samuel Erskine
Rushdon, Northamptonshire, UK

ISBN-13 (pbk): 978-1-4842-4909-3
ISBN-13 (electronic): 978-1-4842-4910-9
https://doi.org/10.1007/978-1-4842-4910-9

Managing Director, Apress Media LLC: Welmoed Spahr
Acquisitions Editor: Joan Murray
Development Editor: Laura Berendson
Coordinating Editor: Jill Balzano

Cover designed by eStudioCalamar

Cover image designed by Freepik (www.freepik.com)

Distributed to the book trade worldwide by Springer Science+Business Media New York, 233 Spring Street, 6th Floor, New York, NY 10013. Phone 1-800-SPRINGER, fax (201) 348-4505, e-mail orders-ny@springer-sbm.com, or visit www.springeronline.com. Apress Media, LLC is a California LLC and the sole member (owner) is Springer Science + Business Media Finance Inc (SSBM Finance Inc). SSBM Finance Inc is a **Delaware** corporation.

For information on translations, please e-mail rights@apress.com, or visit http://www.apress.com/rights-permissions.

Apress titles may be purchased in bulk for academic, corporate, or promotional use. eBook versions and licenses are also available for most titles. For more information, reference our Print and eBook Bulk Sales web page at http://www.apress.com/bulk-sales.

Any source code or other supplementary material referenced by the author in this book is available to readers on GitHub via the book's product page, located at www.apress.com/9781484249093. For more detailed information, please visit http://www.apress.com/source-code.

Printed on acid-free paper

For the love of Azure

Table of Contents

About the Authors

Peter De Tender is the CEO and lead technical trainer at 007FFFLearning (`http://www.007FFFLearning.com`). He has more than 20 years of professional expertise in the Microsoft Infrastructure segment as a consultant, architect, and trainer. He has focused on Microsoft Azure cloud technologies for five years. Based out of Belgium, he travels 87.4% of the time for his true passion, which is providing readiness workshops on Azure. Peter appreciates teaching others in a fun and engaging way. He is a Microsoft Azure MVP, Microsoft Certified Trainer, technical writer, and regular speaker at international conferences on Azure topics. He is active on Twitter @pdtit and @007FFFLearning.

David Rendon is a Microsoft MVP with expertise in Azure. He specializes in enterprise data and applications management in cloud environments. He conducts private training classes globally (India, South America, and the United States) that help companies migrate critical applications to the cloud and train their staff to be certified cloud architects. He is passionate about travel, action-packed tech days with peers, and getting down into the trenches of technology road maps. He is active on Twitter @DaveRndn.

Samuel Erskine has over 20 years' experience in the IT industry and is currently a Cloud Solutions Architect (senior manager). He is focused on cloud technologies with a core competency in Microsoft Azure. He is "multilingual" in his approach, speaking both the language of the business and technology to facilitate the delivery of key organizational objectives. He is a Microsoft MVP, published author, speaker, and blogger at `www.itprocessed.com`. He is active on Twitter @samerskine.

About the Authors

About the Technical Reviewer

James Millar is an independent software developer based in Bristol in the United Kingdom. He has more than ten years of experience in the IT industry and has extensive experience with Azure, AWS, DevOps, release management, and mobile application projects. He has worked with companies such as Microsoft and Sun Microsystems and served clients based in the United States, the United Kingdom, and India.

Acknowledgements

Peter De Tender
This is my sixth book in six years, my third one on Azure, and it still amazes me how much I learn from the writing process; but more importantly, it emphasizes how much love I get from my wife and daughters for allowing me to spend most of my off-business hours on writing and doing what I love doing. I also like to thank my close friends Sam and Dave for jumping in and writing excellent chapters, really helping in upgrading the overall quality of the book. A huge thank you also goes to Jonathan Trull and Tara Larson, directors in Microsoft's Cyber Security team for stepping in when I asked. Lastly, a huge thanks to the Apress team for understanding that writing about a fast-moving and continuously changing topic like Azure leads to massive changes and a little frustration every now and then. But it is so rewarding when it is finished.

David Rendon
A huge thank you to my family for supporting me in all I do.

Samuel Erskine
A big thank you to my loved ones BB and Mimi for letting me borrow time from our weekends to contribute to this book.

Foreword

We have an internal saying, “Microsoft runs on trust.” This motto guides us internally to build solutions that delight our customers and provide the custom-tailored security they need to operate in today’s digital world. Each year we invest $1 billion in cybersecurity and we are dedicated to this commitment, with more than 3,500 professionals protecting, detecting, and responding to threats.

Microsoft Azure is an open, flexible, enterprise-grade cloud computing platform, with more than 100 infrastructure as a service and platform as a service offerings. We maintain 54 Azure regions across the globe, more than any other cloud provider, allowing our customers to leverage the cloud while still meeting their stringent data security, privacy, and sovereignty requirements. Azure also complies with more than 90 different industry and government compliance frameworks, making it easier for our regulated customers to leverage its services.

As a common target for attackers, Azure has been engineered from the ground up to ensure security and resiliency. As with any public cloud, there are shared responsibilities for security between the customer and Microsoft. For example, while Microsoft is solely responsible for the physical security of the data centers and supporting infrastructure that powers Azure, you as the customer retain responsibility for controlling access to data and user provisioning. That’s where the book you hold in your hands steps in. ***Pro Azure Governance and Security*** provides a comprehensive guide for customers to follow, in order to securely deploy and govern workloads within Azure.

The authors share their collective wisdom for operating Azure services at enterprise scale, starting with an explanation of the key governance building blocks of tenants, subscriptions, management groups, resources, and policies. One of the unique advantages of operating in the cloud is that everything is software-defined. This allows customers to create and leverage repeatable code to define and maintain their environments. Azure Policy, which the authors devote an entire chapter to, is a native Azure service that makes it easy for customers to govern their Azure resources, apply security controls at scale, and enforce and audit compliance against established policies and standards.

Azure also contains custom-built solutions that help customers achieve advanced levels of operational security. One of these solutions is Azure Security Center. ***Pro Azure Governance and Security*** intuitively guides you through the capabilities, configuration, and use of Azure Security Center. You will learn how to enlist Azure Security Center for security posture management and enhanced threat protection for cloud workloads. Not surprising, another one of Microsoft's goals is to simplify security for our customers wherever possible. Azure Security Center does this by providing a Secure Score for customers so that they can quickly and easily identify security weaknesses and mitigate them based on Microsoft recommendations and best practices.

Finally, the authors of ***Pro Azure Governance and Security*** wrap up the book, teaching you about our newest cybersecurity solution, Azure Sentinel, a cloud-native security incident and event management (SIEM) solution. It provides limitless scale and speed, and is built to detect threats with built-in machine learning from Microsoft's security analytics experts and researchers. Azure Sentinel was engineered to ease the operational burden on security analysts and includes advanced logic to fuse and collate events into incidents. Further, it offers playbooks to automate common and routine response activities.

If you are tasked with protecting Azure workloads, then ***Pro Azure Governance and Security*** is a must-read and a great reference for those studying to become a Microsoft Certified Azure Security Engineer (`https://www.microsoft.com/en-us/learning/azure-security-engineer.aspx`).

Microsoft is built on trust, and we are devoted to earning that trust by building and operating resilient and secure systems for our customers.

Jonathan C. Trull

Global Director, Cybersecurity Solutions
Cybersecurity Solutions Group
Chief Security Advisor

Microsoft

July 2019

As the Global Director for the Microsoft Cybersecurity Solutions Group, Jonathan leads Microsoft's team of worldwide security advisors and cloud security architects who provide strategic direction on the development of Microsoft security products and services and deliver deep customer and partner engagements around the globe. He serves as a member of Microsoft's Internal Risk Management Committee and is a principal author of the Microsoft Security Intelligence Report.

Jonathan joined Microsoft in 2016 as an experienced information security executive, bringing more than 17 years of public and private sector experience. He was Vice President and CISO with Optiv, where he was responsible for developing and executing the company's information security strategy and program. Prior to his role at Optiv, he was the Chief Information Security Officer (CISO) for Qualys where he was responsible for securing infrastructure and products, bringing security best practices to customers, providing strategic direction on the development of the QualysGuard Security Platform, achieving FedRAMP certification of the Qualys cloud platform, researching real-world threats, and providing guidance on how to address them.

Jonathan has established himself as an innovative security leader and was recently named by the SANS Institute as one of the "People Who Made a Difference in Cybersecurity." He serves as an advisor to several security startups and venture capital firms, participates in the Cloud Security Alliance Top Threats Working Group, and has spoken at major security events such as RSA, Black Hat, Gartner, CSO50, and SANS. He is also the principal author of the Center for Internet Security Azure Security Foundations Benchmark and several open source security tools. He is a Certified Cloud Security Professional (CCSP), Certified Information Systems Security Professional (CISSP), Certified Information Systems Auditor (CISA), and an Offensive Security Certified Professional (OSCP). He completed the Carnegie Mellon University CISO Executive Program and earned a master's degree from the University of North Texas and a bachelor's degree from Metropolitan State University of Denver.

Introduction

The idea for writing an Azure security-oriented book was on my mind for two years, but because of other projects, traveling a lot, and continuous changes in the Azure platform, I decided to put it on the shelf for a while. Until about a year ago, when it became clear that Microsoft was taking cloud security seriously. Seeing how impressive services like Azure Security Center and Azure Policy have become, it would be a shame to not expose that enthusiasm in another book project. But where was I to find time in my already crazy-busy business life, traveling the world, providing Azure workshops, flying on to the next location...?

When talking about the book idea with my close friends and fellow Azure experts, Sam and Dave, during that initial call in June, the enthusiasm was so amazing that we decided to go for it. Honestly, if we mapped the initial outline of topics with the result that you have here in front of you, about 70% would be changed. This includes scrapping chapters and writing new ones.

Azure is a moving target, especially the security services and features it offers. Every few weeks during the writing process, new updates came out, new features were introduced, portal layouts changed, which obviously was a challenge at times. But seeing the beauty and technical completeness of all of these tools, which really help optimize any Azure customer's security posture, put a big smile on our faces. And I'm pretty sure we are only seeing the beginning of the broader potential. In the last few weeks of writing, we were amazed by Azure Sentinel, a first attempt by Microsoft to offer a SIEM as a Service, so we decided to dedicate a chapter to it. And while in the early preview stage for now, it looks rather impressive. But enough of all that. Turn the pages, learn Azure, dive into the security features, and I'm sure this book will bring the same big smile to your face as it did to ours.

In the first chapter, we introduce you to the challenges and advantages an organization has by using public cloud services like Azure, mainly from a governance perspective.

In Chapter 2, we emphasize the importance of building out your Azure tenant and subscription(s) in the correct way, depending on organization structure, complexity, and technical and non-technical requirements.

In Chapter 3, we share our experiences from the field, together with best practices and guidance from the Microsoft Azure product group, on how to name your Azure resources. Although a resource name might look like just a name, there are certain guidelines to follow—especially if you want to be prepared for failure.

Chapter 4 brings you to the technical details of Azure Policy, a service that allows you to govern what can be deployed in Azure. Think of having an Azure administrative role, where you want to lock down the Azure region resources that can be deployed or define which Azure virtual machines sizes cannot be deployed—or pretty much anything else in your Azure environment that you want to streamline. The most technical instrument in Azure today allows you to define settings and validate if /how your active Azure environment is compliant.

In Chapter 5, we guide you through the capabilities and features of Azure Security Center, an end-to-end dashboard and reporting service, focused on all-things security in your Azure and hybrid platform. Starting with the overall options available in the (free) Basic tier, we also discuss the other services that you can use by switching to the (paid) Standard tier. We highlight the importance of Azure Security Center.

Running a security team and managing security in the Azure cloud environment would not be complete without describing the operations and monitoring aspects of the platform, which is exactly what we cover in Chapter 6. Starting with Azure Monitor as the new replacement for OMS, we dive into log analytics and walk you through several other built-in Azure monitoring tools and services.

In Chapter 7, we take it one step further by describing what it takes to enable and implement Azure security in a larger enterprise environment. Topics like automation and self-service are obviously present, but we also provide a helicopter view on how to manage multiple subscriptions by using management groups.

Lastly, in Chapter 8, we introduce you to the (preview) of Azure Sentinel, which is described as a SIEM as a Service. Relying on machine learning, taking information from your Azure subscription, and mixing with input from Microsoft Security Graph, it allows organizations to manage security incidents with a more proactive approach than the typical reactive one.

We hope that you enjoy reading this book and that it helps you learn and understand Azure security by going through the step-by-step instructions that we provide as a walkthrough in each chapter. And finally, we hope that the book helps you optimize your Azure security overall. Do not hesitate to reach out to us when you have questions, doubts, find any mistakes that we made, or if you want to share your enthusiasm.

Happy Azure-ing,

Peter, Dave, and Sam

CHAPTER 1

Introduction to Governance in the Cloud

The cloud, in the context of technology, has many definitions and types—ranging from its simplest form of using shared resources, to a fully automated environment with extreme standardization. What does this really mean in practice, and how is it relevant to your organization?

The answer is simple: technology exists to enable a business to deliver on its vision, mission, and goals. So, very much like using a tool to create an artifact, technology enables businesses of all sizes to generate value in order to deliver on why it exists. Governance maps to the standards of your organization, and typically, the rules of the industry of your business. The focus of this chapter is cloud governance, and specifically, using Microsoft Azure as your cloud technology platform.

This chapter introduces Microsoft Azure Governance components, and explains why it matters and how to go from planning to implementation.

It is important to distinguish between cloud provider (Microsoft) governance and consumer (your organization) governance when you leverage the cloud provider's platform.

Cloud Provider Governance

Cloud providers must adhere to strict controls and processes that not only conform to and exceed industry standards but also provide consumers with inherited governance. Microsoft, for example, ensures that cloud consumers can select locations that adhere to data privacy and sovereignty laws by having data centers all over the world.

P. De Tender et al., *Pro Azure Governance and Security*, https://doi.org/10.1007/978-1-4842-4910-9_1

The Microsoft Trust Center (`www.microsoft.com/en-us/trustcenter/cloudservices/Azure`) explains the important areas that organizations care about and inherit from the cloud provider.

- **Compliance**: Certification of standard compliance
- **Privacy**: Adherence to privacy laws
- **Transparency**: Visibility into your data on the cloud platform
- **Government regulations**: Cloud instances for government workloads
- **Industries regulations**: Alignment to industry-specific regulations

Cloud Consumer Governance

Cloud consumers inherit the provider governance and must apply their specific governance frameworks and organization policies to the environment. This is similar to moving into a serviced apartment block. The apartment block owner (provider) ensures the shared services that you consume are aligned to the right regulations and expectations, and the tenants ensure that their specific rules are applied to their own apartments. The following are some examples of consumer governance areas.

- **Departmental**: Cost centers, locations, and other organizational structural rules
- **Architectural governance**: Internal personalized architecture
- **Technology implementation rules**: Standards applied to technological artifacts
- **Role-based access controls**: Resource access, alignment to operational procedures, and auditing
- **Business continuity**: Recovery, resilience, and contingency
- **Security**: Antivirus and perimeter protection
- **Monitoring and IT auditing**: Log collection and intrusion detection

Figure 1-1 provides a pictorial representation of the two core layers of governance in the Microsoft Azure cloud environment and the cloud resources inheritance.

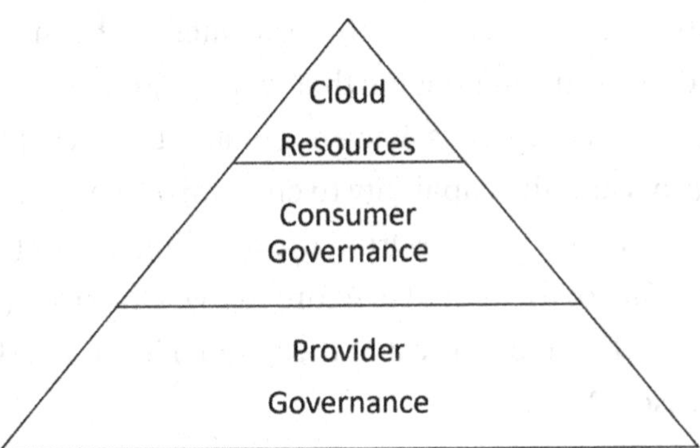

Figure 1-1. *A pictorial representation of the two core layers of governance in the Microsoft Azure cloud environment and the cloud resources inheritance*

Azure Governance Building Blocks

This section introduces the following Azure consumer governance building blocks, which are the relations and dependencies that you must plan for when implementing your public Azure cloud environment.

- Tenants
- Subscriptions
- Resource groups
- Resources
- Management groups
- Policies
- Initiatives
- Blueprints
- Role-based access control (RBAC)

Tenants

A tenant is the top tier of your Microsoft Azure environment. When you sign up for any Azure service for the first time, a tenant is created for you. Each tenant in Azure is unique and the representation of your organization (individual or enterprise). You can consider your organization as the tenant. A tenant is the equivalent of having your own office space in a shared building. You can imagine that your organization has rented space in an office block with other companies. Each company (tenant) has their own office space with access controls and the capability to customize the space as required. Each tenant is separate but consumes services from the building owner (provider), in this case Microsoft. The basic artifact of the tenant is Azure Active Directory (Azure AD), which is like creating your Active Directory forest in the cloud. Figure 1-2 shows the tenant representation in Microsoft Azure.

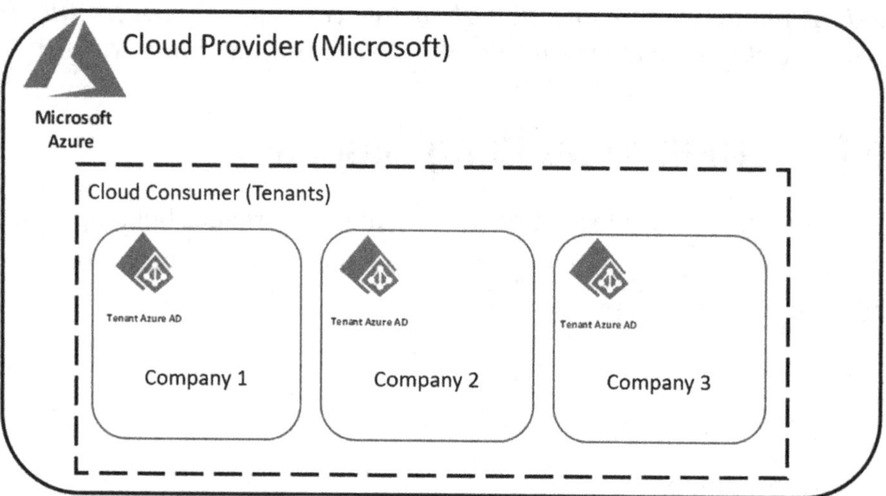

Figure 1-2. *Tenant representation in Microsoft Azure*

You do not need to sign up for an Azure service to get an Azure tenant, but you must have at least one Azure tenant before you can use a paid service, like Office 365. Additionally, a company can create multiple unique tenants.

Subscriptions

The creation and use of an Azure tenant is free and comes with some basic capabilities that are available to all registered Azure consumers. The ability to consume services is enabled through the use of subscriptions. An Azure subscription is required when you need to use the three core cloud service categories.

- **Infrastructure as a Service (IaaS)**: Building and running virtual machines, including traditional infrastructure components as a domain control or database server is an example of IaaS.
- **Platform as a Service (PaaS)**: Database as a Service is an example of PaaS.
- **Software as a Service (SaaS)**: Office 365 is an example of SaaS in Azure.

In essence, you need an Azure subscription to enable and use the SaaS, PaaS, and IaaS capabilities in Azure. A company can have one or more subscriptions linked to a single tenant, as shown in Figure 1-3.

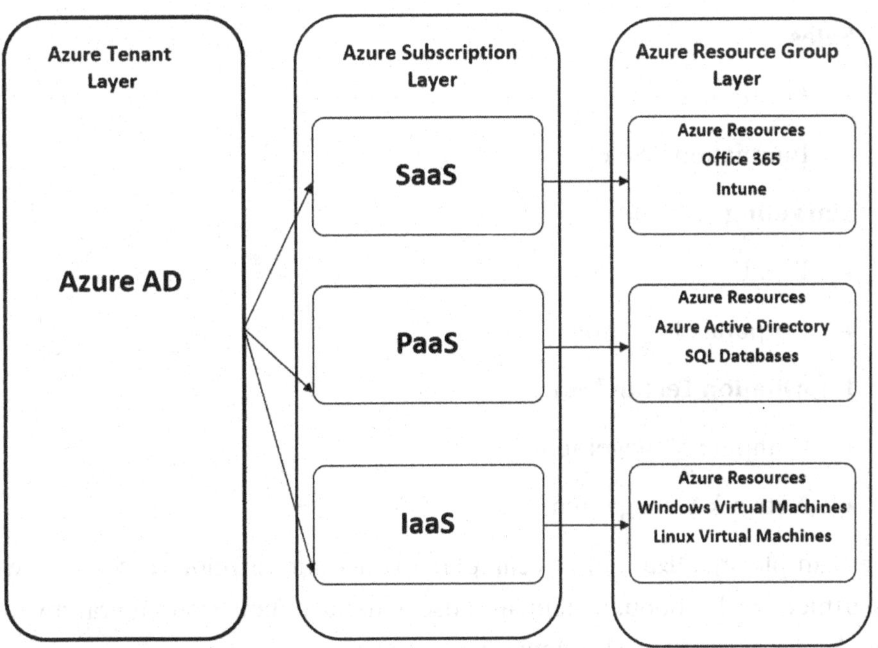

Figure 1-3. *Subscriptions and the relationship to the tenant in Azure*

Management Groups

Management groups are used to group multiple subscriptions linked to one Azure AD tenant. Management groups in Azure allow the organization to create a logical hierarchy for subscriptions. Each Azure AD tenant has a root management group. The root management group is the top level and cannot be deleted but can have the display name changed to reflect the organization (for example, change the name to the company name). You use management groups to group your subscriptions and their respective resources. Once created and organized, management groups are used to implement (scope) your governance policies and initiatives. Policies applied at the management group level are inherited by the assigned subscriptions to that management group and its children, resource groups, and resources.

You create management groups to represent your organization structure. The structure may be aligned to life cycle environments, departments, or some other logical representation. An example organization structure (such as the following) can create a management group hierarchy and subscription assigned appropriately.

Organization Name: NN4 Consultants Limited

Departments:

- **Sales**
  - Local Sales
  - International Sales
- **Marketing**
  - Events
  - Corporate Branding
- **Information Technology**
  - Compute Management
  - Network Management

In the example organization, you can plan to have subscriptions associated with each department and subdepartment, and use a management group hierarchy to assign your organization governance framework.

Figure 1-4 shows the management groups structure used for a logical organization structure.

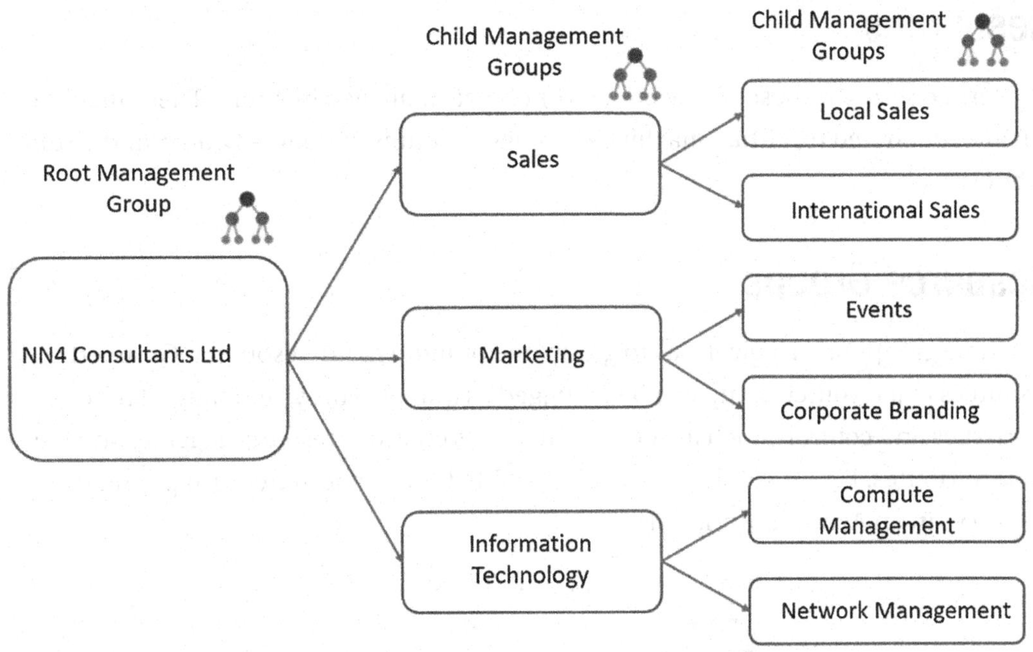

***Figure 1-4.** Example management group structure by departments*

Figure 1-5 shows how subscriptions can be assigned to child management groups.

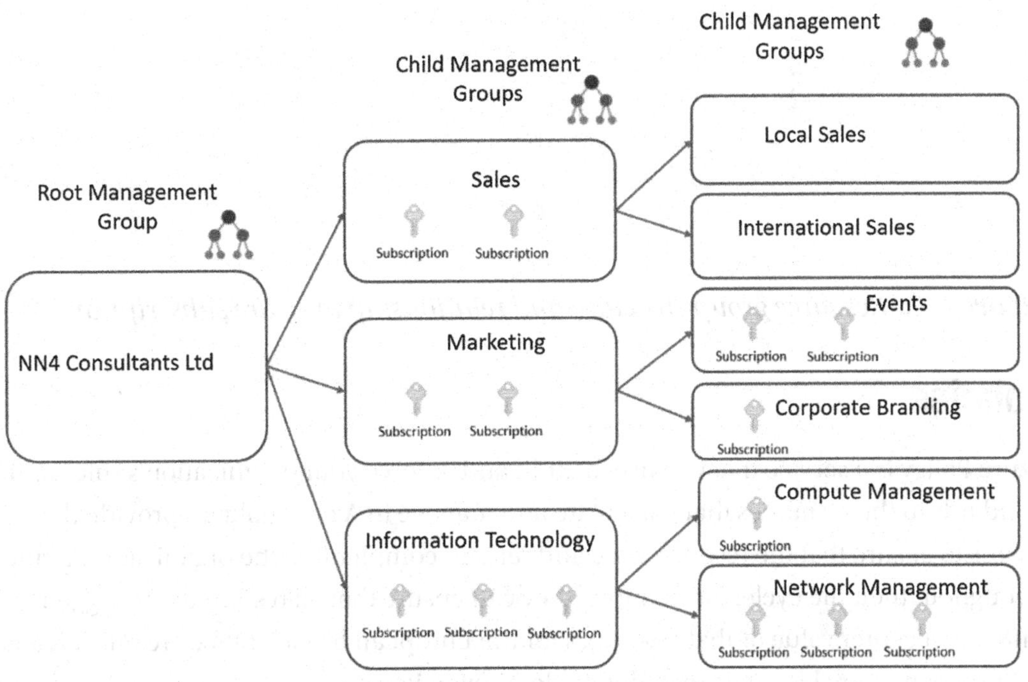

***Figure 1-5.** Subscription assignments to child management groups*

Resources

The term *resource* represents the entities or objects managed in Azure. These include, but are not limited to, virtual machines, storage accounts, virtual networks, and virtual subnets.

Resource Groups

Resource groups are a logical way to group one or more Azure resources. Grouped resources in a resource group can be managed as a single entity, and they all inherit properties and controls, such as role-based access controls, resource tagging, and life cycle attributes. Figure 1-6 shows the relationship between resource groups and the resources in an Azure subscription.

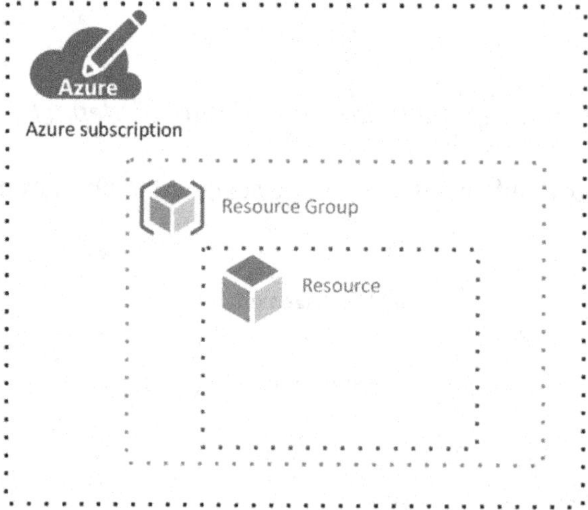

***Figure 1-6.** Resource group structure and relationship to Azure subscription*

Policies

Azure Policy is a service that you use to audit and enforce your organization's rules and standards to the resources that you create and manage in Azure. Policies provide the means to ensure that the resources are and remain compliant to the organizational rules throughout their life cycle; for example, they can ensure that all resources are tagged with a cost center value or that resources for the European branch office are only created in European Azure locations to maintain data sovereignty.

Azure has a number of prebuilt policies that any subscribed tenant can leverage. These built-in policies cover rules that are common to most organizations. You can view and assign these built-in policies using the Azure portal or programmatically.

In the Azure portal, search for "policy", and under Authoring, select Definitions to view the built-in policies available to you, as shown in Figure 1-7.

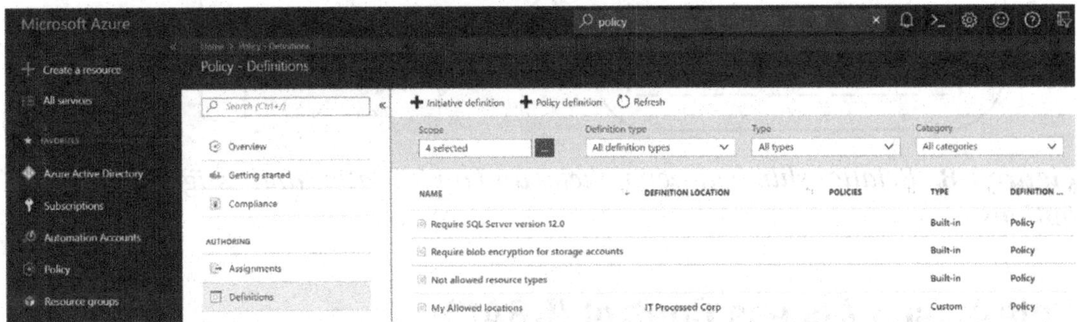

***Figure 1-7.** Azure Policy definition node*

Policies are assigned at multiple levels, known as *scopes*. A scope can be a management group, subscription, or resource group.

Initiatives

Initiatives are a group of one or more policies that are used to audit and/or enforce an organization's governance rules. Similar to policies, Azure provides prebuilt initiatives. Typically, prebuilt policies and initiatives provide a template that you duplicate and customize to suit your specific needs, or you can use the defaults, if appropriate. Figure 1-8 shows the relationship of an initiative to policies and the assignment scope options for an initiative.

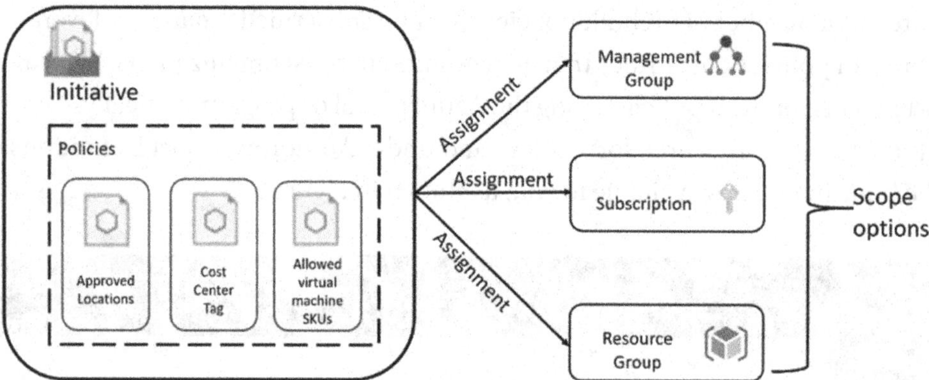

***Figure 1-8.** Relationship between policies and an initiative and assignment scope options*

Role-Based Access Control (RBAC)

Role-based access control (RBAC) is a component of the governance framework for organizations. Policies and initiatives define and enforce how resources should be provisioned to adhere to compliance rules. RBAC ensures that only authorized and approved users have appropriate access to resources. In Microsoft Azure, RBAC has predefined roles that you can use to grant access at the subscription, resource group, or resource level. You have the option to create custom roles to extend and adjust the default role permissions to suit specific requirements or your organization. Figure 1-9 is an illustration of the RBAC structure.

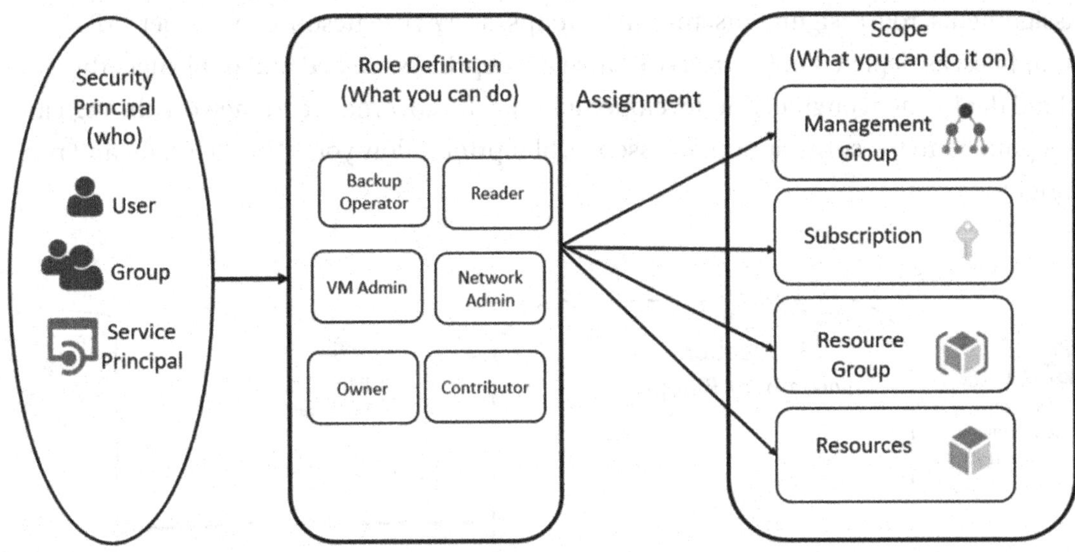

Figure 1-9. *RBAC structure and usage*

Blueprints

Adoption of the cloud, for most entrants, uses the following pattern.

- Trial
- Proof of concept (POC)
- Limited usage
- Full cloud migration

Initially, organizations enroll in limited trials, move into POC with limited controlled usage, and finally, into a full-blown cloud adoption/migration program. This approach previously had a downside; the early initiatives did not always follow organization rules and governance frameworks. As a result, there are a number of brownfield deployments that are live and do not conform to full governance or recommended practices and goals.

Azure Policy and initiatives provide a means to retrospectively audit, and over time, correct these non-compliances and recommend practice drifts. Azure Blueprints, which is in preview at the time of writing, has been introduced to help you build it right from the onset by providing a template framework that incorporates all the governance artifacts and a whole lot more. You create and configure a blueprint to include the policy assignments, role assignments, resource groups, and Azure Resource Manager (ARM) templates, as depicted in Figure 1-10. Once a blueprint is created and published, the cloud deployment engineer or developer inherits the governance framework through an assignment to the subscription. In essence, blueprints allow you to build it right and run it right.

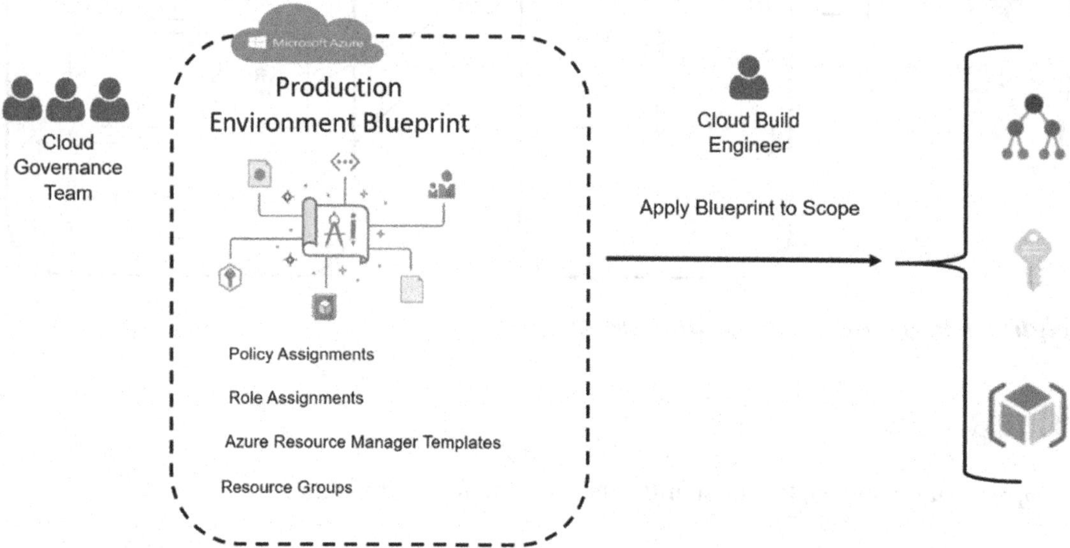

Figure 1-10. *Blueprint illustration with the supported artifact types*

Azure Governance Planning

"Measure twice, cut once" is the principle followed in the carpentry industry. The premise is that to build a strong table, for example, you need to get the right measurements before cutting the wood. If the wood is cut too short, then you will have to join two pieces or more and introduce weakness into the structure. This is very relevant in your Azure governance implementation approach. This section discusses and recommends the planning activities you must perform as a prerequisite to configuring and assigning your governance artifacts.

Planning Categories

- Azure foundational artifacts
- Governance artifacts

Azure Foundational Artifacts

The process of implementing Azure governance requires the cloud custodian to be familiar with and adequately plan for the following.

- Tenants
- Subscriptions
- Resource groups
- Management groups

Planning for Tenants

Planning for and agreeing on the tenant for your cloud environment is the recommended first step. The tenant is key, as it does not only act as the root of the governance tree but also the security principal root.

1. Ensure that the tenant registration is linked and managed by the organization. It is not uncommon to have the Azure registration linked to the sales director's credit card or the default domain provided by Microsoft.
2. Assign appropriate ownership and tenant administrative roles. The tenant roles have rights that impact subscriptions and the child resource groups, and hence, align these roles to the organization's top-tier security authorities and procurement management.
3. In cases where you require full isolation of environments, establishing a separate tenant is recommended; however, note that if you plan to link the Azure AD to an on-premise AD, then only one tenant can be linked to your on-premise AD forest.
4. Agree on which external Domain Name Service (DNS) names that you will assign to the tenant. Assign an appropriate DNS name to the tenant before creating the users that will be players in the management and consumption of the services in your tenant.

5. A tenant is free to create and use, but you need to sign up to premium services to leverage other artifacts of Azure governance. Review the services available in Azure with all the relevant stakeholders, and budget appropriately for the procurement of these services.

The web page at `https://docs.microsoft.com/en-us/Azure/active-directory/develop/quickstart-create-new-tenant` provides information on where to start and how to set up your tenant(s).

Planning for Subscriptions

Planning for subscriptions is the next step after establishing your organization's tenant(s). You may decide to use a single tenant, or in some cases, you may establish a separate tenant still owned by your organization. Subscriptions are the agreements you establish with Microsoft on paying for the consumption of cloud services. There are two categories of subscriptions, which align with the three core categories of cloud services.

- **Microsoft Software as a Service (SaaS) subscriptions**. These subscriptions (at the time of writing) are linked to the Office 365, Intune/EMS, and Dynamics 365 cloud offerings. This type of subscription is integrated into the SaaS offering. The main planning activity is to ensure that you link to the authoritative tenant for your organization. The authoritative tenant acts as your identity and security layer, and provides the users or devices that these subscription models align to for licensing and service charges.
- **Microsoft Platform as a Service (PaaS) and Microsoft Infrastructure as a Service (IaaS) subscriptions**. Unlike SaaS services that are based on specific user accounts consuming the offering, PaaS and IaaS charges are linked to consuming resources that inherit the infrastructure provided by Microsoft. With PaaS or IaaS, you create and manage all the artifacts required for your organization within the subscription.

With SaaS offerings, you need to plan for the following.

- **Licensing authority**. The department or individuals responsible for purchasing licenses; typically, the procurement department. This department must understand the legal aspects of the agreement to ensure that the organization stays compliant with purchasing rules and usage rights.
- **Identity authority**. SaaS offerings require a link to a tenant to provide a trusted identity source. When you sign up for this type of service, you are offered a generic Azure AD tenant; if you have an existing tenant, then you have the option to link to that existing tenant. Optionally, if you have an on-premise identity service like Active Directory, you can also set up synchronization. Synchronizing your on-premise identities with the tenant Azure Active Directory ensures that you only manage one identity and also provide a single sign-on experience for your users when they consume the cloud offering. Figure 1-11 shows the cloud usage options and the link between Azure AD and the on-premise AD.

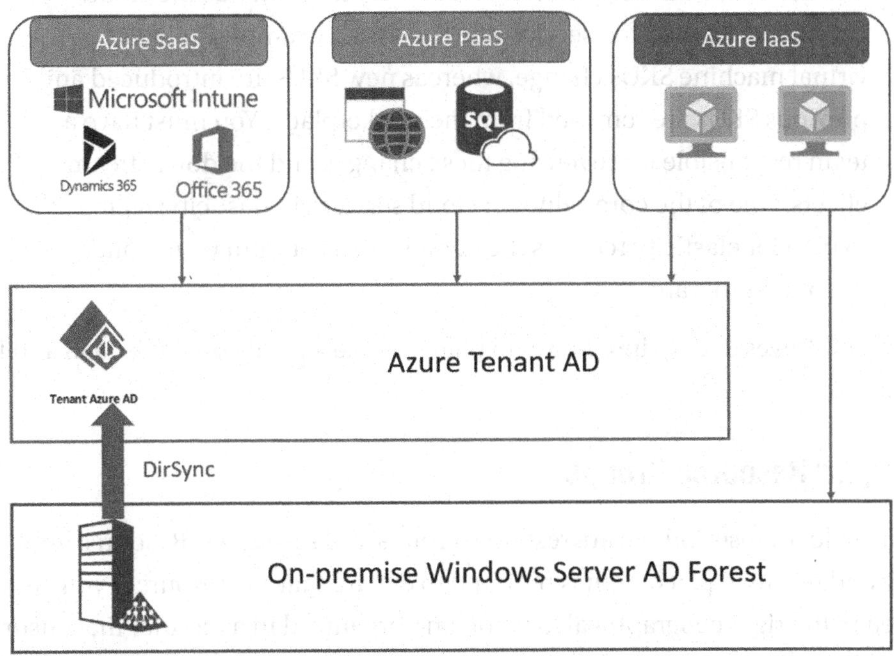

***Figure 1-11.** Subscription options and the link to Azure AD and on-premise AD*

Chapter 2 delves deeper into how you plan, purchase, and consume SaaS subscriptions.

With PaaS and IaaS offerings, you need to plan for the following.

- **Licensing authority**. The department or individuals responsible for purchasing licenses; typically, the procurement department. This department must understand the legal aspects of the agreement to ensure that the organization stays compliant with purchasing rules and usage rights.
- **Policy and security**. Unlike SaaS offerings, you are responsible for the full policies and security framework that you establish for the subscription in order to deliver your own SaaS solutions. Cloud provider SaaS solutions have inherited policies and security frameworks that are managed by the provider. PaaS and IaaS offerings give you full flexibility to create, implement, and manage the policy and security framework for the end-user consumed applications and services you create in these subscriptions.
- **Planning life cycle management**. Plan for the adoption of features and the continual deprecation of features that evolve as the cloud provider enhances the service offering. As an example, in IaaS, virtual machine SKUs change, whereas new SKUs are introduced and previous SKUs are removed from the marketplace. You must have a team responsible for reviewing these changes and the downstream effects. One of the core values of cloud services is elasticity; failing to plan for elasticity reduces the benefits you get from your cloud adoption program.

Chapter 2 delves deeper into how you plan, purchase, and consume PaaS and IaaS subscriptions.

Planning for Resource Groups

The layers below subscriptions are resource groups and resources. Resource group planning and resource placement is required to ensure that the resources you create are placed in the right geographical location and organized in a manner that ensures that the policies that you create for standardization are easy to apply. As example, in

Figure 1-12, you can create a resource group by geographic location to serve the needs of a global organization's adherence to data sovereignty. Figure 1-13 shows an alternative organization strategy, where you create resources groups by life cycle environment (Development, Preproduction and Production) and then by business application types.

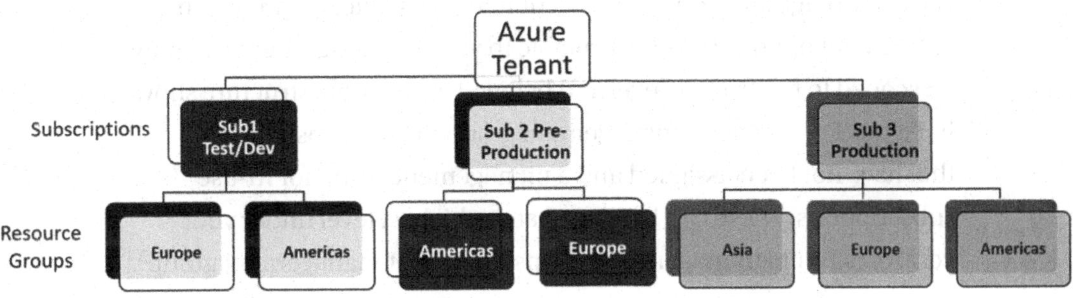

Figure 1-12. *Resource group structure by geographic location*

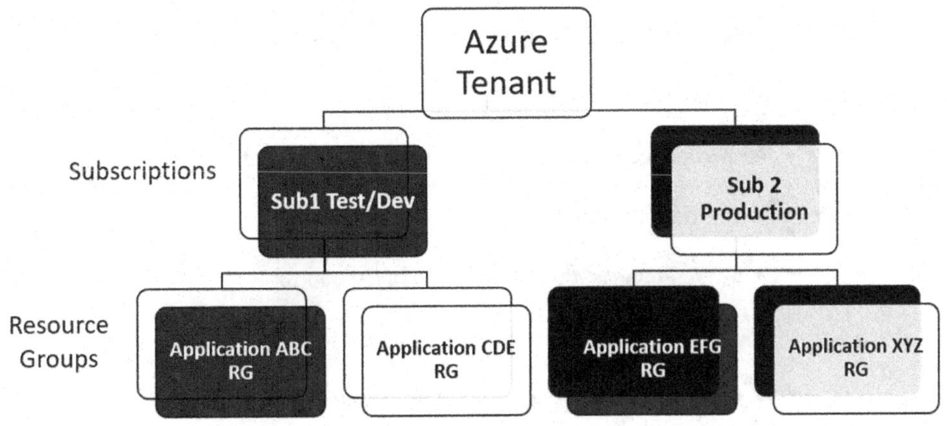

Figure 1-13. *Resource group structure by environment and application type*

Planning for Management Groups

The "Management Groups" section of this chapter introduced what they are and how you typically use them in an Azure environment. This section focuses on how you plan before you create your management group hierarchy.

Management groups in Azure provide two core organizational and management options: where you store your governance artifacts and how you apply these artifacts.

- **Governance artifact placement**. When you create your Azure artifacts, such as policies, initiatives, and blueprints, you are asked to select a storage location. This selection has a significant impact on the assignment options (scope) available to you. The assignment can only be scoped to the storage level and below. The example structure shown in Figure 1-14 creates a management group to hold subscriptions that have not been assigned and a management group for in-use subscriptions. These can be placed at the highest level under your control (as child management groups to the root management group).

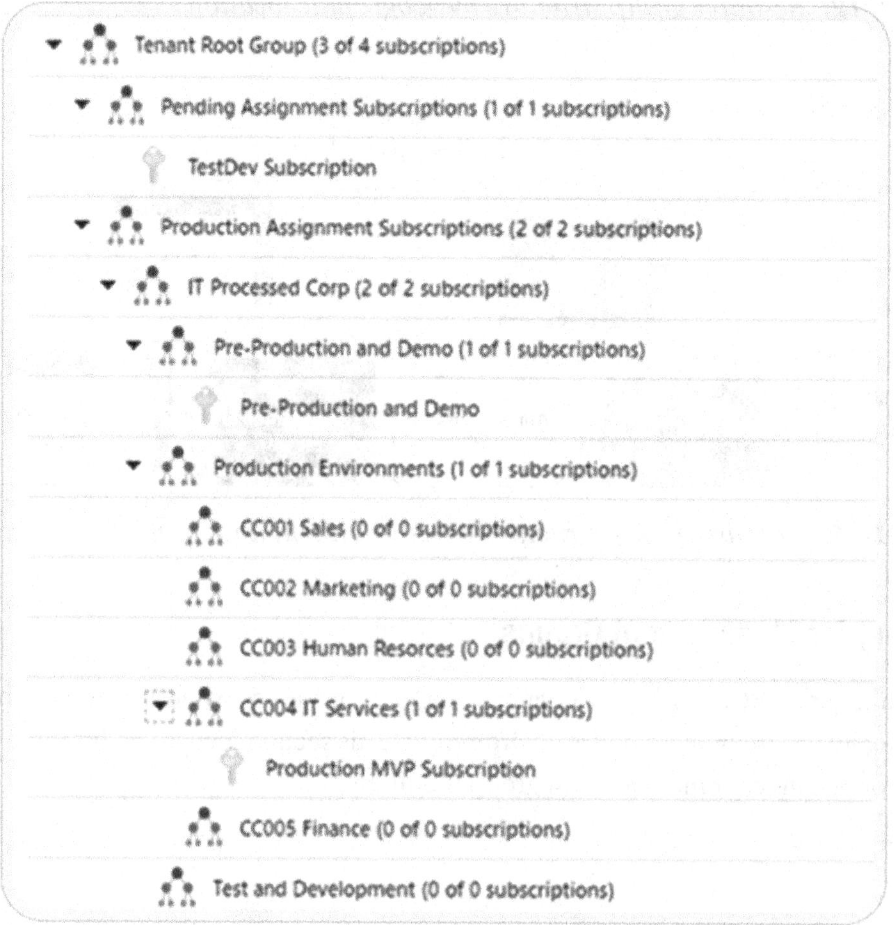

Figure 1-14. *Example management group structure with subscriptions*

- **Governance artifact assignment**. The second category to plan for is how you assign, policies, initiatives, and blueprints. Assignments flow down the management tree, and it is recommended to assign these artifacts at the highest level. You will get the maximum flexibility and least complication if you arrange the management groups in a logical structure to reflect the intended effects of your compliance goals.

  An important area to also plan for is how you use *exclusions*. Exclusions are very powerful but can lead to conflicts and undesired effects if not planned appropriately. Ideally, plan to structure the management groups to mitigate the need to use exclusions in your assignments. Figure 1-15 depicts an assignment structure with exclusions in use.

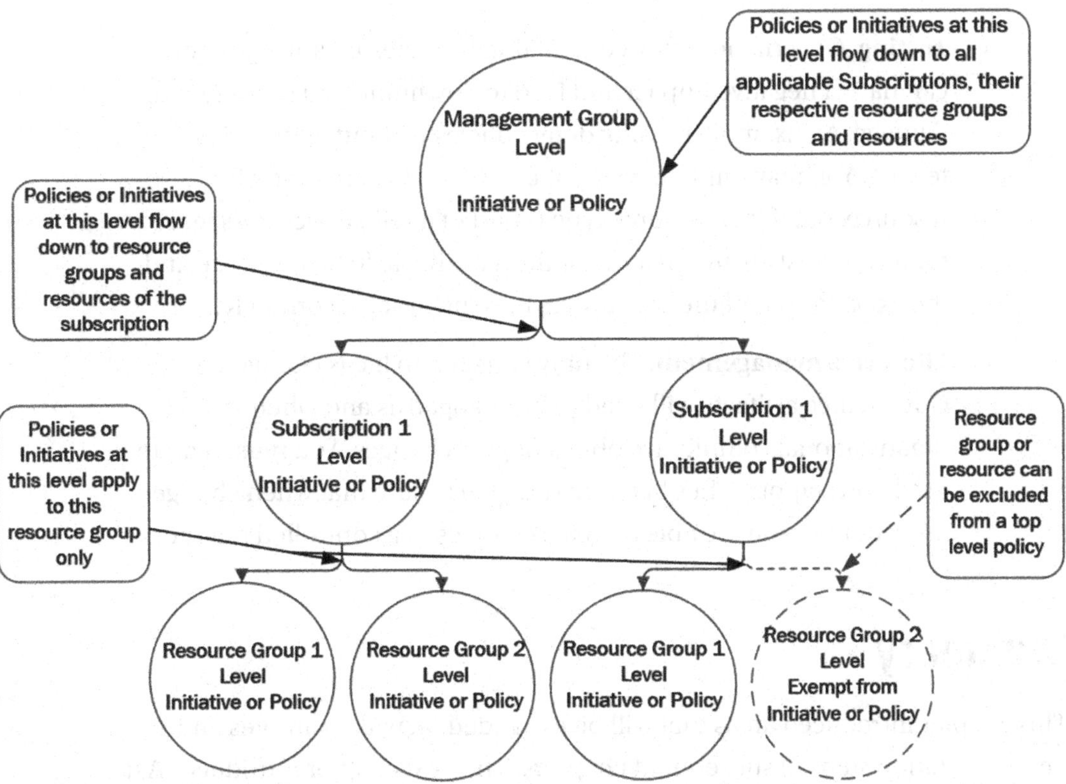

***Figure 1-15.** Planning for policy exclusions*

Planning for Azure Governance Artifacts

The core Azure governance artifacts to plan for are as follows:

- Policies
- Initiatives
- Blueprints

The common areas to take into account for planning are naming conventions, testing, and life cycle management.

- **Naming conventions**. Plan to have and maintain a naming convention for all artifacts. This should be documented and communicated to ensure that all the resources for the management of artifacts follow the same standards.
- **Testing**. Governance enforcement that is not tested appropriately can have a negative impact and lead to downtime and reputational damage. An example is using deny policies without appropriate testing. You may implement a policy to deny the creation of a resource, but if this resource type is part of a self-service offering, then you must ensure that the options available for self-service and the expectations of the consumers have been set accordingly.
- **Life-cycle management**. The only constant in life is change. Governance artifacts will need to be changed as and when an organizational compliance object or goal changes. You must plan to use known approaches like versioning to ensure that when changes are required, you are able to make changes in a controlled manner.

Summary

This chapter introduced areas that will be expanded on with examples and implementation steps in subsequent chapters. The next chapter introduces Azure scaffold for enterprise subscriptions.

CHAPTER 2

Azure Scaffold for Enterprise Subscriptions

When analyzing a migration strategy to the cloud, a fundamental component of correctly managing the applications and infrastructure running on Azure is the correct administration of our subscriptions and the team members that administer them.

In this chapter, we analyze best practices for using a combination of subscriptions, resource groups, and role-based access control to ensure compliance with a set of guidelines in our transition to the cloud.

The previous chapter introduced the Azure consumer governance building blocks.

- Tenants
- Subscriptions
- Resource groups
- Resources
- Management groups
- Policies
- Initiatives
- Blueprints
- Role-based access control (RBAC)

P. De Tender et al., *Pro Azure Governance and Security*, https://doi.org/10.1007/978-1-4842-4910-9_2

Azure Scaffold Pillars

Within a transition from a traditional IT model to an ideal cloud model, Azure scaffolding considers the management of the key components that the cloud impacts on our work teams, such as DevOps, automation, data and analytics, solution architecture, research, and development.

Figure 2-1 shows the key components within Azure scaffolds; it helps us better understand the management of resources in Azure.

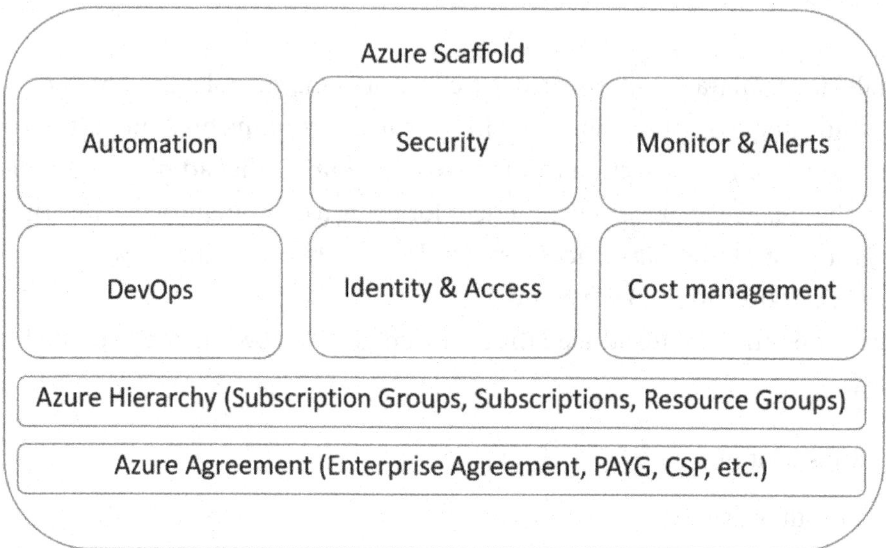

Figure 2-1. *Key components within the Azure Scaffold*

You must consider how you create and manage multiple subscriptions, and access to them, to manage our resources. There are many elements that you must analyze and take into account with a governance model that will ultimately help ensure the success of the transition to the cloud.

So, with an Azure scaffolding governance model, we're talking about the type of agreement you have with your cloud provider—whether it's an Azure Enterprise Agreement, a pay-as-you-go agreement, or so on. Through these different types of agreements, you create several types of subscriptions to provision the key components of our applications that will live in the cloud, which is why we mainly take into account key metrics to design the hierarchy of the governance of subscriptions.

Azure Governance Focus

The following are the key points to consider within an initial hierarchy for managing resources in Azure.

- Management groups
- Subscriptions
- Resource groups

One of the top concerns of organizations is the way operation teams want to use cloud. A lot of the top controls are missing in cloud providers, such as policy controls, auditing controls, and compliances controls. Many times, operations teams have to manually review all of the access and controls before the DevOps teams can provision their resources to the cloud.

Azure provides cloud-native governance so that you have consistent control across all Azure platforms.

Figure 2-2 shows, at a general level, the initial hierarchy for the administration of resources in Azure.

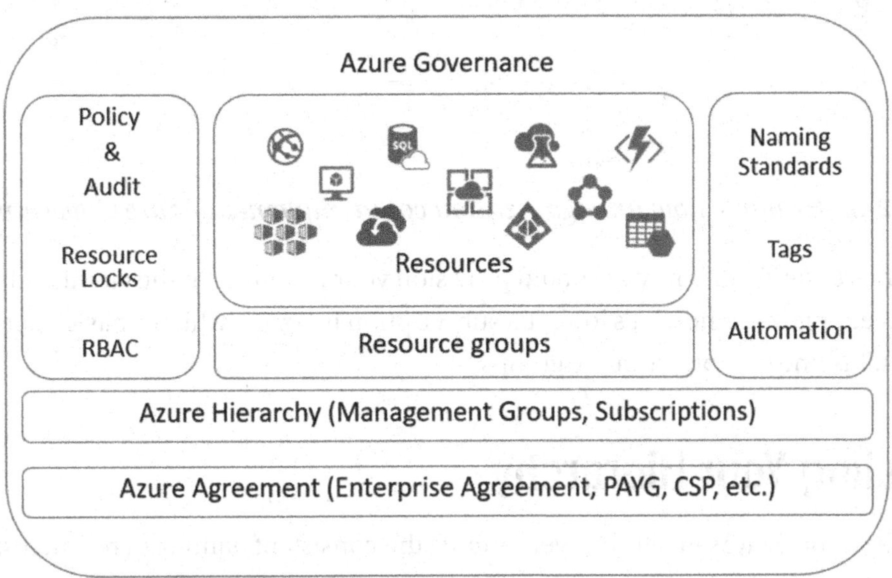

***Figure 2-2.** Initial hierarchy for the administration of Azure resources*

At this level of hierarchy, you must take into account the correct way to provide access to the resources within your subscription, as well as the way you name your resources. For example, on the one hand, you are going to use Azure resource manager policies to control what a specific user can and cannot do with resources called resource actions. On the other hand, you need to be very careful with the standards for naming your resources and assigning labels to better control them.

Here is an example: the iFreeze company wants all users with access to the subscription to be able to create virtual machines only in the US data centers. In addition, these Azure resources adhere to a naming convention to maintain uniform naming standards throughout the subscription.

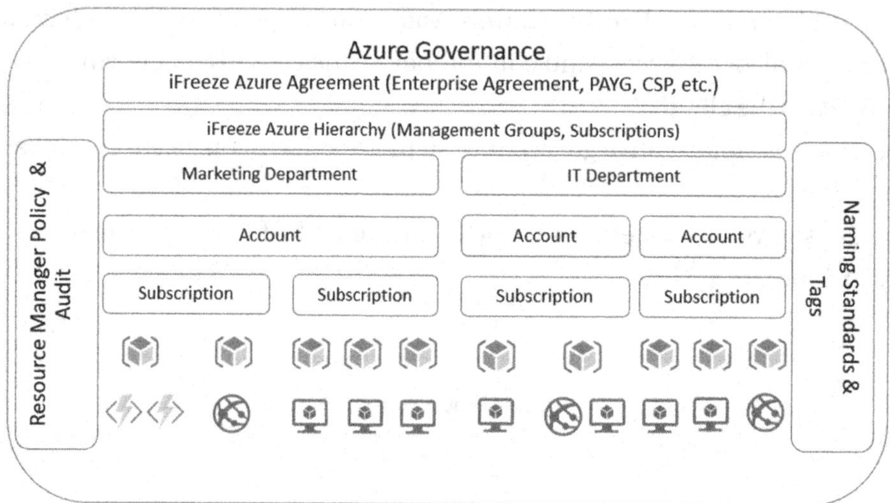

Figure 2-3. *Example how an organization could implement Azure Governance*

For more clarity on how you should provision your resources in the cloud and achieve better governance, let's look at a subscription in Azure, which a basic logical unit that contains one or more resource groups.

Modeling Your Hierarchy

One of the main factors in Azure governance is the consistent naming of resources, starting with our subscriptions. An organization could have several subscriptions, which adds complexity to managing them. This is why Azure provides a feature called *management groups*, which allows you to efficiently manage several subscriptions in a specific organization.

Management groups offer a great way to organize your subscriptions and resources in a hierarchical manner. Consider management groups as a container for one or several subscriptions, which in turn contains the associated resource groups.

Figure 2-4 refers to the management groups presented in Chapter 1.

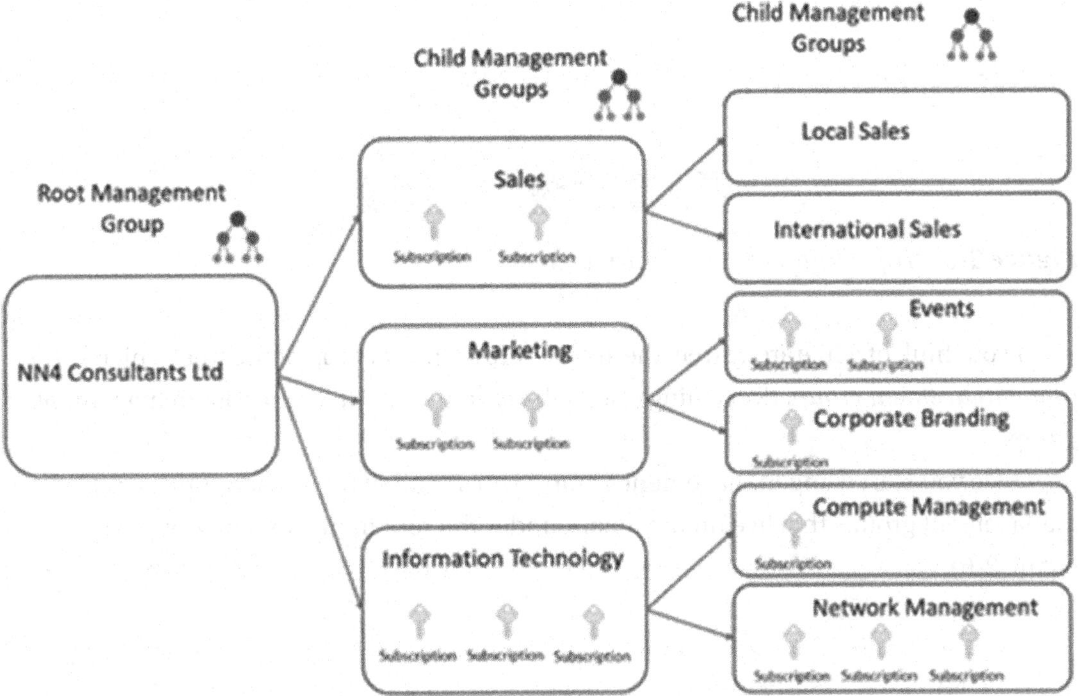

Figure 2-4. *Example of Management Groups*

Looking at this entire governance scenario, management groups is the new object above the subscription level that allows an organization to have management at scale.

Management groups are mainly intended for central management. They offer custom hierarchies and the ability to apply custom policies or RBAC to specific services.

Management Group Use Case

Management groups are a very flexible feature for accessing and managing through the Azure portal, CLI, and REST API. When you go to the Azure portal and look for management groups for the very first time, you see a top management group that is created in each tenant. Figure 2-5 is a screenshot.

No management groups to display

Organize your subscriptions into groups called "management groups" to help you manage access, policy and compliance across your subscriptions. Management groups give you enterprise-grade management at a large scale no matter what type of subscriptions you might have. Learn more

Start using management groups

Figure 2-5. *Top Management Group view*

If you think of a hierarchy tree, there is a node at the very top of the tree, which is the *root management group*. Everything else in the tenant folds up to the root management group.

Once you start using management groups, you see all of the subscriptions or child management groups that live on the tenant under the root management group (see Figure 2-6).

+ Add management group ↻ Refresh

Tenant Root Group

Search by name or ID

Tenant Root Group (details)

NAME
Dave-AzSponsorship-18
Visual Studio Enterprise

Figure 2-6. *Tenant Root Group with Azure Subscriptions underneath*

The main intention of the root management group is to give to your organization the ability to apply policies and RBAC at a top-level scale, as needed.

Figure 2-7 is a functional hierarchy example.

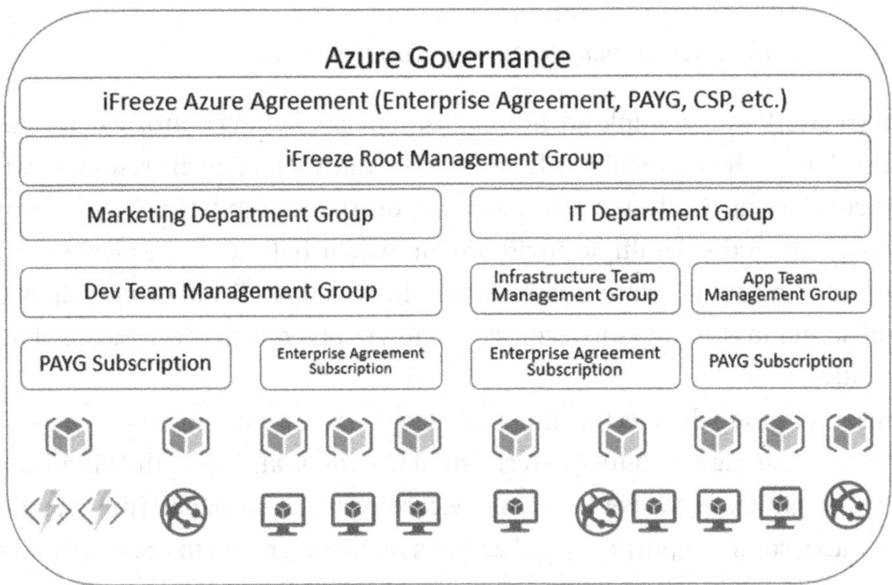

Figure 2-7. *Example of a functional Azure Governance structure*

Please note that tenant admin is the only role that allows you to have access to the root management group level.

A best practice to better simplify management groups governance is to follow the naming standards; for instance, you could have the following scenario:

root management group ➤ *iFreeze* ➤ *Marketing* ➤ *internal website* ➤ *production*

You can create up to 10,000 management groups in a single tenant.

A best practice for managing subscriptions is to consider the hierarchy model of your subscriptions associated with your tenant, as previously discussed. These hierarchies give the guidelines for identifying and assigning a standard nomenclature, which achieves better governance in your cloud environment.

Taking into account a functional pattern, you could assign standard nomenclature to a subscription, as shown in Figure 2-8.

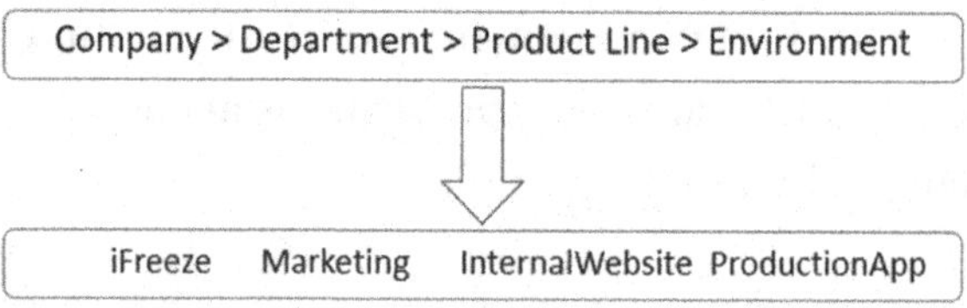

Figure 2-8. *Standard Nomenclature across an organization*

When you work with multiple environments, you have better control over the cost of the subscription and better visibility of the users who are managing the resources within it.

When considering the design of a resources governance model in Azure for multiple teams, workloads, and/or multiple environments, you usually add complexity in the way that a user with an administrator role delegates the responsibility of ownership of the various subscriptions through the resource groups, coupled with the capacity of Azure Policy and RBAC.

The resource group defines the limits and scope of the components in Azure, such as the number of storage accounts, cores, virtual networks, and so forth. It is advisable to use resource groups as the key container according to the workload (that is, group resources with a common purpose) and assign a name that refers to the workload or type of resources.

At this point, you should have a broader picture of how to assign an appropriate governance model to your company. As we reviewed in this chapter, an Azure "scaffold" refers to gathering the right pieces and best practices to have a fully managed cloud environment in Azure.

Summary

Throughout this chapter, we reviewed how Azure governance helps organizations efficiently solve the main concerns of how operational teams use cloud resources, including policy controls, audit controls, and compliance controls through the main hierarchies of management groups, subscriptions, and resource groups.

Additionally, we reviewed how to model hierarchies of management groups to efficiently manage multiple subscriptions in a specific organization, as well as best practices for implementing subscriptions within the organization.

CHAPTER 3

Azure Naming Conventions and Standards

Identifying, organizing, and tracking resources is key in any environment. This is an age-old requirement that continues to be a challenge for technology management teams of all sizes. Naming conventions require a well-thought-out plan before using in all environments. There are a number of reasons that drive this approach; examples include but are not limited to the following.

- **Identification**: Easily identify artifacts in an environment using the name.
- **Organization**: Artifacts can be grouped and structured to facilitate standards.
- **Documentation**: Good naming conventions are self-documenting.
- **Automation**: Automation is simplified and robust with a good naming standard.
- **Search and reporting**: Searching is streamlined and reports are easier to create.
- **Governance and compliance**: Assists with demonstrating governance and compliance when an audit is performed.

This chapter discusses the general recommendations and practices for naming standards and their usage. We also delve into why naming standards are critical to Microsoft Azure Governance components and how to implement them by using example scenarios.

P. De Tender et al., *Pro Azure Governance and Security*, https://doi.org/10.1007/978-1-4842-4910-9_3

Use the approaches and examples as a reference point, but note that your organization may already have reusable standards from areas in on-premise data center management.

This chapter covers

- The case for naming conventions
- Naming standards in action
- Naming at scale with automation

General Recommendations and Standards

The two core objectives of naming standards are clarity and consistency. This can be easier said than done due to how different people define easy. First and foremost, start with what is not allowed. This book is focused on Azure, and in particular, Azure governance. So, what is not allowed in Azure?

The documentation site for Microsoft Azure has a section on naming conventions (`https://docs.microsoft.com/en-us/azure/architecture/best-practices/naming-conventions`). A subsection details the naming rules and restrictions for each resource and service type. Table 3-1 shows examples of some common categories and their rules and restrictions.

Table 3-1. *Examples of Naming Convention Rules in Azure*

Azure Entity	Length	Casing	Valid Characters
Resource Group	1–90	Case insensitive	Alphanumeric, underscore, parentheses, hyphen, period (except at end), and Unicode characters that match the regex.
Tag	512 (name), 256 (value)	Case insensitive	Alphanumeric
Virtual Machine	1–15 (Windows), 1–64 (Linux)	Case insensitive	Alphanumeric and hyphen
Storage account name (disk)	3–24	Lowercase	Alphanumeric

(*continued*)

Table 3-1. (*continued*)

Azure Entity	Length	Casing	Valid Characters
Virtual Network (VNet)	2–64	Case insensitive	Alphanumeric, hyphen, underscore, and period
Subnet	2–80	Case insensitive	Alphanumeric, hyphen, underscore, and period
Network Interface	1–80	Case insensitive	Alphanumeric, hyphen, underscore, and period
Network Security Group	1–80	Case insensitive	Alphanumeric, hyphen, underscore, and period

The next step after identifying what is not allowed is determining your specific naming convention, categorizing, and most importantly, ensuring that it is documented and communicated.

Azure Governance Naming Categories

The common naming categories in Azure Governance are

- Resources in scope of governance
- Resources and artifacts used to implement governance

A starting point for resources in Azure scope of governance is to use the predefined categories in Azure Policy under Definitions, as illustrated in Figure 3-1.

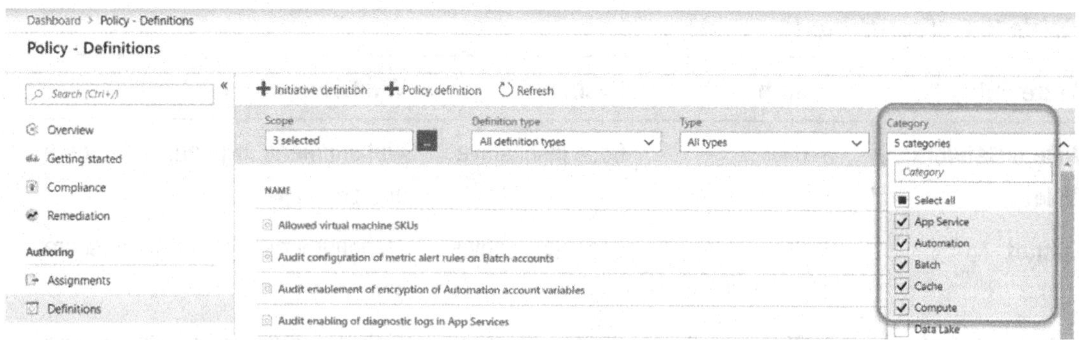

Figure 3-1. *Predefined policy categories in Azure*

The governance team may not be directly responsible for implementing or mandating the naming convention applied to resources in scope. In this case, the governance team should get the details of the naming convention in use before planning for policy assignments.

The naming of resources and artifacts used in Azure Governance fall within the scope of the governance team. The guiding principle is to agree and document conventions and standards that are not only logical but also facilitate automation and reporting. It is also important to note that a naming standard in the cloud environment should be established and maintained from the onset. Retrospectively trying to change the standard can be complex and, in some cases, impossible without first deleting the applicable resources.

Tagging

Tags in Azure provide you with a means to apply additional metadata to your resources. This is a powerful feature that you can use as part of your Azure governance implementation and continual management. Tags give you an additional layer of organization to compliment the naming standards. Note that we are only discussing tags in the context of this governance book; however, tags play a much wider role in Azure.

This section is specific to naming conventions, so in relation to tags that you use for governance, plan the appropriate naming standards. Examples of tags in use for governance are cost center, department, location, and environment values. Is there an agreed cost center naming standard in your organization? Will this standard be the same in Azure, or do you plan to add a prefix or a suffix value to create an Azure-specific standard? Discuss, agree, and document the tag naming standards before you start using the policies that audit or enforce tags.

An example of how tags and their naming standards play a role in governance is illustrated in Figure 3-2, which is a policy example of adding a cost center value to all resources in a specific management group (used to host assigned subscriptions).

Enforce tag and its value on resource groups
Assign policy

SCOPE
* Scope (Learn more about setting the scope)
CC001 Sales
Exclusions
Optionally select resources to exempt from the policy assignment

BASICS
* Policy definition
Enforce tag and its value on resource groups
* Assignment name
Enforce Sales Cost Center tag and its value on resource groups
Description
Enforce the Cost Center Tag value to all resources in this management group
Assigned by
Samuel Erskine

PARAMETERS
* Tag Name
Cost Center
* Tag Value
CC001

Figure 3-2. *Naming example using tags*

Naming Standards in Action

This section provides details and examples of naming conventions for governance artifacts. The following categories are discussed.

- Subscriptions
- Resource Groups
- Management groups
- Policies
- Initiatives
- Blueprints

Subscriptions

All Azure subscriptions have a unique ID and a friendly name. A recommended practice is to rename the friendly name to a standard that is appropriate for your environment.

The original name is typically based on the option that you sign up for when you create the subscription. Pay-As-You-Go and MSDN Visual Studio are two examples. You can change the names to align to their usage and departmental ownership. Follow these example steps to change the subscription name to align with a naming standard that maps to a cost center, department, and life cycle environment.

1. Using a supported web browser, log in to the Azure portal at `https://portal.azure.com`.
2. In the search, type **subscriptions**, and click the subscriptions icon in the results.

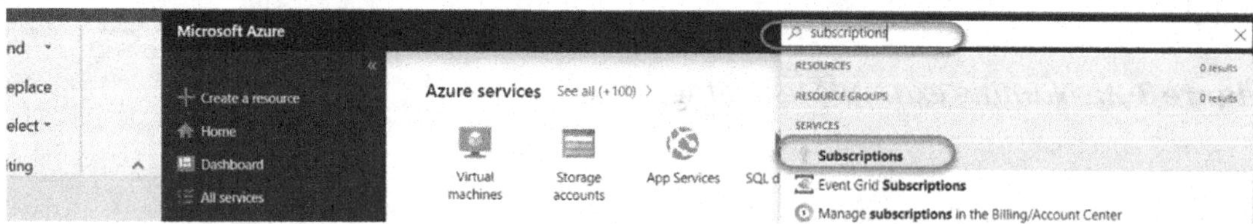

3. You are presented with a list of the subscriptions assigned to you. Click the subscription that you want to rename.

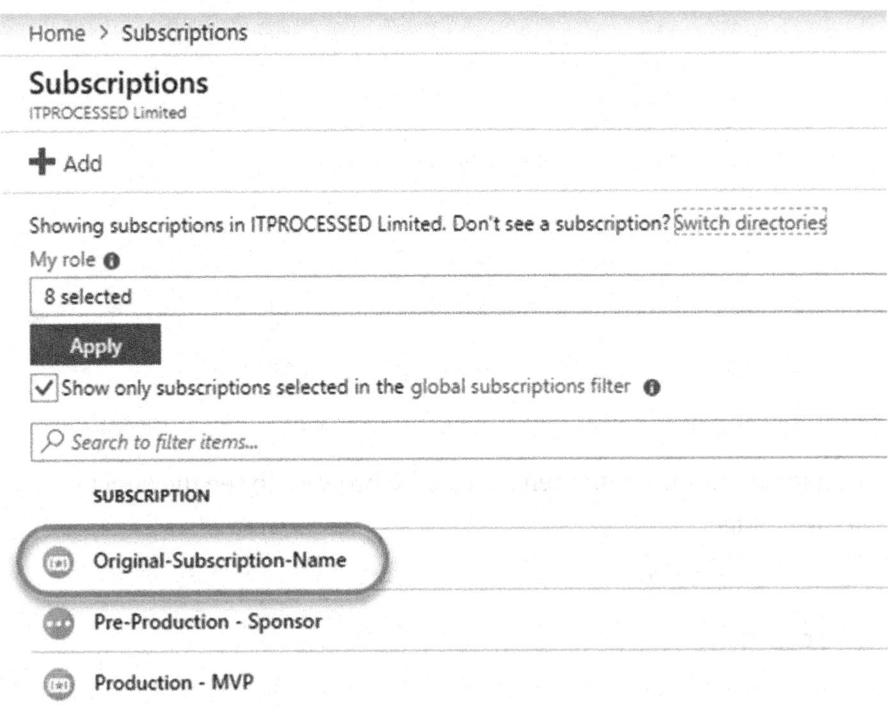

4. Click Rename to bring up the edit subscription name fields.

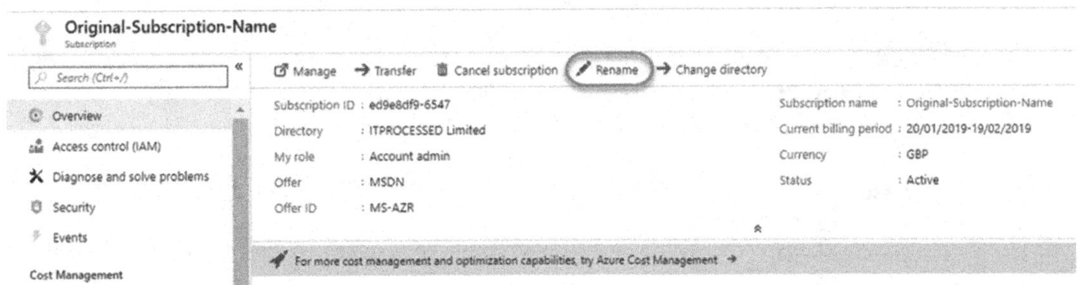

5. Type the new name. Note the time that it takes for the change to take effect. Click Save to complete the change.

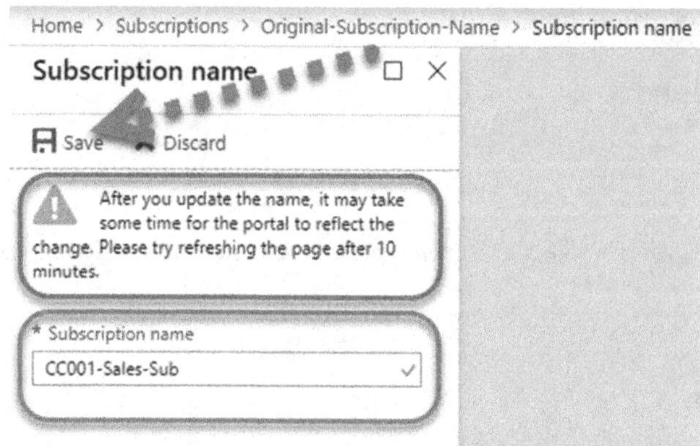

6. Wait for 10 minutes and then refresh the browser to see the effect of the change.

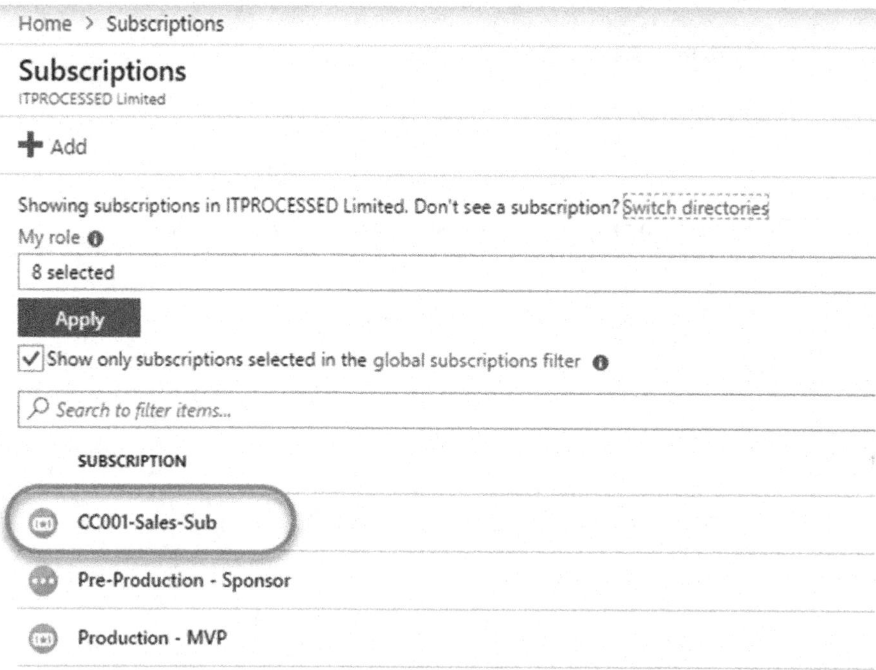

In this example, we applied a logical naming convention based on <Cost Center>-<Department>-<Environment>.

Resource Groups

In Azure, resource groups are used to manage all resources that make up a solution. A solution can be as simple as a virtual machine instance or an n-tier application that includes virtual networks, virtual machine instances, and other related Azure resources. Resource groups are the next layer of grouping under subscriptions. In relation to the Azure governance structure, you have management groups that contain one or more subscription, with each subscription containing one or more resource groups. Resource groups are also used in scoping (how you target policies or initiatives). Establishing a naming convention for resource groups is highly recommended as part of your naming standards strategy in Azure.

The choice of naming standard is up to you, but you must ensure that you follow the rules for naming this Azure artifact. Table 3-2 illustrates some examples of naming conventions for resource groups.

Table 3-2. *Examples of Resource Group Naming*

Standard	Example
<CC>-<ResourceTypes>-RG	CC001-Netw-RG
<CC>-<Environment>-RG	CC001-Dev-RG
<CC>-<AppName>-RG	CC001-App1-RG
<CC>-<Environment>-<AppName>-RG	CC001-Dev-App3-RG
<CC>-<Environment>-< ResourceTypes >-RG	CC001-Dev-Netw-RG

Figure 3-3 is a graphical representation of the examples in the table, showing resource groups created under a subscription called CC001_Sales_Sub.

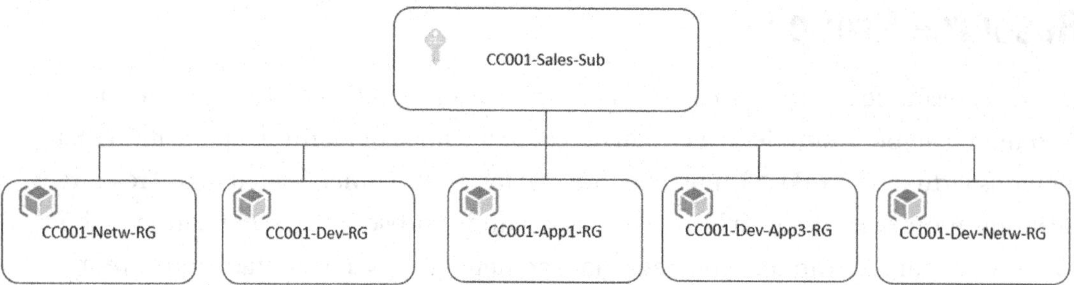

Figure 3-3. *Illustration of resource group naming. Share the agreed naming standards for Resource Groups with teams responsible for creating Azure resources. The teams responsible use this standard to create resource groups either using the Azure portal or automation through PowerShell or the Azure CLI.*

Management Groups

Management groups provide a means to organize your subscriptions to facilitate your Azure governance management, which were introduced in Chapter 1. Management groups must have an appropriate naming standard. You must plan the structure of the management groups to allow simplified operations, while also ensuring that you are following a flexible logical approach. Naming conventions applied to this category should adhere to the organizational structure agreed to for subscription management, role-based security, and governance artifact implementation.

Management groups are hierarchal in nature and require you to plan the naming to allow for flexibility and clarity. Management groups can be up to six levels deep; this does not include the root management level. In total, you can have seven layers if you include the default root management layer. The total number of management groups that you can have is 10,000; remember this is a limit, not a target, so plan to minimize the total number of management groups to avoid complex structures. Figure 3-4 illustrates an example of a five-layer management group structure using a naming convention that starts with a top level assigned or unassigned subscriptions root, which expands into the organization's top structure (R&D and the main company). This further expands to environments and then subdepartments.

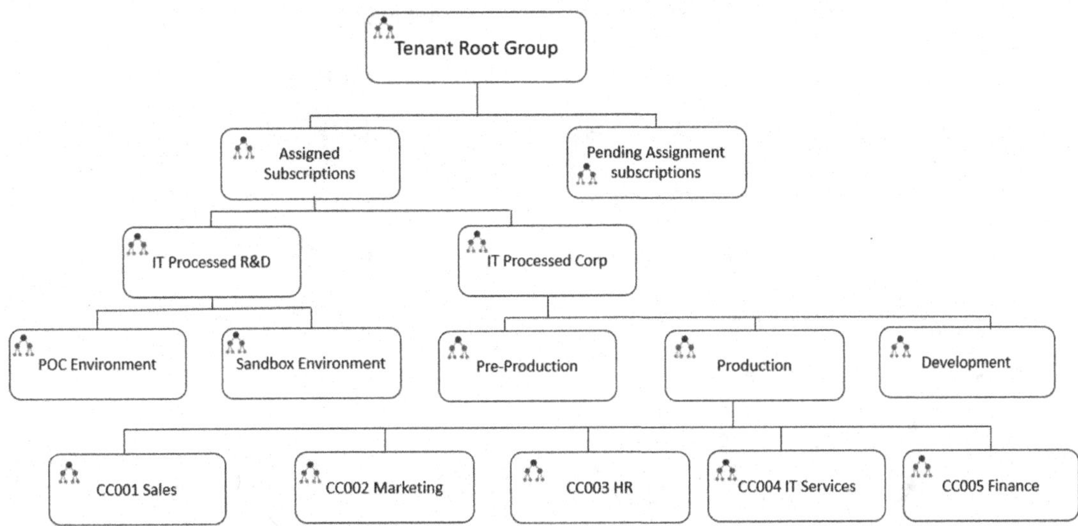

Figure 3-4. *Management group structure planning*

You can get an overview of the current management group structure by using Azure Security Center. Navigate to the Security Center, Policy, and Compliance section and click Security Policy to see a representation of this structure, as shown in Figure 3-5.

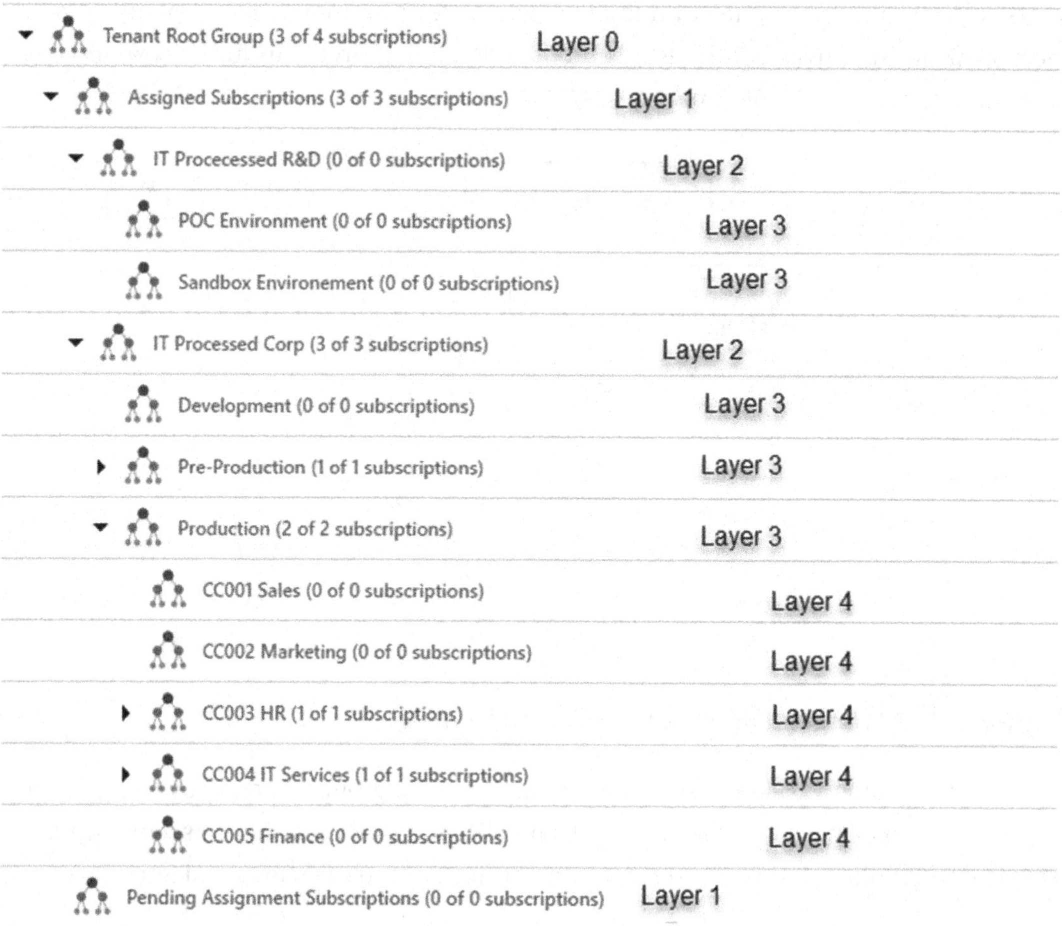

Tenant Root Group (3 of 4 subscriptions) Layer 0
Assigned Subscriptions (3 of 3 subscriptions) Layer 1
IT Procecessed R&D (0 of 0 subscriptions) Layer 2
POC Environment (0 of 0 subscriptions) Layer 3
Sandbox Environement (0 of 0 subscriptions) Layer 3
IT Processed Corp (3 of 3 subscriptions) Layer 2
Development (0 of 0 subscriptions) Layer 3
Pre-Production (1 of 1 subscriptions) Layer 3
Production (2 of 2 subscriptions) Layer 3
CC001 Sales (0 of 0 subscriptions) Layer 4
CC002 Marketing (0 of 0 subscriptions) Layer 4
CC003 HR (1 of 1 subscriptions) Layer 4
CC004 IT Services (1 of 1 subscriptions) Layer 4
CC005 Finance (0 of 0 subscriptions) Layer 4
Pending Assignment Subscriptions (0 of 0 subscriptions) Layer 1

Figure 3-5. *Management group structure hierarchy in the Azure portal*

When creating management groups, you are required to provide a value for the ID and display name. You cannot change the ID without deleting the management group, but you can change the display name at any time. Plan for a logical naming convention for the management group ID, as this can be used in automation. Figure 3-6 shows the creation of the management group dialog box, where you provide the display name and ID.

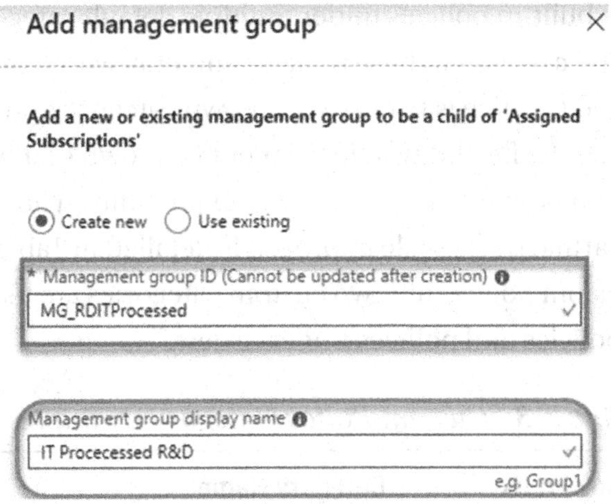

***Figure 3-6.** Management group naming example showing ID and display name*

Management groups are created either with the Azure portal, PowerShell, or the Azure CLI.

Use the following syntax to create a new management group using PowerShell.

```
New-AzureRmManagementGroup -GroupName '<New Management Group ID>'
-DisplayName '<New Management Group Display name>' -ParentId
'<Management Group Parent ID>'
```

Once a management group is created, you can change the display name using the Azure portal or PowerShell. You cannot change the management group ID without deleting the management group.

You can use the following syntax to change the management group display name using PowerShell.

```
Update-AzureRmManagementGroup -GroupName '<New Management Group ID>'
-DisplayName <New Management Group Display name>'
```

Policies

There are three naming categories for policies.

- Policy definition name
- Policy assignment name
- Policy category

Microsoft provides built-in policies under multiple default categories. These policies are not preassigned. You can assign these policies and only worry about the assignment names. A recommended practice is to create your own categories and policies before assigning. This gives you the flexibility to implement your own naming standards and control any customizations, while simultaneously maintaining a library of the default policies as a template artifact. A sample approach is detailed in Table 3-3, where a prefix is used to identify a custom policy, and two custom categories are used to distinguish between production policies and policies under review.

Table 3-3. *Custom Policy Category Examples*

Policy Prefix	Category Name
POL-	ITP Under Review ITP Production

This implements a naming standard that gives a clear view of the purpose of the policies. Figure 3-7 shows the Azure policy definition node listing custom policies with the category and naming standards.

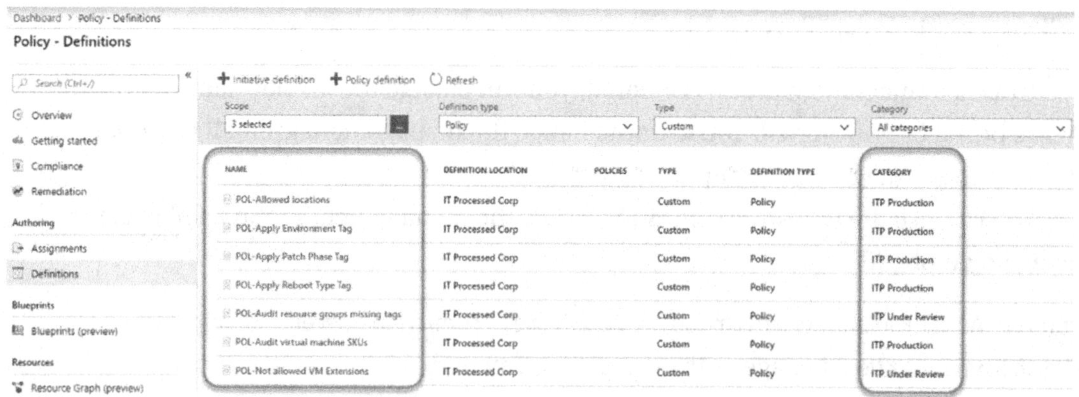

Figure 3-7. *Implementation of policy categories in the Azure portal*

The steps that you take to create a custom policy name and a custom category are performed when you create the policy. You can edit the name and the category of the policy by using the editing option. Figure 3-8 shows these two areas.

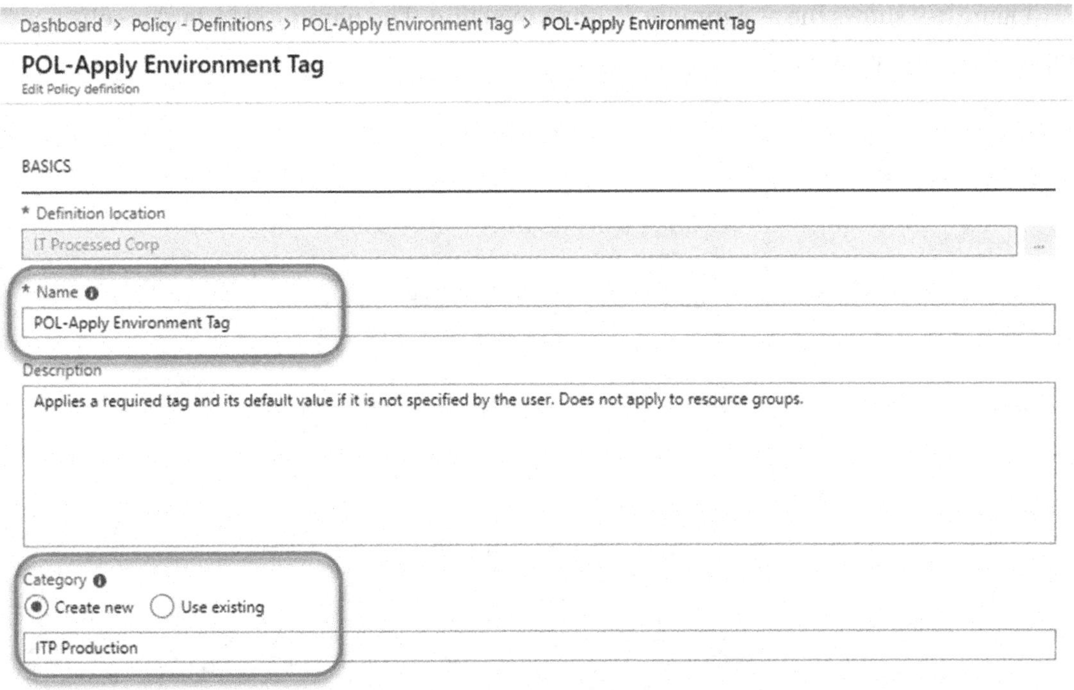

Figure 3-8. *Editing policy names and categories in Azure*

Also note that once a category has been created, you can select the Use Existing option to pick a previously created category (built-in or custom).

Assignment naming standards can also be used to provide further organizational standards to your governance environment. Table 3-4 gives examples of using a standard for assignments.

Table 3-4. *Assignment Name Examples*

Assignment Prefix	Description
Enforce-	Policies that enforce a standard
Auditing-	Policies that are used in audit only mode
ASC	A prefix that is applied automatically by policies assigned through Azure Security Center

Figure 3-9 shows the assignment naming in action. The naming standard is self-explanatory to the portal user.

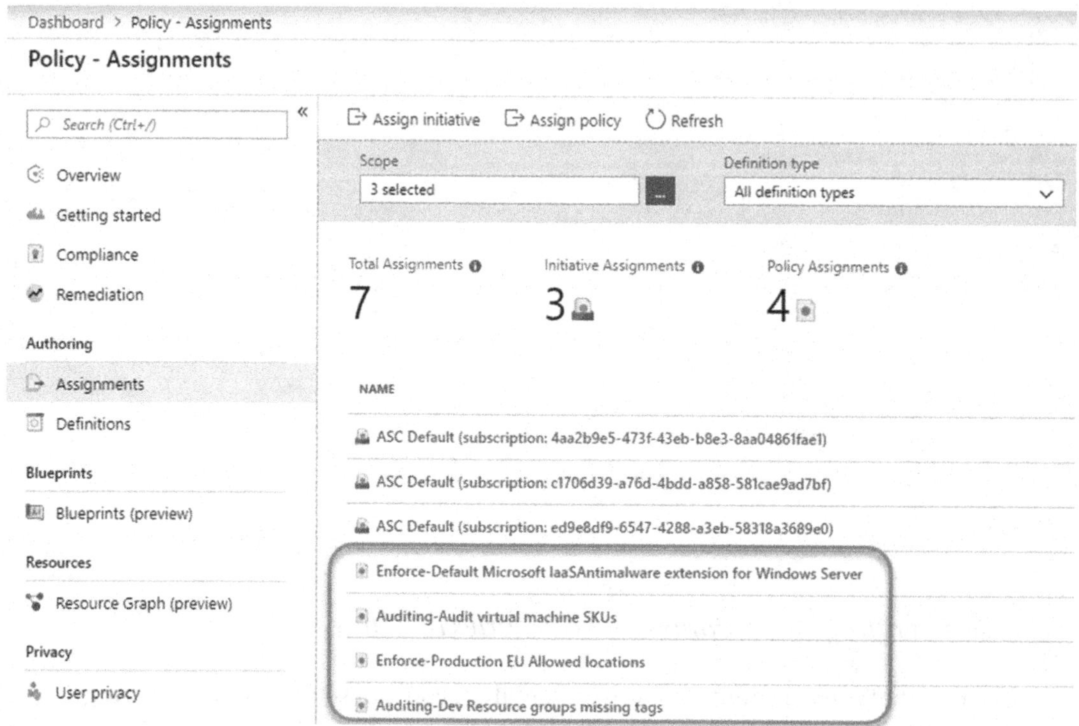

Figure 3-9. *Assignment naming examples*

Initiatives

Initiatives, as discussed in Chapter 1, are a way to group policies in order to have a consistent compliance policy for specific governance and compliance objectives.

Similar to policies, there are three naming categories for initiatives.

- Initiative definition name
- Initiative assignment name
- Initiative category

Microsoft Azure provides built-in initiatives under multiple default categories. These initiatives are not assigned by default. A recommended practice is to create your own categories and new custom initiatives that are planned, scoped, and assigned in line with the governance objectives for your environment. A sample approach for initiative naming is detailed in Table 3-5, where a prefix identifies your custom initiative. The categories for initiatives can be the same as those used for policies.

Table 3-5. *Custom Initiative Category Examples*

Initiative Prefix	Category Name
INI-	ITP Under Review ITP Production ITP POC

This implements a naming standard that gives a clear view of the purpose of the initiatives you create and assign. Figure 3-10 shows the Azure policy definition node listing custom policies with the category and naming standards.

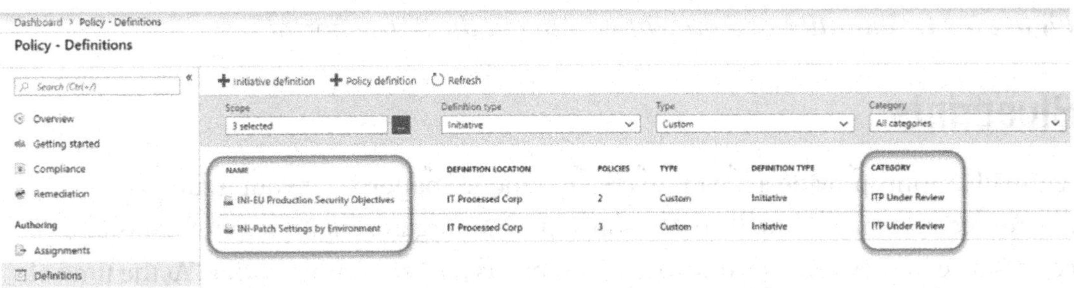

Figure 3-10. *Initiative naming with a custom category*

The steps that you take to create the custom initiative names and a custom category are performed when you create the initiative. You can edit the name and the category of the policy by using the editing option.

Once a category has been created, you can select the Use Existing option to pick a previously created category (built-in or custom). It is important to note that categories may not be available for selection, as this is dependent on the scope option you select. The scope option will only present categories that were created and store at that level when a policy or initiative was created.

Assignment naming standards can also be used to provide further organizational standards to your governance environment. The default assignment name for your initiatives will be the same as the initiative name. You can use the default name or change this name based on your naming standards. Figure 3-11 shows the required initiative assignment naming field, which you can change.

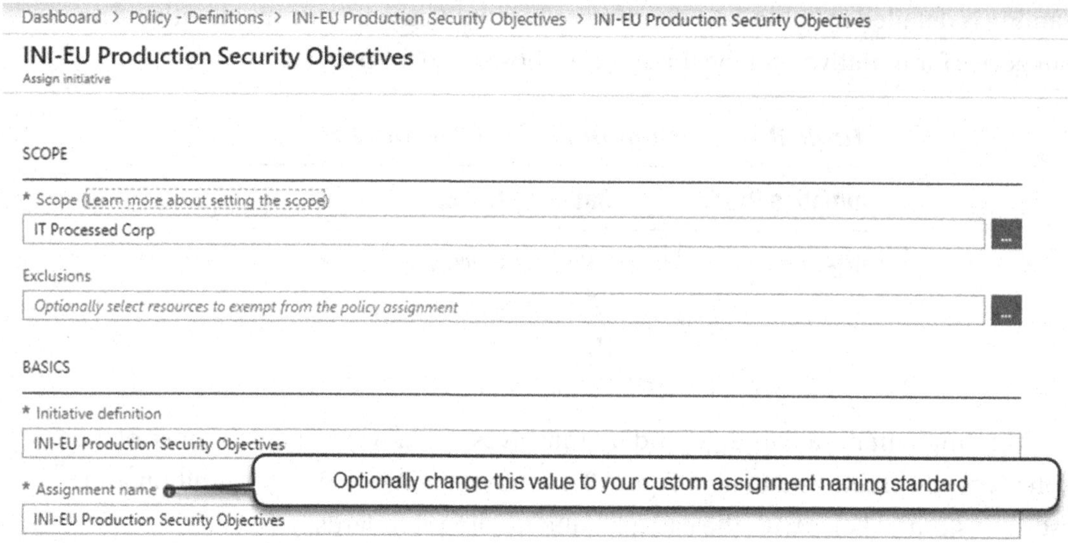

Figure 3-11. *Initiative assignment naming in the Azure portal*

Blueprints

Azure Blueprints provide a means to create standard patterns for your Azure environments, which from the onset adhere to your organization's requirements and compliance framework. The environment scope is an Azure subscription. At the time of writing, Blueprints contain the following.

- Role assignments
- Policy assignments
- Azure Resource Manager templates
- Resource groups

The artifacts contained within Azure Blueprints inherit their naming convention. The naming standard consideration is as follows.

- Blueprint name
- Blueprint version
- Blueprint assignment name

The three areas depend on the life-cycle stage of the blueprint. The relevant life-cycle stages of the blueprint are creation and assignment. Though you can edit a blueprint, you cannot change the blueprint name during the editing operation. For blueprints, it is suggested to use a naming convention with a pattern similar to the one used for subscriptions. The name can be up to 48 characters (numbers and letters), with no spaces or special characters. Table 3-6 provides examples of a blueprint naming convention.

Table 3-6. *Azure Blueprint Naming Examples*

Blueprint Standard	Example
<Lifecycle stage>SubBP	DevSubBP
<Application><Lifecycle stage>SubBP	MyBusinessAppProdSub

When you initiate the create step for a blueprint, you are presented with the blueprint name field and description, as shown in Figure 3-12. Provide the name, and more importantly, a clear description of the usage.

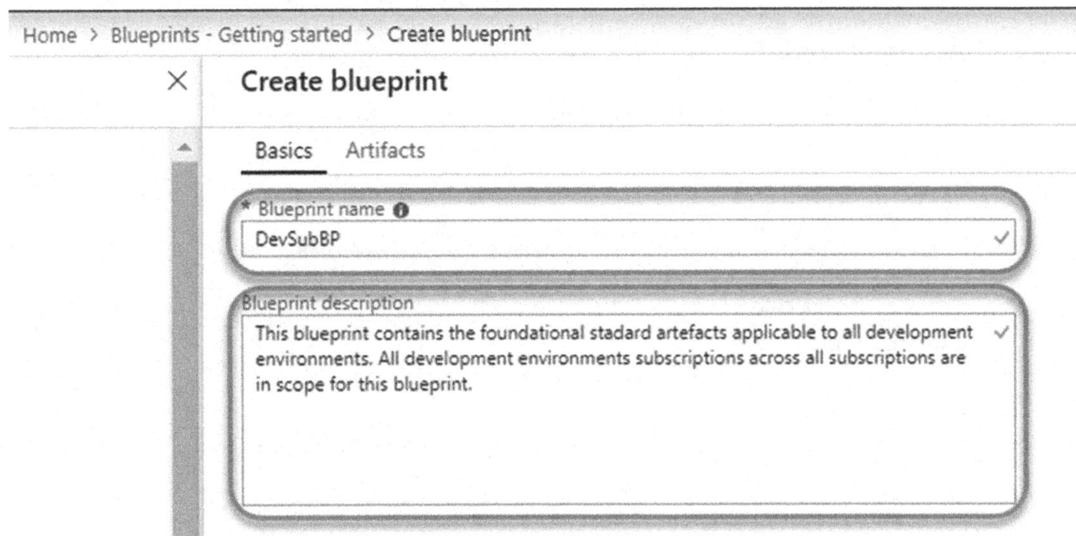

Figure 3-12. *Blueprint name and description in the Azure portal*

The next step in naming a blueprint is the version. The blueprints you create by default are saved as a draft and cannot be used until published. You publish the blueprint when you are ready to use it in assignments. The publishing process requires a mandatory version, and optionally, change notes. The version can be letters, numbers, and hyphens, with a maximum length of 20 characters. It is recommended to use a notation similar to software versions, where the first number denotes a major version and appended incremental numbers denote incremental versions; for example, 1.0 for the first version and 1.1 for a minor change to that version, and 2.0 for the next major version of the same blueprint. Figures 3-13 and 3-14 show examples of this notation in the Azure portal.

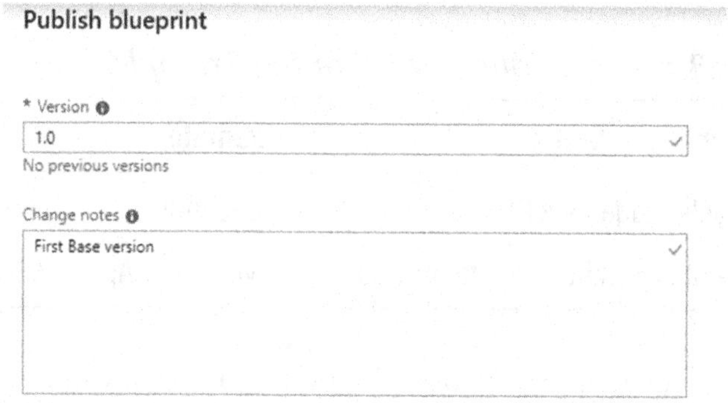

***Figure 3-13.** Blueprint version and change notes*

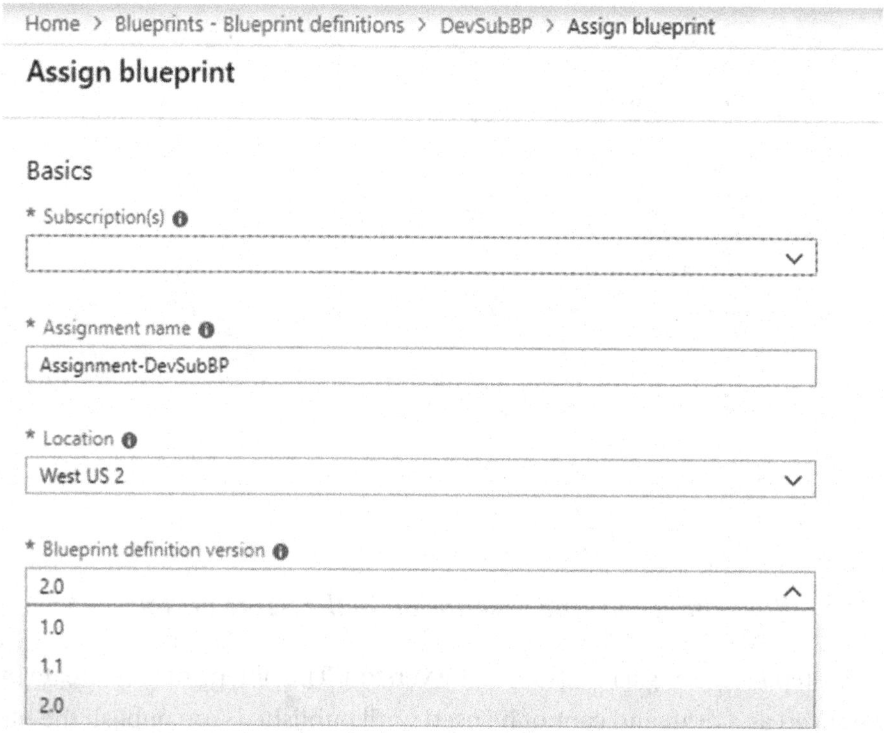

***Figure 3-14.** Blueprint version changes as seen in the Azure portal The latest version of the blueprint is what you will see in the blueprint definitions node. The previous versions are visible and available when you initiate the assignment process.*

The last name component that you can change is the assignment name. You can accept the default assignment name, which is typically the blueprint name with an assignment prefix, or you can use your own defined naming standard.

A final note about blueprint names is that although you cannot rename through the portal, it is possible to achieve this by using an export/import process.

There is a solution in the PowerShell gallery at `www.powershellgallery.com/packages/Manage-AzureRMBlueprint/2.2`, which allows you to export or import an existing blueprint. The import process includes the option to rename the blueprint.

Naming at Scale with Automation

The examples and illustrations in this chapter use the Azure portal for simplicity. In a large enterprise, the naming of Azure resources can be automated and scaled through the use of a variety of options. Examples include using an Azure Resource Manager (ARM) template to create multiple resource groups for a subscription.

You can also use PowerShell or the Azure CLI to automate the naming process for the resources discussed in this chapter.

Additional Links and Examples

There are great examples of Azure naming conventions in the official Microsoft online documentation.

- `https://docs.microsoft.com/en-us/azure/architecture/best-practices/naming-conventions` offers recommended patterns as well as rules and constraints for naming resource types.
- `https://docs.microsoft.com/en-us/rest/api/storageservices/naming-and-referencing-containers--blobs--and-metadata` provides examples of naming of containers, blobs, and metadata.
- `https://docs.microsoft.com/en-us/azure/virtual-machines/windows/infrastructure-example` uses an application workload to demonstrate naming for virtual machines (VM) and the associated resources. The extracts highlight the sections showing the example naming conventions.

"The resulting design must incorporate:

- *An Azure subscription and account*
- *A single resource group*
- *Azure Managed Disks*
- *A virtual network with two subnets*
- *Availability sets for the VMs with a similar role*
- *Virtual machines*

All the above follow these naming conventions:

- *Adventure Works Cycles uses [IT workload]-[location]-[Azure resource] as a prefix*
    - *For this example, "azos" (Azure Online Store) is the IT workload name and "use" (East US 2) is the location*
- *Virtual networks use AZOS-USE-VN[number]*
- *Availability sets use azos-use-as-[role]*
- *Virtual machine names use azos-use-vm-[vmname]"*

*"**Availability sets***

To maintain high availability of all four tiers of their online store, Adventure Works Cycles decided on four availability sets:

- *azos-use-as-web for the web servers*
- *azos-use-as-app for the application servers*
- *azos-use-as-sql for the SQL Servers*
- *azos-use-as-dc for the domain controllers*

Virtual machines

Adventure Works Cycles decided on the following names for their Azure VMs:

- azos-use-vm-web01 for the first web server
- azos-use-vm-web02 for the second web server
- azos-use-vm-app01 for the first application server

- azos-use-vm-app02 for the second application server
- azos-use-vm-sql01 for the first SQL Server server in the cluster
- azos-use-vm-sql02 for the second SQL Server server in the cluster
- azos-use-vm-dc01 for the first domain controller
- azos-use-vm-dc02 for the second domain controller"

The following are examples of two naming standards enforcing automation.

- Sample of enforcing naming standards with Azure policies. `https://github.com/Azure/azure-policy/tree/master/samples/TextPatterns/enforce-match-pattern`
- Sample of enforcing naming standards with ARM templates. `https://github.com/Azure/azure-quickstart-templates/blob/master/1-CONTRIBUTION-GUIDE/README.md`

Summary

This chapter focused on how naming conventions play a key role in planning, implementing, and managing your governance for well-managed cloud environments. Ensure that this critical and value activity is performed consistently to the standards of the organization. The next chapter delves into the implementation and management of Azure policies and initiatives.

CHAPTER 4

Azure Policy Implementation and Management

In Chapter 1, we touched briefly on Azure Policy and the role that it plays in Azure Governance. The following is a recap of the introduction to Azure Policy.

Azure Policy is a service that you use to audit and enforce your organization's rules and standards to the resources that you create and manage in Azure. Policies provide the means to ensure the resources are and remain compliant to the organizational rules throughout their life cycle; for example, they ensure that all resources are tagged with a cost center value or that resources for the European branch office are only created in European Azure locations to maintain data sovereignty.

Azure has a number of prebuilt policies and any subscribed tenant (organization or individual) can leverage. These built-in policies cover rules that are common to most organizations. You can view and assign these built-in policies using the Azure portal or programmatically through command-line tools.

This chapter delves deeper into Azure policy and is split into the following sections.

- Azure Policy Planning
- Azure Policies in Action
- Taking Actions on Azure Policy Results

P. De Tender et al., *Pro Azure Governance and Security*, https://doi.org/10.1007/978-1-4842-4910-9_4

Azure Policy Planning

When it comes to technology, we often forget the importance of planning. This is simply because, unlike other industries, we are able to dive in deep without being blocked. This is simply a case of "just because you can does not mean you should." The following are some building blocks to consider before you dive into creating and deploying policies.

- Azure Policy terminology
- Policy scope
- Policy life cycle

Azure Policy Terminology

- Exclusions

Technological concepts, products, and services often introduce new terms that you must become familiar with in order to maximize their capabilities. This is similar to going to a restaurant and trying to figure out what to order. In a restaurant, the menu lists the dishes, and more importantly, what they mean. In technology, the same term can have multiple descriptions based on a product or a service. Table 4-1 lists the most common and essential terms in Azure Policy and their summarized descriptions. Refer to the Microsoft web page at `https://docs.microsoft.com/en-us/azure/governance/policy/overview` to get additional information on Azure Policy terms and concepts.

Table 4-1. *Azure Policy Terminology*

Azure Policy Terminology	Description
Policy	Azure Policy is a service that you use to audit and enforce your organization's rules and standards to the resources you create and manage in Azure. This is referred to as a policy definition in the Azure portal.
Initiative	One or more policies grouped together to represent a set of applicable compliance objectives. This is referred to as an initiative definition in the Azure portal.
Scope	Policies and initiatives are assigned at multiple levels, known as scopes. A scope can be a management group, subscription, or resource group.

(continued)

Table 4-1. (*continued*)

Azure Policy Terminology	Description
Exclusion	Excluded from the policy or initiative (similar to group policy block inheritance).
Policy Location	Where you store the policy definition. Typically, at a management group level or specific subscription
Assignment	The process of targeting a policy or initiative to a specific scope (Management group, subscription or resource group).

Policy Location

The policies and initiatives definitions that you create and manage must have a storage location. The two options available to store policy and initiative definitions are a management group or a subscription. The location also determines where a policy can be applied. As an example, a policy definition stored at a child management group level cannot be assigned to resources above the child management group or other child management groups at the same level. Once a definition location is selected and saved, it cannot be changed. In Figure 4-1, the effects of selecting the respective management group (MG) or subscription (sub) location for the policy (POL) definitions are as follows.

- **POL-A** can be assigned to all management groups, their child management groups, and respective subscriptions and resource groups.
- **POL-B** can be assigned to all MG-Productions resources, its child management groups, and respective resources below its child management groups. POL-B cannot be assigned to MG-Pre-Production or MG-Development and their respective child resources. The management groups above MG-Production cannot be used as assigned scopes.
- **POL-C** can only be assigned to the CC001-Sales-Sub subscription and its resources groups.

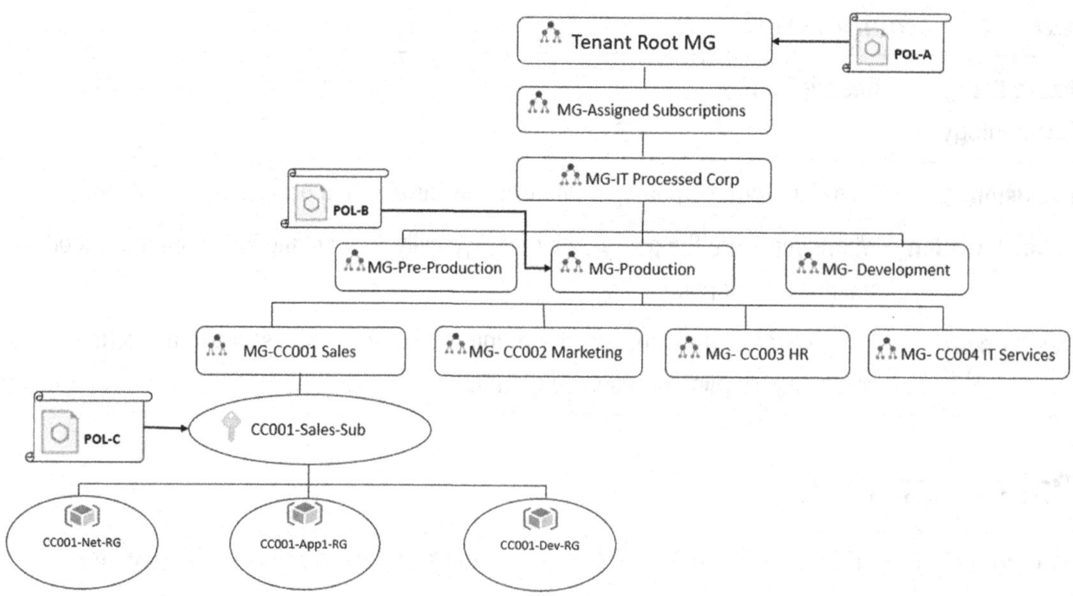

Figure 4-1. *Policy location planning*

The impact of where a policy is located underlines the importance of planning this part of the governance process ahead of creating your definitions. The location can be changed by re-creating the policy, but this would be somewhat inefficient.

Policy Assignment Scope and Exclusions

Policy assignment scope and exclusions are similar to the process of inviting friends and families to an event and the nuances that can ensue when there is no harmony. Imagine a scenario where you want to invite family A and family B, but Uncle Bob in family A does not get along with Uncle Fred in family B. You will have two options: send the invite with instructions to both families not to bring the two uncles, or send individual invites to all except Uncle Fred and Uncle Bob. The two approaches will have the same effect—the question is, which is better?

Policy assignments are similar to the family invite scenario but can get very complex if not planned right. The recommendation is to plan to group your resources using management groups and resource groups structured to account for exclusions. If you know a specific resource need to be excluded from a policy, plan to have these resources in the same management group, subscription, or resource group. Figure 4-2 illustrates a policy scoped to a subscription and all the resource groups in that subscription.

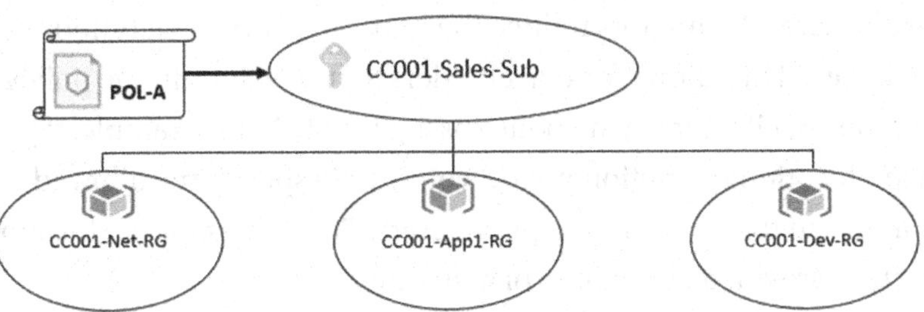

Figure 4-2. *Policy scoped with no exclusions*

Figure 4-3 shows a policy scoped at the subscription level with an exclusion of one resource group (CC001-Net-RG). This is an example of planning for exclusions using a resource group (the policy may not apply to the network resource that you store in that resource group).

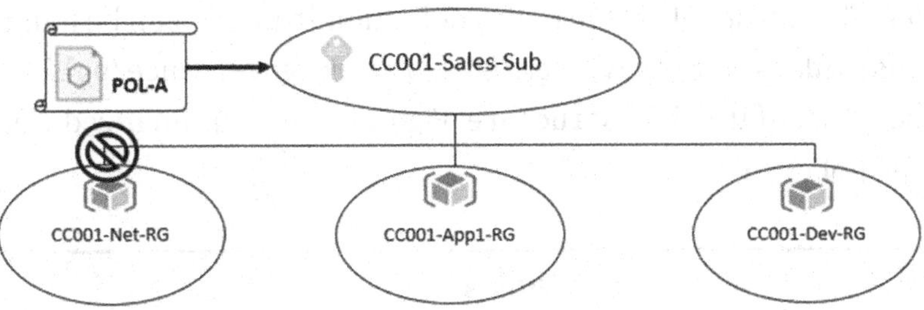

Figure 4-3. *Policy scoped with an exclusion*

Policy Basics

Creating a policy is simple, but before diving in to create one, or using a built-in policy, there are basic rules. A policy definition is structured as follows in a JSON format: mode, parameters, display name, description, and policy rule—logical evaluation and effect.

- **Mode:** This is used to specify which resource type will be evaluated. The two supported modes are All and Indexed. If a mode is not specified, the default is All.
    - **All:** Evaluates all resource types; the default mode
    - **Indexed:** Used for policies that are applicable for tags and locations

- **Parameters:** Parameters reduce the number of policy definitions that you create. This allows for placeholders for the values in the policy that you specify during the policy assignment. As an example, if you have a location restriction policy, you simply specify the allowed locations in the definition as parameters. The values for the locations are then provided at the time of assignment.
- **Display name:** This is the name that you give a policy in free text format.
- **Description:** An optional field that provides further details on the policy and its purpose.
- **Policy rule:** This is the engine of your policy. It has a logical evaluation part to test for conditions, and an effect part to action rules. The full details of the policy definition structure can be found at `https://docs.microsoft.com/en-us/azure/governance/policy/concepts/definition-structure`. Figure 4-4 is a summarized view of the policy rules.

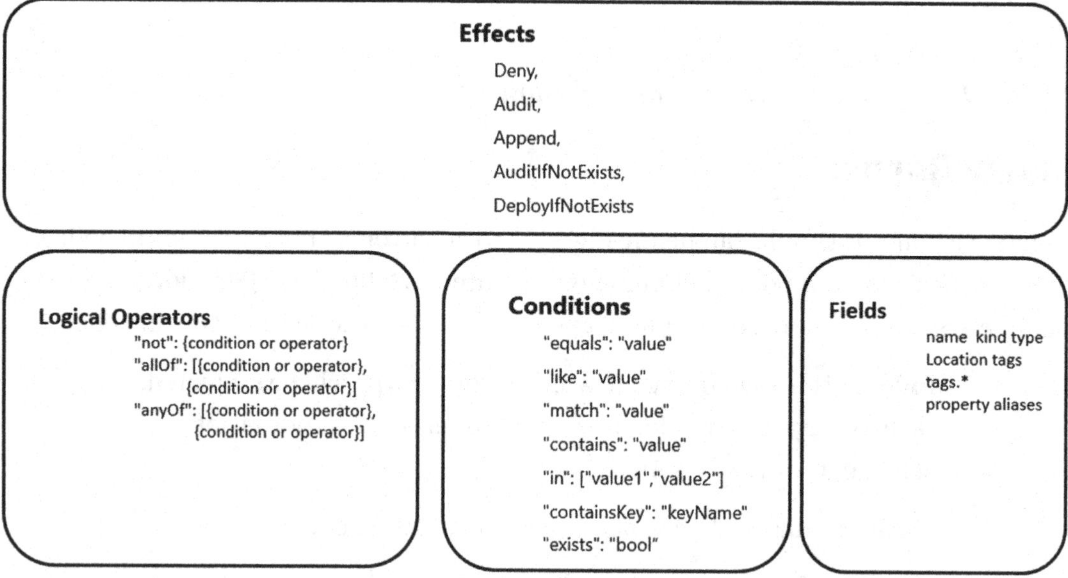

Figure 4-4. *Logical view of Azure Policies and their different operations, conditions and fields*

The following is a sample JSON format illustrating the structure.

```
{
    "properties": {
        "mode": "all",
        "parameters": {
            "allowedLocations": {
                "type": "array",
                "metadata": {
                    "description": "The list of locations that can be
                    specified when deploying resources",
                    "strongType": "location",
                    "displayName": "Allowed locations"
                }
            }
        },
        "displayName": "Allowed locations",
        "description": "This policy enables you to restrict the locations
        your organization can specify when deploying resources.",
        "policyRule": {
            "if": {
                "not": {
                    "field": "location",
                    "in": "[parameters('allowedLocations')]"
                }
            },
            "then": {
                "effect": "deny"
            }
        }
    }
}
```

Azure Policies in Action

Now that we have established policies basics and planning, it is time to see it in action. This section takes you through creating, assigning, and updating policies, and then concludes with using initiatives. This section uses the Azure portal to walk you through the process. First, create a dashboard dedicated to governance and policy management by following these steps.

1. Connect to the Azure portal at `https://portal.azure.com`.
2. Select **Dashboard** in the left navigation pane. Click **+ New dashboard**.

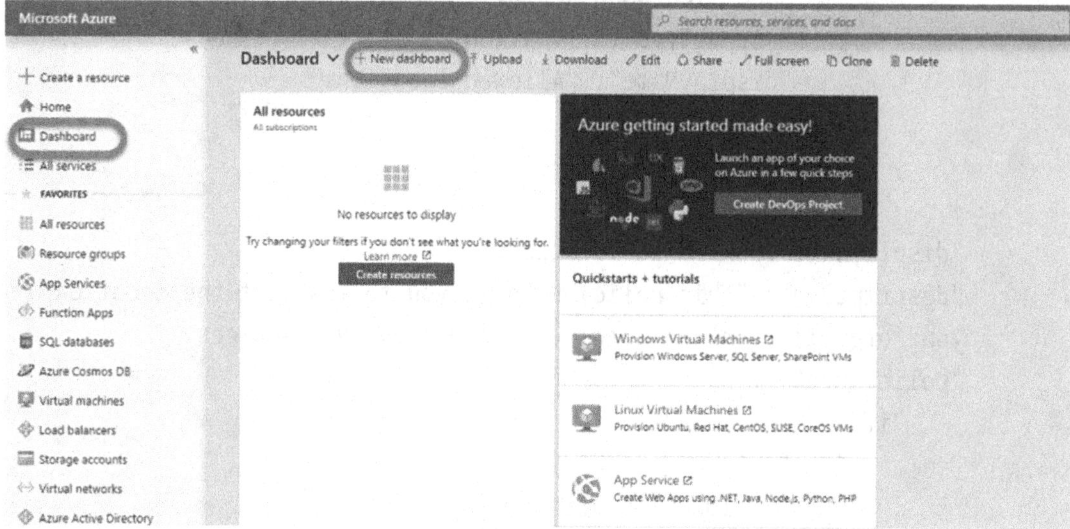

3. Replace the default My Dashboard title with **Governance & Compliance**.
4. Under the Tile Gallery section, click and drag the Markdown tile onto the canvas.

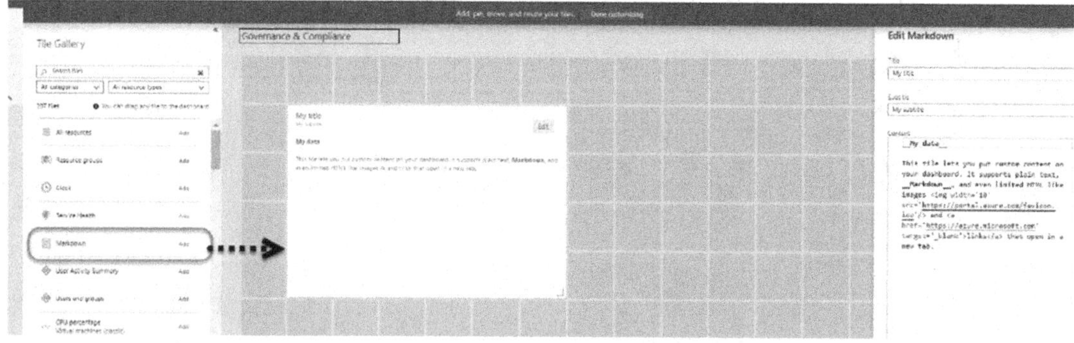

5. In the Edit Markdown section, change the title to **Policy Management** and the subtitle to **Access Policy node by clicking on the Icon.** Use the following code syntax in the Content field.

```
<a href='https://portal.azure.com/#blade/Microsoft_Azure_Policy/
PolicyMenuBlade/Overview' target='_Self'>
<img width='70' src='https://portal.azure.com/favicon.ico'/>
</a>
```

6. Click **Done** to complete Edit Markdown.

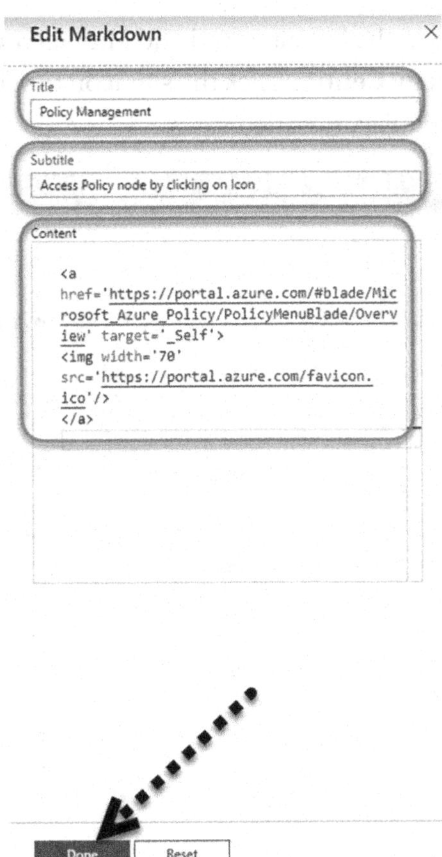

7. Resize the title to your preference and click **Done customizing**.

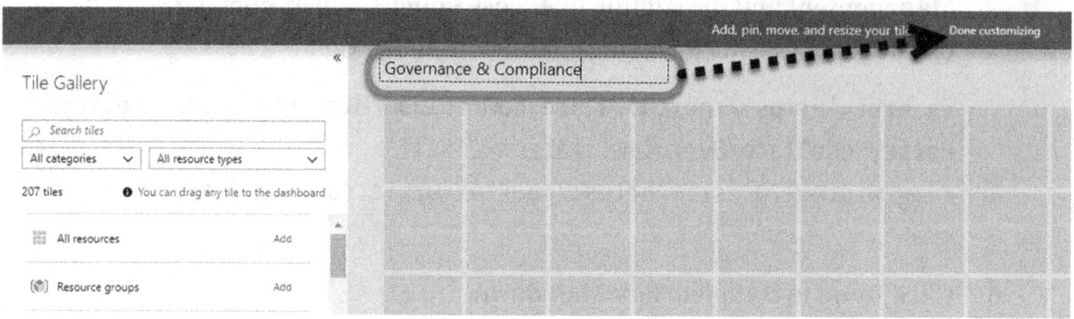

8. Click **All services** in the left pane and add **Management groups**, **Policy**, and **Security Center**. Click the star icon to select and deselect the default Favorites items.

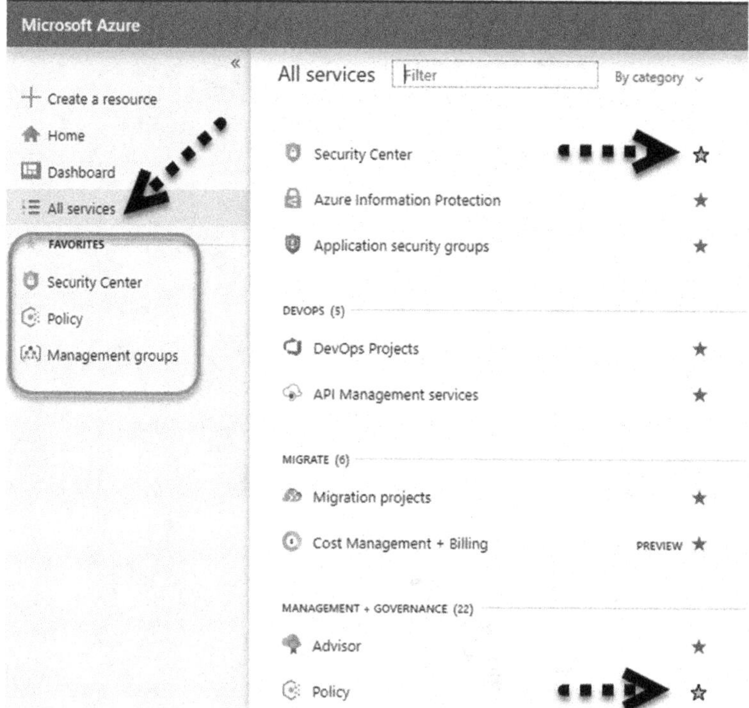

9. Click **Management groups** under Favorites. Click the pin icon to pin the management group tile to the dashboard.

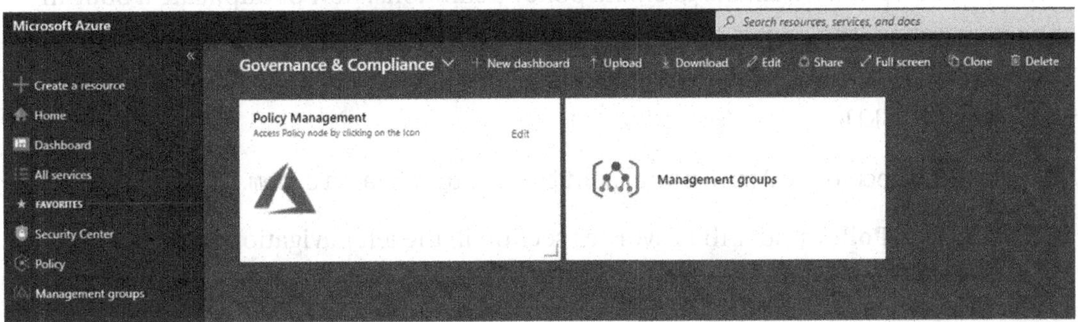

The result is a simple dashboard and focused favorites dedicated to the governance and compliance activities that you perform in the Azure portal. You can find out more about Azure dashboards, and how to customize and share them, at `https://docs.microsoft.com/en-us/azure/azure-portal/azure-portal-dashboards`.

Finally, before moving on to the next section, make sure that you have reviewed the "Azure Policy Planning" section and Chapter 3. The exercises in this chapter use the setup of management groups, subscriptions, and resource groups shown in Figure 4-5 as a starting point.

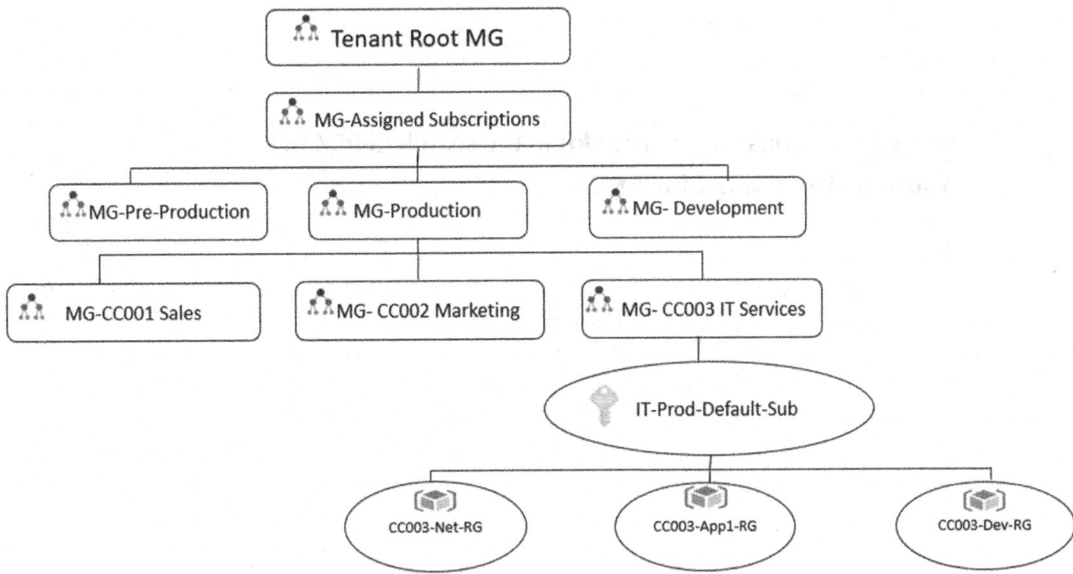

***Figure 4-5.** Management group structure for chapter exercises*

Creating Policy Definitions

There are two options available to create policy definitions: new or duplicate a built-in or custom policy. The easiest option is to use the duplicate option on a built-in policy. The next steps walk you through duplicating a built-in policy to audit allowed virtual machine (VM) SKUs.

1. Connect to the Azure portal at `https://portal.azure.com`.
2. Click **Policy** under the Favorites section in the left navigation bar (this assumes that you followed the previous steps in this chapter).
3. In the Policy blade, select **Definitions**.

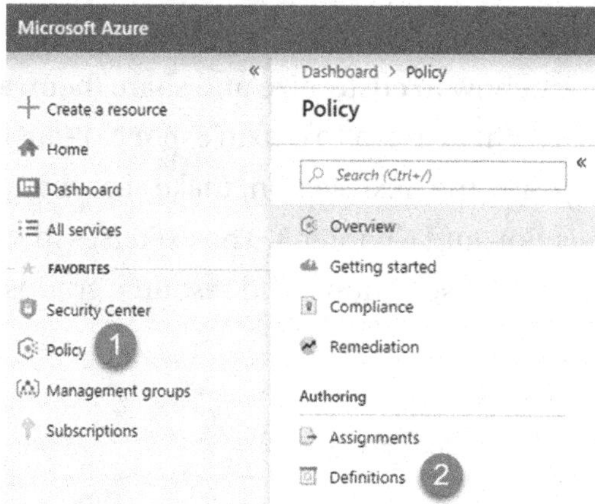

4. In the Definitions blade, type **sku** in the search field. Click **Allowed virtual machine SKUs**.

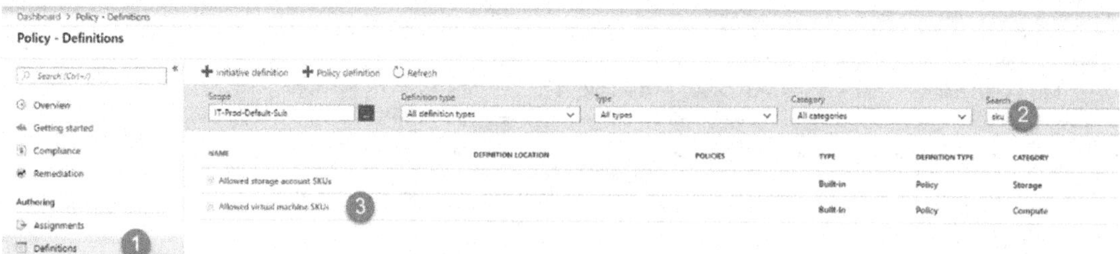

5. You are presented with the built-in policy definition. Click **Duplicate definition**.

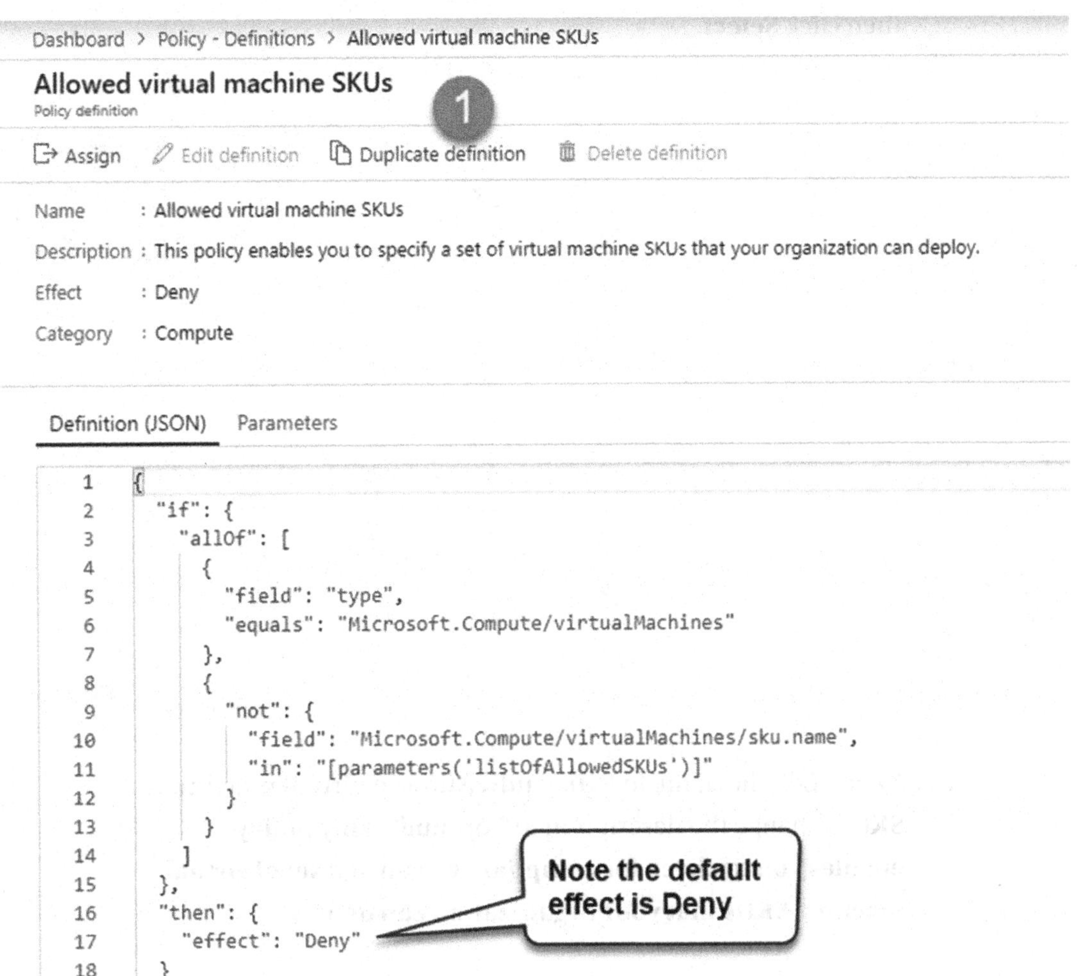

6. Make the following changes.

   a. Definition location: Click **... MG-Assigned Subscriptions**, and then click **Select**.

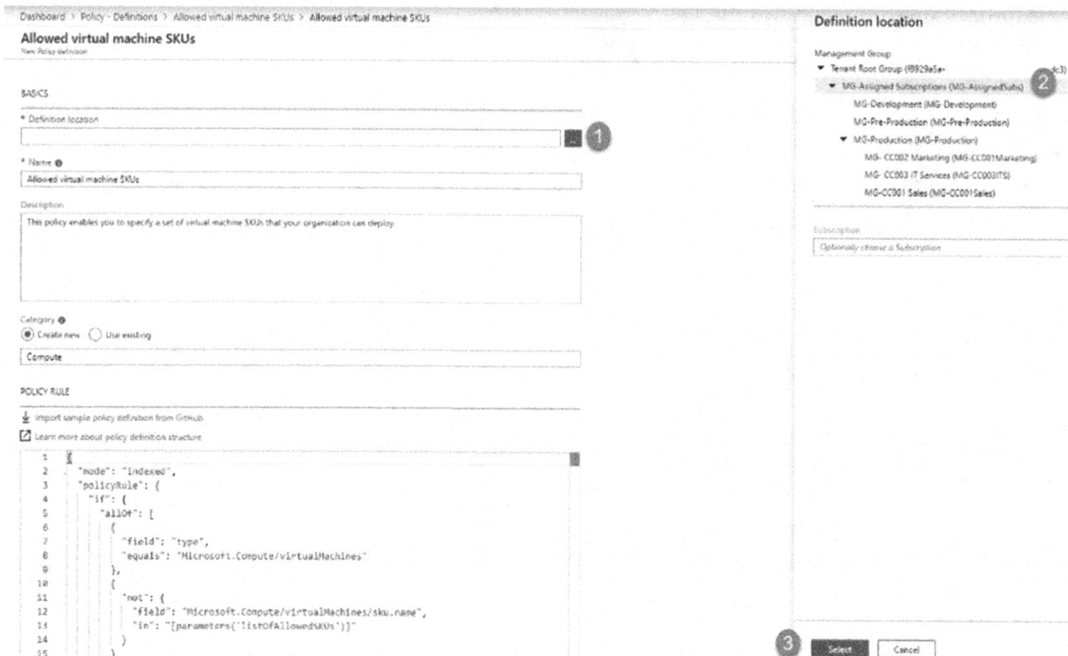

   b. Name: Edit the name to **POL-Audit Allowed virtual machine SKUs**. Change the description to **This audit only policy enables you to check for compliance against a set of virtual machine SKUs that your organization can deploy**.

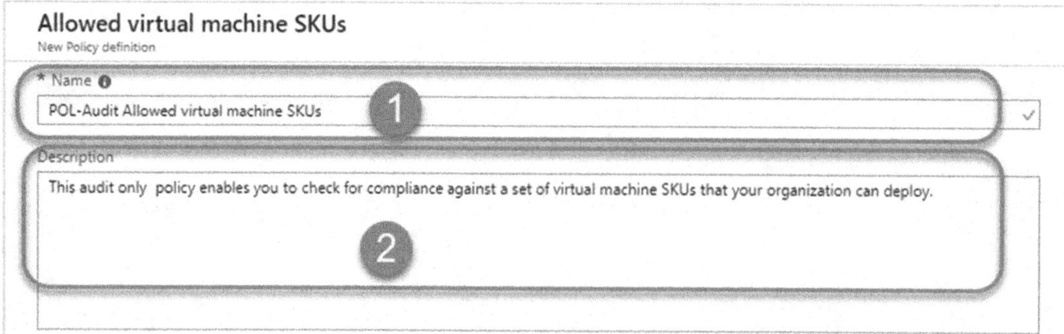

c. Category: Ensure that **Create new** is selected and type **Under Review**. Change the `"effect"` value to `"Audit"` and click **Save** to complete the steps.

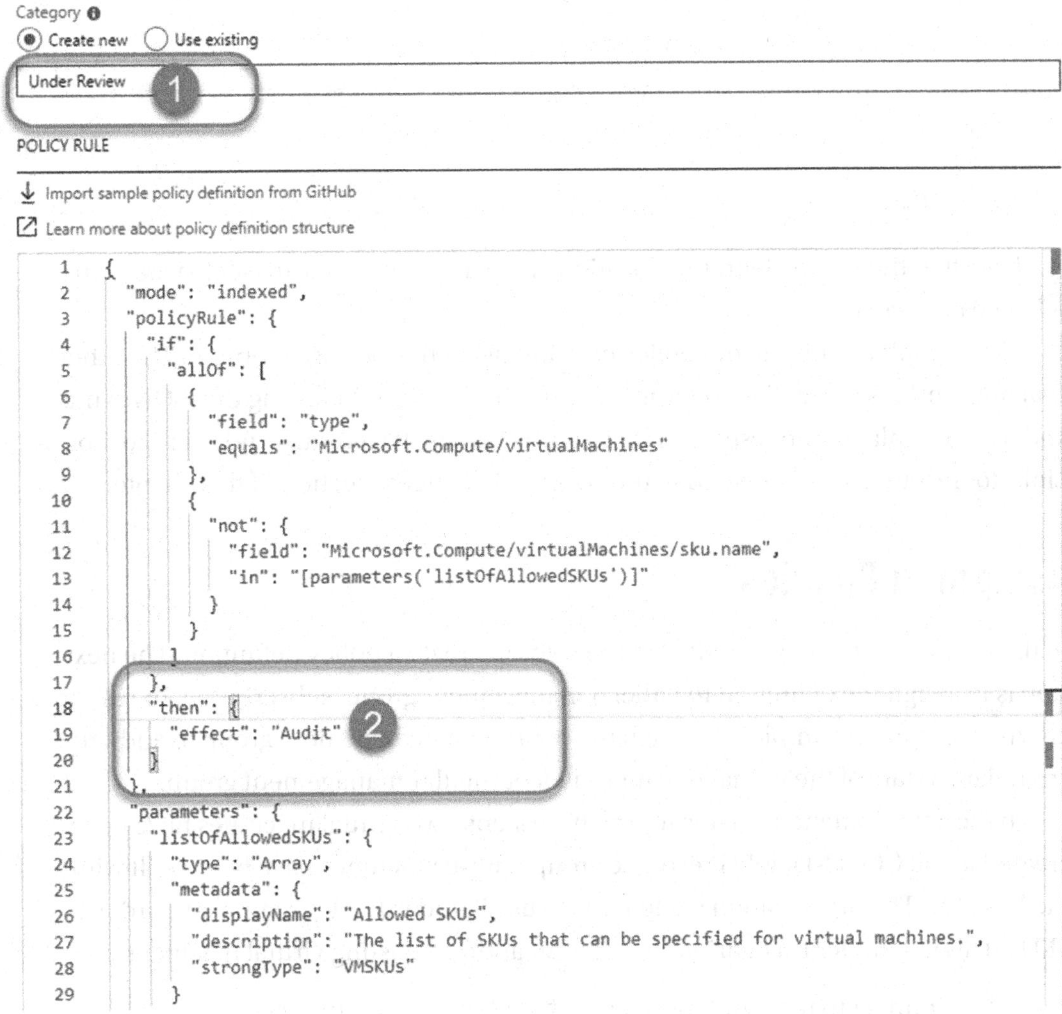

7. Verify that the custom policy has been created by selecting **Definitions** and setting the type filter to **Custom**.

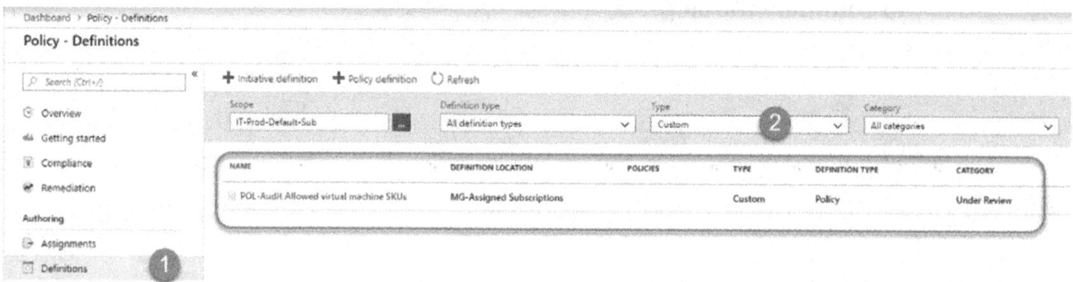

Note that the name, definition location, and category values are set to what you selected and typed.

This completes the custom policy creation using the Duplicate option. The other available options create the policy in an appropriate editor following the JSON syntax and use a template from resources available at Microsoft web sites and Git repositories. Links for resources are provided in the "Useful Resources" section of this chapter.

Assigning Policies

In the previous section, you followed the steps to create a policy definition. The next step is to assign the definition to either a management group, subscription, or resource group. In our next example, we assign the policy to a management group to audit the compliance state of the virtual machines in a particular management group.

In the environment used to capture these steps, two virtual machines have been created in the CC003-Dev-RG resource group. These machines have been built with the B1s SKU. The organization standard is to use Standard_D1_v2 and Standard_D2_v2 SKUs. This assignment scenario is to allow an audit of existing virtual machines.

1. Connect to the Azure portal at `https://portal.azure.com`.
2. Click **Policy** under the Favorites section in the left navigation bar (this assumes that you followed the previous steps in this chapter).
3. In the Policy blade, click **Assignments** and then **Assign policy**.

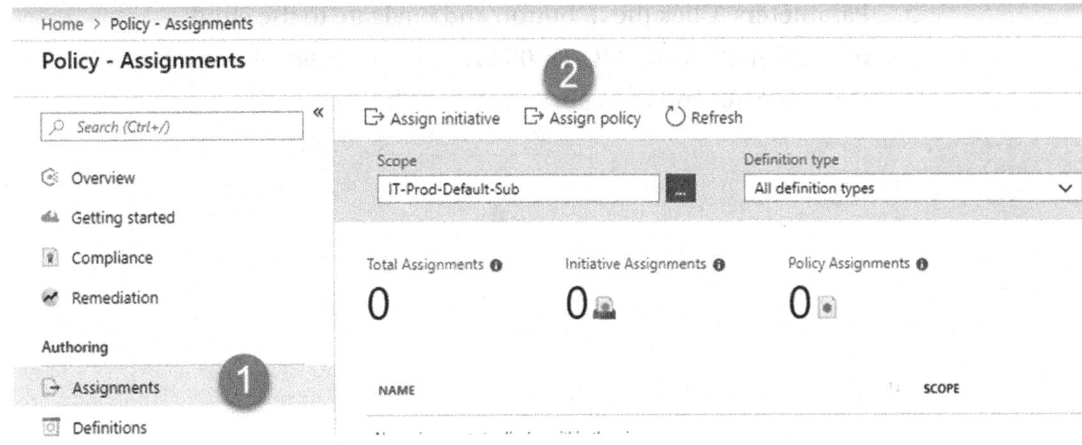

4. Use the following to fill in the details of the assignment page.

    a. Scope: Click the **...** button and select **MG-Production**.

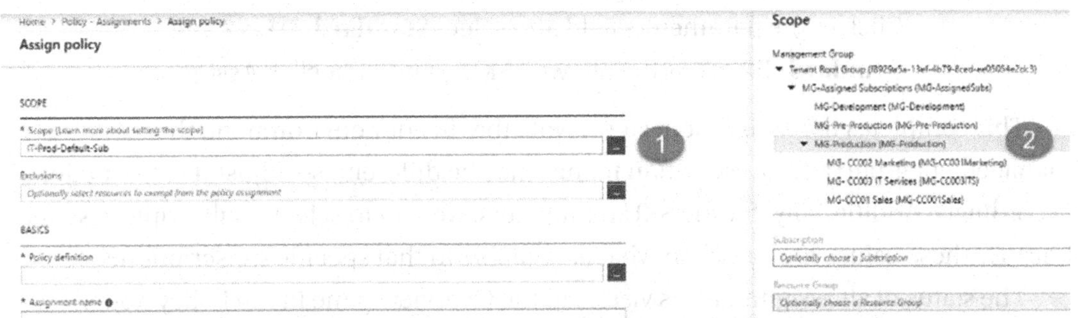

    b. Policy definition: Click the **...** button and change the filter type to **Custom**. Select **POL-Audit Allowed virtual machine SKUs**.

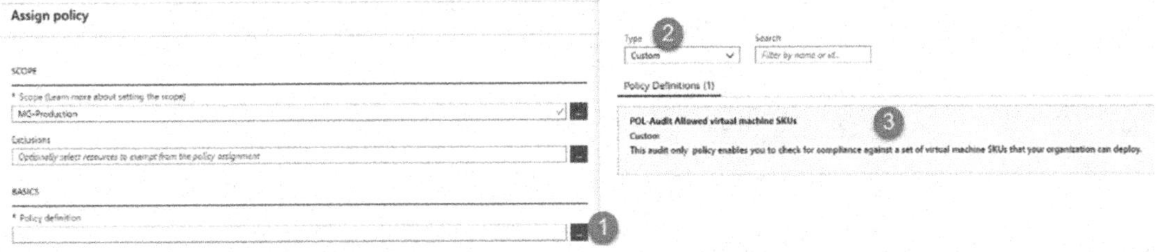

    c. Change the assignment name to **Auditing-POL-Audit Allowed virtual machine SKUs** and provide a description.

d. Parameters: Click the **...** button and navigate to the child management group MG-CC003 IT Services. Select **IT-Prod-Default-Sub**, and then click the **Select** button.

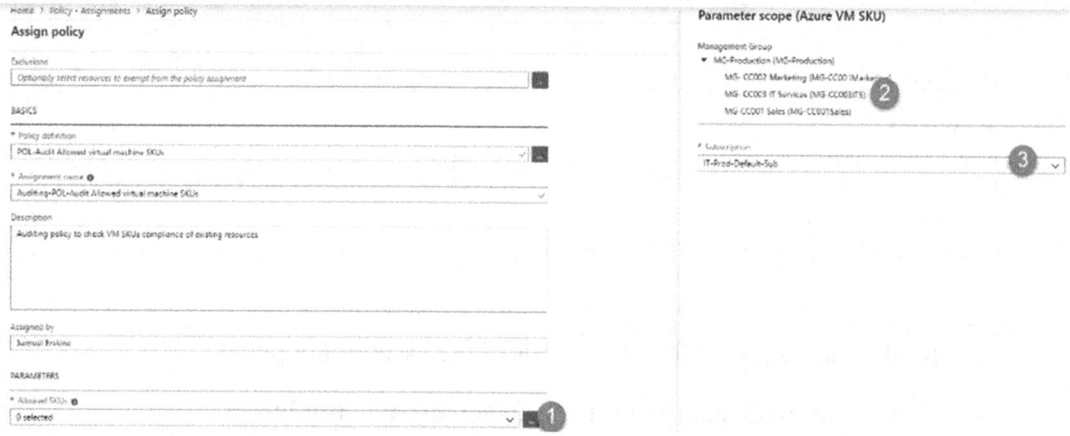

e. Click in the parameters field and select **Standard_D1_v2** and **Standard_D2_v2** as the allowed SKUs, and then click **Assign**.

This completes the assignment steps. Note that in your environment, the management group and subscription names may be different, so adjust the instructions accordingly. Additionally, for the SKU parameters, we had to select a subscription scope because these values are based on what is available in that specific subscription.

The status of all assignments is visible in the Overview pane in the Policy node. When you initially assign a policy, it is marked with a compliance state of **Not started**, as illustrated in Figure 4-6.

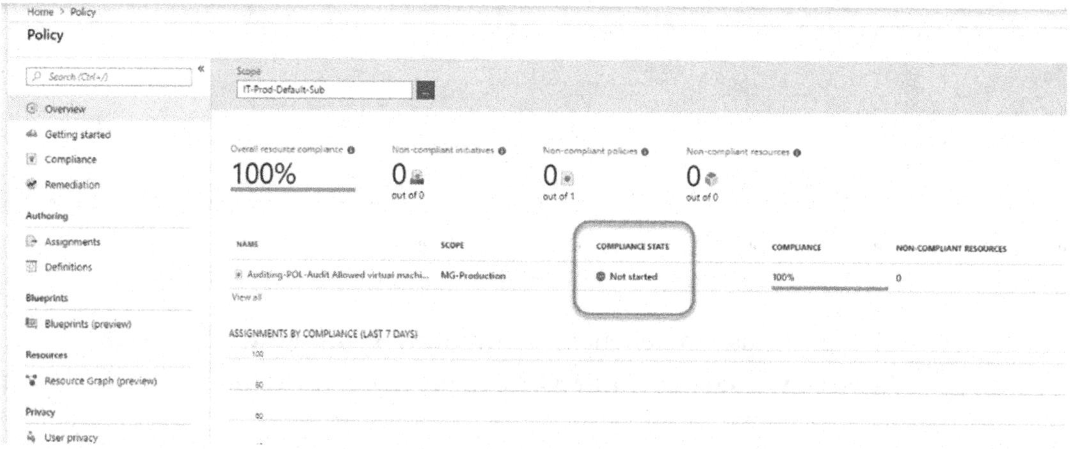

***Figure 4-6.** Initiate state of a policy assignment*

Policies have an evaluation schedule on creation, update, and recurring evaluation. The schedule summary is as follows.

- New Policy/Initiative assignment applied to scope: **30 minutes from assignment**
- Update Policy/Initiative assignment applied to scope: **30 minutes from assignment**
- New resource deployment in scope of Policy/Initiative assignment: **15 minutes from assignment**
- Normal evaluation: **Every 24hrs**

The full details of evaluation and the varying conditions under evaluation can be found at `https://docs.microsoft.com/en-us/azure/governance/policy/how-to/get-compliance-data`. The following is an extract of the details and the recommendations to review the Microsoft web site for changes and enhancements. Azure Policy is a cloud service that continues to evolve, so expect changes.

"Evaluations of assigned policies and initiatives happen as the result of various events:

- *A policy or initiative is newly assigned to a scope. It takes around 30 minutes for the assignment to be applied to the defined scope. Once it's applied, the evaluation cycle begins for resources within that scope against the newly assigned policy or initiative and depending on the effects used by the policy or initiative, resources are marked as compliant or non-compliant. A large policy or initiative evaluated against a large scope of resources can take time. As such, there's no pre-defined expectation of when the evaluation cycle will complete. Once it completes, updated compliance results are available in the portal and SDKs.*
- *A policy or initiative already assigned to a scope is updated. The evaluation cycle and timing for this scenario is the same as for a new assignment to a scope.*
- *A resource is deployed to a scope with an assignment via Resource Manager, REST, Azure CLI, or Azure PowerShell. In this scenario, the effect event (append, audit, deny, deploy) and compliant status information for the individual resource becomes available in the portal and SDKs around 15 minutes later. This event doesn't cause an evaluation of other resources.*

- *Standard compliance evaluation cycle. Once every 24 hours, assignments are automatically reevaluated. A large policy or initiative of many resources can take time, so there's no pre-defined expectation of when the evaluation cycle will complete. Once it completes, updated compliance results are available in the portal and SDKs."*

Once the policy evaluation cycle has completed in our example, the compliance status shows that the two virtual machines are non-compliant. The policy requires either Standard_D1_v2 or Standard_DS2_v2 SKU. The machines are using a Standard_B1 SKU. Figures 4-7 and 4-8 show the overall compliance page and the details of non-compliance to a specific policy.

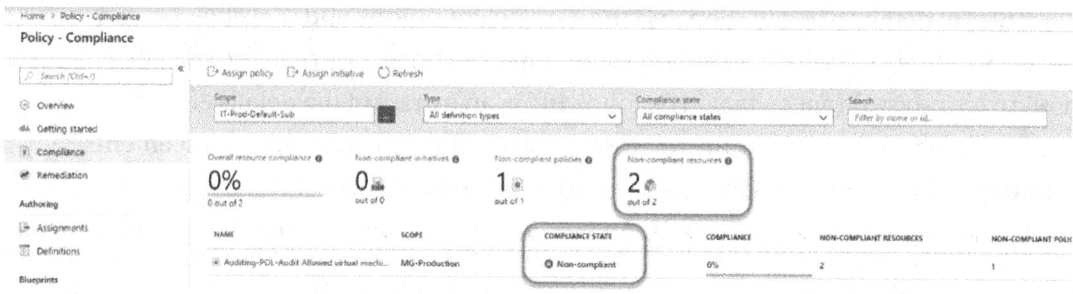

Figure 4-7. *Overall compliance page*

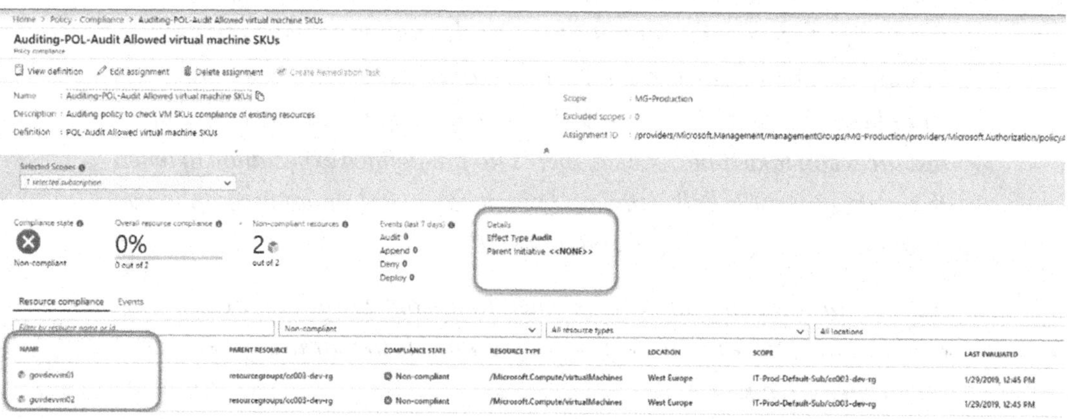

Figure 4-8. *Compliance of a specific policy*

Updating Policies and Assignments

The compliance objectives of an organization change over time. This is due to a variety reasons, including regulator changes and technological advances. The Azure policies that you use to audit or enforce these objectives have to be changed to align. The changes range from minor updates to major updates. Minor updates could be policy name changes or changes to the audit policies.

Major changes include rule effects, changing an audit policy to an enforce policy, and changing the scope (resources in scope of the policy change).

We will use our previous policy example to demonstrate how to address a minor trigger and a major trigger of change to the SKU type policy. The following are our example scenarios.

- **Minor:** Change the category to production and update the description to include the SKUs. The description is important in this case because it enhances the visibility of the policy audits when viewing the compliance state.
- **Major:** Change the policy rule effect from "audit" to "enforce" to ensure that only approved SKUs can be created.

Minor Objective Changes

Minor objective changes include the SKU names in the description and creating a new category called *production* to promote the policy from under review to production ready.

1. Navigate to the Definitions section of the Policy node in the Azure portal.
2. Select **POL-Audit Allowed virtual machines SKUs**, which you created in the previous steps. Click **Edit definition.**

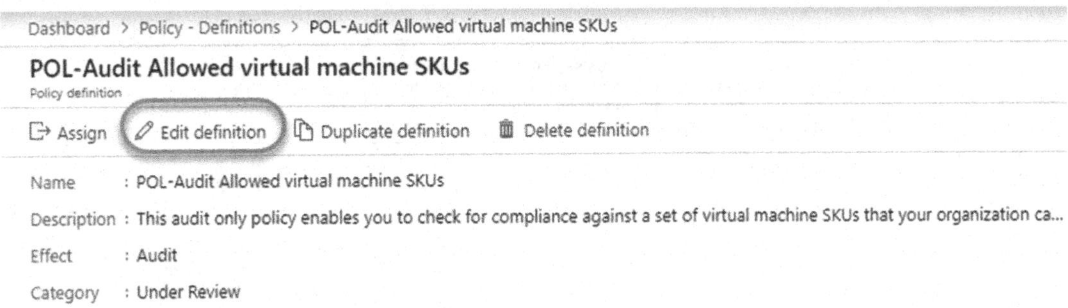

3. Append the following to the description: **The SKUs in scope of this policy are specified in the assignment. Ensure you list the SKUs in the description of the assignment**. Under the category, ensure that **Create new** is selected. Overwrite the existing value with **Production Approved**. Click **Save** to complete the definition update.

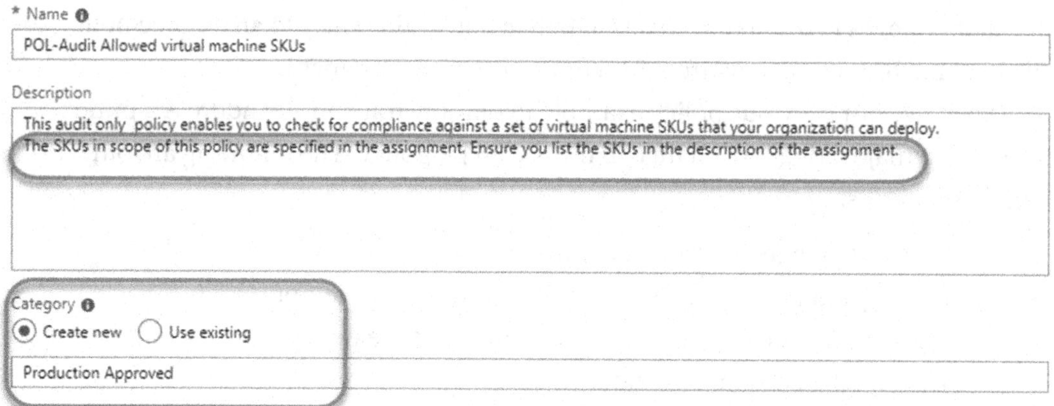

The next steps to the minor change involve editing the policy assignment.

1. Navigate to the Assignments section of the Policy node.
2. Select the previous assignment, **Auditing-POL-Audit Allowed virtual machine SKUs**. Edit the assignment description field to include the details of the SKUs in scope.

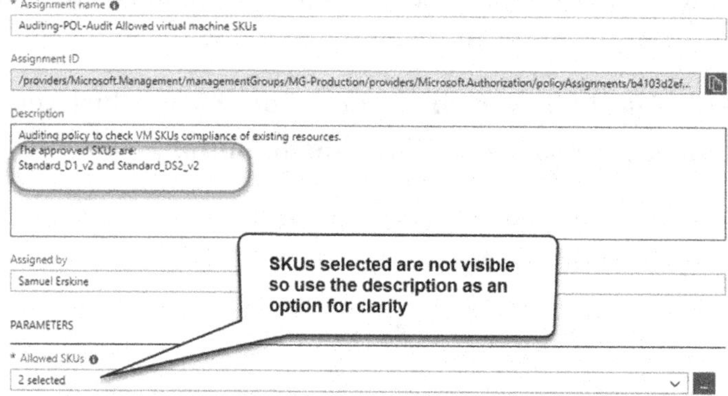

3. Click **Save** to complete the assignment update.

The result of the minor changes is that the policy assigner has clear instructions on the requirements, and the compliance visibility is improved, as illustrated in Figure 4-9.

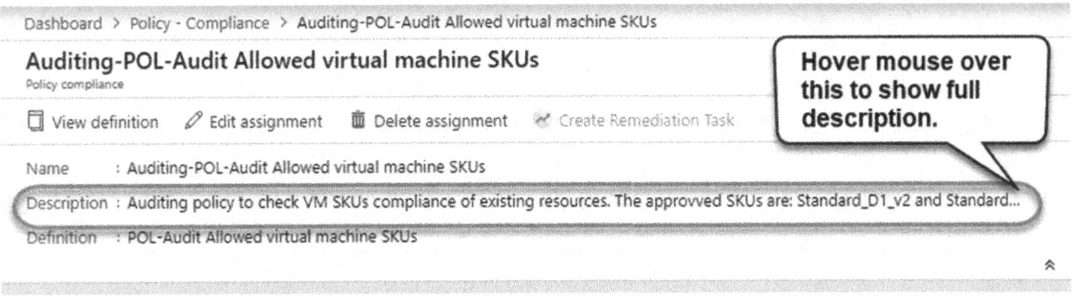

Figure 4-9. *Policy compliance view showing updated description*

Additionally, the category of the definition will show Production Approved when viewed in the definition node.

Major Objective Changes

Change the "`effect`" to "`Deny`" for policy enforcement, and exclude the development resource group from the policy assignment.

1. Navigate to the Definitions section of the Policy node in the Azure portal.
2. Select **POL-Audit Allowed virtual machines SKUs**, as you created in the previous steps, and click **Duplicate definition**.
3. Select **MG-Assigned Subscriptions** as the definition location.
4. Change the policy name to **POL-Enforce Allowed virtual machine SKUs**. Update the description to the following: **This enforcement policy denies the creation of virtual machine SKUs that your organization has not approved for deployment. The SKUs in scope of this policy are specified in the assignment.** Ensure you list the SKUs in the description of the assignment, and that the "`effect`" is "`Deny`".

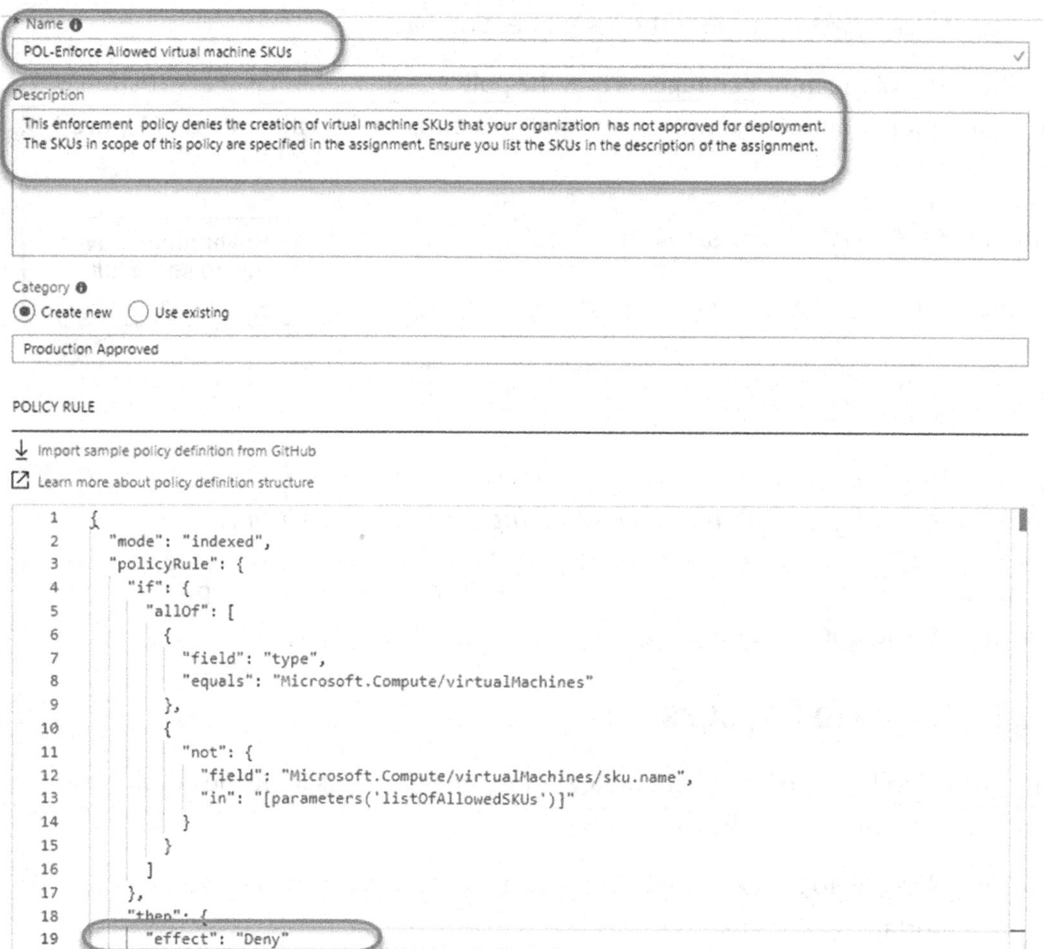

5. Click **Save** to complete the policy update (a new policy is created).

The effect of this change is that we now have two policies. This approach ensures that you follow a process that minimizes the impact of major policy changes. In effect, we have an option to roll back our change and avoid impacting assignments using the previous policy definition.

The second part is to assign the updated policy and allow exclusions.

Exclusions

An exclusion can be set at the management group, subscription, resource group, or specific resource level. You can only set exclusions on resources from one resource group at a time.

Follow the steps in the "Assigning Policies" section of this chapter but with the following changes.

1. Ensure that **IT-Prod-Default-Sub** is selected as the scope and click the **...** button under Exclusions. Select **MG-CC003 IT Services**, and then select **IT-Prod-Default-Sub** in the subscriptions field. Check all resources groups in the subscription to be excluded. Click **Add to Selected Scope**, and then click **Save**.

2. Under **Policy definition**, click the **...** button to select the enforcement policy you created earlier, append **Enforce-** to the assignment name. Type a description that includes the SKUs not allowed, which you select in the Parameters section, and click **Assign**.

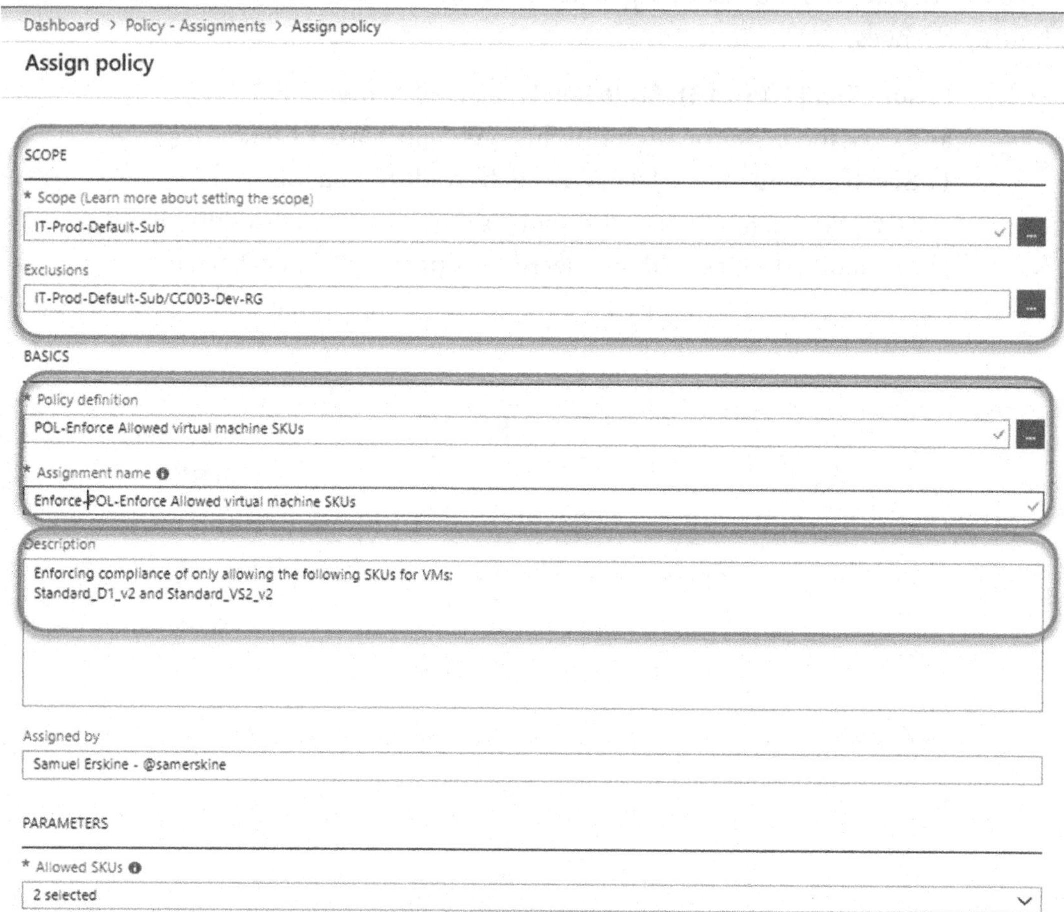

Deny policies like the one used in the example are evaluated and enforced at the time of resource creation. In our example of the allowed VM SKUs, when the Create VM wizard gets to the point of validation, an error is shown, as illustrated in Figure 4-10.

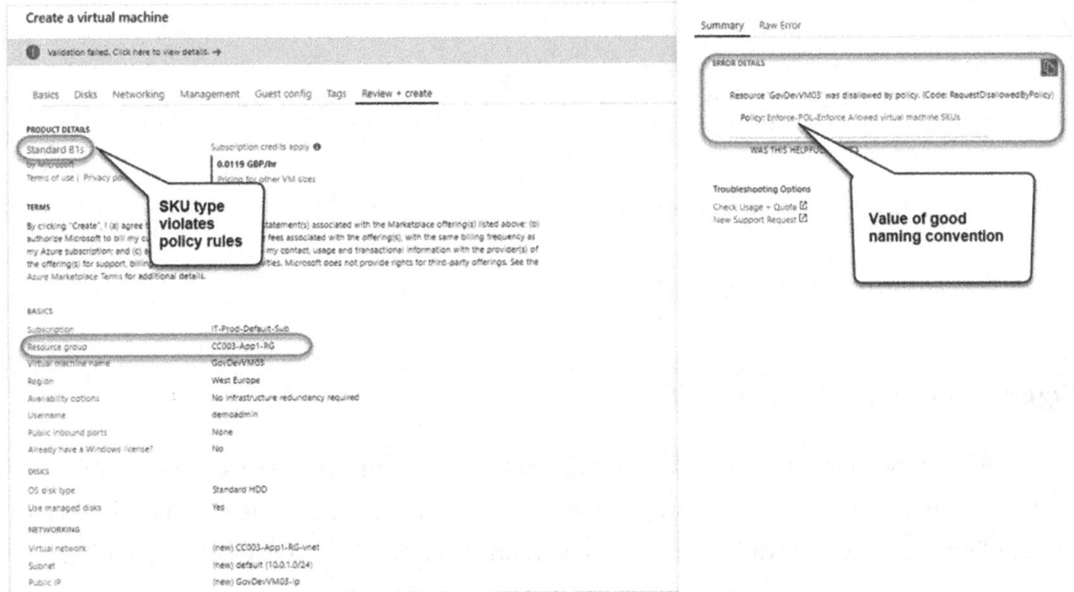

Figure 4-10. *Error showing a violation of a policy at resource creation*

Creating Initiatives

Initiatives are used to group policies to assign one or more compliance objectives. The recommendation is to use an initiative even if all you have is a single policy. This concept is similar to the use of groups instead of individual users when assigning role-based security.

Azure provides a library of built-in initiatives for common organizational compliance objectives that you can use as a starting point. You can view the built-in initiatives available in the Policy node under Definitions. Set the filter under Definition type to see the available initiatives and their respective categories. Figure 4-11 shows the built-in initiatives available in Azure at the time of writing.

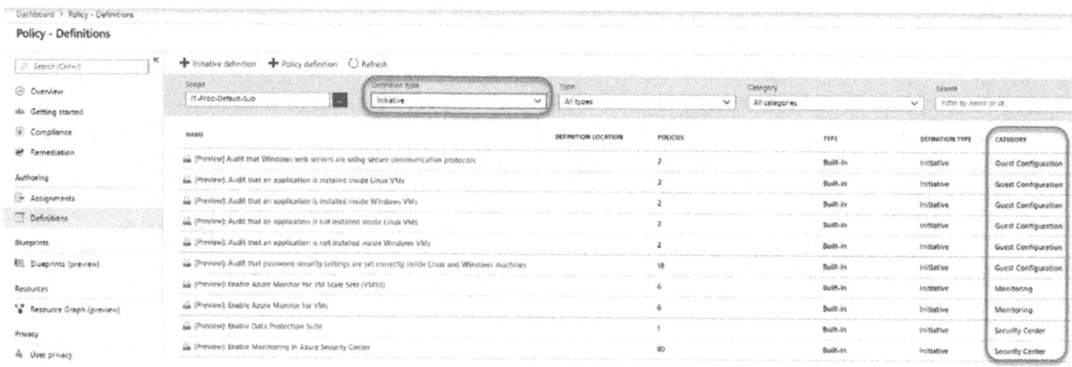

Figure 4-11. *Built-in Azure initiatives*

There are two options available to create initiative definitions: new or duplicate a built-in or custom initiative. The steps to duplicate an initiative are the same as that used for a policy. This section walks you through creating a new initiative. Prior to creating the new initiative in this example, we have duplicated the allowed locations policy and changed the effect type to audit. The two policies are stored in the same definition location. Figure 4-12 shows the two policies. You can create and name your policy to suit your requirements when performing the steps in this exercise.

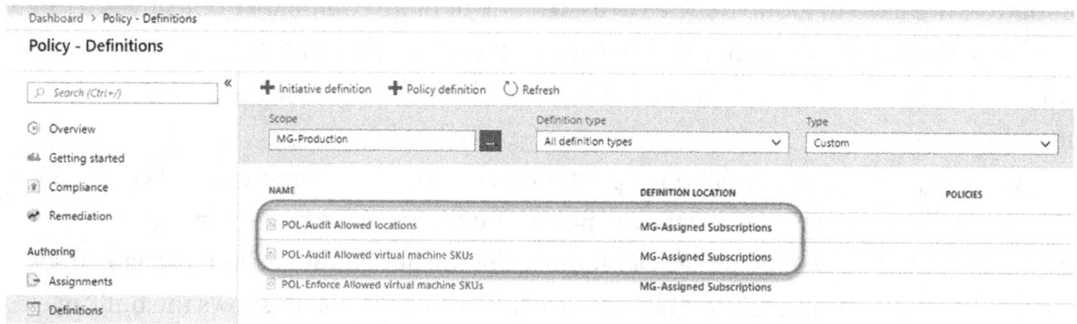

Figure 4-12. *Policies in scope of initiative*

Follow these steps to create a new initiative using two policies.

1. Connect to the Azure portal at `https://portal.azure.com`.
2. Click **Policy** under the Favorites section in the left navigation bar (this assumes you followed the previous steps in this chapter).

3. In the Policy blade, select **Definitions** and click **Initiative definition**.

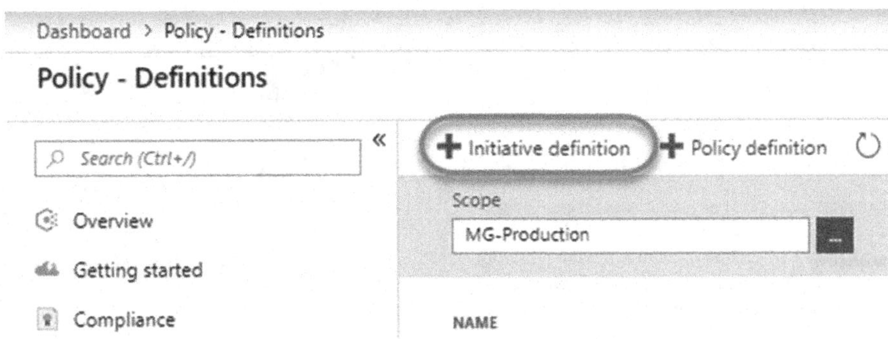

4. Select the initiative location. Provide a name and description. Either create a new category or select an existing category for the initiative.

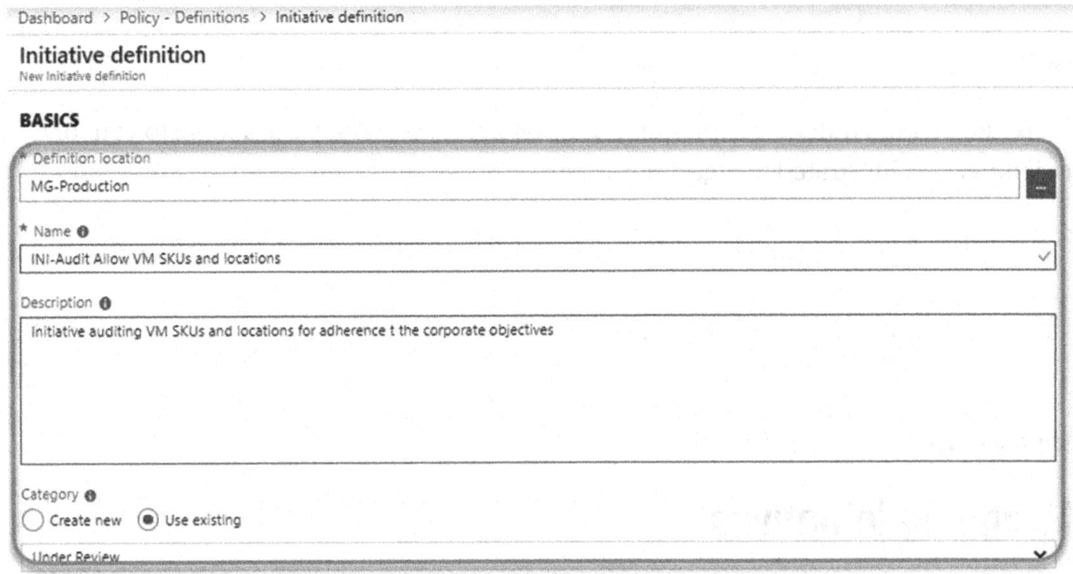

5. Under Available Definitions, select the policies in scope of this definition by clicking the + icon. In the example, we selected the allowed VM SKUs and the allowed locations. These two policies require parameter values. Set the value field for both to **Use Initiative Parameter** to allow the parameters to be set during the initiative assignment. Click **Save**.

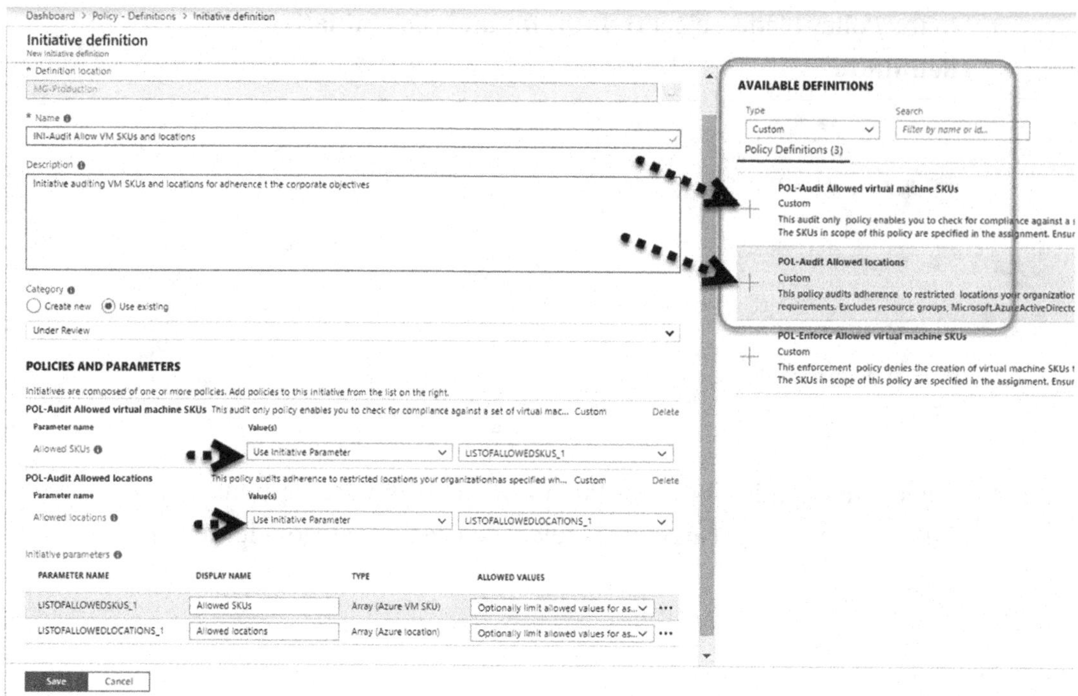

A new custom initiative containing two policies is created. It is available to you for assignment, as illustrated in Figure 4-13.

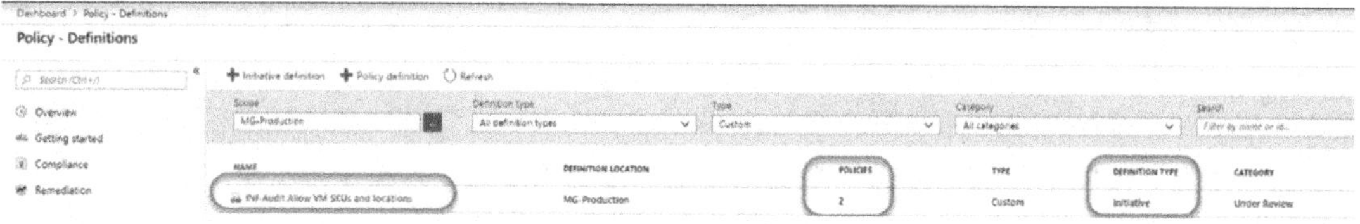

Figure 4-13. *Custom initiative*

Assigning Initiatives

In the previous section, we followed the steps to create a new definition. The next step is to assign the definition to a management group, subscription, or resource group. In our next example, we will assign the initiative to a subscription in order to audit the compliance state of the virtual machines in resources groups in that subscription.

The scenario for the initiative assignment is as follows. The objective is to check for compliance of virtual machines against the corporate-approved SKUs and allowed geographical locations where these virtual machines can reside.

1. Connect to the Azure portal at `https://portal.azure.com`.
2. Click **Policy** under the Favorites section in the left navigation bar, or use the policy management tile if you created the Governance & Compliance dashboard (this assumes you followed the previous steps in this chapter).
3. In the Policy blade, click **Assignments** and then click **Assign initiative**.
4. Click the **...** button under Scope and navigate to the subscription under the MG-CC003 IT Services child management group. Select IT-Prod-Default-Sub (in our environment, yours may defer, so select as appropriate) and then click **Select**.

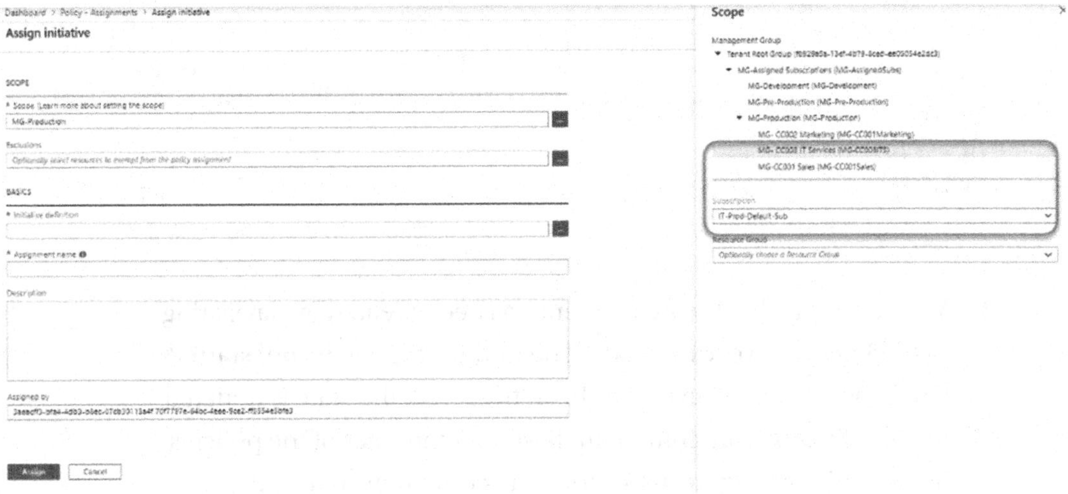

5. Edit the assignment name to your standard, provide a description, set the parameter values for the two policies, and click **Assign**.

6. You can verify that the assignment has been created by navigating to the Policy – Overview blade. The initial state will be not started. Once the evaluation cycle has been triggered, the state is updated to compliant or non-compliant, based on the rules of the policies in the initiative. Figure 4-14 shows the compliant state of the initiative assigned in the example.

NAME	SCOPE	COMPLIANCE STATE	COMPLIANCE	NON-COMPLIANT RESOUR...	NON-COMPLIANT POLICIES
Audit-INI-Audit Allow VM SKUs and locations	IT-Prod-Default-Sub	Non-compliant	0%	15	2
Auditing-POL-Audit Allowed virtual machine SKUs	MG-Production	Non-compliant	0%	2	1
Enforce-POL-Enforce Allowed virtual machine SKUs	IT-Prod-Default-Sub	Compliant	100%	0	0

***Figure 4-14.** Policy and initiative states*

We can drill further into the compliance status by clicking the initiative and then clicking the policy showing non-compliance to view the resources that do not meet the objectives. In our case, using the allowed locations, the parameter values were set to North Europe and West UK. Figure 4-15 shows that the resources are all in West Europe, which is the reason for the non-compliance to that policy.

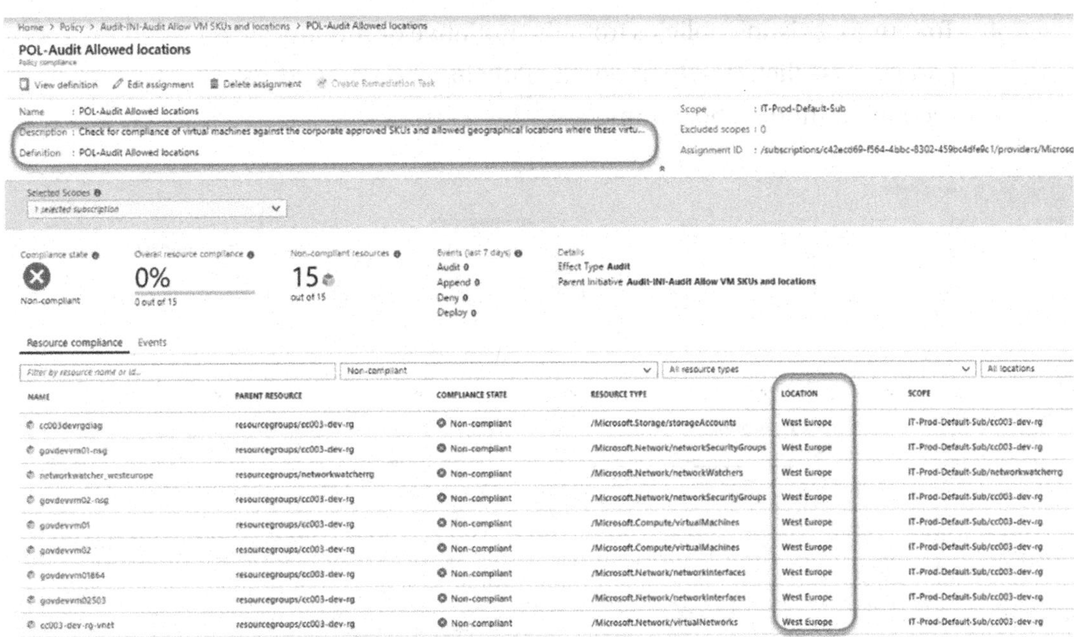

***Figure 4-15.** Compliance status of the policy with an initiative*

When you assign an initiative, it is important to review and ensure that the policies that you include are not assigned separately through other policy assignments. This is to ensure that the same policy is not assigned multiple times to the same resource(s).

Updating Initiatives

The value of using initiatives instead multiple policies is that you can update one or more compliance objectives from one place. You update an initiative by either adding or removing policies or updating the policy definitions contained within the initiative.

The following are the steps to add or remove policies from an initiative.

1. Navigate to the Policy node and select **Definitions** in the Azure portal.
2. Select the initiative to be edited, and then select **Edit Initiative**.
3. To add additional policies, select the required policy/policies from the Available Definitions section.
4. To remove existing policies from the initiative or modify parameters, click **Delete** under the Policies and Parameters section, or modify the parameters.

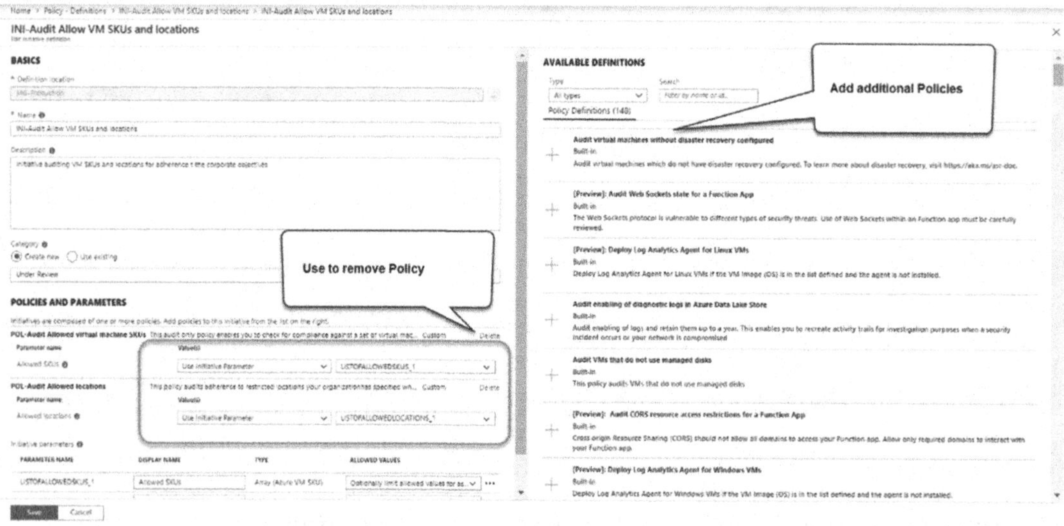

5. You can also change the initiative's name and definition.

6. Click **Save** to complete the necessary update(s).

In addition to using the Azure portal for creating and updating policies/initiatives, you can also use PowerShell or Azure CLI to perform the same actions. The Chapter 7 provides examples of using automation through PowerShell and command-line options. For examples, refer to `https://docs.microsoft.com/en-us/powershell/module/azurerm.resources/?view=azurermps-6.13.0#policies`.

Taking Action on Policy Results

The follow-up actions that you can take on policy results depend on the rules, conditions, and effect specified in the policy. There are six policy effects available.

- Append
- Audit
- AuditIfNotExists
- Deny
- DeployIfNotExists
- Disabled

Append

Append adds fields to the target resource during a create or update. Examples include adding tag values, like environment resource owner. The following is an append effect JSON that specifies an environment tag (key/value pair).

```
{
   "properties": {
      "displayName": "Apply tag and its default value",
      "policyType": "BuiltIn",
      "description": "Applies a required tag and its default value if it is
      not specified by the user.",
      "parameters": {
```

```
            "tagName": {
               "type": "String",
               "metadata": {
                  "description": "Name of the tag, such as Environment"
               }
            },
            "tagValue": {
               "type": "String",
               "metadata": {
                  "description": "Value of the tag, such as Development"
               }
            }
         },
         "policyRule": {
            "if": {
               "field": "[concat('tags[', parameters('tagName'), ']')]",
               "exists": "false"
            },
            "then": {
               "effect": "append",
               "details": [
                  {
                     "field": "[concat('tags[', parameters('tagName'), ']')]",
                     "value": "[parameters('tagValue')]"
                  }
               ]
            }
         }
      },
      "id": "/providers/Microsoft.Authorization/policyDefinitions/2a0e14a6-
      b0a6-4fab-991a-187a4f81c498",
      "type": "Microsoft.Authorization/policyDefinitions",
      "name": "2a0e14a6-b0a6-4fab-991a-187a4f81c498"
}
```

Audit

Audit is the equivalent of a report-only mode. The rule checks for a condition and reports as compliant if true and non-compliant if false. No action is taken. It is the condition used in most of the exercises so far in this book.

AuditIfNotExists

AuditIfNotExists can be confusing to understand, but in essence, it is similar to Audit. Audit checks for the compliance of a resource to a specific condition, such as allowed VM SKUs; however, AuditIfNotExists is more aligned to checking if a resource property or artifact exists. An example is checking whether anti-malware extensions are enabled. This effect type also reports back true or false but does not have remediation (deploy instructions as part of the `then` portion of the definition). The following code snippet is an example of checking for the existence of anti-malware extensions on a virtual machine.

```
{
    "if": {
        "field": "type",
        "equals": "Microsoft.Compute/virtualMachines"
    },
    "then": {
        "effect": "auditIfNotExists",
        "details": {
            "type": "Microsoft.Compute/virtualMachines/extensions",
            "existenceCondition": {
                "allOf": [{
                        "field": "Microsoft.Compute/virtualMachines/
                        extensions/publisher",
                        "equals": "Microsoft.Azure.Security"
                    },
                    {
                        "field": "Microsoft.Compute/virtualMachines/
                        extensions/type",
                        "equals": "IaaSAntimalware"
```

```
                    }
                ]
            }
        }
    }
}
```

Deny

The Deny effect is used to prevent the creation of resources that do not meet a condition. In the case where a resource already exists and does not meet the condition, then a non-compliance state is reported. An example is preventing VMs from being created that do not use an approved SKU. When evaluating creation, the effect will throw an error message and prevent the creation.

DeployIfNotExists

DeployIfNotExists is similar to AuditIfNotExists; the difference is that it can deploy a template for remediation based on the non-compliance condition. When non-compliant is returned for this effect type, it is not auto-remediated. You will need to create a remediation task to complete the process using the template defined in the policy.

Disable

This effect type disables the policy and is the equivalent of not evaluating. This is a useful effect in initiatives, where one or more policies can be disabled during testing without impacting the other policies or removing the policy from the initiative assignment. The effects' order of precedence is documented at `https://docs.microsoft.com/en-us/azure/governance/policy/concepts/effects`.

Requests to create or update a resource through Azure Resource Manager are evaluated by policy first. Policy creates a list of all assignments that apply to the resource, and then evaluates the resource against each definition. Policy processes several of the effects before handing the request to the appropriate resource provider. Doing so prevents unnecessary processing by a resource provider when a resource doesn't meet the designed governance controls of policy.

1. **Disabled** is checked first to determine if the policy rule should be evaluated.
2. **Append** is then evaluated. Since append could alter the request, a change made by append may prevent an audit or deny effect from triggering.
3. **Deny** is then evaluated. By evaluating deny before audit, double logging of an undesired resource is prevented.
4. **Audit** is then evaluated before the request going to the resource provider.
5. After the resource provider returns a success code, **AuditIfNotExists** and **DeployIfNotExists** evaluate to determine if additional compliance logging or action is required.

Table 4-2 shows a summary of different condition effects based on the resource state.

Table 4-2. *Summary of Condition Effects*

Resource State	Effect	Policy Evaluation	Compliance State
Exists	Deny, Audit, Append*, DeployIfNotExist*, AuditIfNotExist*	True	Non-Compliant
Exists	Deny, Audit, Append*, DeployIfNotExist*, AuditIfNotExist*	False	Compliant
New	Audit, AuditIfNotExist*	True	Non-Compliant
New	Audit, AuditIfNotExist*	False	Compliant

**The Append, DeployIfNotExist, and AuditIfNotExist effects require the IF statement to be TRUE. The effects also require the existence condition to be FALSE to be non-compliant. When TRUE, the IF condition triggers evaluation of the existence condition for the related resources.*

Remediation Options

The effect settings you select for the policies you assign will determine your remediation options. You have two options available for remediation: manual and automatic.

Manual Remediation

Manual remediation can be performed using the Azure portal or command-line options. This would depend on the policy objective and the complexity of remediation. As an example, updating the tag for the environment will be simpler than changing the virtual machine SKU. The manual remediation option will be more aligned with policies that are set to audit only. This is the first scenario for using Azure policy for existing environments that were set up before the compliance objects were agreed on or mandated for your organization.

Automatic Remediation

The second option is automatic remediation. This can be triggered through the policy service using the remediation node or your own automation tools and scripts that target the resources that are out of compliance.

The option for remediation through the policy services is applicable to policies that use the DeployIfNotExists effect. You first assign a policy with the specified effect, and then create a remediation task to target non-compliant resources. The remediation task uses a security principal known as the *managed identity*, which is granted the security role appropriate to perform the remediation. The managed identity can be automatically created using the Azure policy definition or created manually. The following example walks through creating a DeployIfNotExists policy, assigning it to resources and creating a remediation task. All the steps are performed using the Azure portal.

We will use a duplicate of the built-in policy deploy default—Microsoft IaaSAntimalware extension for Windows Server. The steps are as follows.

1. Connect to the Azure portal at `https://portal.azure.com`.
2. Click **Policy** under the Favorites section in the left navigation bar (this assumes you followed the previous steps in this chapter).
3. In the Policy blade, select **Definitions**.
4. In the Definitions blade, type **anti** in the search field and select **Deploy default Microsoft IaaSAntimalware extension for Windows Server**.
5. You are presented with the built-in policy definition for the policy. Click **Duplicate definition**.

6. Make the following changes.

   a. Definition location: Click the **...** button, and then click **MG-Assigned Subscriptions**. Click **Select**.

   b. Name: Edit the name to **POL-Enforce Deploy default Microsoft IaaSAntimalware extension for Windows Server**. Leave the default description.

   c. Category: Ensure that **Create new** is selected and type **Can Remediate**. Click **Save**.

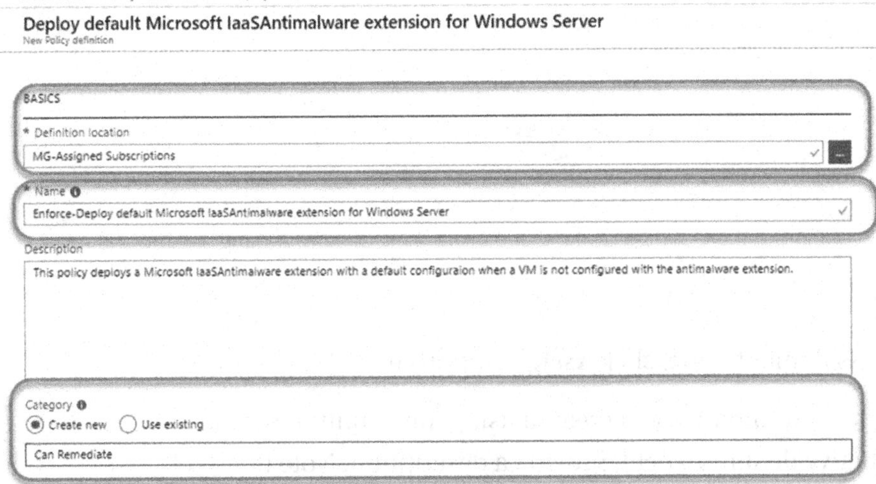

7. Verify that the custom policy has been created by selecting definitions and setting the type filter to **Custom**. Notice that the name, definition location, and category values are set to what you selected and typed.

8. Follow the steps used to create a new initiative to create one called **INI-Mandatory Default Extensions**.

   a. Initiative location: MG-Assigned Subscriptions

   b. Initiative name: INI-Mandatory Default Extensions

   c. Initiative description: Default extensions required for Windows Servers

d. Category: Can Remediate

e. Available Definitions: Select the new policy you created in the earlier steps.

9. Click **Save**.

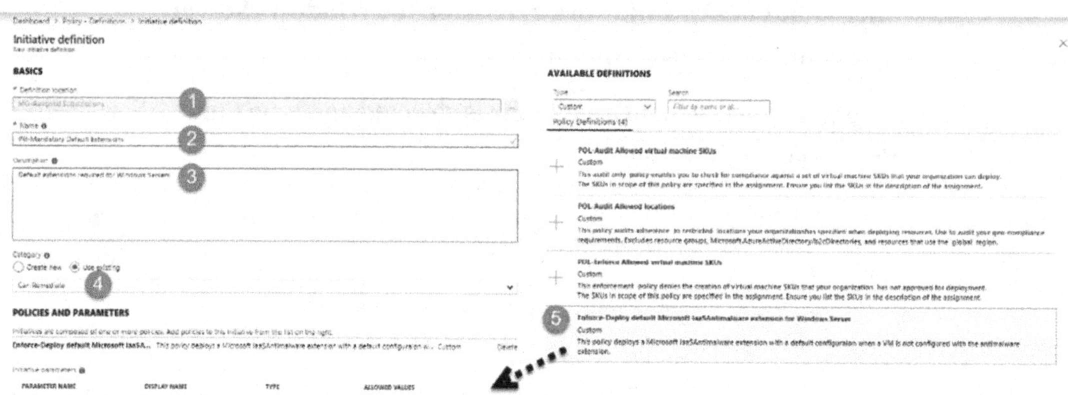

10. In the Assignment node, click **Assign initiative**.

11. Select the new initiative you created using the **...** button next to the initiative definition field, provide a description. Note that Create a Managed Identity is automatically checked because the policy in this initiative has a DeployIfNotExists effect. Click **Assign** to complete the assignment.

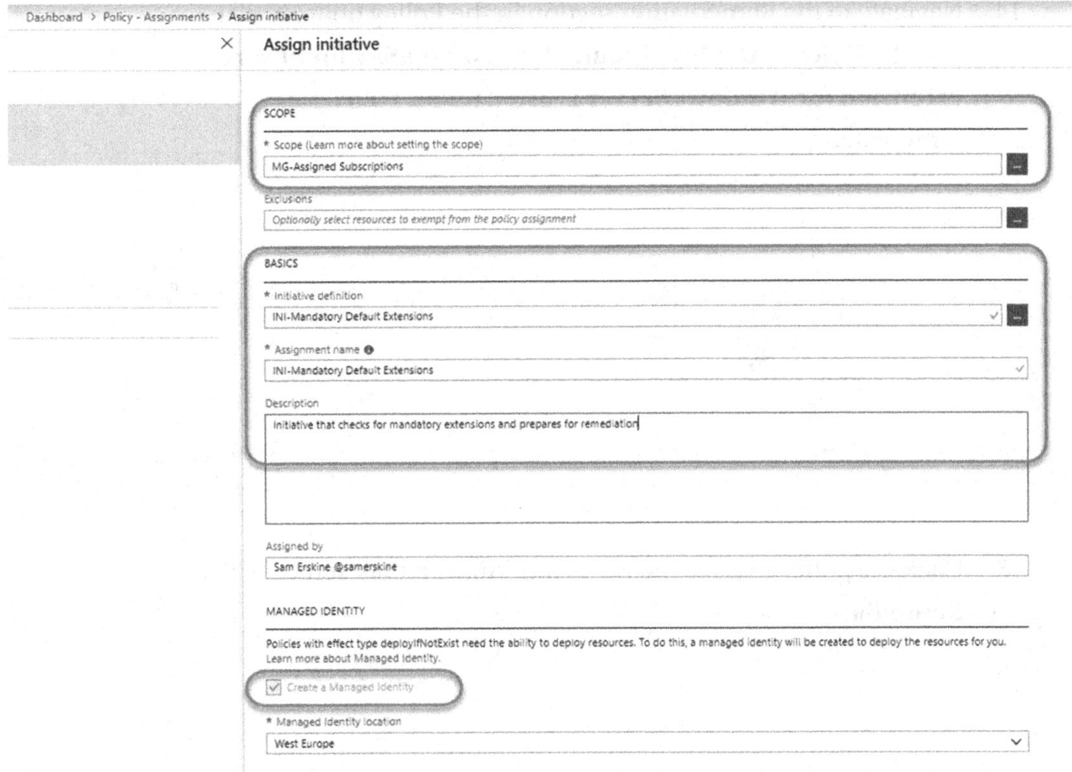

12. Wait for 30 minutes for the initial evaluation cycle to complete before moving on to the next step. This should be the case when the Compliance State changes from not started to non-compliant.

13. This initiative shows as non-compliant in our environment because the virtual machines in scope do not have the anti-malware extension.

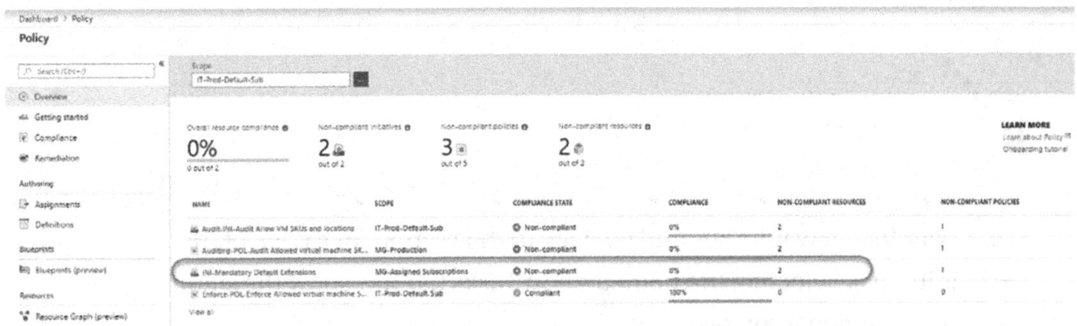

14. Navigate to the Remediation section in the Policy node. Notice that the **Enforce Deploy default Microsoft IaaSAntimalware extension for Windows Server** is listed under Policies to remediate.

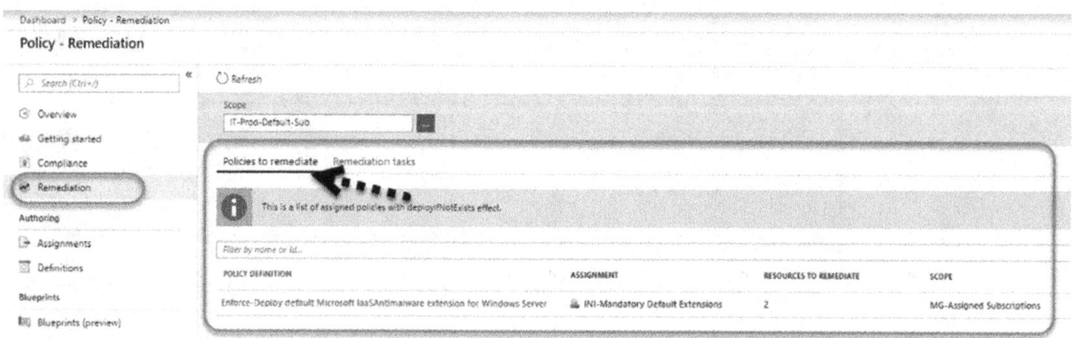

15. Click the policy to go to the **New remediation task** screen. Click **Remediate**.

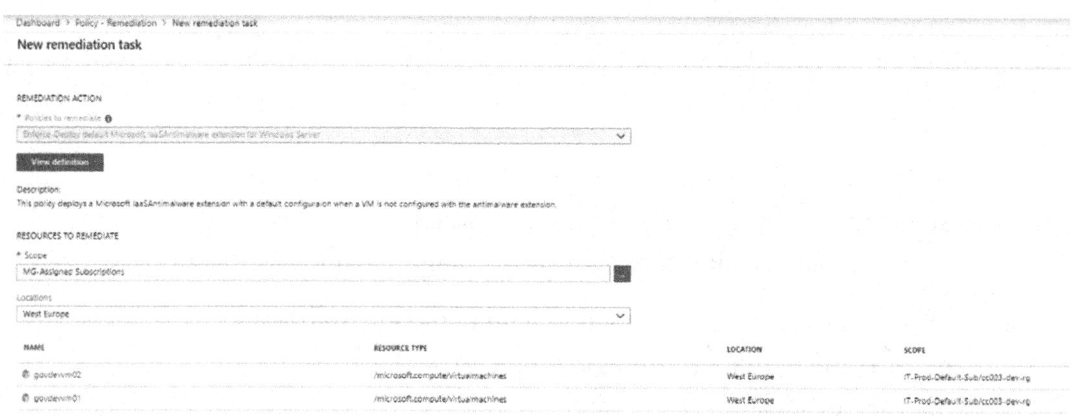

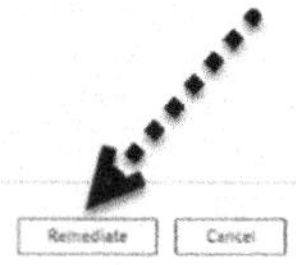

16. Wait for a few minutes and go back to the compliance page of the initiative. Selecting the Remediation Tasks tab will show the status of the remediation task.

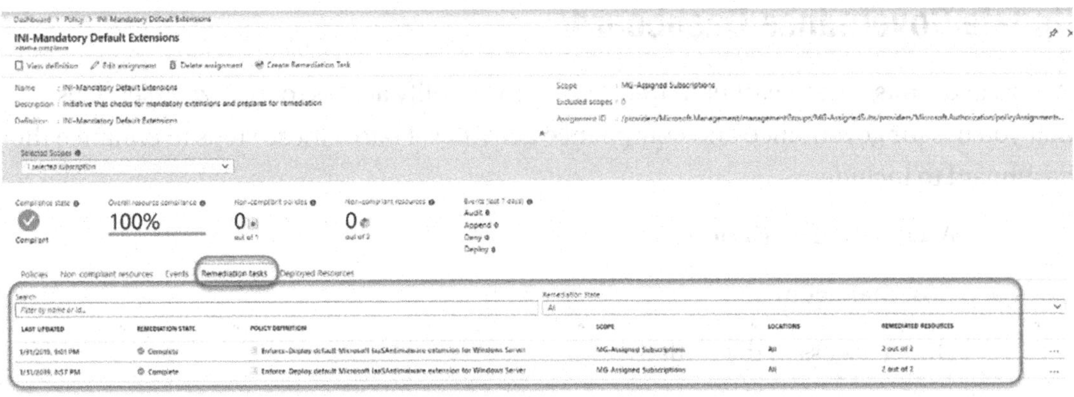

17. You can also verify that the extension has been installed on a resource in scope. In this case, the virtual machine shows that the remediation was successful.

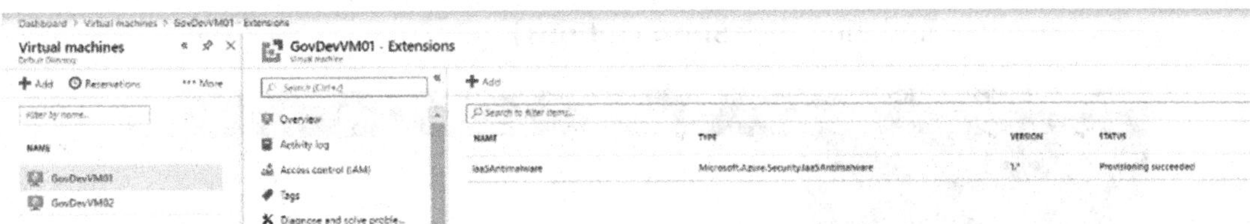

18. Finally, notice that the initiative compliance has now changed to compliant.

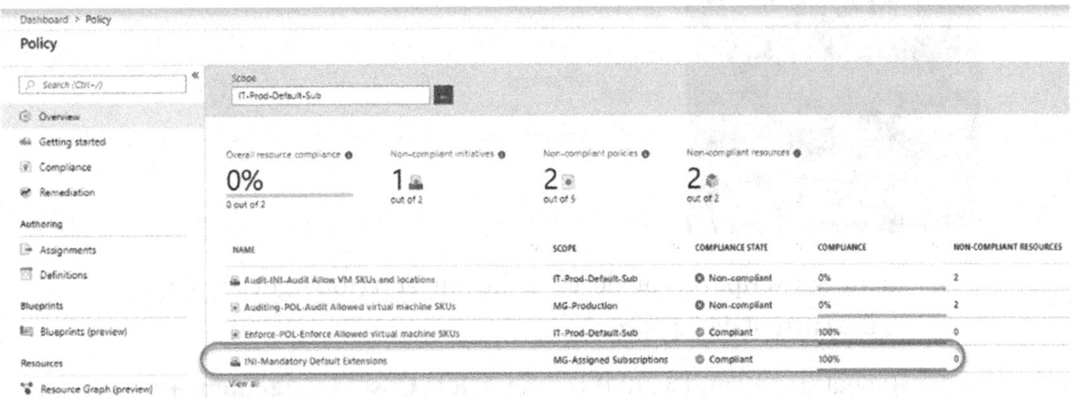

There are numerous resources available, including the official Microsoft sites with examples of other remediation-capable policies.

Update Governance Dashboard

We created a dashboard earlier in the chapter to simplify access to the Azure services that you use for governance and compliance activities. Follow these steps to enhance the dashboard to include

- Access to subscriptions
- Cost management
- Direct access to the initiatives

1. In the Azure portal, click **Dashboards** and select the dashboard that you created.
2. Click **Subscriptions** under Favorites (if you did not follow the steps to add subscriptions to the Favorites section, click **All services** and then click **Subscriptions**).

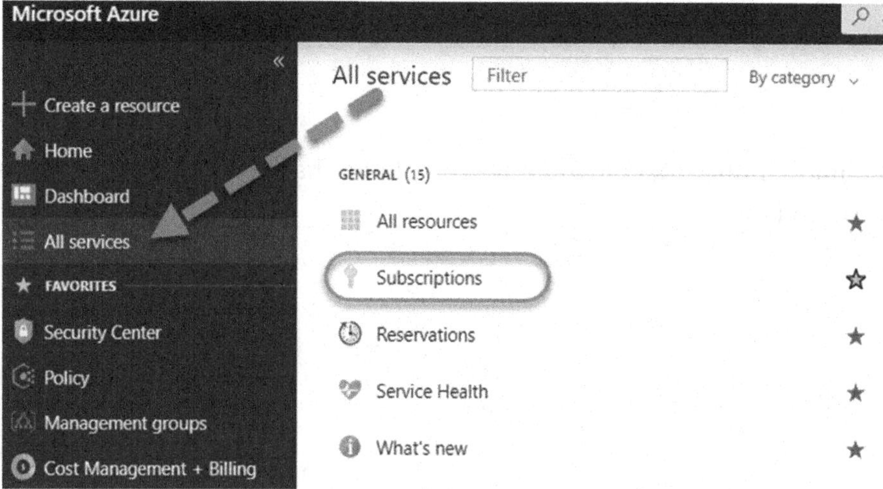

3. In the Subscriptions blade, click the pin icon (top right) to pin to the current dashboard.
4. Repeat steps 2 and 3 but this time, select **Cost Management + Billing**.

5. Navigate to the Policy blade. Click **Compliance** to show the compliance state of all policy and initiative assignments. Set the type filter to **Initiative**.

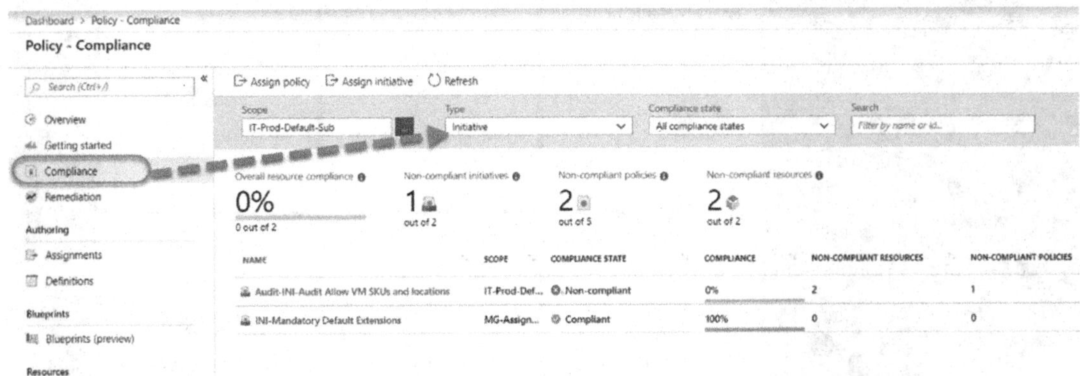

6. Click **Audit-INI-Audit Allow VM SKUs and location** to open the initiative blade. Click the pin icon on the top right to place on the dashboard.

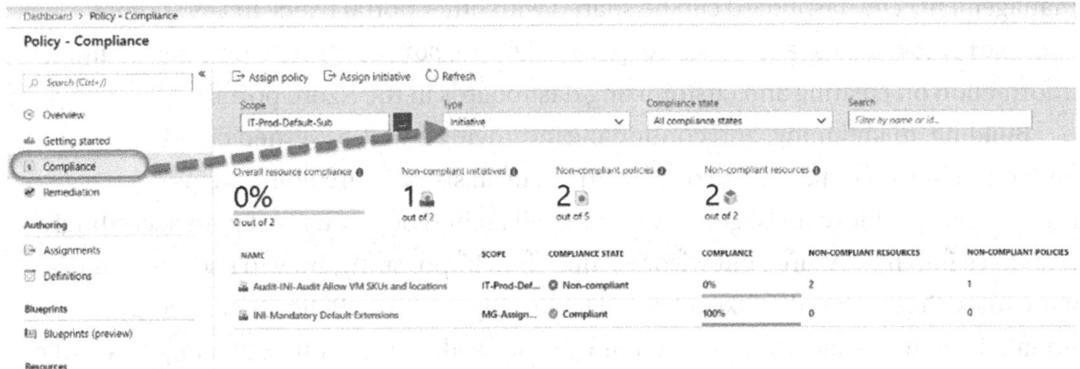

7. Repeat step 6; but this time, select the second initiative.

8. Return to the dashboard. You should now have the original dashboard updated to include Subscriptions, Cost Management + Billing, and the two initiatives.

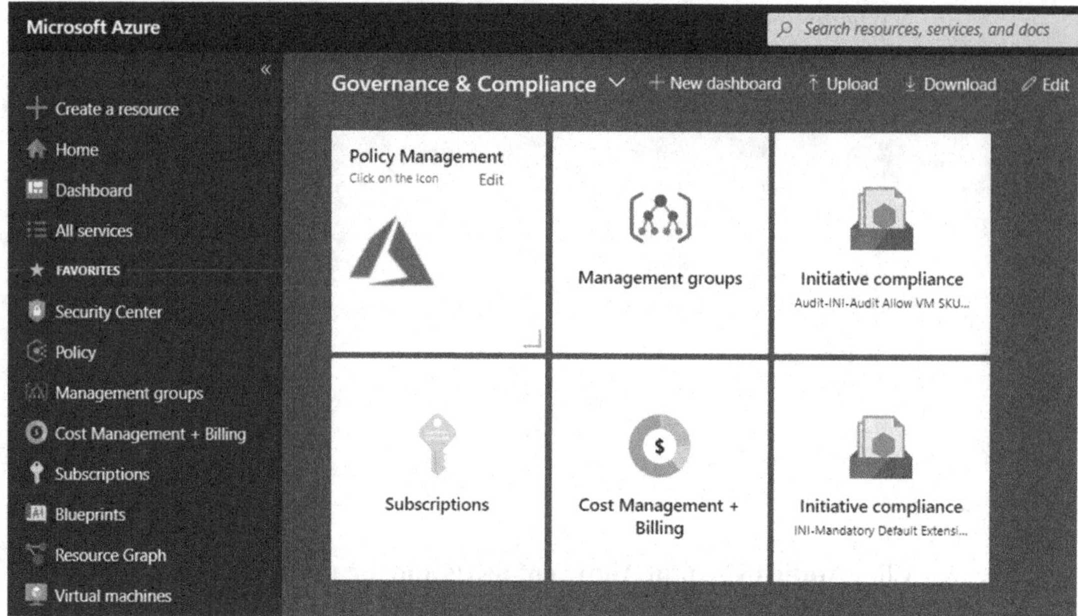

You now have a focused dashboard dedicated to governance and compliance management. The dashboard can be shared with other portal users. `https://docs.microsoft.com/en-us/azure/azure-portal/azure-portal-dashboards` has additional information on creating and customizing dashboards in the Azure portal.

Building, maintaining, and continually improving a well-governed cloud environment is foundational to organizations of all sizes. Azure Policy helps organizations achieve these goals. Similar to all technology, you must plan accordingly and delve into how Azure Policy works, and more importantly, how to use it to achieve your goals. Remember that like all cloud technologies, Azure Policy is constantly updated and new features are continually introduced, so review these changes as part of your overall governance process.

Summary

This chapter started with how to plan for your policies and initiatives, then delved into policies and initiatives in action, and concluded with remediating non-compliance to policies. The next chapter walks you through the Azure Security Center.

CHAPTER 5

Azure Security Center

Azure Security Center is Microsoft's centralized dashboard solution for all things security, whether in Azure or in a hybrid topology.

This chapter walks you through the following.

- What Azure Security Center is
- How to enable and use Azure Security Center
- How to protect your Azure and on-premises resources
- Using Azure Security Center to protect your data
- Enhancing security by following ASC recommendations
- Azure Security Center advanced features and capabilities
- Security Score and how to optimize

What Is Azure Security Center?

Azure Security Center is an Azure service that aims to optimize an organization's security and the overall protection of its resources. Resources can run in Azure and comprises Azure IaaS and PaaS objects. By deploying the Azure Microsoft Management Agent onto virtual machines or physical servers, once can extend Azure Security Center to report on hybrid systems as well.

Many organizations are moving workloads to the cloud, or deploying new workloads in the cloud, to optimize their security posture. This is a funny twist from several years ago, where organizations did not trust public cloud computing that much. We remember several situations in classroom trainings and customer meetings, where a public cloud was out of the question "because it is not secure." Things have changed over only a couple of years! That is obviously a good thing. As soon as we started working with

P. De Tender et al., *Pro Azure Governance and Security*, https://doi.org/10.1007/978-1-4842-4910-9_5

Azure, we were true believers of its enhanced security. Because, face it, security is really the baseline of any public cloud environment. Or, said differently, if public cloud would not be secure, there would not even be a need for public cloud.

That said, cloud security is a shared responsibility. The cloud provider (Microsoft in this Azure world) is mainly responsible for the physical data center, up to the hypervisor if you want. When you as a customer deploy virtual machines on top, you need to take control of the virtual machine security. Think of system hardening, network security, administrative access, and the like. When using Platform as a Service, Microsoft is even more responsible for handling security, as it goes all the way up to the application itself. Think of running Azure web apps, SQL Azure, and other such serverless solutions. As a customer, you are mainly responsible for securing the data, and less for taking control of the underlying systems, because that is probably not even possible.

Security is part of all layers of the public cloud environment.

The good news is that Azure Security Center has the capabilities to tackle and report on each of these layers in an Azure environment, as well as in a hybrid cloud scenario.

Security Challenges

Any organization, no matter if it is a small or medium sized business, or a multinational, they all face identical security challenges. The larger or more publicly known the organization is, the larger the attack surface might be. Yet, sometimes even a small start-up can be a security target.

Depending on what they are doing as a core business, which intelligence or information systems they use, and who their competition is, an organization should always "assume breach." (We will talk more about this later.)

With that in mind, any organization's security challenges can be summarized in three different pillars.

a) Attacks are becoming more and more advanced

b) Systems are changing fast

c) Security experts are hard to find

Allow us to explain each of these challenges more in detail.

Advanced Attacks

Some of you might remember the long-gone days of annoying computer viruses. While the initial intention was to infect the machine, some of those viruses were far from the recent CryptoLocker and alike. (Some examples from the mid-1980s were Ping Pong, where every 30 seconds some characters on a screen would just drop or start bouncing, and AIDS Trojan, which encrypted all the files on your hard drive. So CryptoLocker wasn't all that new after all.)

If you think about how many Internet-facing applications we are using on a day-to-day basis, even to do our corporate job, it is no surprise attacks are becoming more and more advanced. From connecting our machine in the morning, checking emails, or storing files in a cloud storage system like OneDrive, Dropbox, or Google Drive, to connecting to cloud SaaS apps like Office 365— every application is an attack surface.

Systems Are Changing Fast

We all face frustration when a Windows Update is installed right as we start an important presentation. But hey, they are for a good reason—security. Eighty percent of all software updates are related to fixing security issues. When looking at how easy it is to deploy new virtual machines on Azure, it is important that each of these workloads is secure "out of the box." Next to that, how can we make sure that our workloads are always secure, even the ones we deployed weeks or months back? And what if those systems are not (always) deployed and managed by the IT team?

Security Experts Are Hard to Find

The third statement is a bold one. Think back to where this section started; organizations from any size, small to multinational, face these security challenges. In larger organizations, it should be no surprise that IT teams are taking ownership of systems' security hardening. What about smaller organizations? They sometimes believe that their systems and applications are secure, and they are not under attack. (*Who would be interested in our company?*) In this fast-changing world of systems, it is hard to catch up. And knowing that IT environments are becoming more and more complex, especially when extending to public cloud environments and cloud SaaS applications, it is not possible to keep all systems under control.

Azure Security Center to the Rescue

We will talk a lot more about all the security and protection features that Azure Security Center brings to the table, but since we are still in the overview section, let's position ASC from a high level and discuss how it helps tackle the aforementioned challenges.

Protection at Cloud Speed

Azure Security Center runs as a cloud service in Azure, meaning it relies on the cloud itself, to offer this service. Starting from the initial activation (nothing needs to be deployed or installed), Azure Security Center is operational in seconds. Starting from the Azure subscription in which it was activated, it immediately starts learning from the running services and resources, and starts reporting on their security state. Detecting security vulnerabilities is lightning fast; remediation reporting is done within minutes. Even fixing the security issues usually only requires a few clicks.

Real-Time, Built-In Threat Protection

Outside of all the other advanced security features and solutions, one of Azure Security Center's core services is to provide real-time threat protection. By learning your deployed resources, both Azure and hybrid, Azure Security Center provides a list of security recommendations and security alerts for you to take action on.

No Security Experts Required

As bold as the statement around security experts was before, this should be understood in the same way. We obviously still need security experts, and honestly the more the better, but the way Azure Security Center assists with reporting and alerting about security issues in your environment, the security officers in an organization should not be the only people able to understand how to fix the issues. Again, ASC can help here by using a lightweight approach in providing recommendations and security alerts.

How Azure Security Center Is Organized

When you open Azure Security Center for the first time, without any modifications to the dashboards, it looks like what's shown in Figure 5-1.

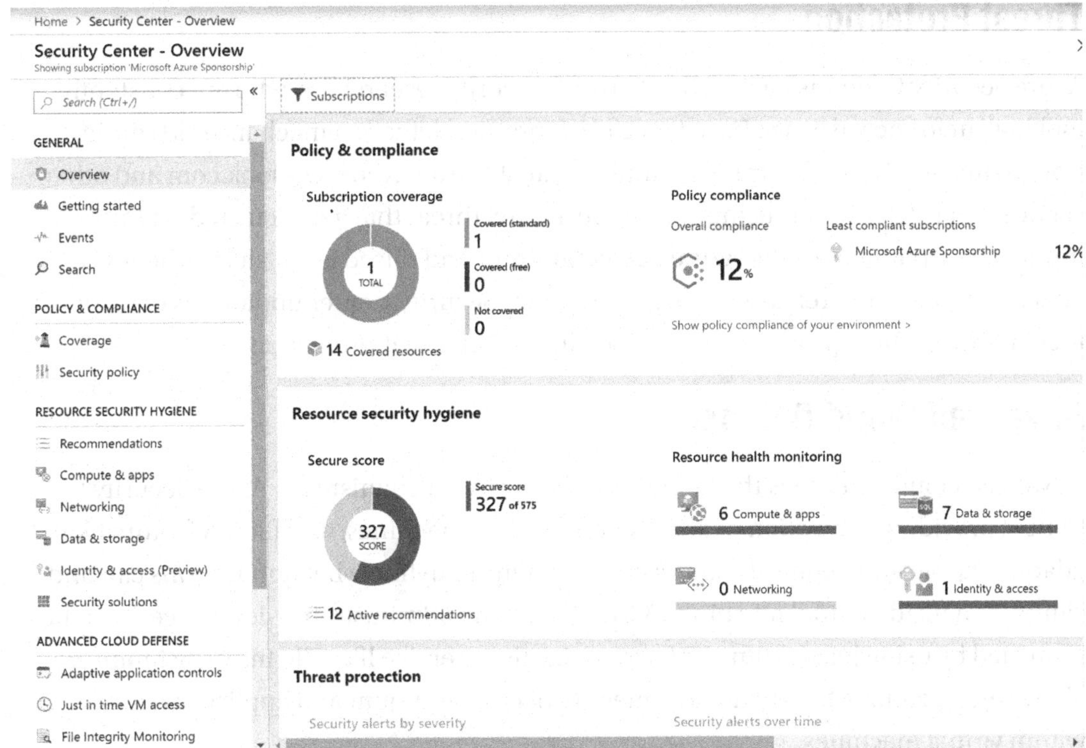

***Figure 5-1.** Azure Security Center – Overview Dashboard*

We will go over every aspect of Azure Security Center in more detail later on, but this is the high-level structure in which it is organized.

Policy and Compliance

In the Policy and Compliance section, Azure Security Center reports about your overall Azure subscription compliance. You can drill down to the specific Azure policies being configured in your Azure environment. A nice feature here is the overall secure score (12%) for this section (based on our sample environment, there seems to be some room for improvement and optimization).

Resource Security Hygiene

The Resource Security Hygiene section is where you get an immediate view on your infrastructure security, highlighting compute and apps, networking, data and storage, and identity and access. A secure score option (327 in the example) and a summary of security optimization recommendations for your specific environment are provided.

Threat Protection

Azure Security Center is backed by Microsoft security researchers, who are constantly looking out for new threats. Based on global Internet detection mechanisms (coming from Azure and Office 365 traffic scanning, but also from Xbox, Outlook.com and other services) that Microsoft is using continuously, any threat that gets detected is almost immediately handed over to Azure Security Center and raised as an alert. Whenever attackers update and release new exploits, Azure Security Center updates its detection mechanisms, which provides a very powerful tool in threat protection.

Advanced Cloud Defense

Advanced cloud defense is the last group of security mechanisms in Azure Security Center, providing protection of applications, virtual machines, and files. A feature like adaptive application controls allows organizations to define what applications can and cannot run inside virtual machines. Virtual machine administrative-level access can be protected by using just-in-time VM access. Lastly, a service like File Integrity Monitoring, allows organizations to validate the integrity of critical system and application files within virtual machines.

Automation and Orchestration

Azure has an extensive built-in automation tool known as Azure Automation. This service allows you to execute so-called runbooks, and automating just about any task against your Azure resources, as well as against your hybrid-running infrastructure. However, in case of Azure Security Center, automation is driven out of security playbooks, a service that actually relies on Azure Logic Apps workflows. A security playbook is a collection of steps and procedures that can be executed from ASC, once it is triggered out of a security alert.

Azure Security Center Cost

Before we move over to the more technical aspects of enabling and configuring Azure Security Center, it is important to understand its cost model.

Azure Security Center is offered in two different pricing tiers.

- Free edition
- Standard edition

Free Edition

The Azure Security Center Free edition is what everyone gets as part of an Azure subscription. It provides the core security features that we covered in the Overview section—namely policies, security assessment, and security recommendations.

Standard Edition

The Standard edition is an add-on to the Free edition; it extends several of its capabilities outside of Azure; for example, it allows you to integrate with hybrid clouds, whether public or private. The Standard tier also provides advanced threat detection, relying on behavioral analytics and machine learning.

The Standard edition can be enabled as a free trial for 30 days. After 30 days, you have to calculate the cost of consumption, depending on the specific Azure Security Center features you want to use, as well as what your environment looks like.

All pricing information can be reviewed on the Azure pricing page at `www.azure.com/pricing`. For Azure Security Center-specific pricing, go to `https://azure.microsoft.com/en-us/pricing/details/security-center/`.

Figure 5-2 shows the pricing structure at the time this book was written.

Pricing

RESOURCE TYPE	FREE TIER	STANDARD TIER
Virtual Machine	Free	~$14.60/Server/Month Included data - 500 MB/day
App Services	Free	~$14.60/App Service/Month
SQL DB	Not Available	~$15/Server/Month
MySQL (Preview)	Not Available	~$7.50/Server/Month*
PostgreSQL (Preview)	Not Available	~$7.50/Server/Month*
Storage (Preview)	Not Available	$0/10K Transactions*

* Pricing displayed is preview price. Price will change at GA. For details on ASC features by resource, please refer to the resource specific documentation

Figure 5-2. *Azure Security Center - Pricing structure*

Estimate around $15 USD per month for each virtual machine or App Service you want to protect with Azure Security Center. (Note that pricing can vary per region, where the information in Figure 5-2 is for Central US at the time of writing.)

Section Summary

In this section, we provided a high-level overview of Azure Security Center, including how it helps organizations optimize their security posture in cloud and hybrid environments. We gave a quick overview of the core capabilities and cost.

In the next section, you learn how to enable Azure Security Center and how to start using its core built-in capabilities and features.

Enabling Azure Security Center

Now that you have a good understanding of the core capabilities and features of Azure Security Center, we imagine that you want to move it up a notch by effectively exploring the service in the Azure portal. And that's exactly what we are going to do in this section.

Enabling ASC Free Edition

The good news is that there is nothing really to be enabled, as the service is already baked into your Azure subscription. At least for everything that is related to the Free edition's capabilities. (Later on, we'll show you how to enable the Standard tier).

While there are a couple of different ways to navigate around in the Azure portal, the "easiest" path would be this one.

1. From the Azure portal, select **All services**.

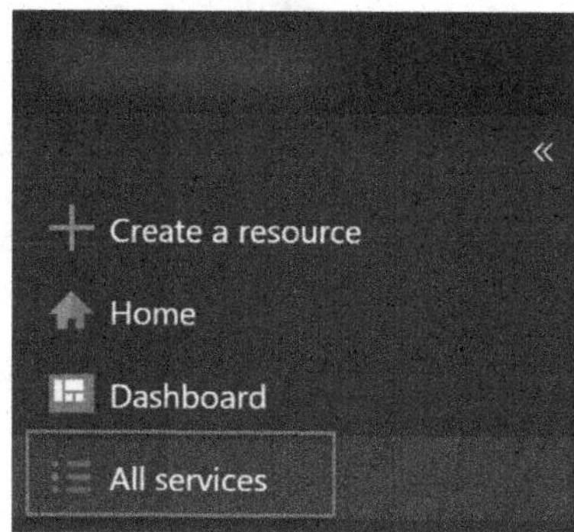

2. From the list of services, search for **security**. This brings up a list of all Azure services with the word *security* in its name. Here, notice Security Center.

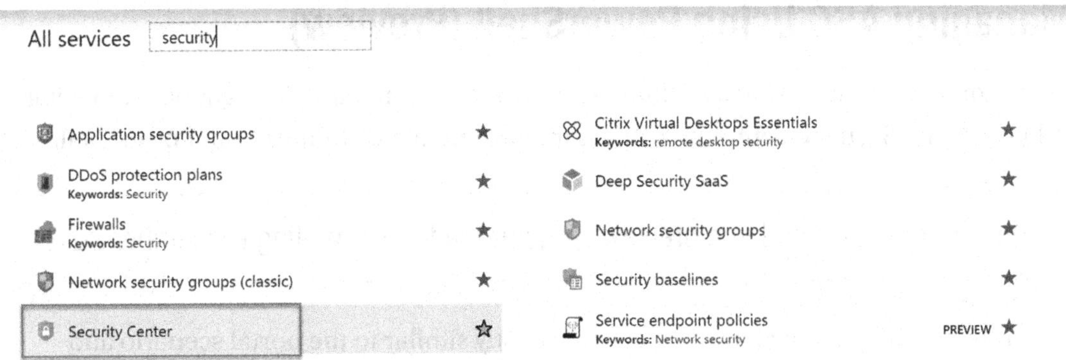

3. If you want to add Security Center to your list of Favorites in the Azure portal, click the star icon.
4. Click **Security Center** to open its blade in the Azure portal.

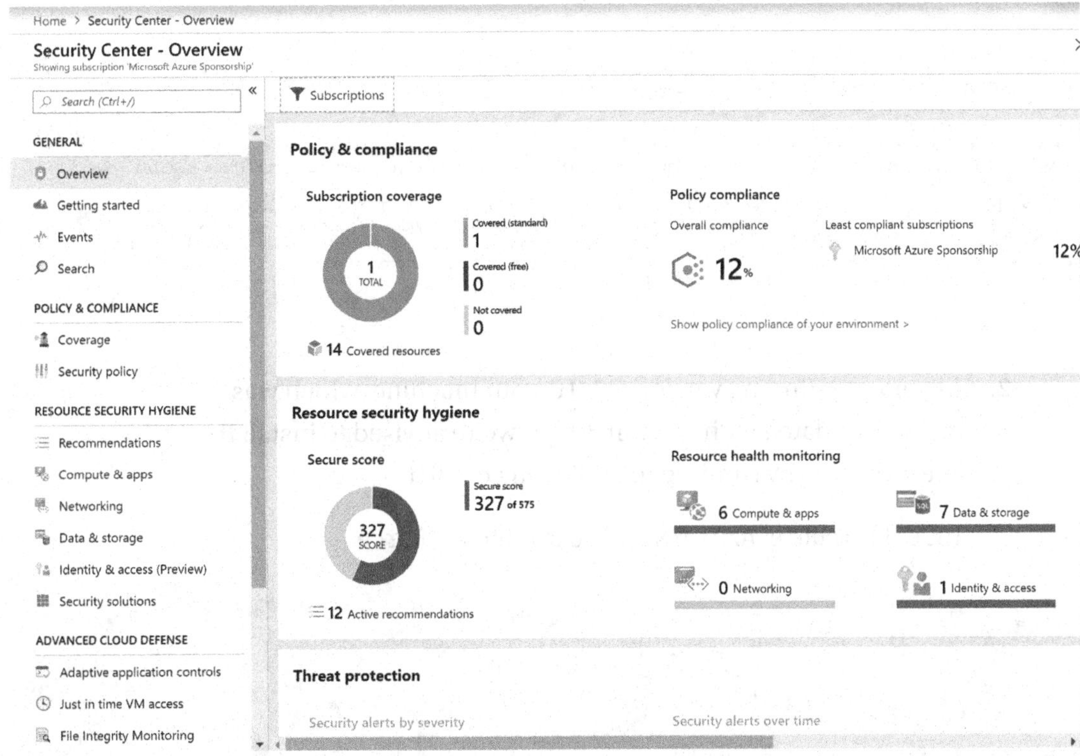

Note that the content in the Overview pane may be different from what's shown here, depending what you have running within your Azure subscription. If you are first enabling Azure Security Center before any other Azure resource, the Overview pane is empty. If you already have resources running, Azure Security Center reports on the security state of these resources.

Managing ASC Using PowerShell (Preview)

In the context where you have multiple subscriptions to manage, it might be interesting to know Azure Security Center now offers management capabilities from PowerShell.

Note This was offered in a preview stage at the time of writing (December 2018).

From an ASC perspective, the steps are mostly similar to the portal scenario and involve the following.

1. Install the latest version of Azure PowerShell, opening the PowerShell shell with administrative rights.

   ```
   install-module -name azureRM -allowclobber
   ```

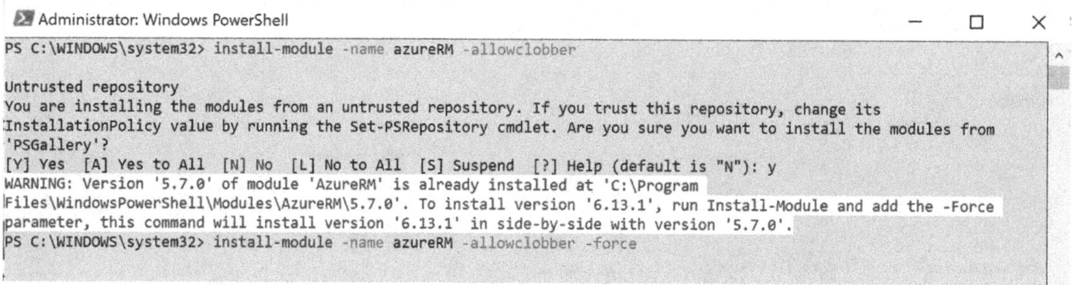

2. As we were running version 5.7.0 on our machine, which was recently updated with version 6.13.1, we're advised to install the latest version, by running the following cmdlet.

   ```
   Install-module AzureRM -allowclobber -Force
   ```

```
Installing package 'AzureRM'
   Installing dependent package 'AzureRM.IotHub'
   [ooooooooooooooooooooooooooooooooooooooooooooooooooo                    ]
  Installing package 'AzureRM.IotHub'
     Unzipping
     [ooooooooooooooooooooooooooooooooooooooooooooooooooooooooooooooooooooooo  ]
PS C:\WINDOWS\system32> install-module -name azureRM -allowclobber -force
```

3. The AzureRM.Security module is offered through PowerShellGet, so we have to make sure this is running in the latest available edition too.

   ```
   Update-Module -Name PowerShellGet
   ```

4. Next, we need to install AzureRM.Profile, requiring a specific version 5.5.0. (Again, this is preview and might have changed by the time that you read this.)

   ```
   install-module -name azurerm.profile -requiredversion 5.5.0
   ```

5. Now, we can install the actual AzureRM.Security Module, by executing the following cmdlet.

   ```
   install-module -name azurerm.security -allowprerelease
   ```

6. Once the module is installed, load it by firing off the import-cmdlet.

   ```
   import-module azurerm.security
   ```

7. Next, log on to your Azure subscription, with an account that has administrative access (RBAC) to Azure Security Center.

   ```
   Connect-azurermaccount
   ```

```
PS C:\WINDOWS\system32> update-module -Name PowerShellGet
PS C:\WINDOWS\system32> install-module -name azurerm.profile -requiredversion 5.5.0
PS C:\WINDOWS\system32> install-module -name azurerm.security -allowprerelease
PS C:\WINDOWS\system32> import-module azurerm.security
PS C:\WINDOWS\system32> connect-azurermaccount

Account        SubscriptionName              TenantId                              Environment
-------        ----------------              --------                              -----------
in      it.be  Microsoft Azure Sponsorship  70681eb4-8dbc-                         AzureCloud
```

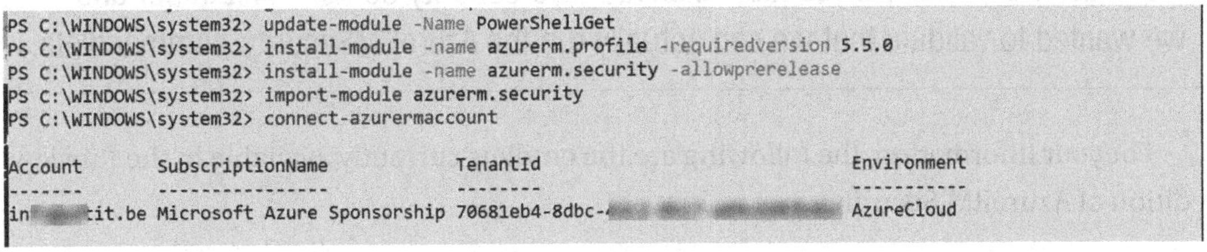

8. Validate that you can read some of the security alerts by running the following cmdlet.

   ```
   Get-AzureRMSecurityAlert
   ```

Administrator: Windows PowerShell

```
Id                   : /subscriptions/0a407898-c                                                  ojumpVMRG/providers/
                       Microsoft.Security/locations/centralus/alerts/2518592039914304162_80d3bda9-da05-420b-8f24-c68f5dd7
                       eaae
Name                 : 2518592039914304162_80d3bda9-da05-420b-8f24-c68f5dd7eaae
ActionTaken          : Detected
AlertDisplayName     : Suspicious authentication activity
AlertName            : Login_BF_ValidUserFailed
AssociatedResource   : /subscriptions/0a407898-c077-                                               jumpVMRG/providers/
                       Microsoft.Compute/virtualMachines/jumpvm
CanBeInvestigated    : True
CompromisedEntity    : jumpvm
ConfidenceReasons    : {}
ConfidenceScore      :
Description          : Although none of them succeeded, some of them used accounts were recognized by the host.
                       This resembles a dictionary attack, in which an attacker performs numerous authentication
                       attempts using a dictionary of predefined account names and passwords in order to find valid
                       credentials to access the host.
                       This indicates that some of your host account names might exist in a well-known account name
                       dictionary.
DetectedTimeUtc      : 11/24/2018 10:00:08 PM
Entities             : {Microsoft.Azure.Commands.Security.Models.Alerts.PSSecurityAlertEntity}
ExtendedProperties   : {[activity start time (UTC), 2018/11/24 22:00:08.5695837], [activity end time (UTC), 2018/11/24
                       22:59:48.1166965], [attacker source IP, IP Address: 46.246.123.6], [attacker source computer
                       name, Unknown]...}
InstanceId           : 80d3bda9-da05-420b-8f24-c68f5dd7eaae
RemediationSteps     : 1. Enforce the use of strong passwords and do not re-use them across multiple resources and
                       services
                       2. In case this is an Azure virtual machine and source IP is available, add the source IP to NSG
                       block list for 24 hours (see
                       https://azure.microsoft.com/en-us/documentation/articles/virtual-networks-nsg/)
                       3. In case this is an Azure virtual machine, create an allow list in NSG (see
                       https://azure.microsoft.com/en-us/documentation/articles/virtual-networks-nsg/)
ReportedSeverity     : Low
ReportedTimeUtc      : 11/24/2018 11:45:39 PM
State                : Active
SubscriptionId       : 0a407898-c077-442d-8e17-71420aa82426
```

Note The output will be different in your environment; it might not even report alerts at all, especially if you just enabled Azure Security Center. Most importantly, we wanted to validate that we can actually run the AzureRMSecurity-commandlets.

For your information, the following are the cmdlets currently available in the Preview edition of AzureRM.Security.

```
Get-AzureRmDiscoveredSecuritySolution
Get-AzureRmExternalSecuritySolution
Get-AzureRmJitNetworkAccessPolicy
Get-AzureRmSecurityAlert
Get-AzureRmSecurityAutoProvisioningSetting
Get-AzureRmSecurityCompliance
Get-AzureRmSecurityContact
Get-AzureRmSecurityLocation
```

```
Get-AzureRmSecurityPricing
Get-AzureRmSecurityTask
Get-AzureRmSecurityWorkspaceSetting
Remove-AzureRmJitNetworkAccessPolicy
Remove-AzureRmSecurityContact
Remove-AzureRmSecurityWorkspaceSetting
Set-AzureRmJitNetworkAccessPolicy
Set-AzureRmSecurityAlert
Set-AzureRmSecurityAutoProvisioningSetting
```

Since these are all still in preview mode, we won't mention them anymore throughout this chapter, unless it's giving capabilities that are not available or too hard to manage from the Azure portal. We hope that we teased you enough to look at the state of PowerShell for Azure Security Center.

Enabling ASC Standard Edition

As you learned from the introductory section, Azure Security Center gives you even better security optimization features when using the Standard edition. Keep in mind enabling this edition comes with a cost per month, but if you ask me, it is definitely worth it! You can't be secured enough.

1. From the Azure Security Center, select **Getting started**. Next, click **Upgrade**.

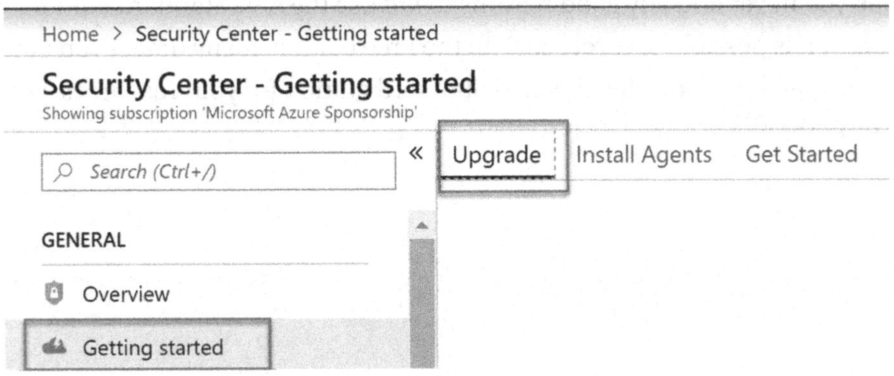

Here, click the **Start Trial** button. Assuming you already passed the 30 days trial, you are greeted with a message.

^ Trial already used on all subscriptions. Click here to choose subscriptions to upgrade

2. Click the **Upgrade** button.
3. After a few minutes, the workspace should switch to **Upgraded**.

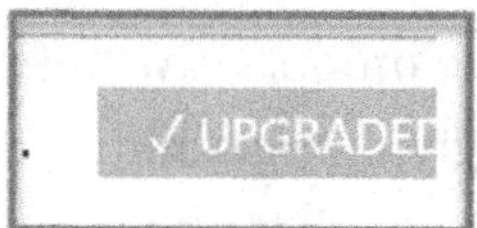

4. Refresh the Azure portal. In Azure Security Center - Getting Started, you see a new message.

˅ All set! All of your Azure subscriptions and workspaces are already fully protected with the standard plan

Good job! You are now ready to start using all capabilities provided by Azure Security Center.

Switching Back Editions

While we hope you never find any good reasons to *not* use the ASC Standard edition, we want you to know it is possible to revert back to the Free edition at any time. Even better, you can granularly enable or disable the paid Standard edition for your resources. So it is not really all or nothing.

1. From Azure Security Center, select **Security policy**.

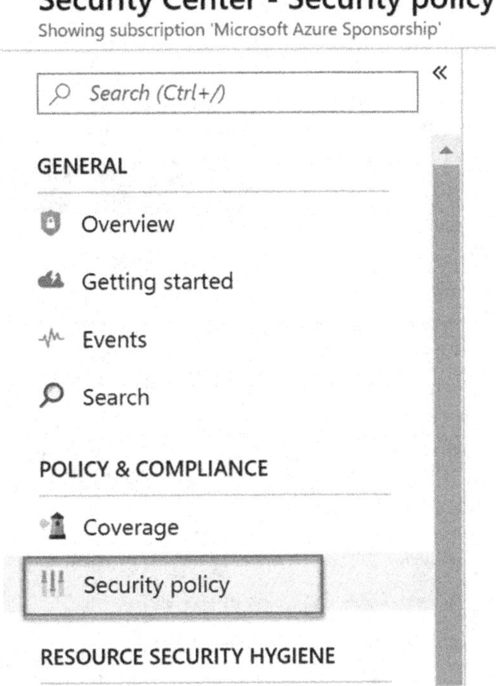

2. This shows you the different management groups and subscriptions for which you have security policies configured. Select your Azure subscription, and click **Edit settings**.

Policy Management

Manage the security policies by choosing a subscription or management group from the list below. In order to define additional polici

Click here to learn more >

3 MANAGEMENT GROUPS 1 SUBSCRIPTIONS 1 WORKSPACES

Search by name

NAME	POLICY INITIATIVE ASSIGNMENT(S)	COMPLIANCE	COVERAGE	SETTINGS
Tenant Root Group (1 of 1 subscriptions)	Limited permissions		---	
HR-pdtit (0 of 0 subscriptions)			---	
HRAppGrp (0 of 0 subscriptions)			---	
Microsoft Azure Sponsorship	ASC Default (subscription: 0a407898	13%	Standard	Edit settings >
PDTOMSWorkspace	---	---	---	Edit settings >

3. This opens the Settings blade. Here, select **Pricing tier**.

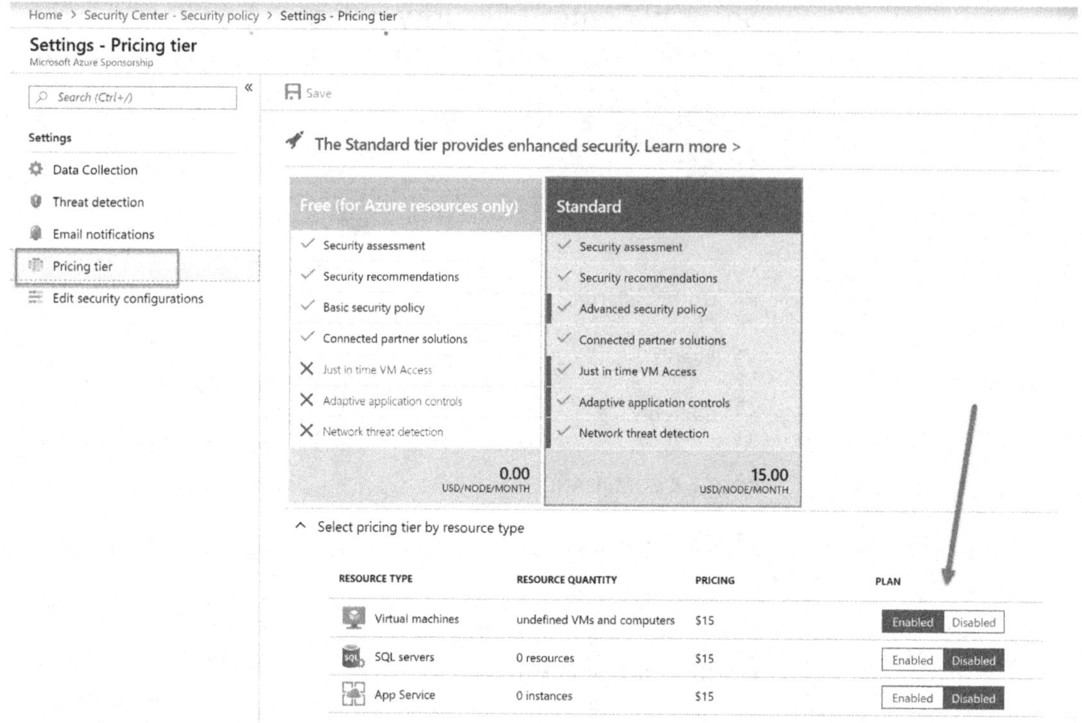

Select the Free tier if you ever want to switch back from Standard. Also, you can decide (per the resource type) if you want to enable the plan or not.

Section Summary

In this section, you learned how to enable both the Azure Security Center Free edition, as well as how to upgrade to the Standard edition.

Collecting Data in Azure Security Center

Now we have Azure Security Center (Free or Standard edition) enabled in our Azure subscription, we will move over to the next important task, configuring how our systems and applications—remember, this can be both Azure resources and non-Azure resources—report back to Azure Security Center.

Because after all, if there is no data in ASC, it cannot provide you any security alerts and recommendations.

You already found out that several Azure resources automatically are picked up by ASC, and it automatically starts generating security information about these. While this should go fine for most of the supported Azure-running resources, it is still good to know how this happens more in detail. At the same time, we will walk you through the steps required to configure hybrid-running systems and applications.

Collecting Data from Azure Virtual Machines

Azure Security Center collects data from Azure virtual machines, Azure App Service, and SQL Azure infrastructure and databases. To gather virtual machine data, Security Center relies on the Microsoft Monitoring Agent. Yes, you might have heard about this agent before. This is the same agent that is installed when using Operations Management Suite (OMS) and Log Analytics. Through this agent, security information like system updates, endpoint protection presence and status, as well as more general security information and event logs is being read from the VM itself and copied to the allocated workspace for analysis.

While installing this agent is possible in a manual way out of OMS Log Analytics or deploying it as a virtual machine extension, a safer and more secure way (making sure all VMs are reporting) is enabling Security Center for automatic data collection, which is done as follows.

1. From within Azure Security Center, select **Security policy**.

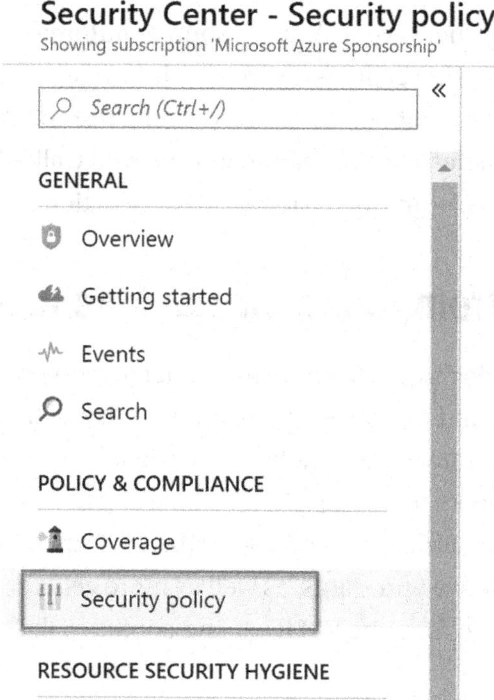

2. Select the Azure subscription, and choose **Edit settings**.

Policy Management

Manage the security policies by choosing a subscription or management group from the list below. In order to define additional polici

Click here to learn more >

3 MANAGEMENT GROUPS 1 SUBSCRIPTIONS 1 WORKSPACES

Search by name

NAME	POLICY INITIATIVE ASSIGNMENT(S)	COMPLIANCE	COVERAGE	SETTINGS
Tenant Root Group (1 of 1 subscriptions)	Limited permissions		---	
HR-pdtit (0 of 0 subscriptions)			---	
HRAppGrp (0 of 0 subscriptions)			---	
Microsoft Azure Sponsorship	ASC Default (subscription: 0a407898·	13%	Standard	Edit settings >
PDTOMSWorkspace	---	---	---	Edit settings >

3. This opens the Settings - Data Collection blade. Here, set Auto Provisioning to **On**.

Security Center collects security data and events from your resources and services to help you prevent, detect, and respond to threats. Learn more >

Auto Provisioning

This enables the automatic installation of the Microsoft Monitoring Agent on all the VMs in your subscription. If enabled, any new or existing VM without an installed agent will be provisioned. Learn more >

4. Next, specify the workspace you want Azure Security Center to use. This is the default generated by ASC; or, you can allocate to use an existing one. (Since we were already using OMS Log Analytics prior to enabling ASC in our subscription, like a lot of customers in the field, we chose the OMS workspace as the target.)

Workspace configuration

Data collected by Security Center is stored in Log Analytics workspace(s). You can select to have data collected from Azure VMs stored in workspace(s) created by Security Center or in an existing workspace you created. Learn more >

○ **Use workspace(s) created by Security Center (default)**

Connect Azure VMs to report to workspaces created by Security Center

◉ **Use another workspace**

Connect Azure VMs to report to selected user workspace

PDTOMSWorkspace

5. You have the option to gather additional raw data, like Windows Security Event Log information, by enabling the **All Events** setting under **Store additional raw data**.

Store additional raw data

You can store raw events, logs, and additional security data in your Log Analytics workspace. This data allows you to perform auditing, investigation, and analysis of your threats.

Windows security events

Select the Windows security events to be collected and stored. When you change your selection from None, you start to pay for the stored events
For additional details

(●) **All Events**
All Windows security and AppLocker events.

( ) **Common**
A standard set of events for auditing purposes.

( ) **Minimal**
A small set of events that might indicate potential threats. By enabling this option, you won't be able to have a full audit trail.

( ) **None**
No security or AppLocker events.

6. Click the **Save** button on top of the blade to save your settings.
7. Depending on your setup, you might see a warning pop up, asking you to change the selected workspace for configured Azure VMs. Here, confirm with **Yes**. This guarantees that all deployed VMs will point back to the same workspace.

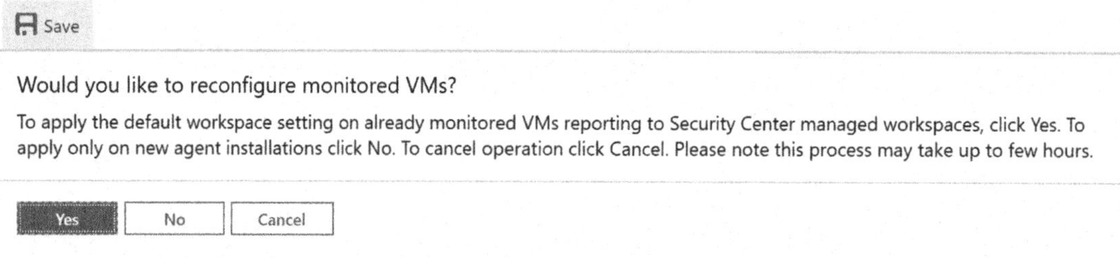

Save
Would you like to reconfigure monitored VMs?
To apply the default workspace setting on already monitored VMs reporting to Security Center managed workspaces, click Yes. To apply only on new agent installations click No. To cancel operation click Cancel. Please note this process may take up to few hours.
Yes
No
Cancel

Note Organizations might have restrictions in place that do not allow all VMs to report to a single workspace. Several of our customers have OMS Log Analytics workspaces for different purposes, being used by different IT teams. Some have workspaces based on workloads, other have workspaces defined per location of resources, and so forth.

8. From a deployed—and running—Azure virtual machine, select **VM Extensions**. Notice that the MicrosoftMonitoringAgent is showing up here, with a provisioning succeeded status. This confirms that the MMA agent is installed successfully. (If you don't have an Azure VM deployed yet, this might be a good time to do so and validate that the agent will be installed automatically.) If an Azure VM is deployed but not running, the information will be unreliable until the VM is started and running successfully.

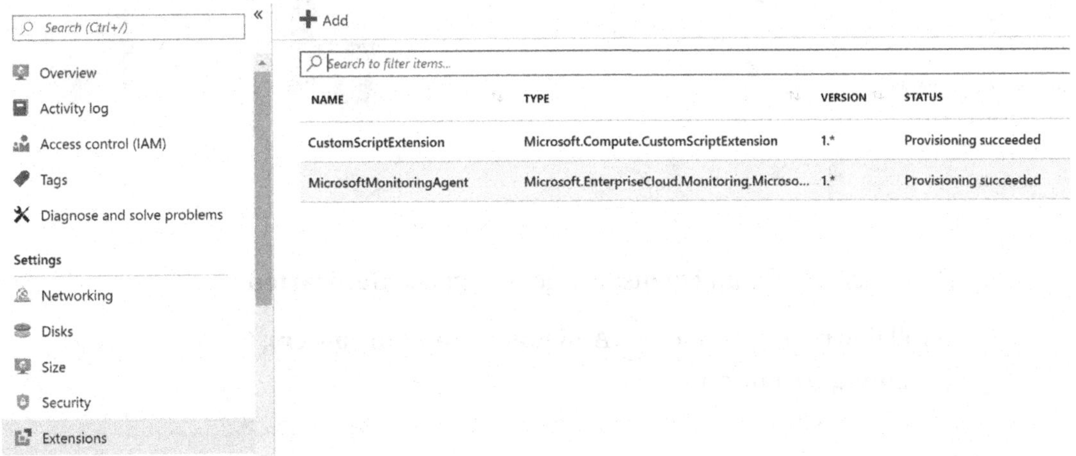

Collecting Data from Non-Azure Virtual Machines

Security Center helps secure and protect both Azure-running VMs and non-Azure-running VMs. They can basically run anywhere: on-premises, in another cloud, in Hyper-V and VMware, and technically, they could even be physical servers.

The only component that we need to build the integration between Azure Security Center and the endpoint is the Microsoft Monitoring Agent.

Let's walk through the different steps on where to find this agent, since the updated portal from September 2018 is a little bit misleading here.

1. From Azure Security Center, select **Get Started**.

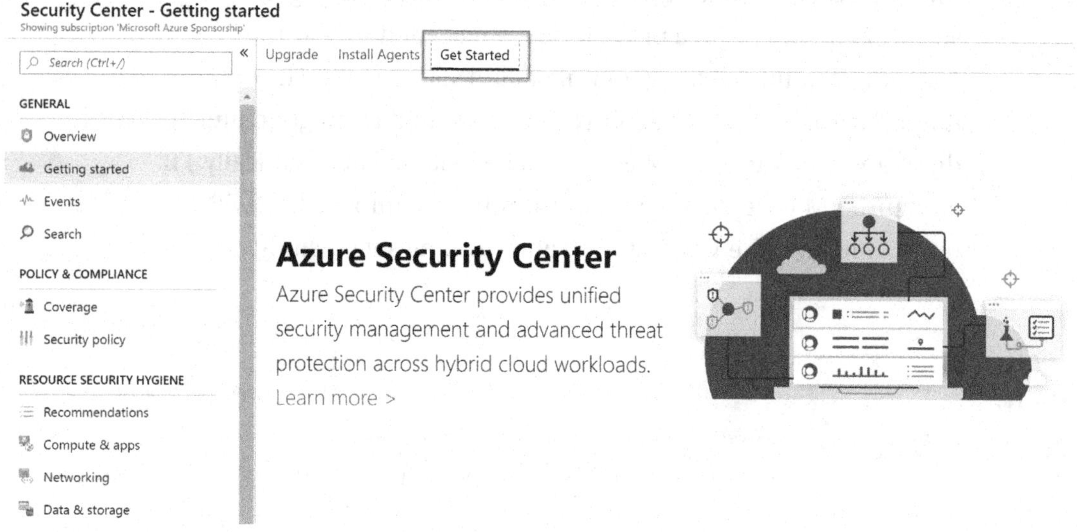

2. Here, instead of going to Install Agents, choose **Get Started**.
3. Scroll down a bit, and notice **Add non-Azure Computers**. Click the **Configure** button.

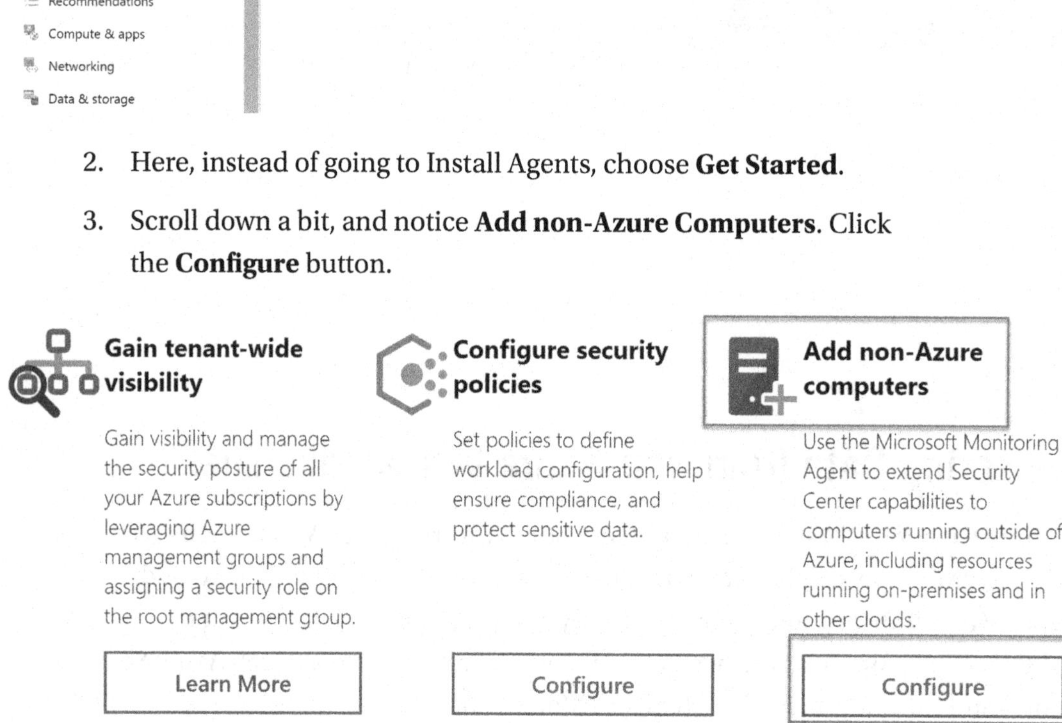

4. This opens the **Add new non-Azure computers** blade. Select the **Azure Security Center** workspace that you want to use for these VMs, and click the **+ Add Computers** button.

Add new non-Azure computers

A Log Analytics workspace is required in order to onboard non-Azure computers to Security Center.

Choose an existing workspace or add a new workspace , and follow the instructions how to connect computers to it. Learn more about workspaces and how Security Center uses them >

Adding computers to workspaces with no Security solution will not protect them under Azure Security Center.

WORKSPACE NAME	VMS & COMPUTERS	SUBSCRIPTION	
PDTOMSWorkspace	1	Microsoft Azure Sponsorship	+ Add Computers

5. This opens the Direct Agent blade, showing you more information on where to download the latest version of the Microsoft Monitoring Agent for both Windows 32- and 64-bit, as well as for Linux OS. Next, it also provides you the workspace ID and security keys that is required when installing the MMA agent onto the actual VM workload.

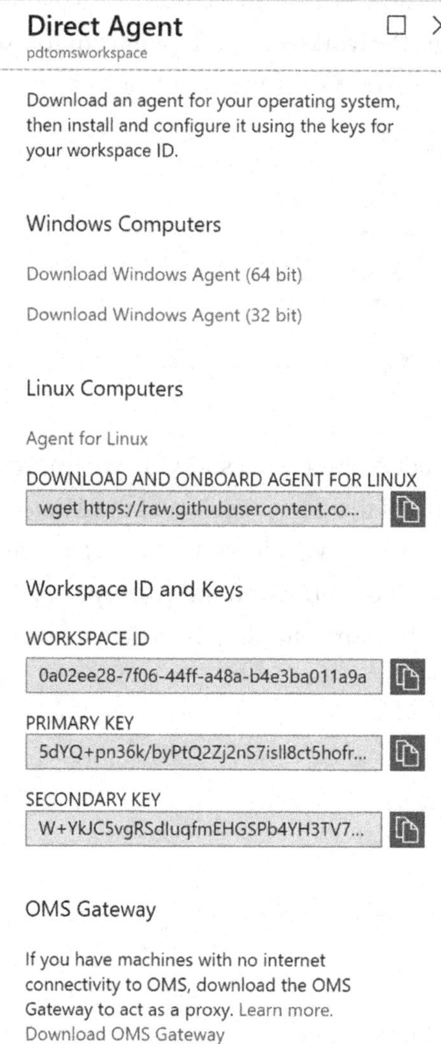

6. Easiest to copy this information for later retrieval when you are actually installing the agent onto a source virtual machine.

Note Chapter 6 is dedicated to management and monitoring, and extensively covers OMS Log Analytics, as well as how to deploy the Microsoft monitoring agent manually or by using automation. Head over to that chapter for further details.

---

7. Once the agent is successfully installed on your non-Azure-running VM, you should validate if Azure Security Center receives data from it. From Azure Security Center, browse to Compute & apps.

8. From the blade, go to **VMs and Computers**. This shows a list of currently connected machines.

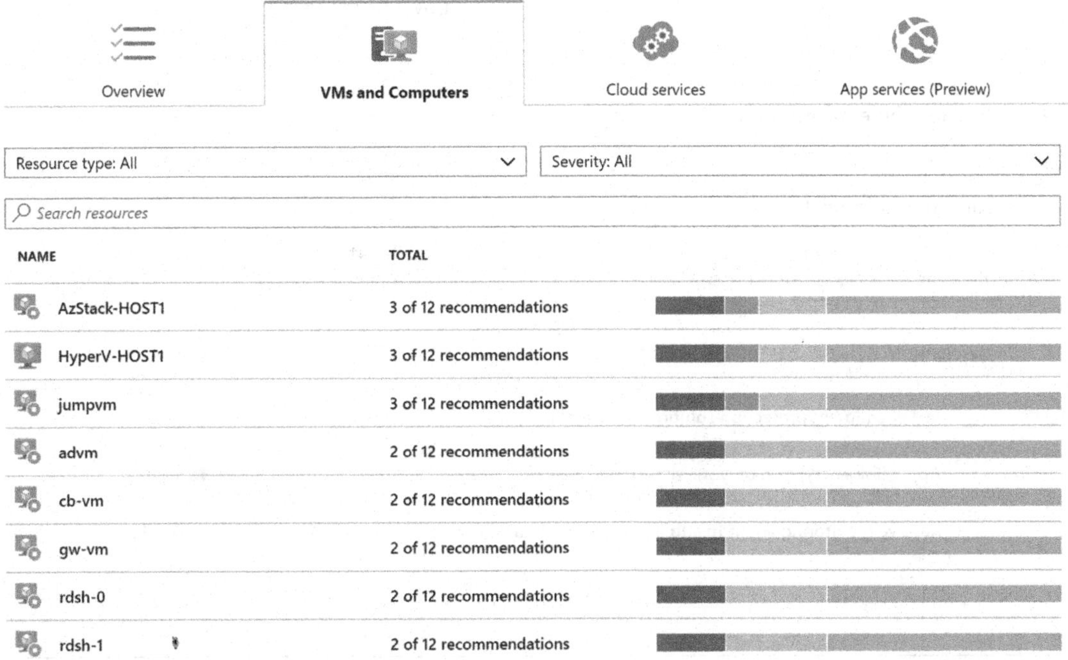

9. Selecting any of the machines opens a more detailed blade, exposing security health for that specific machine and provides details on security recommendations, passed assessments, and unavailable assessments.

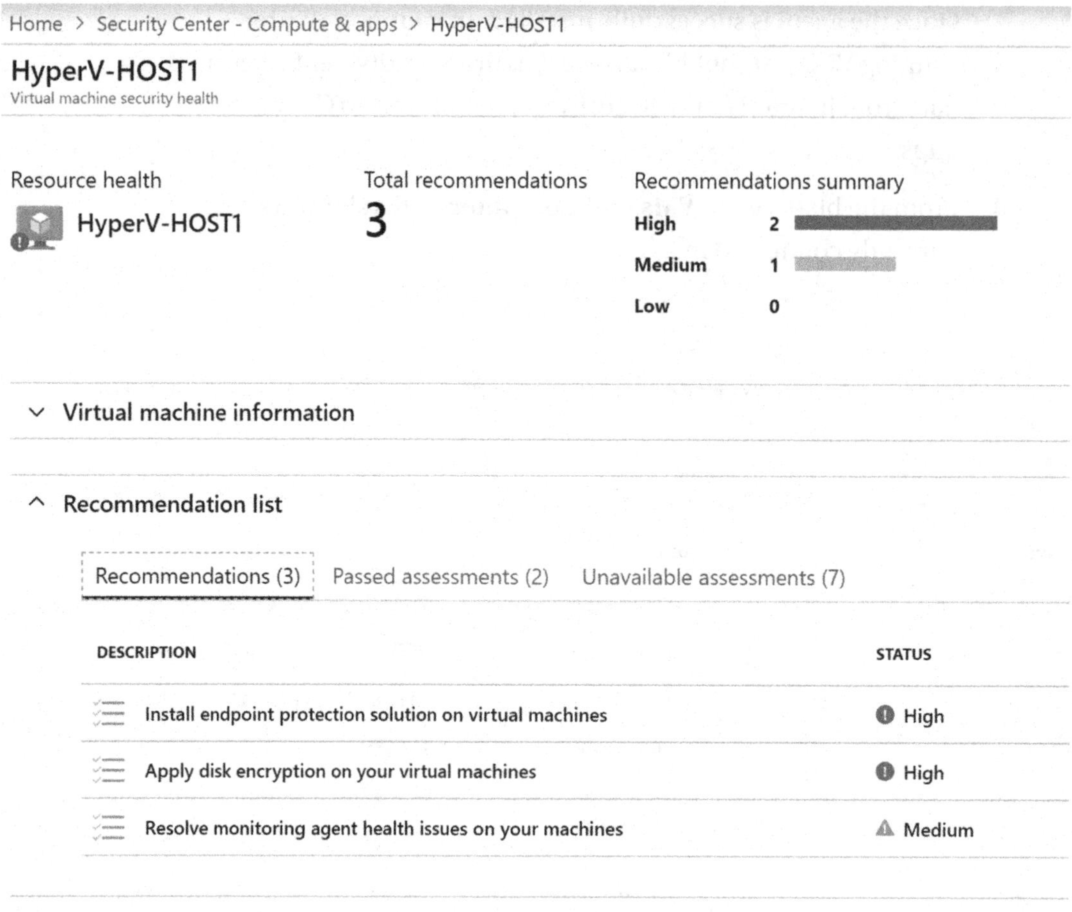

Home > Security Center - Compute & apps > HyperV-HOST1

HyperV-HOST1
Virtual machine security health

Resource health: HyperV-HOST1

Total recommendations: 3

Recommendations summary

High	2
Medium	1
Low	0

Virtual machine information

Recommendation list

Recommendations (3) | Passed assessments (2) | Unavailable assessments (7)

DESCRIPTION	STATUS
Install endpoint protection solution on virtual machines	High
Apply disk encryption on your virtual machines	High
Resolve monitoring agent health issues on your machines	Medium

---

Note Assessments (and how to configure them for your environment) are explained in the next section.

Section Summary

In this section, you learned about how Azure Security Center collects data from Azure virtual machines and non-Azure machines, relying on the Microsoft Management Agent.

Configuring and Defining Security Assessments

We closed the previous section by pointing to assessments, and we are continuing the same subject to make sure that you get a good understanding of what these are and how you can manage them.

One of the Azure Security Center policies that you can create is an *assessment policy*. It is a set of rules and validations that you configure in a rule base, which is then mapped against a system's configuration state. Eventually pinpointing if your system is compliant with the assessment rule base you defined in the assessment configuration file.

Technically, the assessment configuration file is using a JSON syntax structure, starting from a default definition. Next, as an organization you can create your customized assessment definition file and applying these to all VMs that are linked to a certain workspace. At any time, you can revert back to the default configuration provided by Azure Security Center.

Operating System Security Definition

As a starting point, Azure Security Center relies on a set of more than 150 security rules that specify the operating system's hardening state, the firewall rules applied, audit policies, password policy settings, and more.

Some of you might remember having configured these from Active Directory Group Policy or local machine Group Policy registry keys in the past. But with more and more systems not being Active Directory domain integrated anymore, another solution needed to be put in place. An ASC security assessment is an alternative solution.

The security baseline list published by the Azure Security Center team is available at `https://gallery.technet.microsoft.com/Azure-Security-Center-a789e335`. The file is an Excel worksheet that lists the rules as a baseline for different Windows operating systems (2008–2016), as well as a baseline for the Linux OS.

The baseline itself is using the Common Configuration Enumeration (CCE) to assign unique identifiers for the several configuration rules, as published at `https://nvd.nist.gov/config/cce`. So you could call it an open standard.

If you look at the Excel sheet from the TechNet Gallery link, and check for Windows Server 2016, its content looks like the following, for a total of 138 security settings.

```
DataSource           BaselineRegistryRule
BaselineId           221cdf46-aef5-4120-bb00-fdc70afd7432
```

```
Id                    3715ec67-6cd4-49c0-8c82-27001a0e332b
OriginalId            e745b4e7-6c95-414c-89ab-34f3bb0bed85
CceId                 CCE-37615-2
Name                  Ensure 'Accounts: Limit local account use of blank
                      passwords to console logon only' is set to 'Enabled'
Type                  Registry
ExpectedValue         1
Severity              Critical
AnalyzeOperation      Equals
Enabled               TRUE
Hive                  LocalMachine
RegValueType          Int
KeyPath               System\CurrentControlSet\Control\Lsa
ValueName             LimitBlankPasswordUse
AuditPolicyId
SectionName
SettingName
LGPO path             Computer Configuration\Policies\Windows
                      Settings\Security Settings\Local Policies\Security
                      Options\Accounts: Limit local account use of blank
                      passwords to console logon only
LGPO setting          Enabled
Description           This policy setting determines whether local
                      accounts that are not password protected can be
                      used to log on from locations other than the
                      physical computer console. If you enable this policy
                      setting, local accounts that have blank passwords
                      will not be able to log on to the network from
                      remote client computers. Such accounts will only
                      be able to log on at the keyboard of the computer.
                      The recommended state for this setting is:
                      `Enabled`.
Vulnerability         Blank passwords are a serious threat to computer
                      security and should be forbidden through both
                      organizational policy and suitable technical
```

	measures. In fact, the default settings for Active Directory domains require complex passwords of at least seven characters. However, if users with the ability to create new accounts bypass your domain-based password policies, they could create accounts with blank passwords. For example, a user could build a stand-alone computer, create one or more accounts with blank passwords, and then join the computer to the domain. The local accounts with blank passwords would still function. Anyone who knows the name of one of these unprotected accounts could then use it to log on.
Impact	None - this is the default configuration.

This rule base lists all the common security configuration options for the operating system, defining a default setting, a severity level, and the impact. Based on this information, Azure Security Center generates recommendations and alerts on how to optimize the security of your systems. It's great!

Defining the Security Assessment Baseline in Azure Security Center

Now that you have more background on assessment information and where the rule base comes from, it is important to know how to configure this baseline for use in Azure Security Center.

At first, if you are OK with the rule base as it is, you don't have to make any changes. However, assuming that you want to make changes, this is the process to follow.

1. From Azure Security Center, select **Security policy**.
2. Select your Azure subscription and click **Edit settings**.
3. This brings you to the Settings pane. Select **Edit Security configurations**.

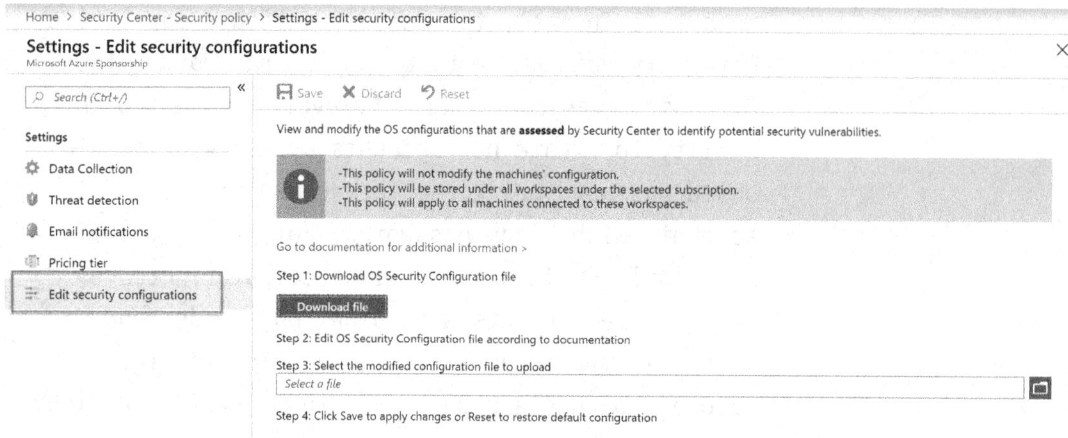

4. Next, click **Download file**, and save the file to your local machine. Notice it is in JSON format.

5. Open the file in a text editor like Visual Studio Code, Visual Studio, or Notepad++ (with the JSON viewer add-on installed). You should recognize the rule base from our previously described example from the Excel sheet, as the JSON structure is almost identical to that one. For example, let's search for the same entry described earlier using its CCE code CCE-37615-2. In Visual Studio Code, the result looks like this.

{} BaselineConfiguration.json ×

CCE-376

```
    },
    {
      "rules": {
        "baselineRegistryRules": [
          {
            "hive": "LocalMachine",
            "regValueType": "Int",
            "keyPath": "SYSTEM\\CurrentControlSet\\Control\\Lsa",
            "valueName": "LimitBlankPasswordUse",
            "ruleId": "385cc232-e49c-4ce1-bd8c-4c835968c46a",
            "originalId": "051cdac6-2234-4eb7-85eb-db391c469557",
            "cceId": "CCE-37615-2",
            "ruleName": "Accounts: Limit local account use of blank passwords to console logon only",
            "baselineRuleType": "Registry",
            "expectedValue": "1",
            "remediationValue": "1",
            "severity": "Critical",
            "analyzeOperation": "EQUALSORNOTEXISTS",
            "source": "Microsoft",
            "state": "Enabled"
          },
```

6. Imagine that you removed certain rules from the rule base or changed specific parameters (e.g., modifying an expectedValue from 1 to 0, basically disabling the security check), the next step involves uploading your changed JSON file to Azure Security Center.

7. From the same location in the Azure portal where you downloaded BaselineConfiguration.json, you can also upload it again. This is done in step 3 from the listed steps. Browse to your new JSON-file, and commit the changes by clicking the Save button.

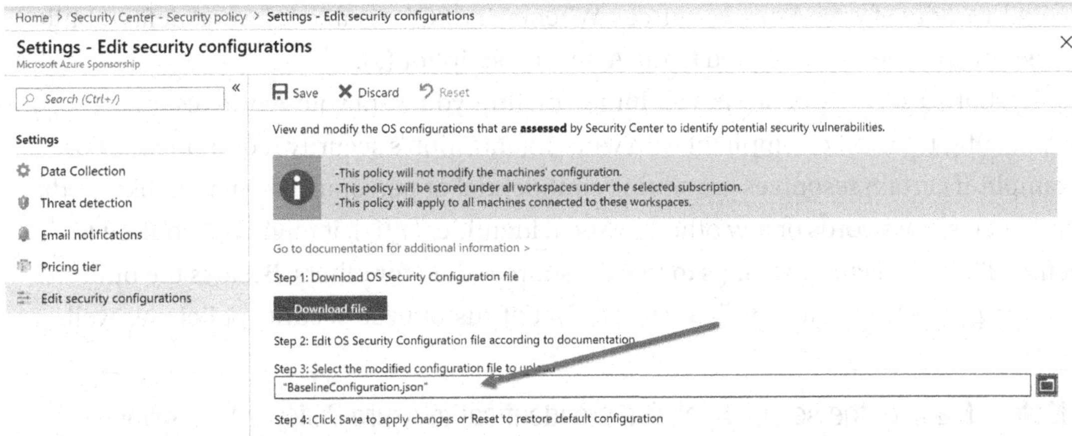

8. If you ever want to make other changes to the baseline, repeat the same procedure by uploading the newest JSON file that you have. Similarly, if you ever want to go back to the original Azure Security Center default baseline, use the Reset button.

Section Summary

In this section, you learned about Azure Security Center baseline assessments, where the rule base information comes from, and how you can change this baseline rule base, by importing an updated JSON-file and applying it into ASC.

Azure Security Center Security Policies

The previously described assessment rule base helps identify any security issues for Windows and Linux machines. But you already know that Azure Security Center can help in securing more than just (virtual) machines. A huge part of this security detection capability is based on security policies.

What Are Security Policies?

Similar to the overall Azure policies that are used for governance of your Azure environments, as described in Chapter 3, security policies assist with optimizing the overall security of your Azure resources. Whenever ASC is enabled, several default built-in security policies are assigned to the Azure subscription(s).

In short, a security policy is a definition on how you want your Azure resources to be configured, to be compliant with your organization's security requirements. For example, if certain resources are storing confidential or personal information like credit card details, passwords or any other personal identifier (PID), it might be required to define different security settings to these resources than for others. Besides the built-in security policies, you can configure its own set of customized security policies as well.

Note Many of the security policies are identical to Azure Policy, which involves topics that we already discussed, like management groups, how to assign policies to multiple subscriptions, and the definitions of a rule, initiative, and assignment. Refer to Chapter 4 if you are not that familiar with these definitions or concepts.

Managing the Built-In Security Policies

A critical component to understanding how Azure Security Center operates is a view of the built-in security policies. For each of the configured policies, a different effect can be defined, which can be any one of the following: Append, Audit, AuditIfNotExist, Deny, DeployIfNotExist, or Disabled.

Let's have a look at the default configuration.

1. From Azure Security Center, select **Security policy**.
2. Select the Azure subscription or management group for which you want to check the security policy.

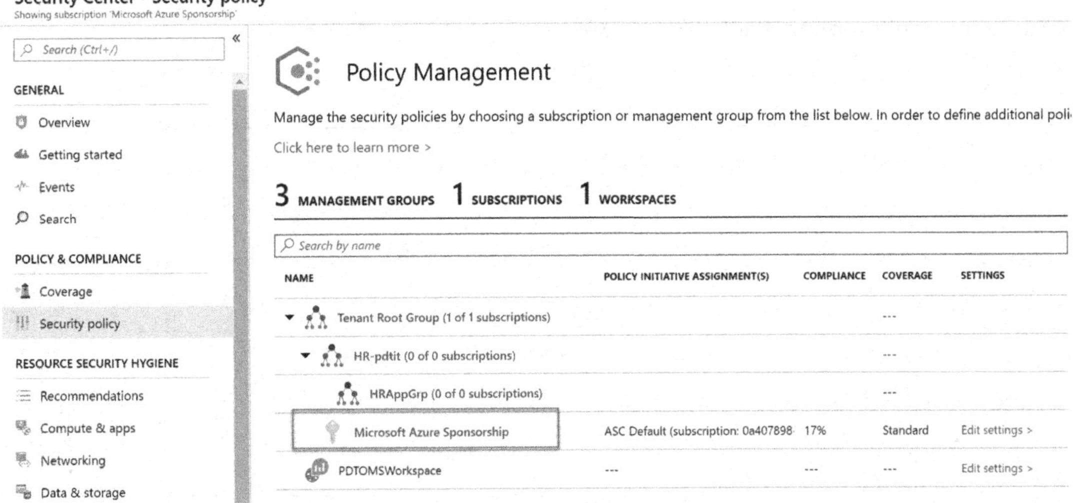

3. This opens the details on the security policy.

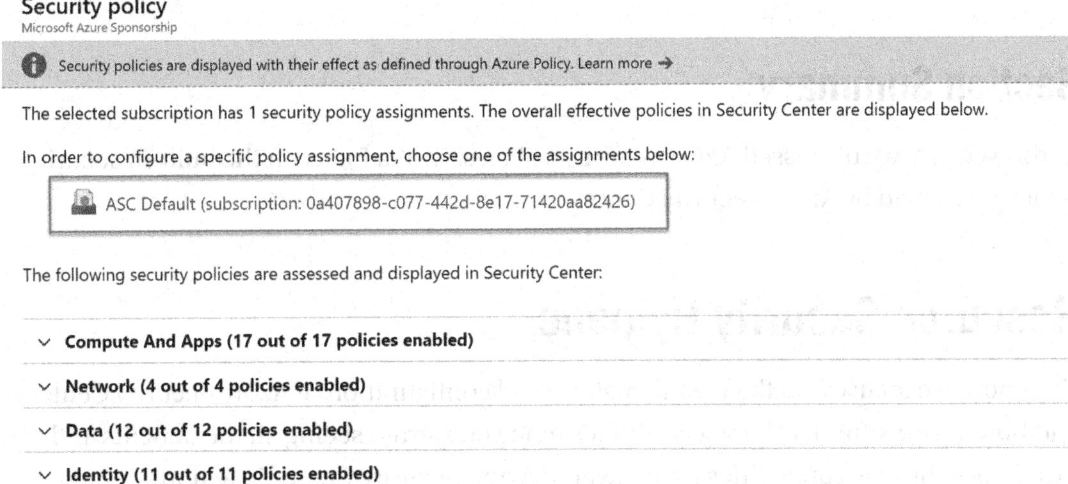

4. To make changes to the default setting of this security policy, select the **ASC Default** policy.

5. This opens the policy in edit mode, which allows you to make changes where needed. You can change the scope, define exclusions, alter the policy name, or modify parameters.

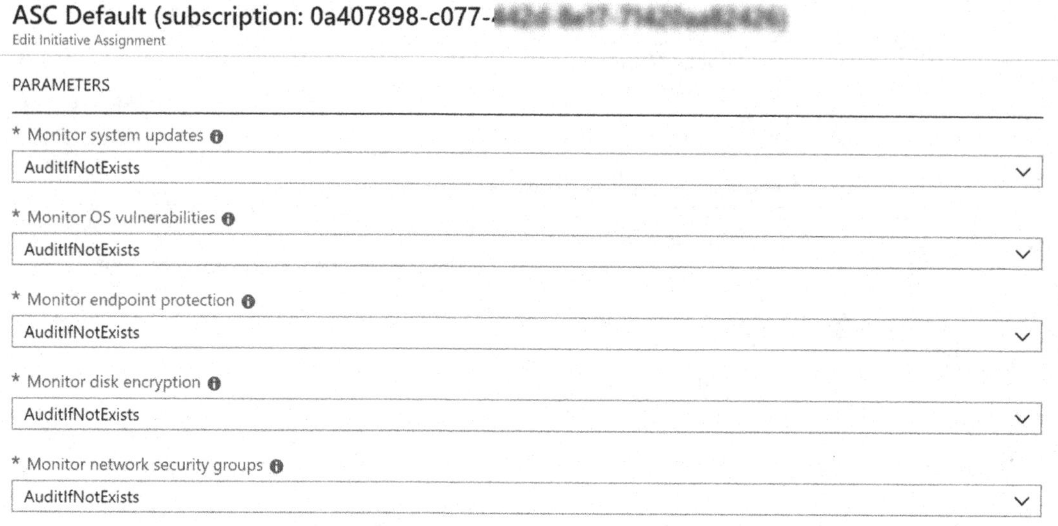

Note that changes are applied immediately.

Section Summary

In this section, we discussed Azure security policies, with a focus on the built-in security policies assigned by Azure Security Center.

Resource Security Hygiene

Until now, we focused on the overall higher-level configuration of Azure Security Center and how it works “under the hood.” But it’s time you started seeing all the benefits and experience the true capabilities and power of Azure Security Center in action.

Note Azure Security Center can only report and alert on Azure resources and the non-Azure systems that it sees. To have a good experience on what ASC can report on, it is recommended to have several Azure resources deployed, as otherwise, there is not much to report on. In our sample scenario here, we deployed a few Azure VMs, both Windows and Linux, an Azure web app, a SQL Azure database, and created a few users in Azure Active Directory. The output of ASC's reporting and alerting is heavily depending on how these Azure Resources are deployed. So don't be surprised if the results in your environment are different from in ours.

One of the key features of Azure Security Center provides security recommendations, which really helps organizations optimize their security posture for all reported systems and applications. Within ASC, this is allocated in the Resource Security Hygiene part of the console.

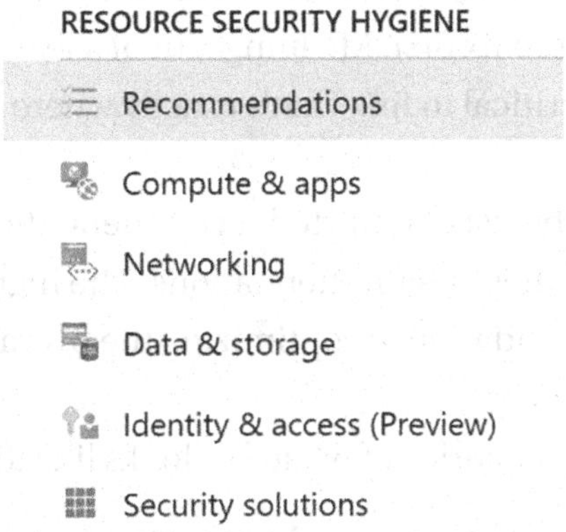

Figure 5-3. *Resource Security Hygiene section in the Azure Security Center portal view*

This section is split into several buckets.

- **Recommendations**. This is an overall listing of security recommendations, secure scores, and resource health monitoring; it contains subsection recommendations.
- **Compute & apps**. Contains filtered security recommendations, specifically for (virtual) machines, Azure and non-Azure, as well as Azure App Service (preview) and Containers (preview).

- **Networking**. Contains filtered security recommendations specifically for Azure virtual networks and network security groups, and provides access to Network Map.
- **Data & storage**. Contains filtered security recommendations specifically for SQL Azure and Azure storage accounts.
- **Identity & access**. Contains filtered security recommendations, specifically for Azure identity and subscriptions, and Azure Key Vault
- **Security solutions**. Here you can configure integration with third-party security solutions like anti-malware or SIEM, Azure advanced Identity Protection or Microsoft Advanced Threat Analytics.

Secure Score

One of the main challenges in managing an organization's security as a security analyst or security officer—besides getting a clear view on all the security risks and required protection—is deciding what to fix first. Meaning, out of a list of reported issues, how do you decide what is most critical to fix? That's exactly where a secure score comes in rather handy.

Starting from analyzing the list of reported recommendations, the secure score allocates a "score" to each of these recommendations. The higher the score, the more critical the reported recommendation for optimizing the overall security health of your environment.

Let's walk through some scenarios of what this looks like in our sample setup.

1. From Azure Security Center, go to **Recommendations** under the Resource Security Hygiene section.

Security Center - Recommendations
Showing subscription 'Microsoft Azure Sponsorship'
Search (Ctrl+/)
POLICY & COMPLIANCE
Coverage
Security policy
RESOURCE SECURITY HYGIENE
Recommendations
Compute & apps
Networking
Data & storage
Identity & access (Preview)
Security solutions
ADVANCED CLOUD DEFENSE
Adaptive application controls
Just in time VM access
File Integrity Monitoring
THREAT PROTECTION
Security alerts
Secure score
393 SCORE
Secure score 393 of 720
16 Active recommendations
Resource health monitoring
8 Compute & apps
7 Data & storage
1 Networking
1 Identity & access
Search recommendations
RECOMMENDATION
SECURE...
RESOURCE
Enable MFA for accounts with owner permission... +50 1 of 1 subsc...
Install system updates on your machines +40 1 of 8 virtua...
Enable Network Security Groups on virtual mac... +20 1 of 2 virtua...
Install endpoint protection solution on virtual m... +18 7 of 8 virtu...
Require secure transfer to storage account (Prev... +17 6 of 7 stora...
Apply disk encryption on your virtual machines +15 8 of 8 virtu...
Disable unrestricted network access to storage ... +15 7 of 7 stora...

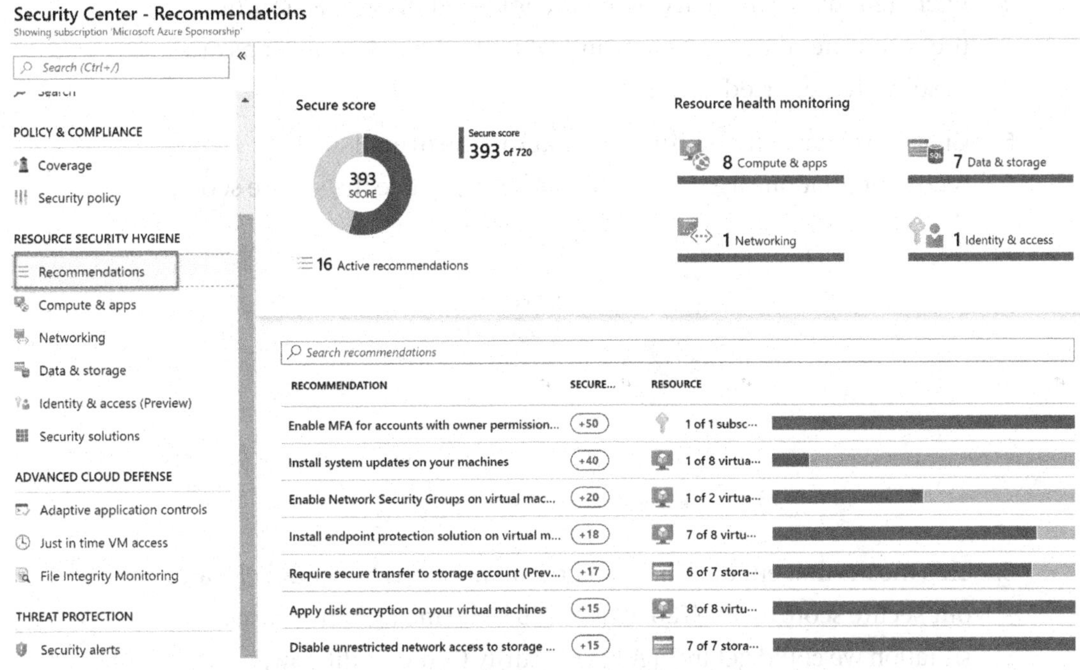

2. Notice the list of recommendations. For each of the recommended actions, a value is listed in the secure score column.

3. Click a value to get more information on that specific recommended item. For example, we selected the first item with a score of +50.

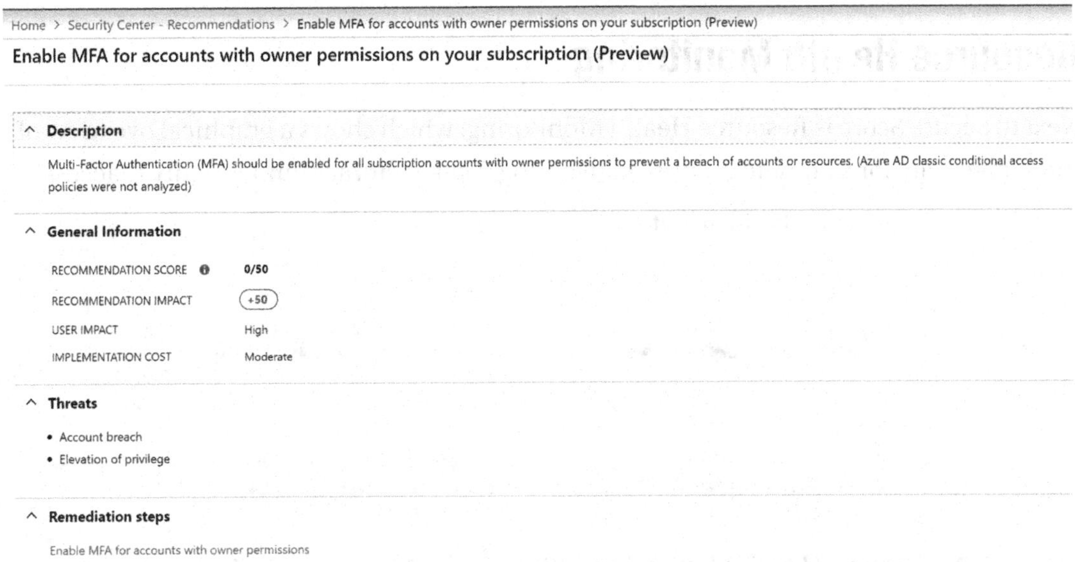

Home > Security Center - Recommendations > Enable MFA for accounts with owner permissions on your subscription (Preview)
Enable MFA for accounts with owner permissions on your subscription (Preview)
Description
Multi-Factor Authentication (MFA) should be enabled for all subscription accounts with owner permissions to prevent a breach of accounts or resources. (Azure AD classic conditional access policies were not analyzed)
General Information
RECOMMENDATION SCORE 0/50
RECOMMENDATION IMPACT +50
USER IMPACT High
IMPLEMENTATION COST Moderate
Threats
Account breach
Elevation of privilege
Remediation steps
Enable MFA for accounts with owner permissions

4. Each item has a summary of the recommendation, a description, the recommendation impact, and what the remediation steps are to solve the reported issue.

5. Close this item, which brings you back to the overall recommendations list. On top of this blade, notice the secure score.

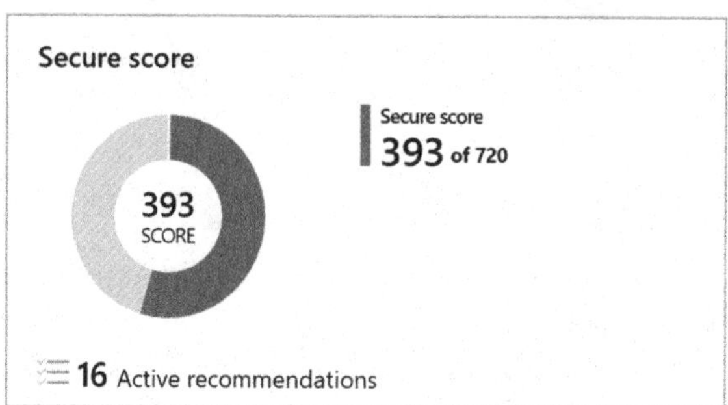

6. This means that out of 16 listed recommendations, we could elevate our secure score to 393/720, where 720 is the maximum secured situation we could get from Azure Security Center until now, based on the information it has gathered from the setup. Think of it differently by fixing the 16 recommendations that we're moving from 0 to 393! It is rather impressive to get that information in a split second. Without Azure Security Center and the secure score feature, it would take a lot more time to analyze the different security alerts and issues, and deciding which one(s) are more critical than others.

Resource Health Monitoring

Next to Secure Score is Resource Health Monitoring, which shows a graphical overview of the secure state for Compute & apps, Networking, Data & storage, and Identity & access.

Figure 5-4. *Resource Health Monitoring options in the Azure Security Center portal view*

Honestly, this is nothing more than a summarized graphical view that allows you to be redirected to the detailed recommendations for each topic.

Securing Network Resources

As mentioned in the high-level overview on resource security hygiene, Azure Security Center also recognizes and detects security issues in the networking layer of your Azure resources. Besides listing out the different security recommendations for your networking resources, ASC has another pretty powerful tool to assist in detecting network security issues—Network Map. Next, it also provides another new feature called Hardening Network Security Groups. (It is currently still in limited public preview, which requires product group activation in your subscription.)

Network Map

Network Map is a graphical interface within ASC, highlighting any Azure Networking Resources, together with their dependencies and security issues, if any. The Network Map topology is drawn automatically by Azure Security Center itself. Let's walk through the core steps on how it can be used.

1. From Azure Security Center, in the Resource Security Hygiene section, select **Networking**.

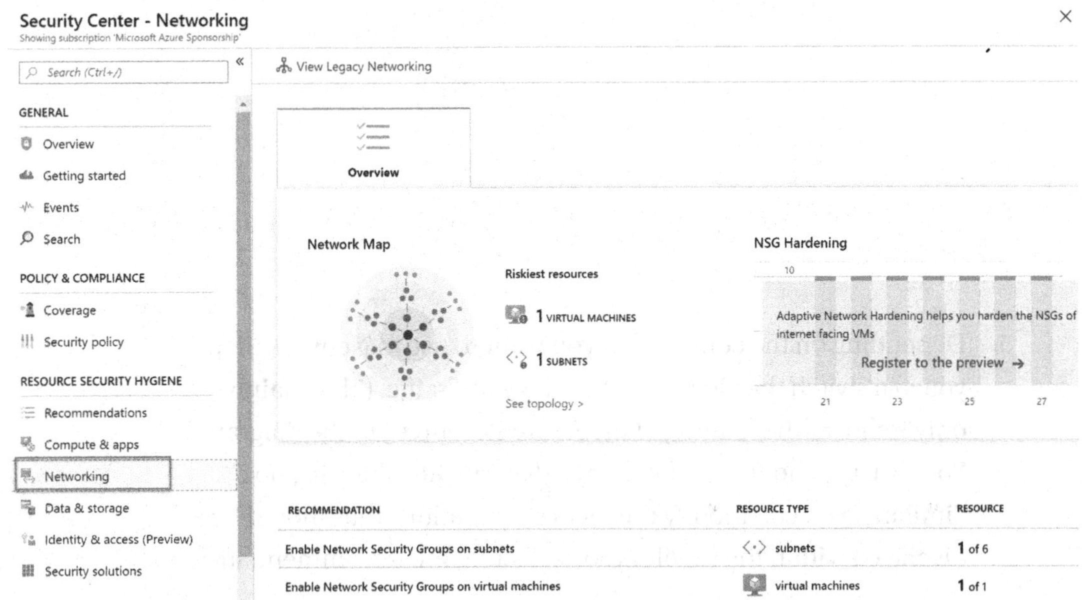

2. This opens the Networking blade of Azure Security Center, showing the Network Map, NSG Hardening, and networking resources-related recommendations to fix detected security issues.

3. Click the **Network Map** diagram.

4. This opens a more detailed topology map of the different Azure Virtual Networks you have, together with any other Azure resources connected to it, like virtual machines and storage accounts.

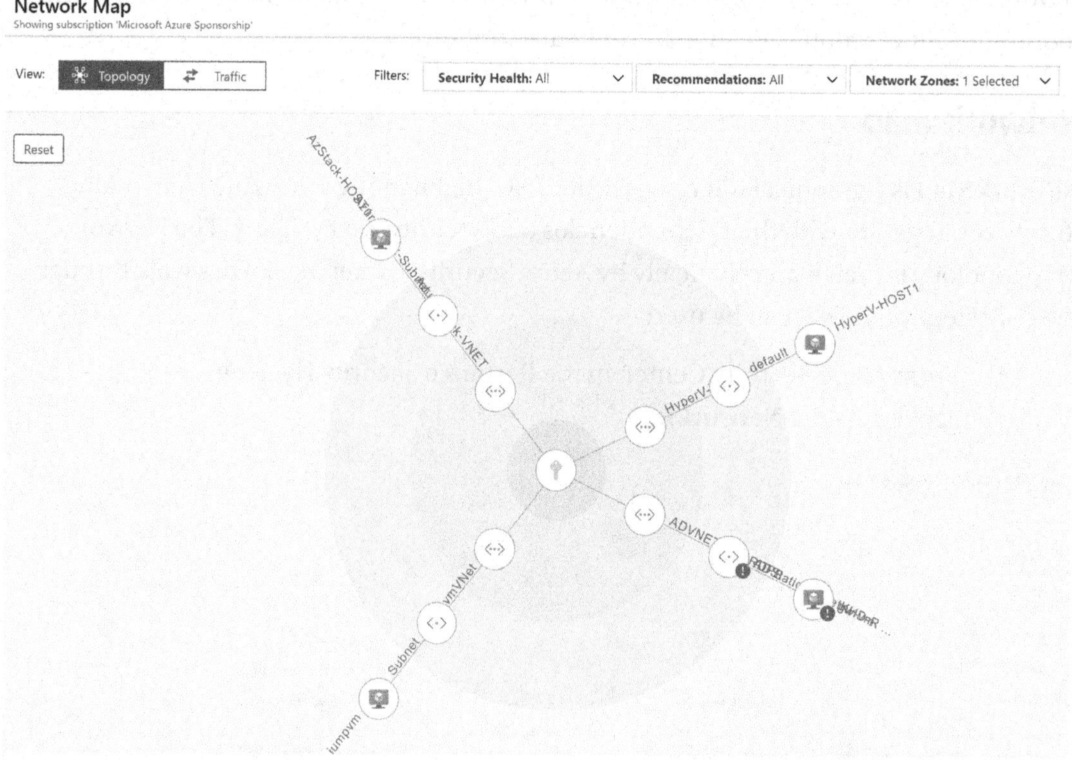

5. Depending on the context that you want to use in Network Map, you can switch the view from Topology to Traffic. (This mainly only removes the naming of the Azure Resources in the diagram.) You can also modify the filters by selecting the Filters list box. Similarly, you can modify the recommendations that should be displayed within the topology, by selecting the Recommendations

list box. Lastly, you can modify the network zones, showing the Azure internal VNets only, or including the Internet-facing ones.

6. By making these selections, and activating all filters, recommendations, and network zones, the diagram (for our sample scenario of Azure Resources), changes to the following topology. This shows more information in the same topology diagram.

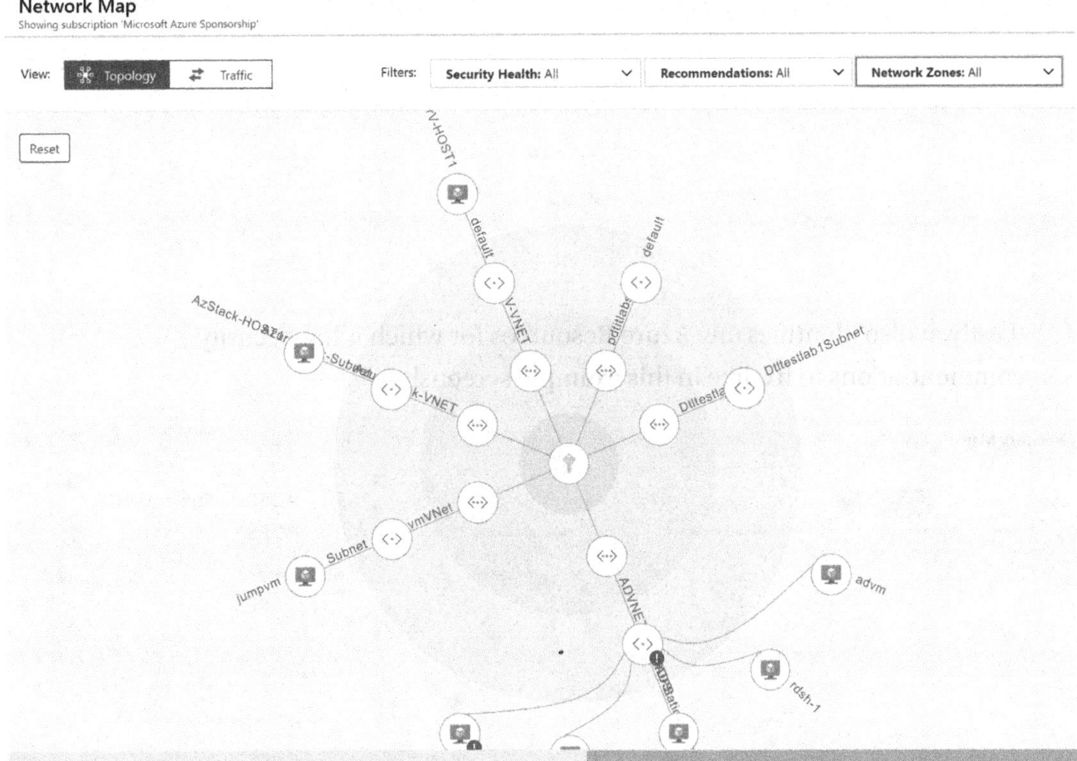

7. Let's drill down on some of these details listed in the diagram itself. By scrolling the mouse wheel up/down, you can zoom in/zoom out of the network map. (There is also a button for that if you don't have a wheel mouse.) Selecting any of the Azure resources in the diagram shows you more information about that specific resource.

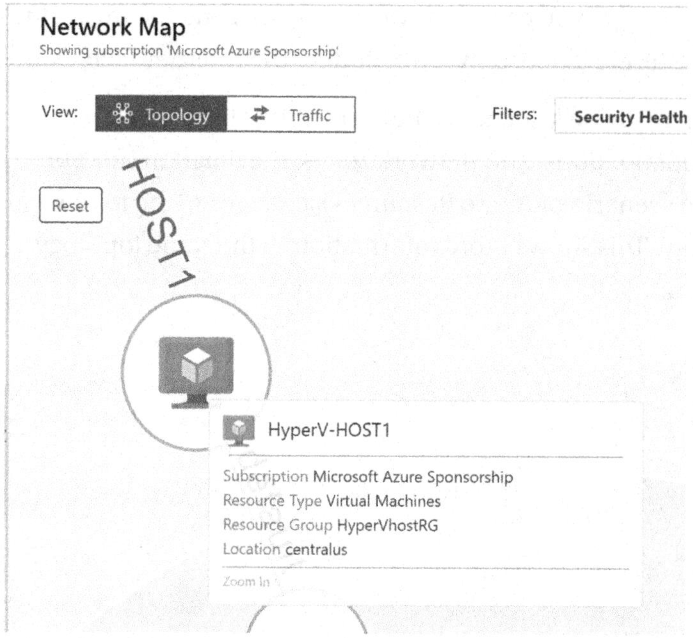

Lastly, it also identifies any Azure Resources for which it has security recommendations to fix, like in this example screenshot.

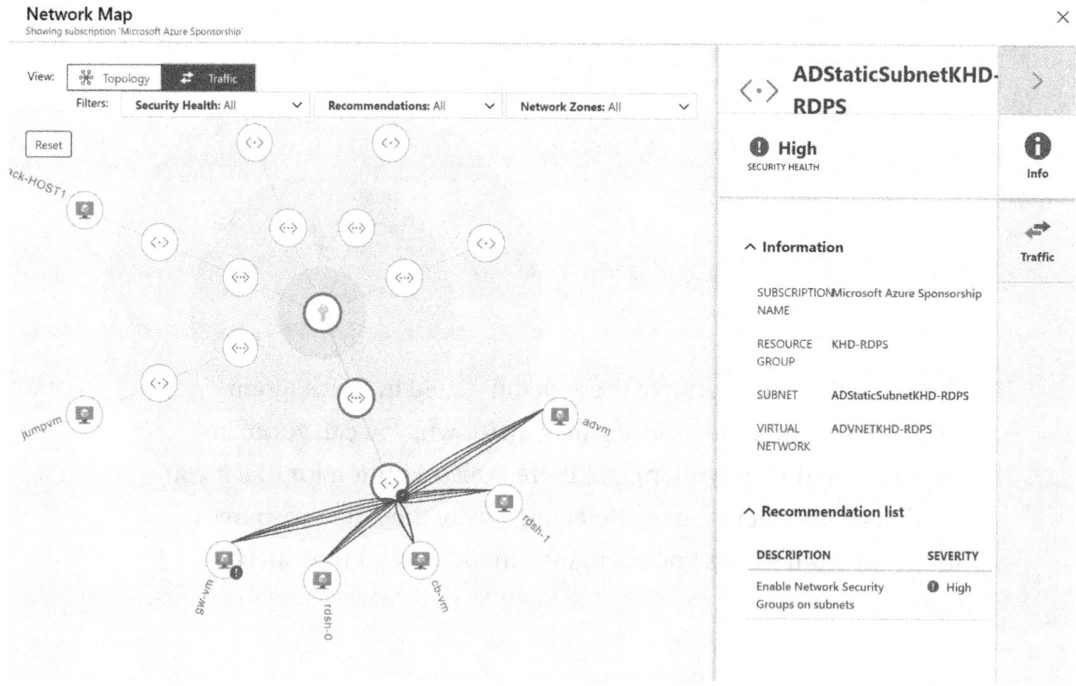

8. From the view shown in the screenshot, notice the Info and Traffic buttons on the right. The information section lists information about the selected resource, including VNet, subnet, resource group, as well as descriptions of any recommendations to fix.

9. Now, click the **Traffic** button. This shows you a detailed overview of all Inbound and Outbound network traffic, including Azure Resource, as well as configured TCP and UDP ports.

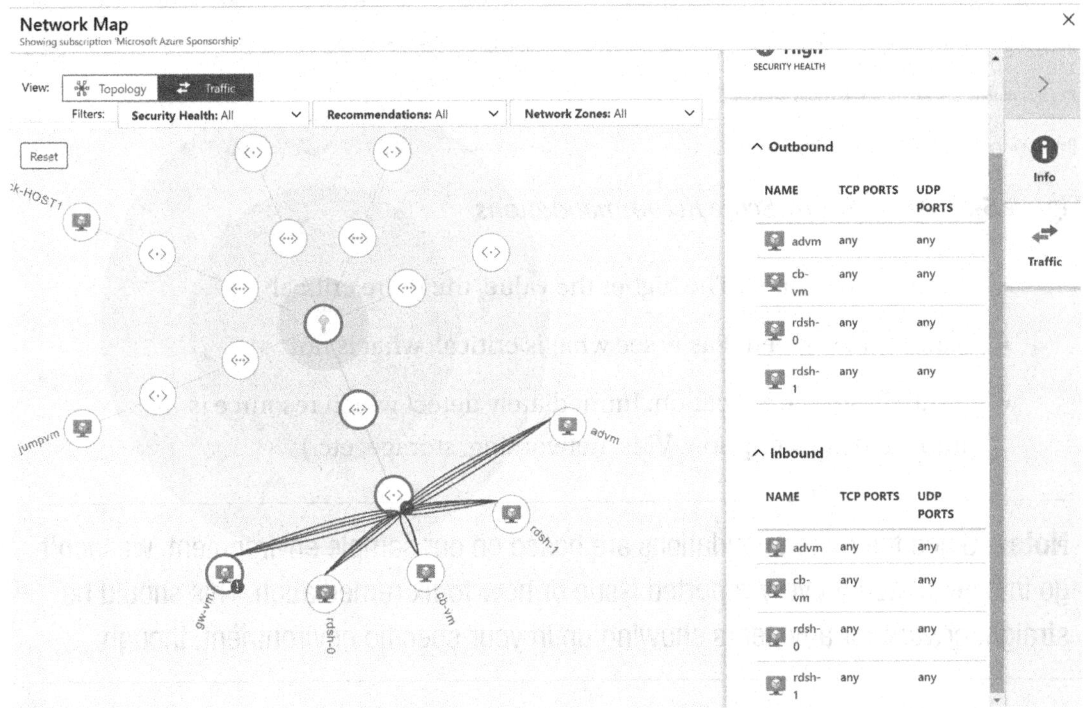

That's about all we can share about Network Map, a valuable addition to Azure Security Center.

Fixing Recommendations

With the help of a secure score, the idea is to easily build up a list of recommended actions, based on the criticality (the value) of the reported item.

For each item, a clear description is given on how to remediate it, and which resources are impacted. The colored lines quickly tell you how critical the situation might be for a given resource.

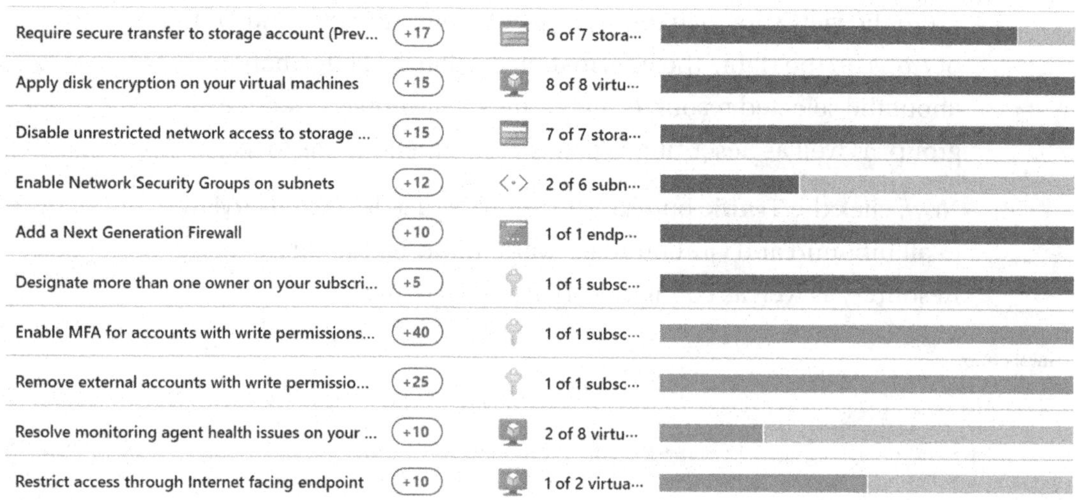

Figure 5-5. *Azure Secure Score Recommendations*

- Secure score value: The higher the value, the more critical
- Red/orange/green: Easily see what is critical, what is not
- Azure Resource allocation: Immediately detect which resource is impacted (subscription, VMs, networking, storage, etc.)

Note Since the recommendations are based on our sample environment, we won't go into detail about every reported issue or how to fix remediation. This should be straightforward for any items showing up in your specific environment, though.

Azure Security Center allows for integration with third-party security solutions, outside of Azure Security Center. Think of the SIEM solutions that you are already using, but also Microsoft security solutions like Azure Active Directory Identity Protection, or Microsoft Advanced Threat Analytics. The main reason for setting up such integration is to have a "single pane of glass" around your security state, and adding additional security-related information from other platforms into your Azure Security Center.

Integrating with Microsoft Advanced Threat Analytics

Advanced Threat Analytics (ATA) is a Microsoft security solution that is installed on the on-premises network and performs network traffic analysis for suspicious behavior. Based on analyzing authentication, authorization, and information-gathering traffic from DNS, Kerberos, NTLM, RPC, and others, it learns about your users' typical behavior and builds a profile around that. Whenever traffic points out that some action is outside of a profile, it is flagged as suspicious. For example, imagine that a certain user—a typical end-user or an administrative user—tries to open a remote session to a server, like RDP or SSH, and never did this before. This would be detected as suspicious by ATA. Or, imagine a cyber-attack approach, where certain listeners have been installed on the network, exposing data at a certain moment in time. That never happened before. It would also be detected by ATA. A last example we can share outside of the cloud is the "pass the ticket" attack. This involves trying to log on with an authenticated Kerberos ticket, passing it on from one machine to another—and a lot more. For more information on ATA, we recommend the product website at `https://docs.microsoft.com/en-us/advanced-threat-analytics/what-is-ata`.

The integration between ATA and Azure Security Center means that the logging information from ATA (alerts, reports, etc.) can be shown in Azure Security Center. So instead of having to look at multiple consoles for security information, ASC can become your prime dashboard.

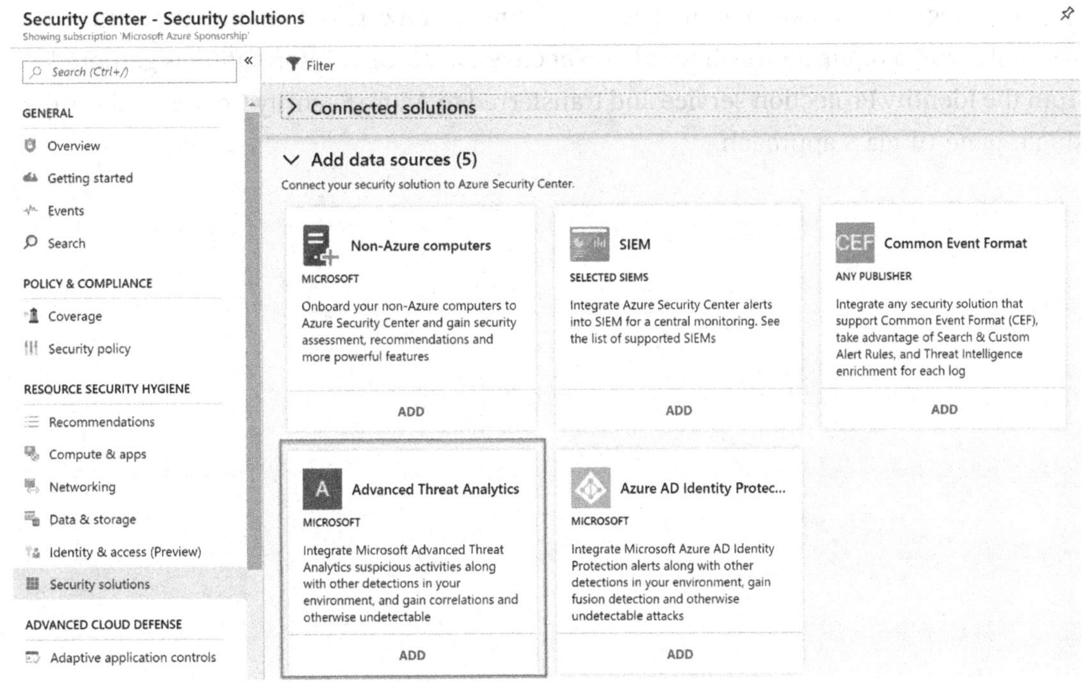

Figure 5-6. *Azure Security Center - Add data sources snap-in*

The integration encompasses the following steps.

1) From your ATA on-premises server console, go to the syslog server settings. Use IP-address 127.0.0.7 with port 5114.

2) Enable all syslog notifications within the ATA portal.

3) Install the Azure Security Center Windows agent (the Microsoft Monitoring Agent) onto the ATA server, and register this machine into the ASC workspace.

This triggers Azure Security Center to recognize and alert on the notifications received from the Advanced Threat Analytics Server, like the security alerts that it handles from other sources.

Integrating with Azure Identity Protection

Azure Active Directory Identity Protection is an Azure identity service, assisting in securing your cloud-based identity accounts from being compromised, recognizing identity attacks, and helping with detecting overall identity security issues.

The integration between Azure Security Center and Azure AD Identity Protection is mainly from a reporting/dashboard perspective. All security information is gathered from the Identity Protection service and transferred to Azure Security Center to allow the single-pane-of-glass approach.

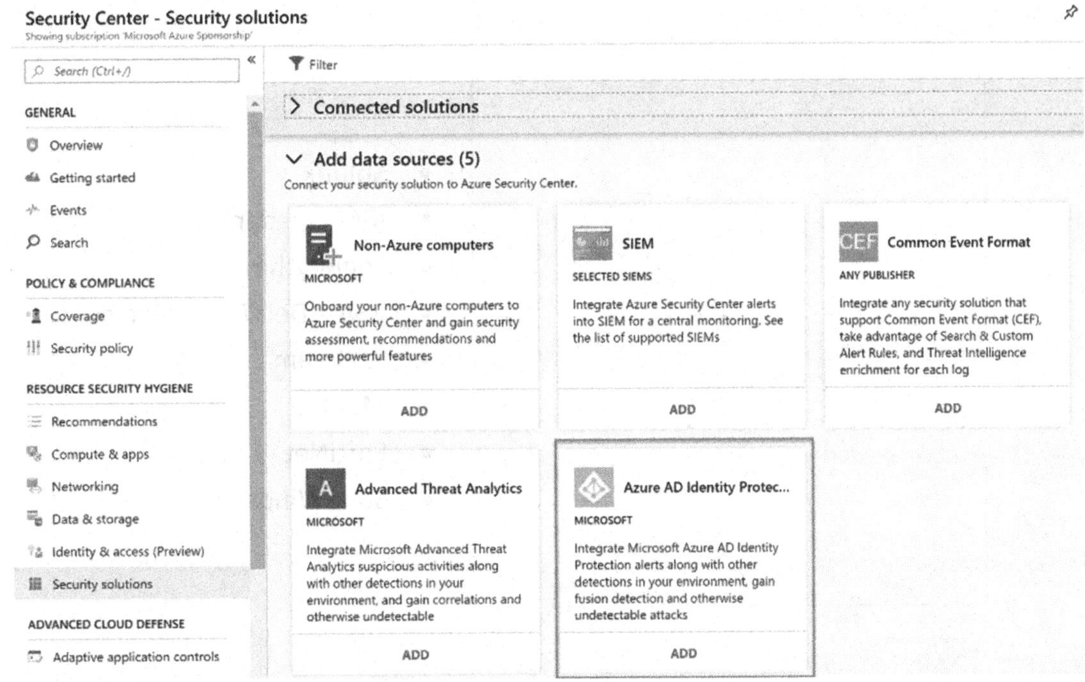

Figure 5-7. *Azure Security Center - Azure AD Identity Protection snap-in*

Since identity protection is already running in Azure, no connectors or syslog configurations need to happen. Once the Identity Protection service is operational, you need to "add" it to Azure Security Center from within the Security Solutions. That's it. Information will show up under the Identity & Access pane, next to other more general alerts from Azure Identity, if you are not using the Premium P2 features.

Integrating with Other SIEM Solutions

SIEM is the abbreviation for *security information and event management*. In many (larger) enterprise organizations, these solutions have been around for a long time and are as critical to the IT teams as an ERP or CRM system is to the business teams.

As reported by Gartner's Magic Quadrant for SIEM solutions, there are big players in the field.

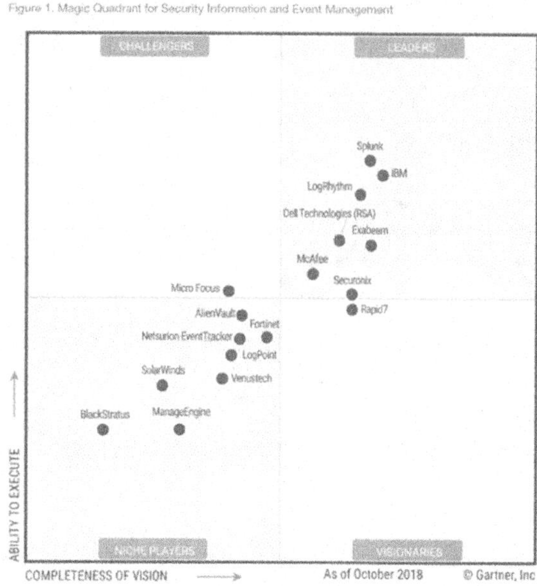

- Splunk
- IBM QRadar
- LogRhythm
- RSA – Dell Technologies
- Exabeam
- McAfee
- FortiNet
- SolarWinds

Figure 5-8. *Gartner Magic Quadrant for SIEM solutions*

Splunk is probably the most popular, or at least the one most people have heard about.

Similar to the dashboard capabilities of Azure Security Center, such SIEM solutions are offering similar features, but most probably with a different scope than what Azure Security Center supports. So instead of trying to pull information from this SIEM platform to ASC, it makes much more sense to port information from ASC to this SIEM solution. And that's exactly what this integration here offers.

As we don't want to force anyone to start using Splunk, we are not describing how to establish this integration specifically. And honestly, ASC supports a lot more platforms than Splunk, so that wouldn't be fair to all other solutions available. However, allow us to share at least the high-level approach on how to make this integration work, as it relies on other Azure Platform service components like Azure Monitor and Azure Event Hub.

ASC relies on Azure Event Hub, a PaaS component that allows you to retrieve and send telemetry information, such as monitoring data, notifications, and alerts.

Next, security information from Azure Activity Log is transferred onto Azure Event Hub.

Lastly, you need to configure the integration from your SIEM solution to pick up the events from Azure Event Hub.

SIEM Integration

This section details steps for exporting security data to a SIEM including how to set up SIEMs and monitoring tools. Security Center must be configured in your Azure subscription before starting. Security alerts produced by Security Center are published to the Azure Activity log. Azure Monitor enables you to get your Activity log data to an Event Hub where it can be read by a SIEM.

Figure 5-9. *SIEM integration flow from the Azure Portal*

The following SIEM solutions can integrate with Azure Security Center.

- IBM QRadar
- Splunk
- SumoLogic
- ArcSight
- Syslog Server

Section Summary

In this section, we discussed how ASC assists with handling security events by providing recommendations, secure scores, and security solutions, which allow integration with third-party platforms. We'll close this topic by reminding you that SIEM integration fits better in the overall monitoring and management strategy, as it relies on a lot more than what Azure Security Center is reporting on.

Advanced Cloud Defense

Advanced cloud defense is the next big area in which Azure Security Center provides several nice but extremely powerful protection and security features. It really provides mechanisms that truly safeguard your Internet-connected virtual machines.

Protection and security at this level is offered by three different services.

- **Adaptive application controls.** Based on the concepts of AppLocker before, Application Controls assists with securing VMs by allowing only specific applications to run on those VMs and blocking all non-allowed software like malicious code or unauthorized applications.
- **Just-in-time VM access.** Just-in-time (JIT) VM access is a control mechanism, operating at the network traffic level of any for JIT Access configured VM, allowing or blocking remote admin access, based on a combination of RBAC and Azure NSGs. As such, dramatically reducing the attack surface of non-authorized remote management, but even authorized admin access can be time-limited.
- **File Integrity Monitoring.** File Integrity Monitoring is a solution that validates changes to an operating systems core system files and registries, and determines if they are malicious or not, indicating an attack on the system or core applications.

We will dive into each of these services, describing what they do and guiding you through how to configure them, by relying on our sample scenario of Azure deployed resources.

Just-in-Time VM Access

Configuring just-in-time VM access is not really a big deal, and after having been using it at several of our customers for their real critical servers, we're actually wondering why this is not enabled by default for all virtual machines. But that's where Azure Security Center comes in handy, as it is clearly making you aware of the fact that you should enable this. Even better, whenever you have deployed an Azure VM, for which you allow direct Internet-connected remote management (RDP or SSH), the Azure portal is showing a security warning, suggesting enabling JIT VM Access for that VM.

Without configuring any settings, JIT VM access relies on Azure Security Center intelligence and categorizes all of your VMs in three different states.

- **Configured.** This group lists all the VMs that have JIT VM access enabled.
- **Recommended.** This group contains all VMs for which JIT VM Access would be a good option to enable; these are the VMs that have direct remote management from the Internet enabled.

- **No recommendation**. this group contains all VMs for which ASC cannot detect if JIT VM access is recommended or configured. In most cases, this is because the VMs are offline. But it might also be because they have no NSG rules configured. It might be because those VMs are still running or deployed in Azure Classic, so ASC cannot work with them.

Let's walk through the actual configuration steps on how to enable JIT VM access for one of our sample scenario VMs. (This VM is a regular Azure VM, for which we configured direct Internet-connected RDP access.) This is the best "trigger" to get JIT VM access as a recommended option to be enabled.

1. From Azure Security Center, navigate to **Just in time VM access**.
2. Notice the three different categories of virtual machines.

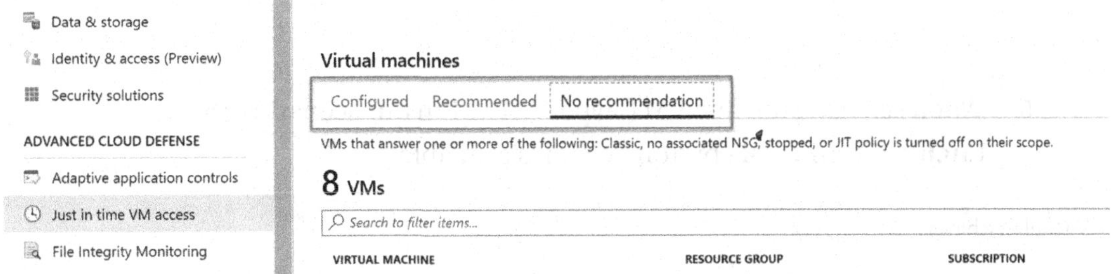

3. Select the **No Recommendation** option, which lists all VMs in our sample scenario that are offline for now (shutdown). Therefore, ASC has no idea what to do with them.

8 VMs

Search to filter items...

VIRTUAL MACHINE	RESOURCE GROUP	SUBSCRIPTION
Missing Network Security Group (2 VMs)		
gw-vm	KHD-RDPS	Microsoft Azure Sponsorship
jumpvm	KHD-RDPS	Microsoft Azure Sponsorship
Other (6 VMs)		
advm	KHD-RDPS	Microsoft Azure Sponsorship
cb-vm	KHD-RDPS	Microsoft Azure Sponsorship

ASC tries to help us as much as possible by allocating a reason why those VMs are in this category. As you can see, two VMs have no network security group rules configured; whereas for the other VMs, no specific reason (Other) is given.

4. Select Recommended. In our sample scenario, it lists two VMs with a critical security severity.

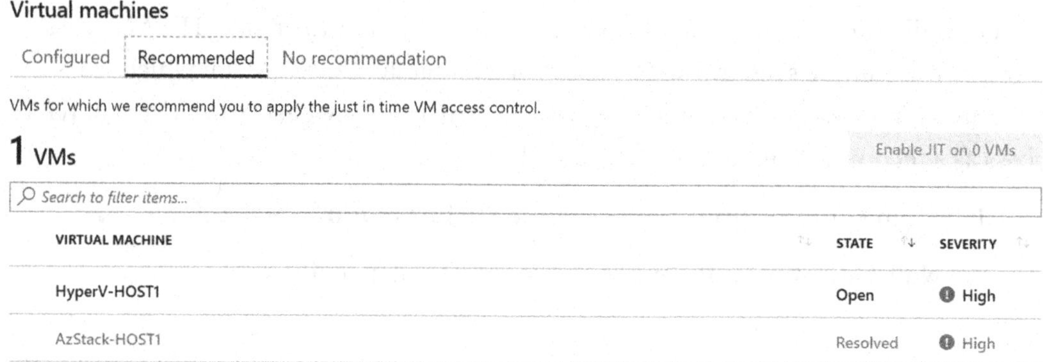

5. When selecting the first VM (HyperV-Host1 in our scenario), the **Enable JIT on 1 VMs** button becomes available.

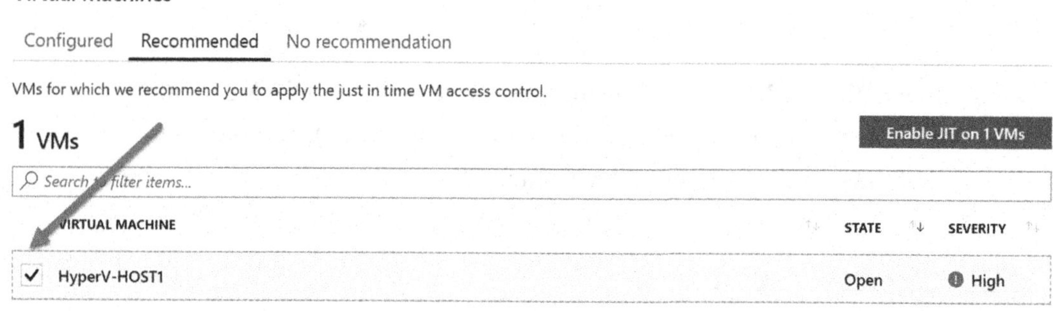

6. Click the **Enable JIT** button. This opens the recommended port and time allocation configuration setting blade.

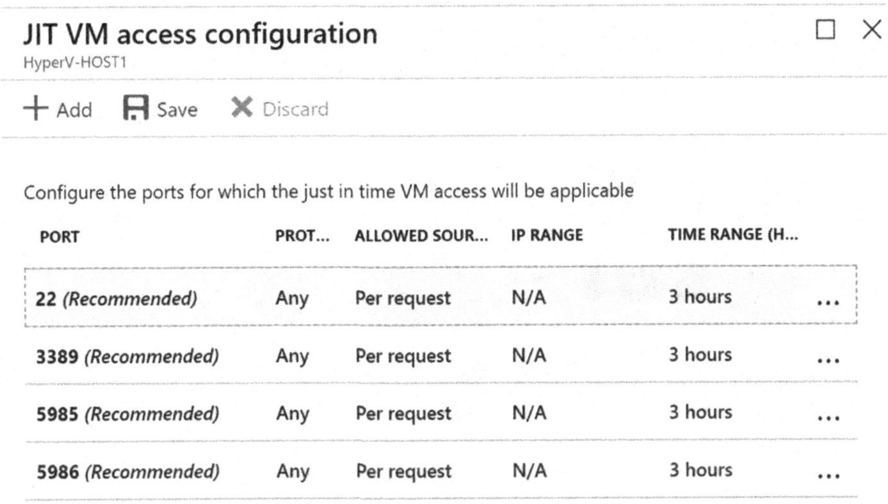

JIT VM access configuration
HyperV-HOST1

+ Add Save Discard

Configure the ports for which the just in time VM access will be applicable

PORT	PROT...	ALLOWED SOUR...	IP RANGE	TIME RANGE (H...	
22 *(Recommended)*	Any	Per request	N/A	3 hours	...
3389 *(Recommended)*	Any	Per request	N/A	3 hours	...
5985 *(Recommended)*	Any	Per request	N/A	3 hours	...
5986 *(Recommended)*	Any	Per request	N/A	3 hours	...

7. This shows the default ports that are used for remote management of a Windows Platform (SSH, RDP, WS-Management and Remote PowerShell). Click the **...** button for the line with port 22. This allows you to delete this line. (SSH is typically used on a Linux machine, not on Windows, so it can be removed.)

8. Similarly, click the line with port 3389. This opens the port settings blade, which allows you to make any modifications to the specific port configuration, like TCP, UDP, changing the port number (e.g., 33890 instead of 3389), and define the time window for access. You can also limit the source IP addresses from where remote management is allowed.

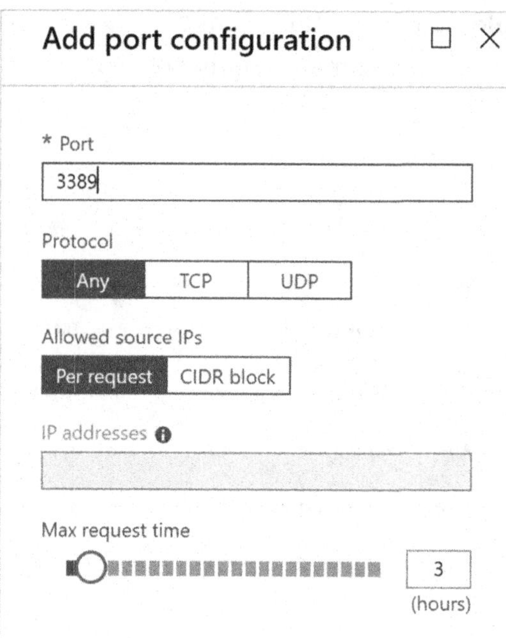

9. Save any changes made to this port configuration.

10. Back in the JIT VM access blade, navigate to the **Configured** tab. Note that the VM server for which we enabled JIT VM access is listed now.

Virtual machines

Configured Recommended No recommendation

VMs for which the just in time VM access control is already in place. Presented data is for the last week.

1 VMs

Request access

Search to filter items...

VIRTUAL MACHINE	APPROVED	LAST ACCESS	LAST USER
HyperV-HOST1	0 Requests	N/A	N/A

11. When you try to open a remote desktop connection to the VM, you see that it is not working.

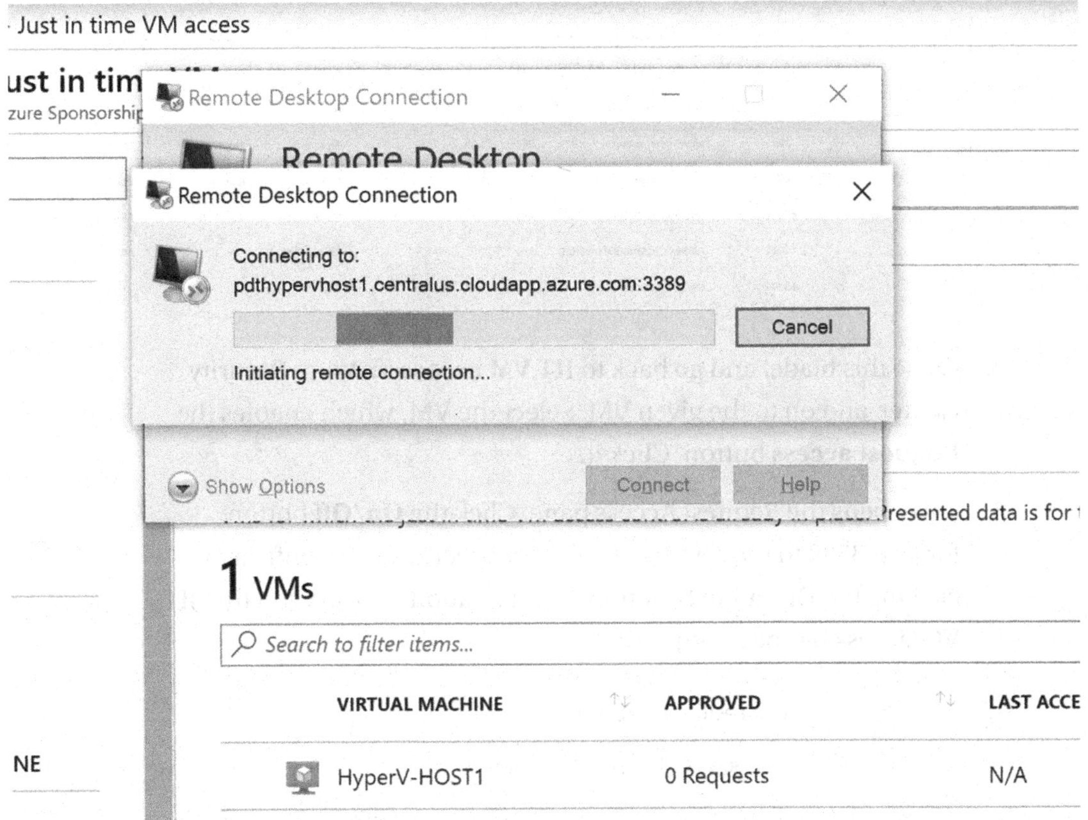

12. This means that half of the solution we want is in place now. This is a "secured" VM, because it is now blocking RDP access from the public Internet. Let's validate where this technically is defined.

13. From the Azure portal, go to **Virtual Machines**, and select the given VM (HyperV-host1 in our scenario). Next, go to Networking. Three new rules are added to the Network Security Group rule base, pointing to JIT VM settings and denying access.

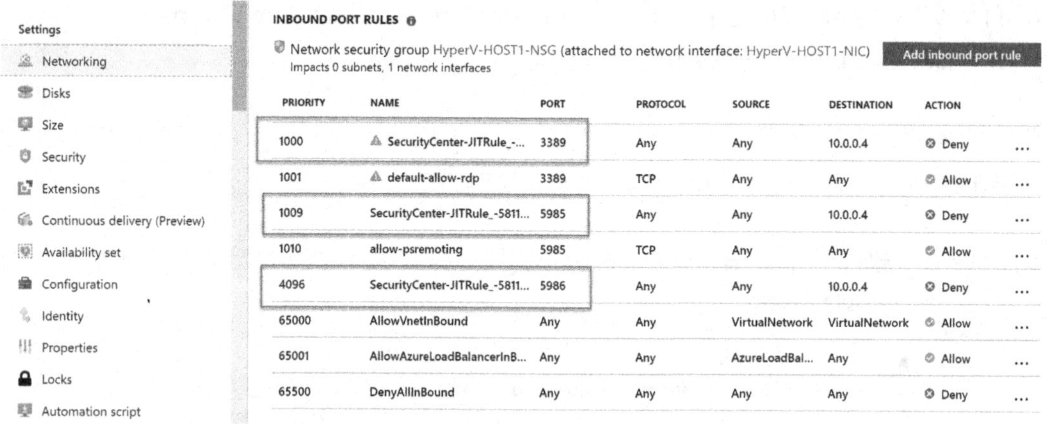

14. Close this blade, and go back to **JIT VM access** in Azure Security Center, and on to the given VM. Select the VM, which enables the **Request access** button. Click it.

15. This opens the Request Access pane. Click the **On/Off** button for port 3389 to request access for that specific port. Confirm by clicking the **Open Ports** button. A notification informs you that JIT VM access has been requested.

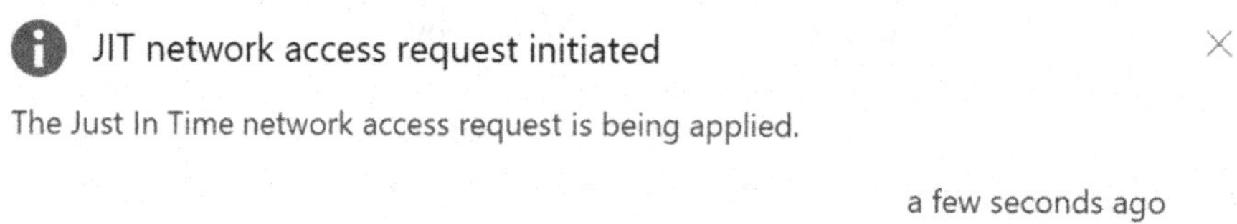

JIT network access request initiated
The Just In Time network access request is being applied.
a few seconds ago

16. Switch back to the given VM and validate the networking and network security group rules. Notice that a new temp rule has been added, allowing port 3389 from the public Internet IP address of our client.

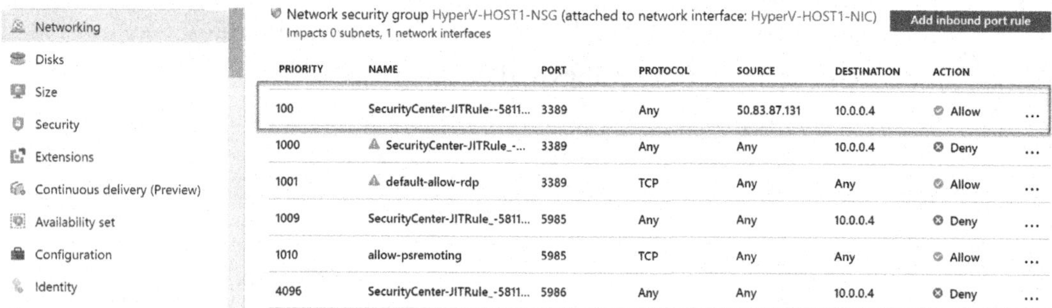

17. Attempting an RDP session to this VM's public name or IP address allows remote desktop connection this time. Confirm that JIT VM access is working as expected. (You could validate it again three hours later, and notice that RDP access doesn't work anymore.)

18. All activity related to this VM has been written to the Azure Activity Log. To see which entries are in there that are related to JIT VM access, go to **JIT VM access** in the Azure Security Center portal, and click the **...** button for the given VM.

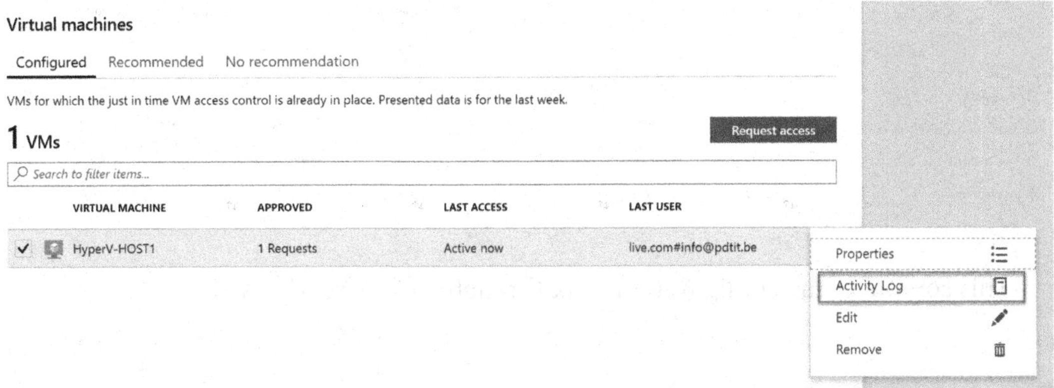

19. Click **Activity log** in the context menu. This opens the Azure Activity Log, which shows the specific events for this VM, filtered for JIT VM access.

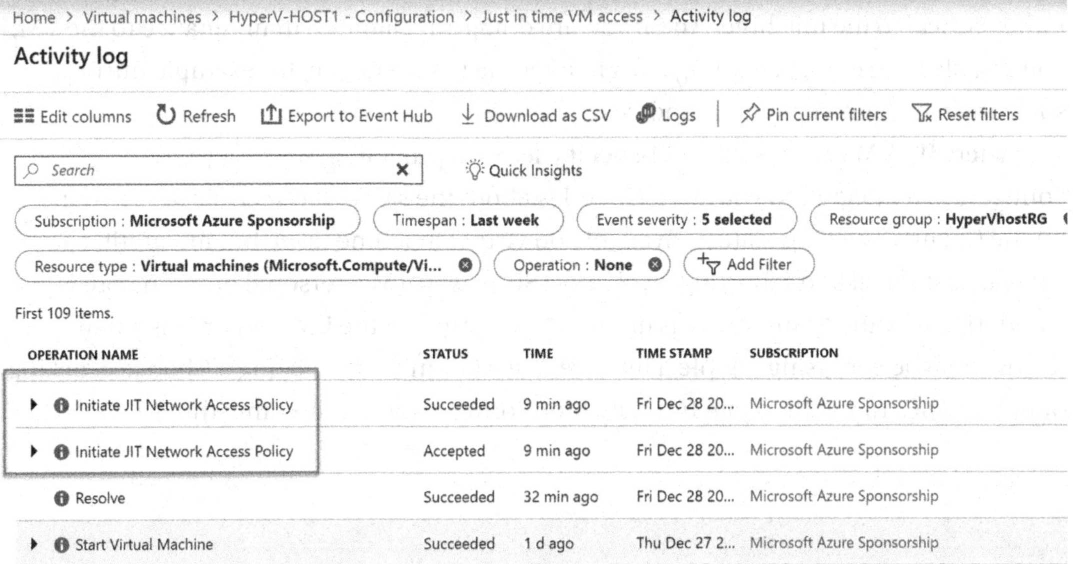

20. To clean up the JIT VM access configuration for the VM, from the context menu, select **Remove**. Confirm the remove from the pop-up message.

21. When checking from the virtual machine networking configuration, notice that the JIT VM access rules have been removed from the NSG rule base.

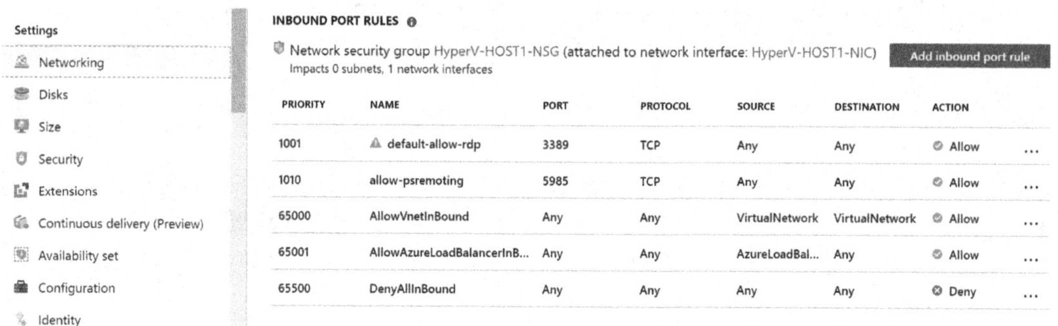

This completes the configuration walk-through of JIT VM access.

File Integrity Monitoring

From the short introduction on File Integrity Monitoring, you know that this should be a service that is enabled by default for all virtual machines. It is basic in functionality, but yet so powerful! Because after all, whenever a system file or registry key is changed, that's rather critical to the machine. And if you are doing any planned maintenance to the VM, you disable this setting, enabling it again after the maintenance, for example during a software installation or system updates.

Where JIT VM access was a VM-specific feature, providing reporting and configuration integration within ASC, FIM is about the same. It is technically relying on the Change Tracking feature, available on virtual machine level, but integrating at a larger scale level and reporting level into ASC as well. (My personal opinion here is wondering why the terminology is different, rather giving the impression it is a new feature, maybe confusing people a bit here. We wouldn't mind seeing a Change Tracking option in ASC, rather than File Integrity Monitoring, which is the same thing.)

Let's walk through the configuration steps to see it work.

1. From Azure Security Center, go to **File Integrity Monitoring**.

File Integrity Monitoring

Choose a workspace to view its File Integrity Monitoring dashboard

WORKSPACE NAME	TOTAL CHA...	TOTAL COM...	LOCATION	SUBSCRIPTION	
defaultworkspace-0a407898-c077-...	0	0	East US	Microsoft Azure Sponsors...	
defaultworkspace-0a407898-c077-...	0	0	West Europe	Microsoft Azure Sponsors...	ENABLE
pdtomsworkspace	0	3	West Europe	Microsoft Azure Sponsors...	ENABLE

2. Select the workspace for which you want to activate FIM. Click **Enable**. This opens the detailed blade for FIM. Here, all VMs that are registered in the workspace are listed, for both Windows Server and Linux operating systems. (It might take some time before all VMs are detected, so refreshing or checking back regularly might be required.)

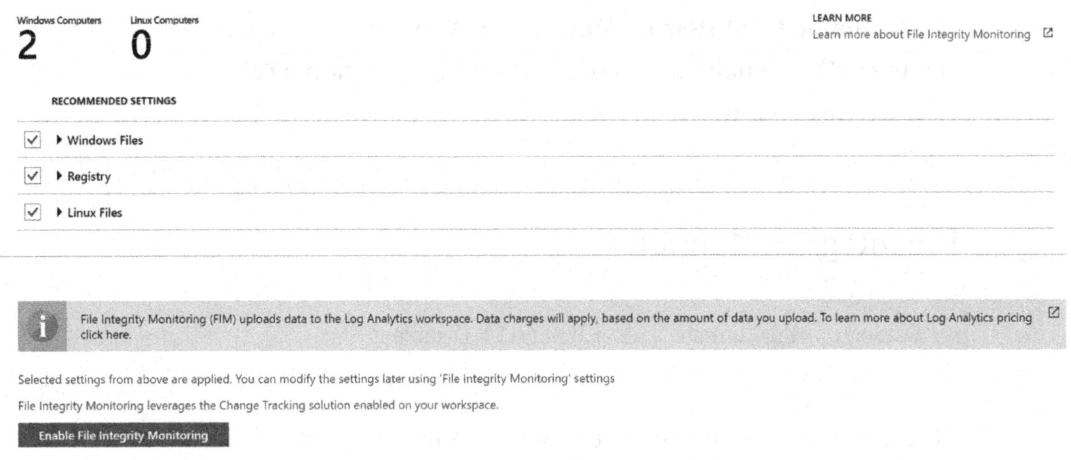

3. For each of the three items (Windows Files, Registry, Linux Files), FIM lists which files and settings were checked. Click any of the three items to see the details.

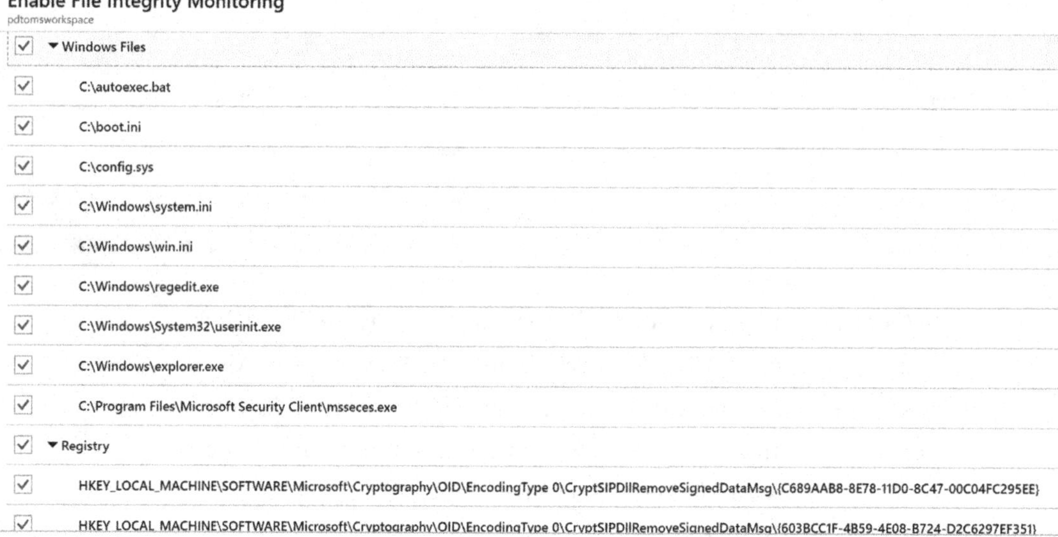

4. Click **Enable File Integrity Monitoring**. Wait for it to become enabled. Once enabled, go back into its configuration by clicking the settings button.

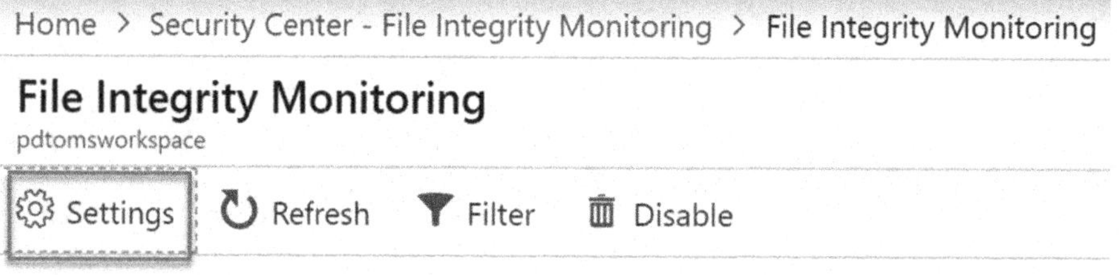

5. The listed files and registries are not the only ones that can be checked, as you can customize this list yourself. For example, if you want to make sure no tampering or attacks happen on business-critical software, like a line-of-business application, you can easily add this folder or even a specific file to this list. Whenever a change happens to this folder, it triggers the FIM alert.

6. From the FIM settings workspace configuration, select **Windows Files** and then click the **Add** button to edit the list of Windows files and folders to be checked. Complete the fields, pointing to a "dummy" folder that we will create on the VM later on. Set Recursive to **On**, which allows FIM to check the full directory.

Add Windows File for Change Tracking ×

Save | Delete | Discard

Enabled

True | False

* Item Name

LOB folder check

Group

Custom

* Enter Path

c:\fimtets*

Recursion

On | Off

Upload file content

True | False

7. Save the changes, and see the items being added to the list of Windows files.

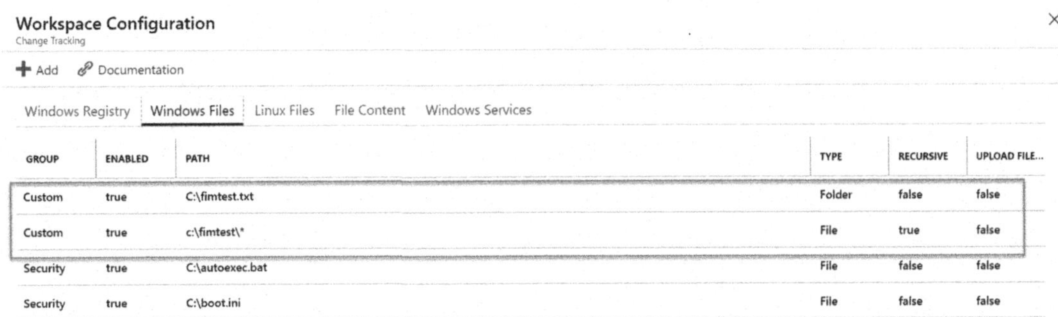

Workspace Configuration
Change Tracking
Add
Documentation
Windows Registry
Windows Files
Linux Files
File Content
Windows Services
GROUP | ENABLED | PATH | TYPE | RECURSIVE | UPLOAD FILE...
Custom | true | C:\fimtest.txt | Folder | false | false
Custom | true | c:\fimtest* | File | true | false
Security | true | C:\autoexec.bat | File | false | false
Security | true | C:\boot.ini | File | false | false

8. Connect to any of the VMs listed and make changes to the monitored system files and/or registry. For this scenario, create a **c:\fimtest** folder and a **fimtest.txt** file inside the folder.

9. Wait a few minutes, and check the FIM portal for reported changes.

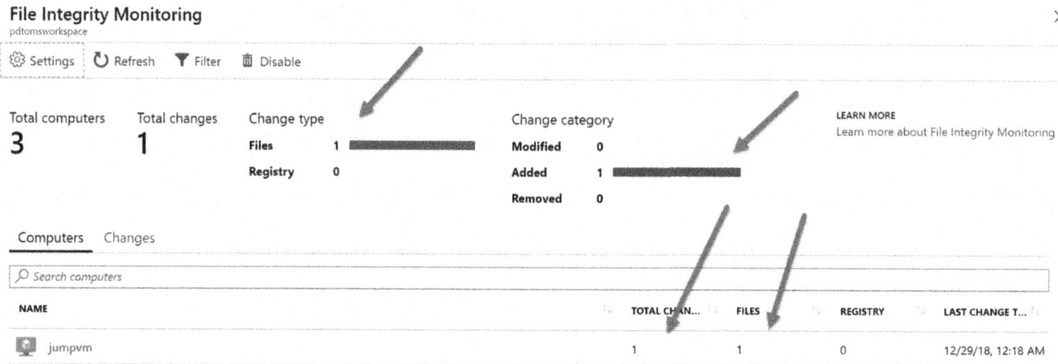

10. Select **Changes**, which shows the list of changes made to the VM.

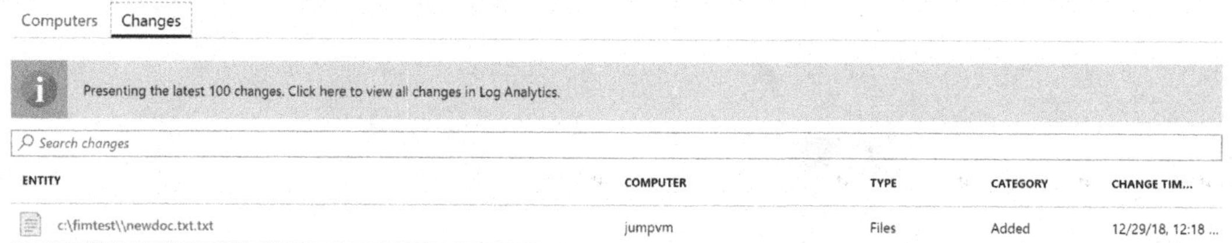

11. Select the change item, which shows you more information about the effective change to the system.

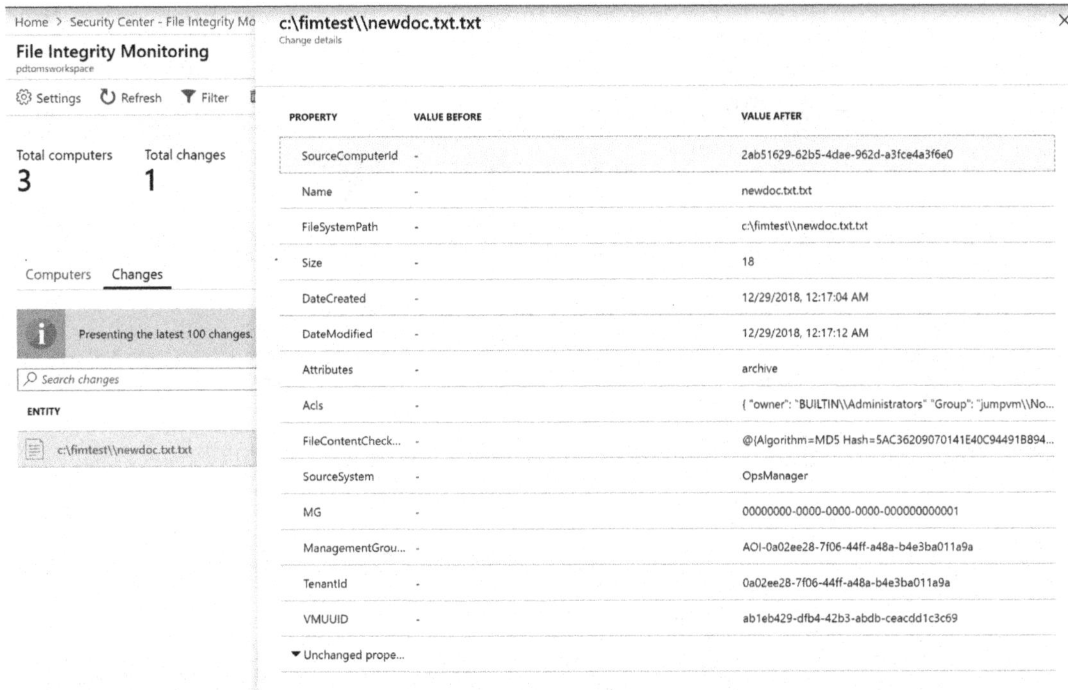

12. Since there is no data in the Value Before column, this means a new file/folder was created.

13. Another way to get a view of the changes that occurred on your system is to select the VM. Return to the FIM portal and select the VM. This redirects you to Log Analytics, which runs a query on changes to files and registries.

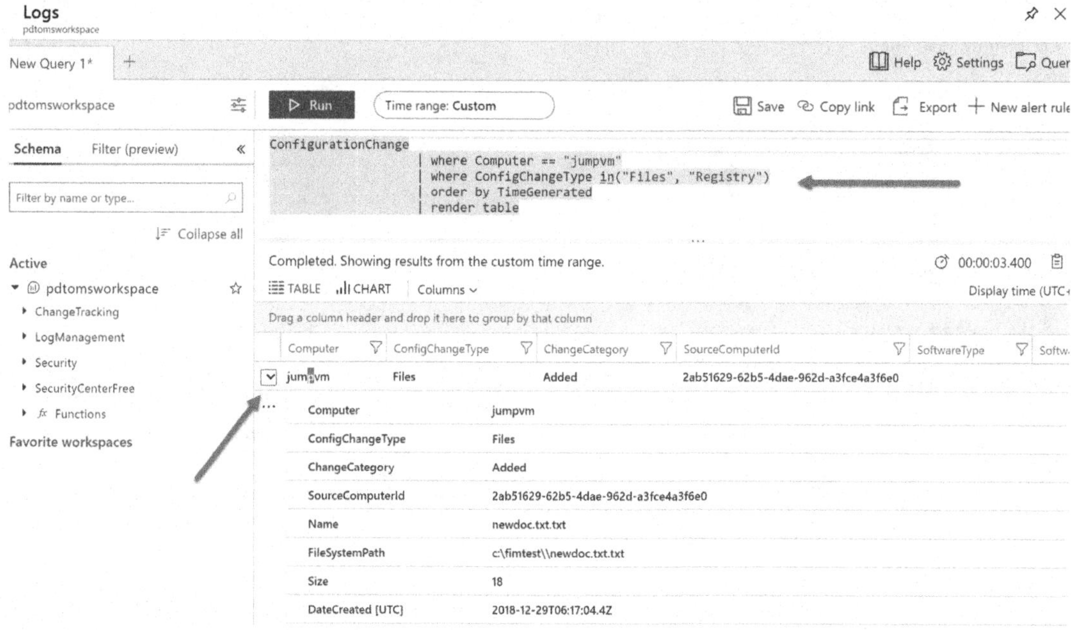

This way, you can run more powerful queries across multiple systems, rather than going through each system individually.

Section Summary

This section discussed the Cloud Defense topic in Azure Security Center, highlighting its capabilities and features. Zooming in on just-in-time VM access and File Integrity Monitoring, what they are, how to configure and use them. Two additional super-powerful features from a security perspective, which should not be left out when optimizing the security posture of your virtual machines.

Threat Protection

This is one of our favorite parts of Azure Security Center because it assists with detecting any malicious attacks from or within your Azure environment. (And yes, both Windows and Linux systems are supported!)

This is another Azure Security Center feature for which you need to have the Standard edition.

Face it, every system is under attack nowadays, and not just the ones that are directly connected to the Internet. We all know those stories from large companies like Twitter, Uber, Marriott, and so many more, having become the victim of malicious attacks from inside the network, running malicious code on their internal systems, sometimes implemented months or years before the actual attack happens. And most of these are not protected by anti-malware solutions running on the systems.

Typical security defense measures put in place on the outside of the network, inside perimeter zones and on the internal surface of systems are ok. Most often, they also come with a downside: they generate a lot of noise, making it hard to detect the actual attacks among all the other alerts being reported.

Once more, that's where Azure Security Center proves its usage. Out of the intelligence analyzed by Microsoft security researchers, Azure Security Center threat protection is very well positioned to assist you with focusing on the real attacks, next to providing real-time alerts. But on top of that, the gathered information comes from a broad spectrum of sources within Microsoft, known as Microsoft Security Graph. All Internet-connected systems within Microsoft (think of Outlook.com, Azure, Office 365, Dynamics 365, but also Xbox and others) provide that much information on what happens on the Internet. In a typical scenario, whenever an attack is detected on any of these platforms, this information (e.g., the source IP address) is transferred to Microsoft Security Graph and integrated with Azure threat protection almost immediately. So whenever a connection occurs to your Azure-running workloads from any of these suspiciously flagged IP address sources, it is reported, and you are alerted by Azure Security Center.

Besides recognizing patterns on the Internet, threat protection also learns from traffic analysis of your Azure resources, the Azure internal networks, and any connected partner solutions. (Jump back to the "Security Solutions" section if you want more information on the systems that are supported and integrate with ASC.)

Another source mechanism that makes threat detection within Azure Security Center really powerful because it has deep integration with machine learning technologies, which helps identify threats across multiple cloud systems and services that could not be detected before. Machine learning analyzes the information received from different sources.

- Telemetry information from Microsoft Security Response Center, Microsoft Digital Crime Unit, and other Microsoft cloud-connected platforms
- Malicious behavior analysis
- Detecting anomalies in system behavior, using statistical profiling

As this security domain is continuously evolving, it is really hard to describe all the details about how these different detection mechanisms work, and how they are put in place. A good source of reference from the Azure Security Center team is at `https://docs.microsoft.com/en-us/azure/security-center/security-center-detection-capabilities`.

Simulating Attacks

One of the big challenges in describing or even using threat protection is the ability to show which attacks are being detected. One option is to wait and do nothing until something shows up. A better approach is to run "attack simulators," not just for the fun of it, but as a detection testing mechanism. After all, you can never be secured enough.

When testing threat protection during the writing of this book, we relied on a free tool called APT Toolkit. It is probably one of the easiest ways to test your infrastructure security detection mechanism and protection procedures. APT Toolkit is available as a free download on GitHub at `https://github.com/NextronSystems/APTSimulator/releases`. A more descriptive page on what the tool does at `https://github.com/NextronSystems/APTSimulator#advanced-solutions`.

Installing and running this tool is super easy.

1. From within your Azure VM, download the APT Toolkit install files from the /releases repo on GitHub.
2. Extract the zip-file to the local machine.
3. From within an administrator command prompt, run **APTSimulator**.bat.

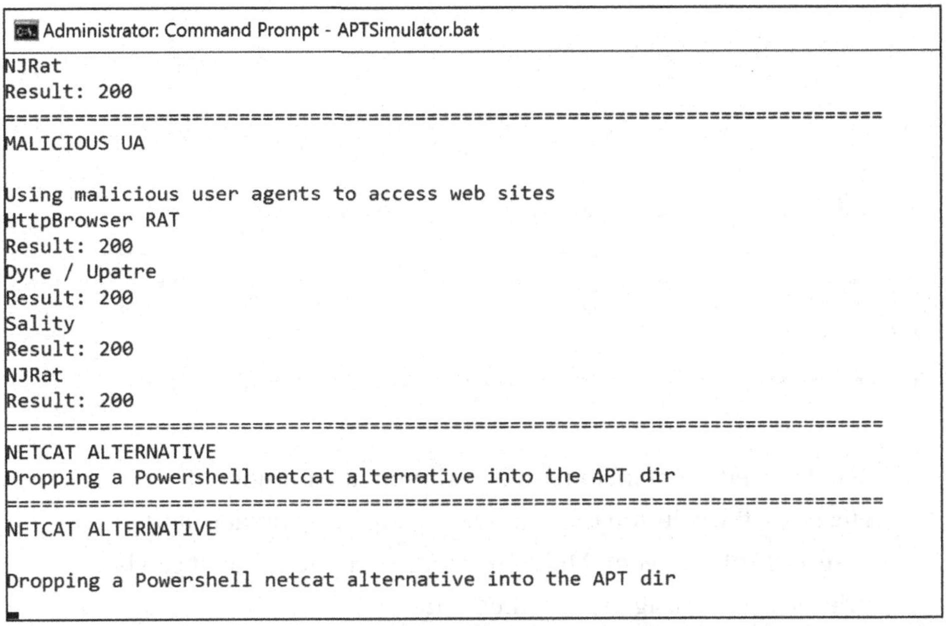

```
Administrator: Command Prompt - APTSimulator.bat
NJRat
Result: 200
==========================================================================
MALICIOUS UA

Using malicious user agents to access web sites
HttpBrowser RAT
Result: 200
Dyre / Upatre
Result: 200
Sality
Result: 200
NJRat
Result: 200
==========================================================================
NETCAT ALTERNATIVE
Dropping a Powershell netcat alternative into the APT dir
==========================================================================
NETCAT ALTERNATIVE

Dropping a Powershell netcat alternative into the APT dir
```

4. It runs through a set of attack simulations, which mimics that your machine is under attack and full of malicious code.

5. Repeat this process a few times if no alerts show up in Azure Security Center threat protection right away.

How Threat Protection Reports Attacks

If you followed the preceding simulation steps (or used any other simulation tool), ASC threat protection should be able to pick up the security attacks and alert about it.

1. From Azure Security Center - Threat Protection, select **Security Alerts.**

2. This opens a list of all detected attacks on a timeline, as well as showing you a listing of these attacks.

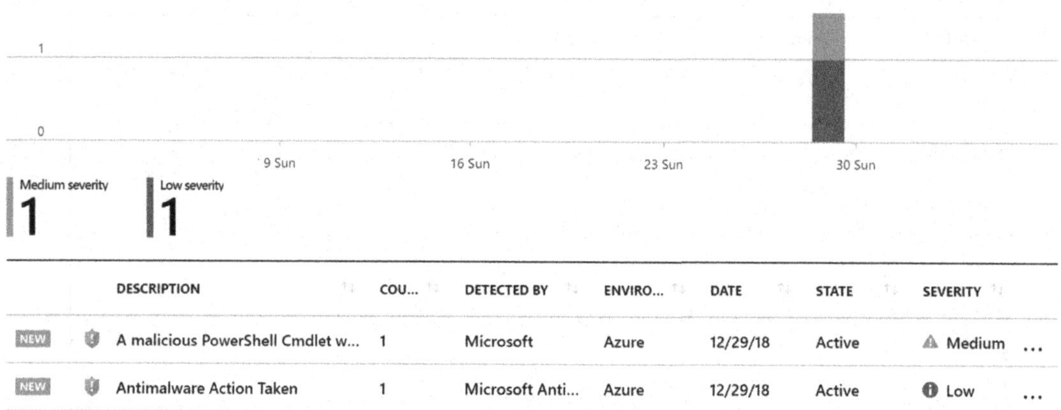

3. Each detected event includes a description, the number of detections, the solution that detected the security breach, and the severity of the event. More information about an event can be retrieved by selecting the specific event.

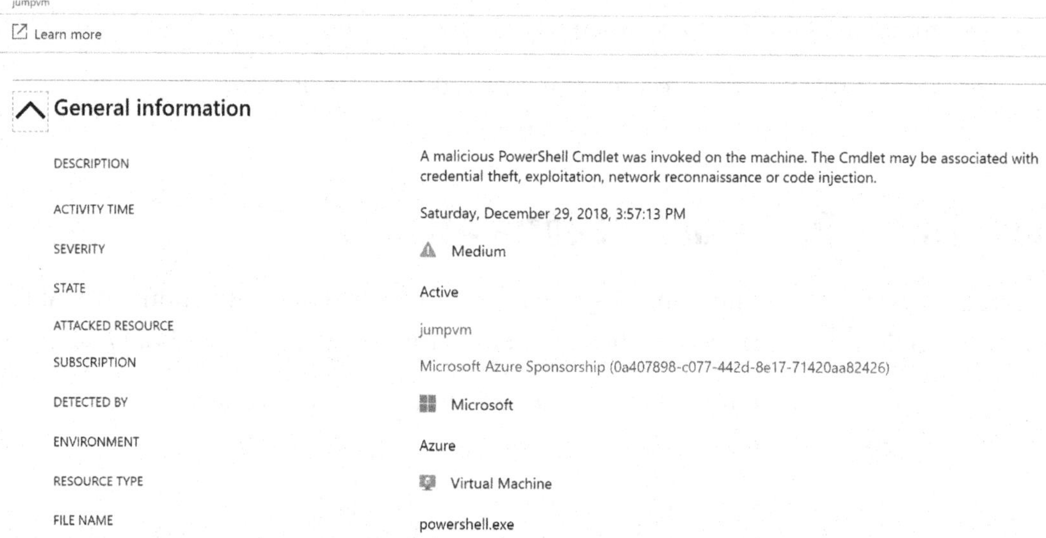

So far, we know there has been a malicious PowerShell cmdlet invoked on the machine we are using in the simulation. But how and why does ASC detect this as a security attack, and more importantly, what is the aggressive impact of this attack? This is where the threat protection's investigation feature comes to the rescue.

Click Investigate. This opens Investigation Dashboard (Preview), which provides a nicely detailed dashboard for the specific event.

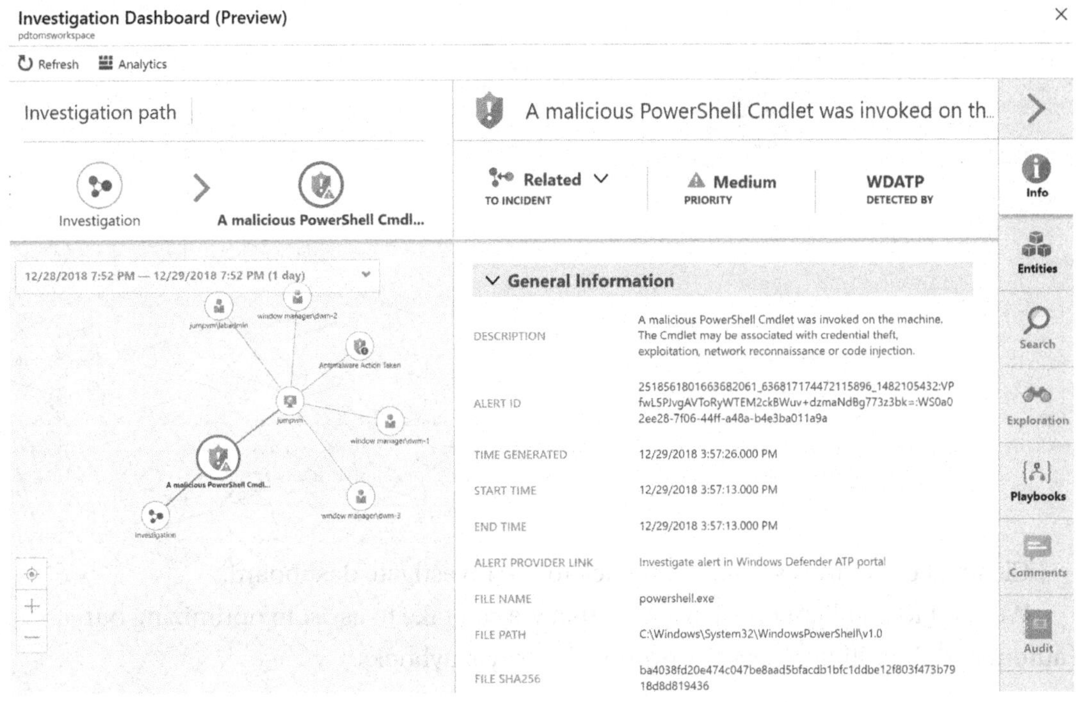

It helps you truly understand the impact of the attack. Starting from the topology view, it shows the different user accounts involved (labadmin, as well as different Windows Manager system processes, but also what system was under attack (jumpvm), the attack itself (PowerShell cmdlet), but also the remediation (Windows Defender on the VM). Remember when we talked about threat protection working together with other solutions? Windows Defender is a nice example. And no, it doesn't work because it is a Microsoft tool; it reports the incident when you have other anti-malware solutions running.

Next to the topology diagram, there is a decent amount of information about the attack: what it involved, the time it ran, which process was involved, and things like that.

Azure Log Analytics is another integration.

1. To use it, click the **Analytics** button. This opens Log Analytics.
   One small thing that is missing is the actual query to run. But you can update this yourself easily enough.

2. Type **SecurityAlert** in the query field, and click **Run**. This will bring up the two security events from our simulation again.

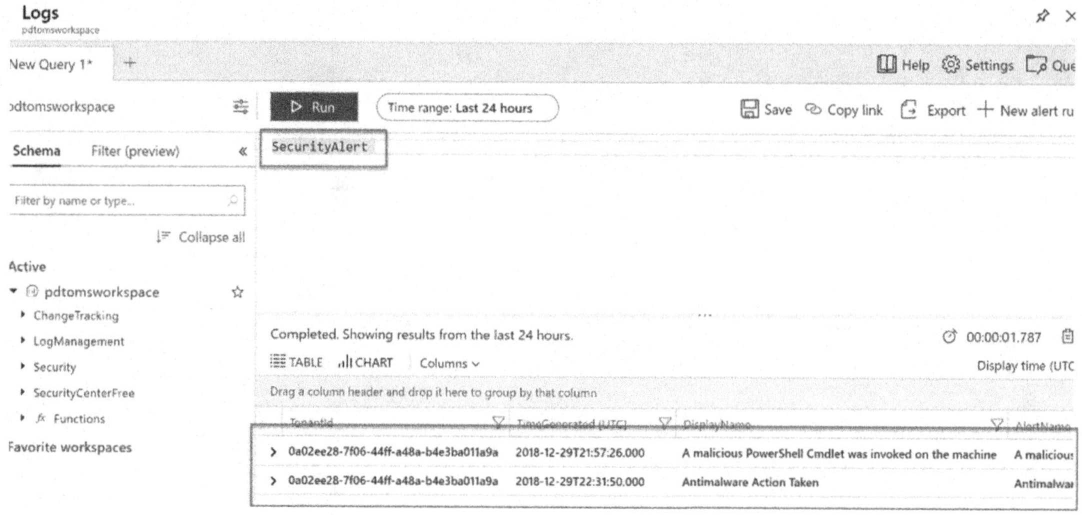

Closing Log Analytics brings you back to the Investigate dashboard.

We want to highlight one last action that we can take to assist in optimizing our (automated) handling of security events: security playbooks.

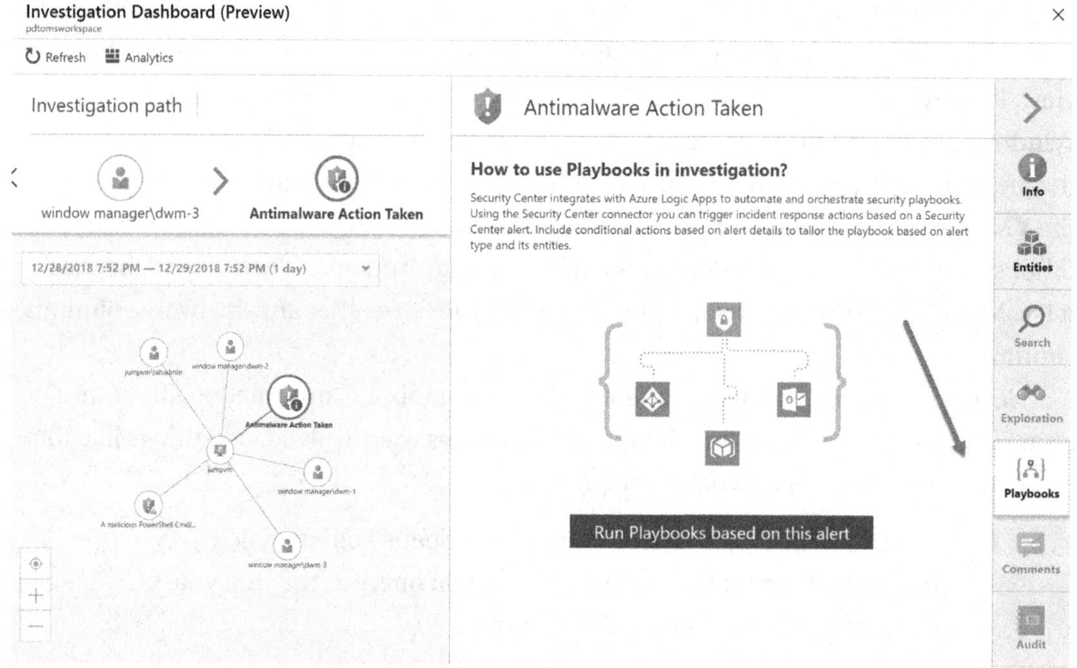

But that's a topic important enough by itself.

Section Summary

This section introduced you to threat protection, another powerful security attack and analysis solution within Azure Security Center. You learned about its capabilities, as well as how to simulate surface attacks using open source tools. Lastly, you learned how threat protection assists with the investigation process by offering the investigate dashboard.

Security Playbooks

So far, we covered most of the functionalities within Azure Security Center that help in reporting and alerting about security incidents and attacks. But besides the alerting aspect, another huge part of fixing your security attack is fixing the issues.

One solution we talked about earlier to help you in this was Security Recommendations, where Azure Security Center offers you much like a case-by-case recommended solution to fix the reported issue. This is a great way to help you optimize your security posture, but it's not a viable solution to mitigate a larger security attack because you are looking for an automation tool—and that's exactly the purpose of security playbooks.

Overview of Security Playbooks

Why is there another automation tool in Azure besides Azure Automation? Security playbooks are actually based on a workflow automation tool in Azure: Logic Apps.

By going through a sequence of procedures, much like a step-by-step scenario, security playbooks reacts on a trigger, for example out of an event or an alert. As it is technically based on Azure Logic Apps, but focusing on the security templates in there. (FYI: Azure Logic Apps is a business workflow tool that allows automation processes for business tools like Office 365, DocuSign, SAP, GotoMeeting, and many others.)

This also means that security playbooks are in analogy with the pricing of Azure Logic Apps, thus not being part of the Azure Security Center consumption cost. For more information on Logic Apps pricing, refer to `https://azure.microsoft.com/en-us/pricing/details/logic-apps/`.

Building a Security Playbook Workflow

1. From Azure Security Center, go to Automation and Orchestration. Select **Playbooks**. (Another approach is to go to the Investigation dashboard and select **Playbooks.**)

   And to be complete, you can start creating these directly from **Azure Logic Apps** as well. Starting from a prebuilt security template or creating a new one from scratch.

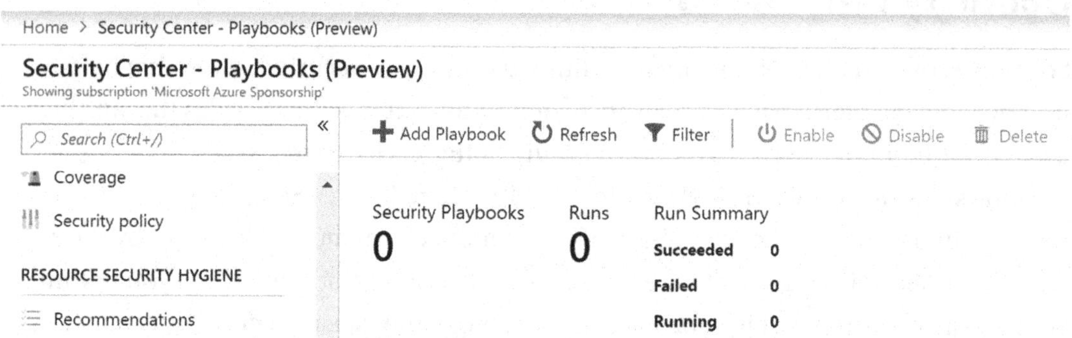

2. Click **Add Playbook**. This opens the Logic App blade, which allows you to create a new Logic Apps resource. Complete the necessary information, such as the Logic App name, resource group, and the location where you want it to be created.

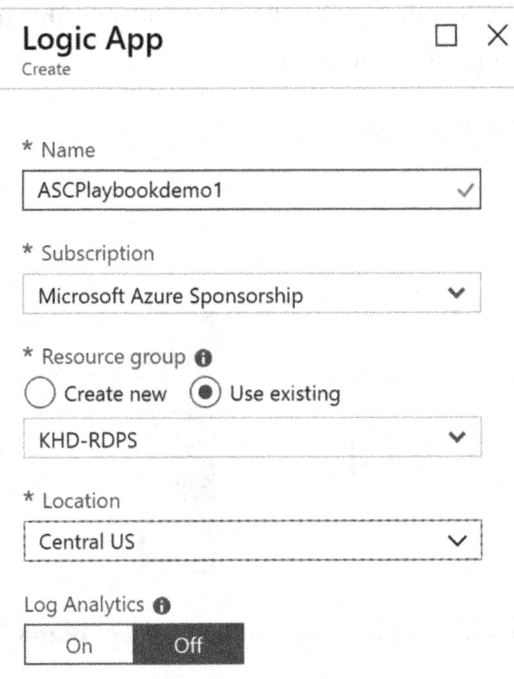

3. Wait for the playbook to be created.

Playbooks

Search playbooks

NAME	STATUS	TOT...	RU...	SU...	FAI...	SUBSCRIPTION	LOCATION	TRIGGER KI...
ASCPlaybookdem...	Enabled	0	0	0	0	Microsoft Azure S...	Central US	Not defined

4. Once created, select the playbook to customize it. This redirects you to Azure Logic Apps designer.

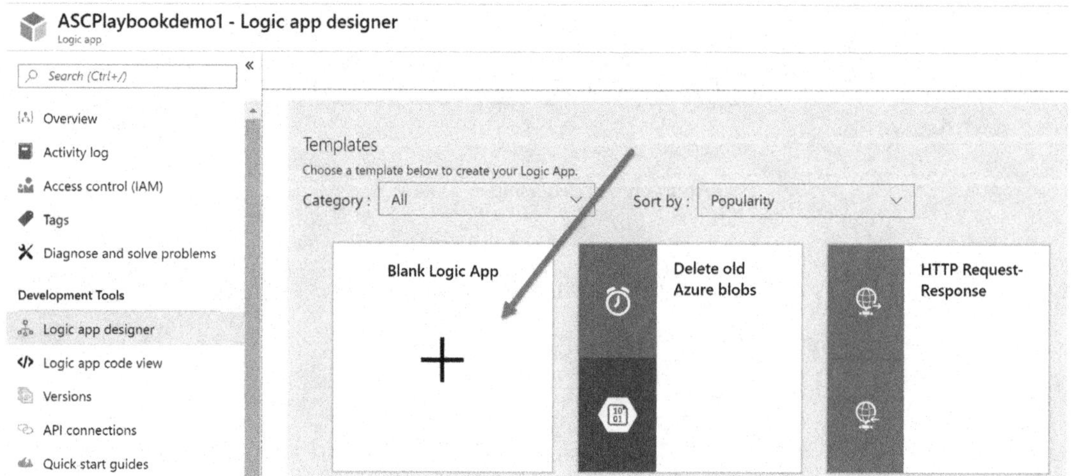

5. Scroll down to the Templates section, and select **Blank Logic App**.

6. Search for **Azure Security Center** and select **All**. This shows **When a response to an Azure Security Center alert is triggered**. Click this.

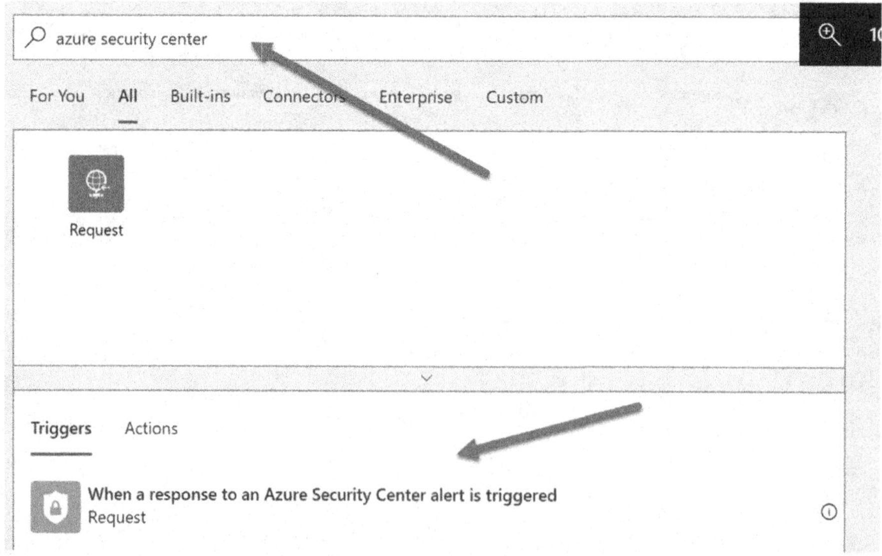

7. The workflow designer opens. Here you can add the different actions that happen as part of the workflow.

8. From here, you can integrate with about 200 connectors, from an extensive list of third-party vendors, as well as Microsoft. To keep it easy and simply introduce you to the capabilities, let's trigger the actions to

   a) send an email

   b) redeploy the Azure VM that's impacted, from an Azure Resource Manager template

9. In the Logic App Designer, click **New step**.

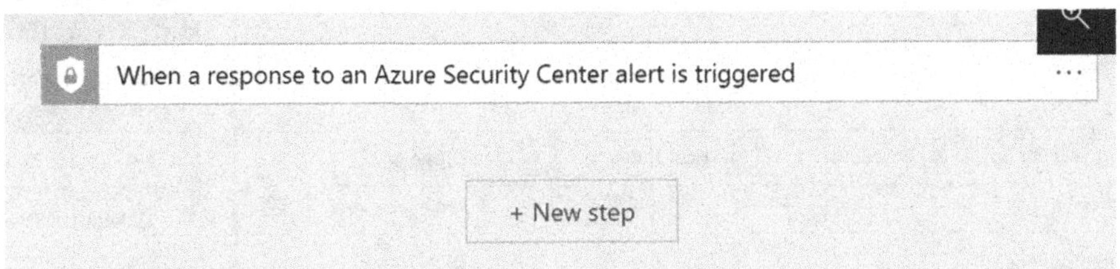

10. Search for **email**. This shows a list of all connectors providing email functionality. Select **Office 365 Outlook**. From the list of Actions, select **Send an email**.

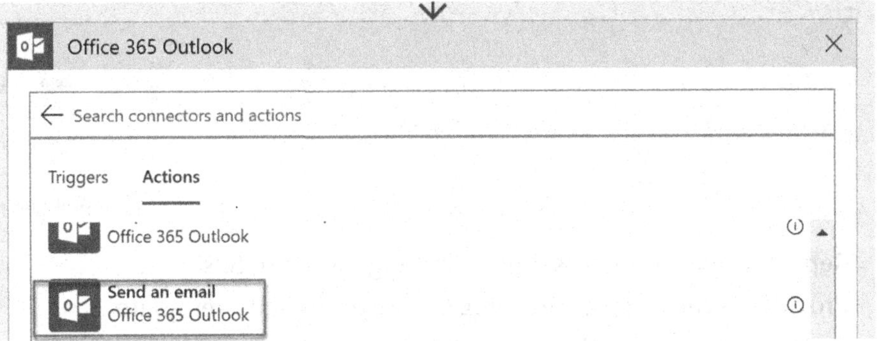

11. When asked to sign in, provide your Office 365 credentials, which are needed to get access to the Office 365 Logic Apps connector. In a typical organization setup, we recommend using a generic account for this; for example, secplaybooks@company.com. As such, you know that the Office 365 integration is driven out of that security playbooks user account mailbox.

12. In the **Send an email** window, complete the required information for the email subject, as well as the body of the email. For example, type **Security Playbook trigger** in the Subject field. This will be a static subject for each email sent by playbooks. In the Body field, we can make use of dynamic content. Select some interesting fields from the list; for example, Alert Severity, Description, Host Name, and Start Time. (This information changes for actual security alerts.)

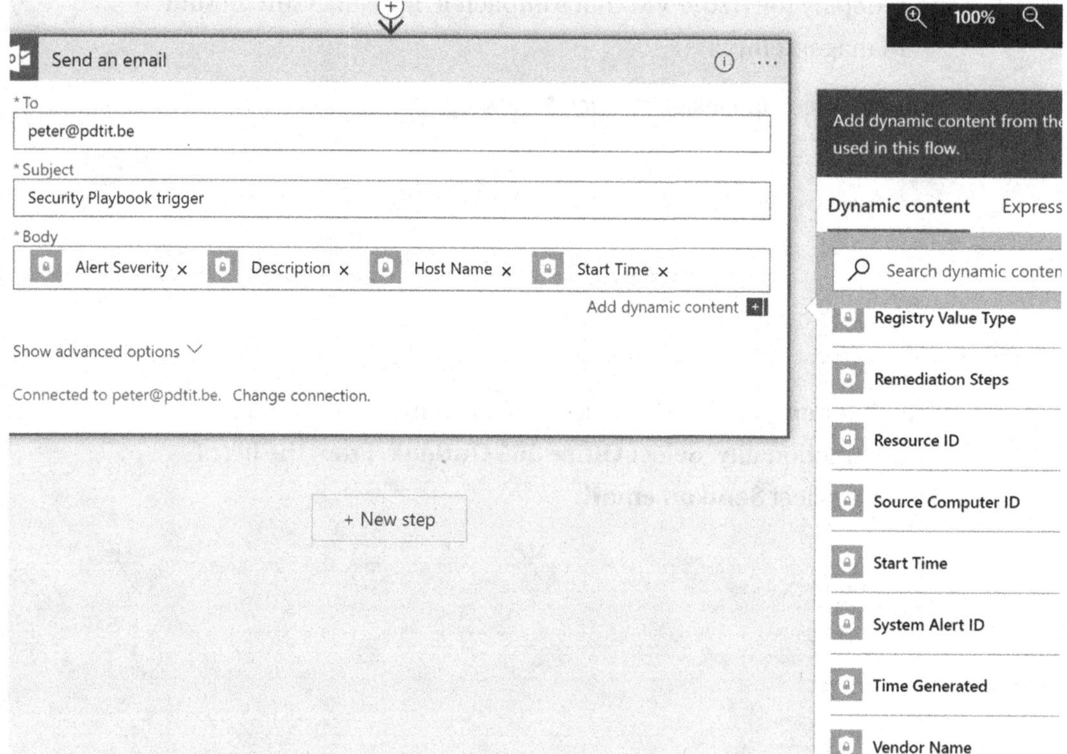

13. Repeat similar steps, this time searching for Azure Resource Provider as the trigger, and using Create or **u**pdate a template deployment as the action. Complete the information from your Azure subscription, such as subscription ID, the resource group where you want this template to run, and the link to the actual ARM template.

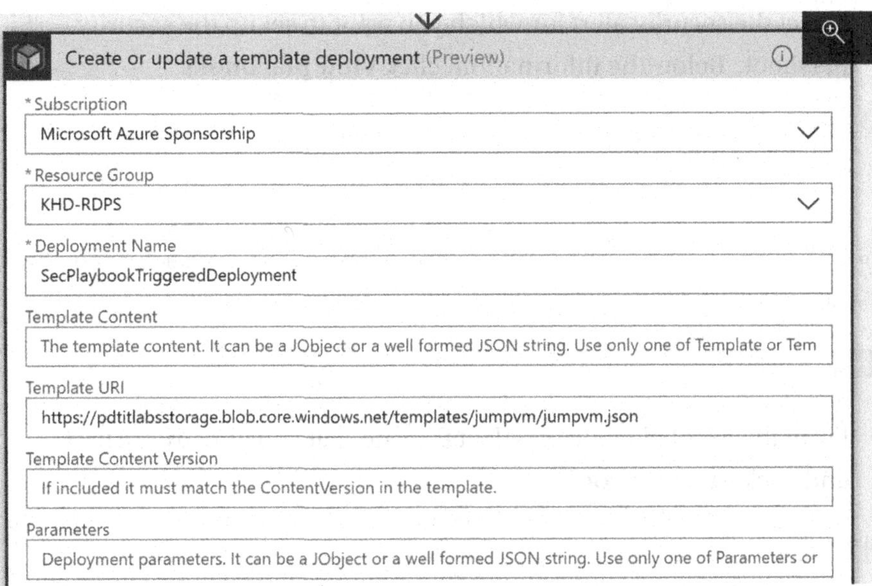

Feel free to use this template link as an example: `https://pdtitlabsstorage.blob.core.windows.net/templates/jumpvm/jumpvm.json`. It is a basic VM template deploying a Windows 2016 VM in its own VNet; it does nothing harmful.

14. Save this workflow. This completes the creation process.

Configuring Security Playbook Triggers

Now that the security playbook is configured, the last thing that we need to do is integrate it into our Azure Security Center alerts. Meaning, setting up that whenever an alert is generated for which we want to execute this playbook, it needs to get triggered.

1. From Azure Security Center - Threat Protection, select **Security Alerts.**

Medium severity 1 | Low severity 1

		DESCRIPTION	COU...	DETECTED BY	ENVIRO...	DATE	STATE	SEVERITY	
NEW		A malicious PowerShell Cmdlet w...	1	Microsoft	Azure	12/29/18	Active	Medium	...
NEW		Antimalware Action Taken	1	Microsoft Anti...	Azure	12/29/18	Active	Low	...

2. Select the security alert for which you want to set up the security playbook. Below the information, click **View playbooks**.

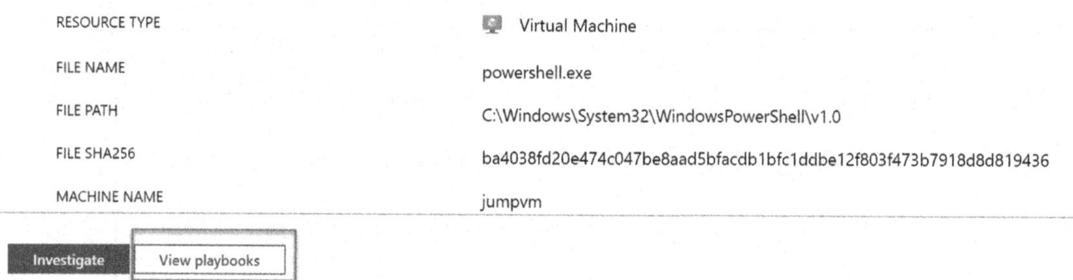

3. From the list of playbooks, select the one that you already created, and click **Run playbook**.

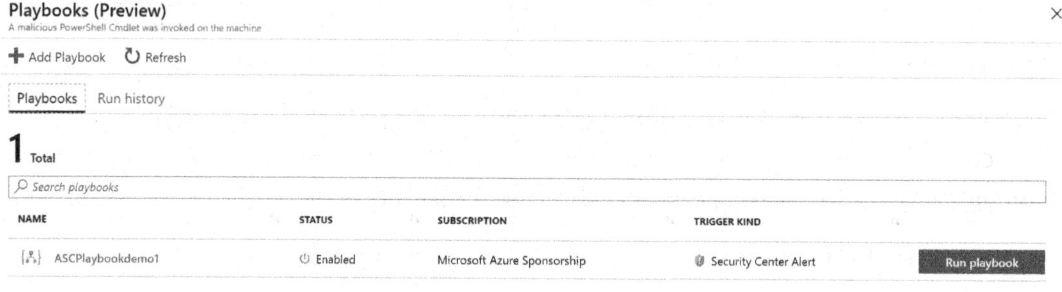

4. Read the notification from Azure, which informs you about the triggered event.

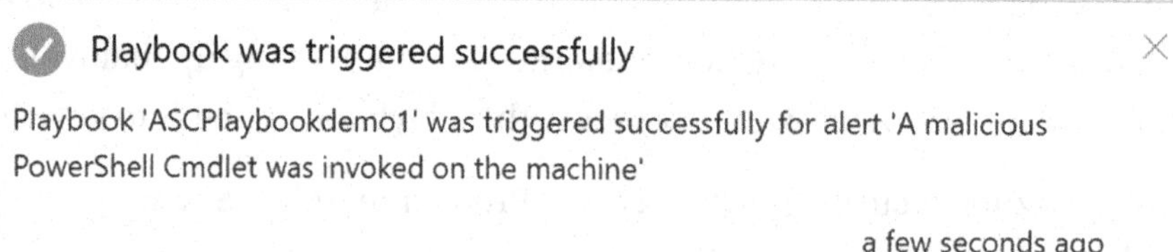

5. Check if you received an email and if the ARM template deployment was triggered and running.

   a) If the email was sent successfully, all details are in the subject and body.

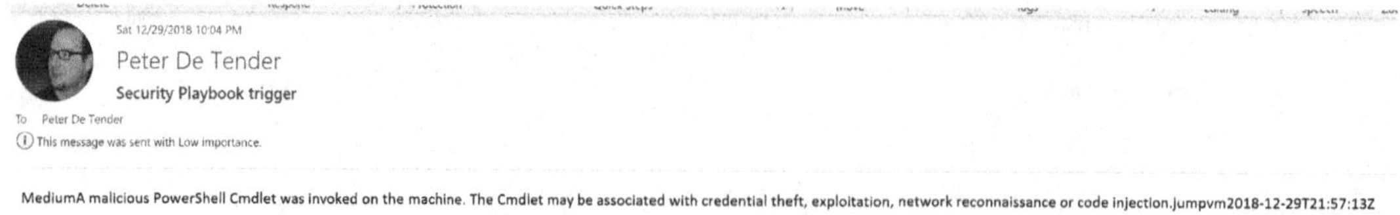

b) To see if the ARM template deployment also works as expected, go to the Azure Resource Group you specified, select Deployments, and look for the last deployment state.

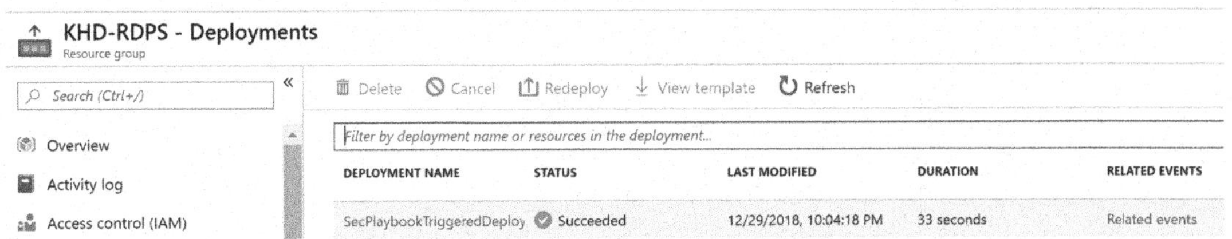

This completes the successful configuration of the security playbook, starting the trigger, and running the actions.

Section Summary

In this section, you learned about Azure security playbooks, a powerful mechanism to run workflows based on events and alerts.

Chapter Conclusion

Thank you for going with us through the details of Azure Security Center. We started this chapter with a high-level introduction to Azure Security Center, where it is positioned within the Azure portfolio of services. You learned about all the built-in features and capabilities for both the Free and paid Standard editions. Next, you journeyed through the more technical and security-oriented services provided by Azure Security Center, such as security policy, resource security hygiene, advanced cloud defense, threat protection, and security playbooks.

After going through all the walk-through scenarios, you should have a very good understanding of what Azure Security is and where it can help you optimize your security posture.

CHAPTER 6

Optimizing IT Operations Using Azure Monitor and Log Analytics

Microsoft Azure provides a large number of hybrid cloud services that allow us to extend our infrastructure and applications in new ways to improve not only their performance but also provide us with a platform that offers one of the most important capabilities for IT administrators: capacity of monitoring and diagnostics to proactively manage our applications.

Azure Monitor provides IT developers and administrators with the appropriate tools for monitoring IaaS, PaaS, and SaaS along with open source integrations that allow extending the critical capabilities for any organization so that they can proactively improve the delivery of their applications, which improves the visibility of the infrastructure where the application is hosted, the networks, and most importantly, the security and the capacity to recover the resources of the data center.

This chapter reviews the services that Azure Monitor provides to implement a robust solution to monitor and obtain an analysis of infrastructure and applications in the cloud, and shows you a way in which digital transformation impacts how we carry out an adequate strategy for the design of monitoring our infrastructure and applications in hybrid environments.

We will architect an efficient IT infrastructure operations and diagnostics strategy based on the iFreeze case, analyzing the business objectives and solving the business needs.

P. De Tender et al., *Pro Azure Governance and Security*, https://doi.org/10.1007/978-1-4842-4910-9_6

Business Overview

iFreeze manufactures high-quality freezers that are used in various everyday industries, such as bars, restaurants, grocery stores, and warehouses to store food, beverages, or flowers. With an excellent name in the industry, iFreeze continuously sought to expand its business to other vertical markets, and it is now also a leading brand for industrial freezers in the mortuary and healthcare sectors.

In addition to nine central sites around the world, iFreeze has about 100 other smaller sites spread across different continents. Mainly due to the low number of users on each site, and without having local IT operations, no further details are provided. All sites and hubs around the world are connected using an MPLS-WAN connection when it is available. If MPLS-WAN connectivity is not possible, VPN devices are deployed to establish a site-to-site connection, connecting to the MPLS cloud WAN through any of the nearby hub sites.

Most of the physical servers were completely replaced with Hyper-V Server 2012 R2 fiver years ago. Only a few servers are not yet virtualized. After a four-year update cycle, they finalized their migration project of standardization and consolidation of data centers to the following ones in 2013.

- Hypervisor: Windows Server 2012 R2
- Operating system: Standardized in Windows Server 2012 R2, although some Windows Server 2008 R2 and Windows Server 2016 also run
- Some manufacturing applications run on Apache servers with MySQL databases in the Red Hat Enterprise operating system
- Main applications: Own architecture of three levels developed internally.
- Framework applications: .NET, which runs on a clustered IIS farm that connects to the SQL Server 2012 R2 database clusters. The application is somewhat redundant by providing high availability of Hyper-V replication at remote sites.
- The backup is managed by System Center Data Protection Manager 2012 R2.

- End-user applications: Due to its familiarity with Exchange Server, iFreeze decided to migrate all mailbox data to Exchange Online/ Office 365.

Approximately four years ago, in conjunction with their next IT renovation project at that time, the CTO and solution architects experimented with the Amazon AWS and Microsoft Azure public cloud platforms, primarily to run virtual machine workloads. Since completing their internal consolidation of the data center, they predicted the next IT migration project, scheduled for mid-2019, with the intention of maximizing the use of the cloud.

The following lists the company's business objectives.

- Minimize the impact on the integration of DevOps scenarios. iFreeze will continue its IT operations and the development teams will continue their existing mode of operations.
- iFreeze must be able to proactively monitor any status of the current infrastructure and applications in order to maximize RPO and minimize RTO in addition to taking care of the integrity of data.
- Adapt as much as possible; existing development and testing platforms in IaaS or preferably PaaS / SaaS environments in order to have a reduction and optimization of costs.
- While IT operations are pretty well standardized in their operating systems, iFreeze must reduce the provisioning and maintenance time of its infrastructure in a simple and agile way.
- iFreeze must implement a solution to obtain better visibility on SaaS and PaaS applications to speed up productivity and have better integrity using corporate credentials.

Let's review which Azure services can help achieve these business objectives.

Understanding the Different Azure Components That Provide Monitoring

One of the main challenges with traditional data centers is the way that administrators provision and manage monitoring solutions that provide effective visibility into the operation of their applications. Azure provides turnkey solutions to monitor on-premises and cloud resources in a way that facilitates integration into hybrid environments.

Azure Monitor allows us to collect, analyze, and manage telemetric data—both in the cloud and in local environments. In general, cloud native applications often depend on different types of Azure resources, whether they are App Services instances, virtual machines, containers, networks, firewalls, storage accounts, databases, and so on.

This solution allows us to understand how applications work and identify potential points of failure to reduce the risk of a downtime in service.

Azure provides tools to enable the monitoring of Infrastructure as a Service through (a) Azure Monitor that collects metrics and logs, which is composed of three basic categories: activity logs, metrics, and diagnostic logs; (b) Application Insights; and (c) Log Analytics.

Note Azure Monitor's terminology is constantly changing. We are using the latest terminology that best fits the purpose of understanding the monitoring capabilities.

Which Method Should I Use?

The most basic answer to this question is: The method that allows you to have greater control and visibility of your application.

First, you need to keep in mind what kind of data you can get from each of these services and what actions you can take once you get a specific type of data.

In our case study, you could implement Log Analytics so that iFreeze could obtain log and metric logs of Azure services (through Azure Monitor) from virtual machines hosted on Azure and on-premises for a flexible analysis of consumption, and later take some particular action, for example, optimize IaaS resource costs by updating the size of virtual machine instances.

Or, iFreeze could use Application Insights to analyze the behavior of its .NET Framework applications to reduce provisioning and maintenance time in a simple and agile way.

Understanding the Different Azure Components Providing Diagnostics and Logging

For a better understanding of Azure Monitoring services, take a look at the diagram. It simplifies the main categories and their functionalities.

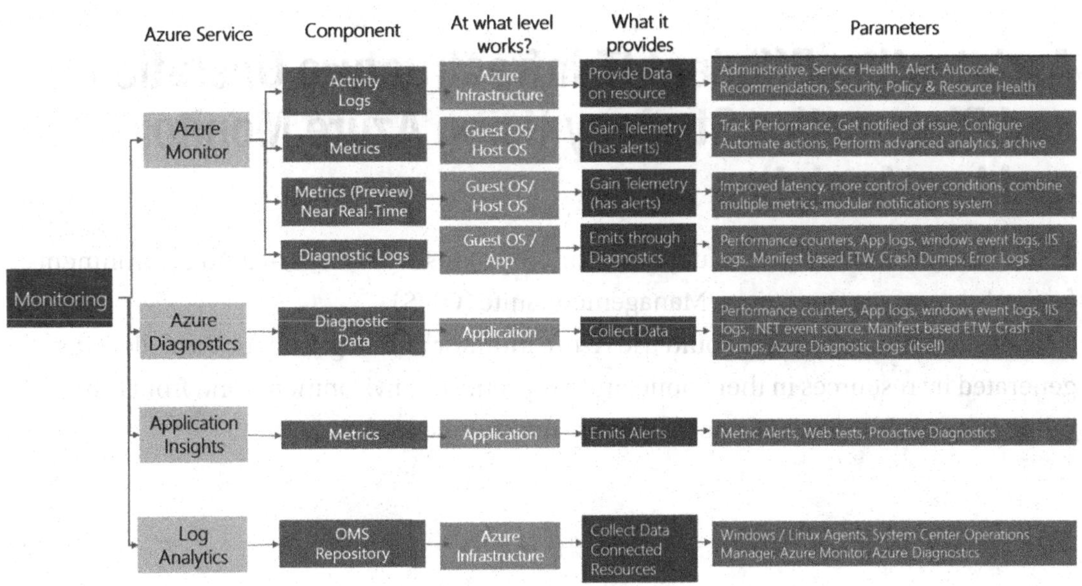

***Figure 6-1.** Overview of different Azure Monitoring services*

Note Diagnostic Extended Logs is equivalent to Azure Diagnostics, although in the official documentation, this service can be considered within Azure Monitor to better understand Azure Monitoring. We emphasize Azure Diagnostics separately.

As you can see, depending on the approach, we can select some services of Azure Monitor and Log Analytics to design the monitoring strategy for IaaS. Alternatively, we could assign Metrics (Preview) and Application Insights if our goal is to monitor PaaS or SaaS.

An important consideration is the alerts that Azure provides within these monitoring components. An alert executes queries to the record in an interval or period of time. If the result of the query to the record matches some previously established criteria, an alert record is created.

Once an alert record is created, we can generate an additional configuration to take an action, or in this case, a group of actions to execute another process related to the alert. For example, we could implement an alert to check the percentage of CPU used in a certain virtual machine; if the percentage of CPU used is greater than *N*, we can generate an action or a group of actions (in this case, automate the scaling of said virtual machine instance).

Architecting Efficient IT Infrastructure Operations and Diagnostics Strategy Using Azure Monitor and Log Analytics

Azure Monitor enables you to fully monitor on-premises and cross-cloud environments, formerly known as Operations Management Suite (OMS).

Let's review how iFreeze could use Azure Monitor and Log Analytics to collect data generated by resources in their cloud and on-premises environments and from other monitoring tools to provide analysis across multiple sources.

Solution Design

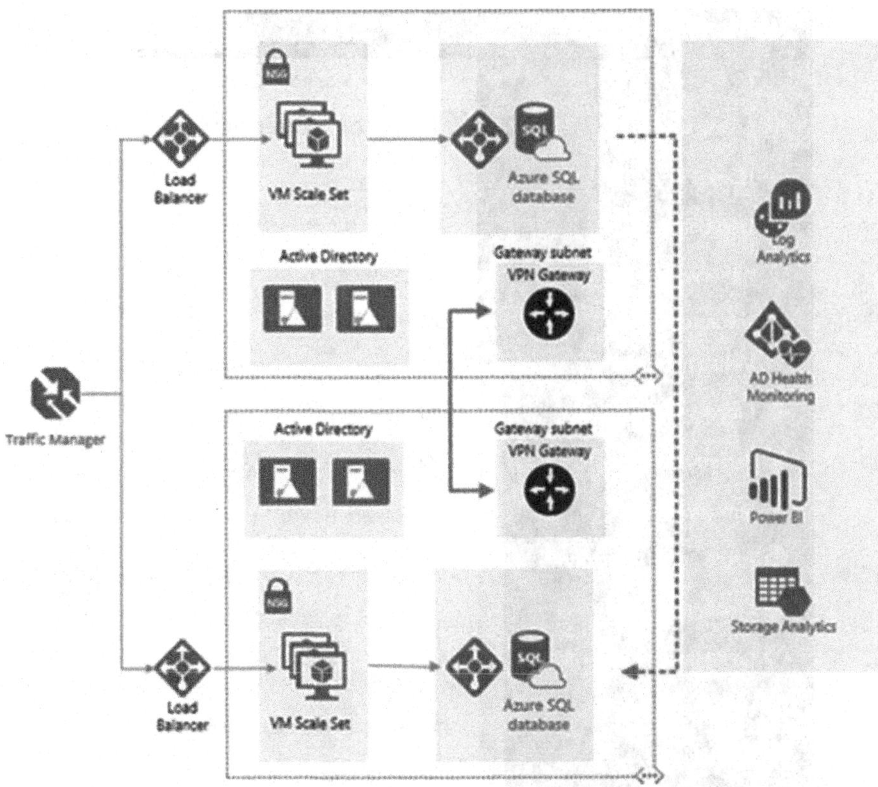

***Figure 6-2.** Azure Monitoring Solution design sample diagram*

Now let's get a bit more practical and review the step-by-step process to set up a workspace to collect all the necessary data to proactively monitor resources. We assume that you previously deployed the resources shown in the diagram above. You can select a different region where the service is available.

1. Go to the Azure portal and look for Monitor. Click **Logs**, as shown below.

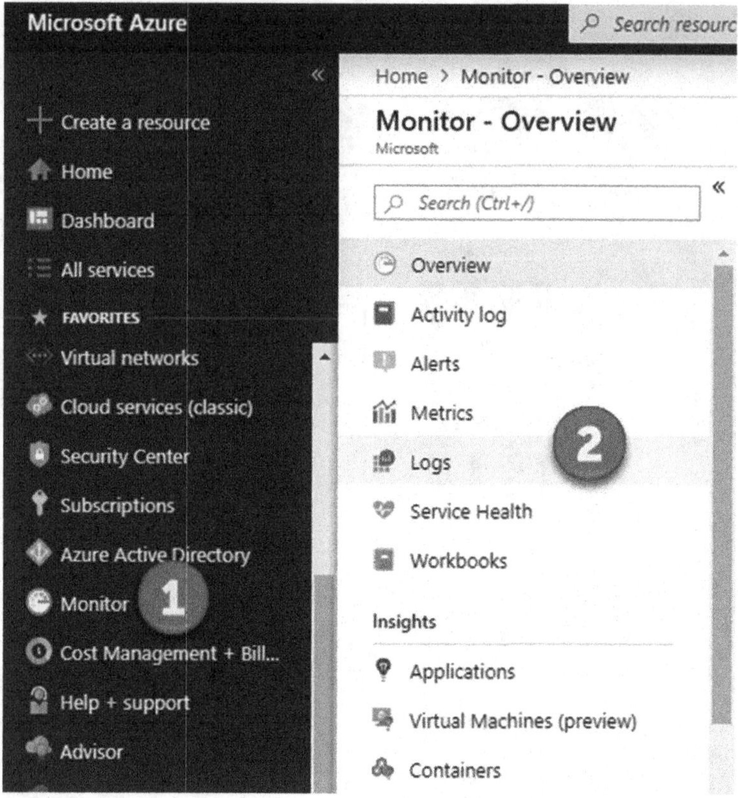

Now we will create our new Log Analytics workspace, where we will store all the data from our resources.

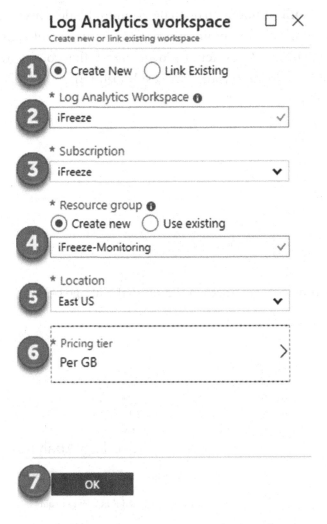

2. Once the Log Analytics workspace is created, go to the main menu and select **More services**. Type **monitor** and select **Monitor service**.

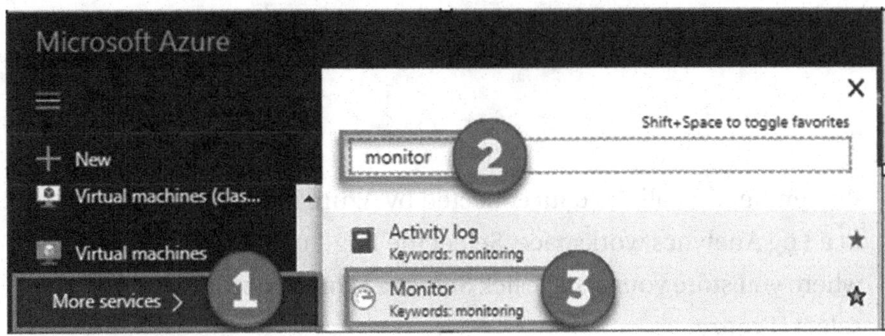

1. Click the **Monitor** option to open the Monitor blade. This blade brings together all your monitoring settings and data into one consolidated view. Click **Activity log** to ensure that you get the recent log activity from your current subscription.

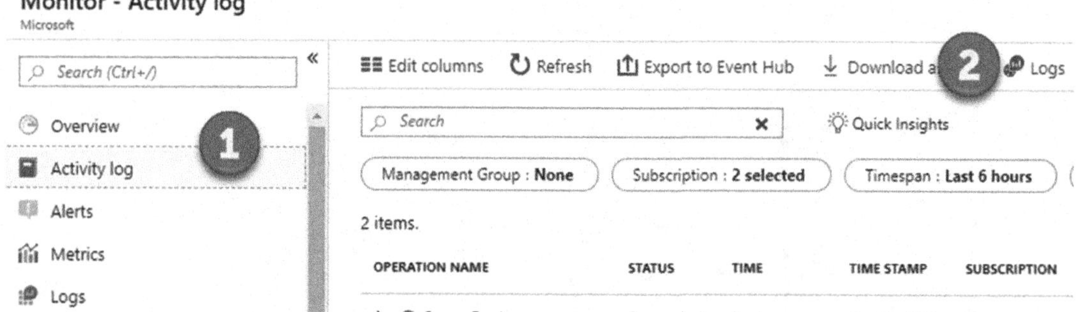

2. The first time, you get a screen similar to the image below.

Get started with Log Analytics

Gain insights into Azure activities using log search and visualization

Please click "+ Add" button to begin

3. Click **Add**.

4. Remember that all the data collected by Azure Monitor is stored in a Log Analytics workspace. Select the Log Analytics workspace, where you store your data. Click **Select a Workspace** and then select **iFreeze**.

Note As of writing time, Log Analytics was not available in all Azure regions, so be careful when choosing the region for your workspace.

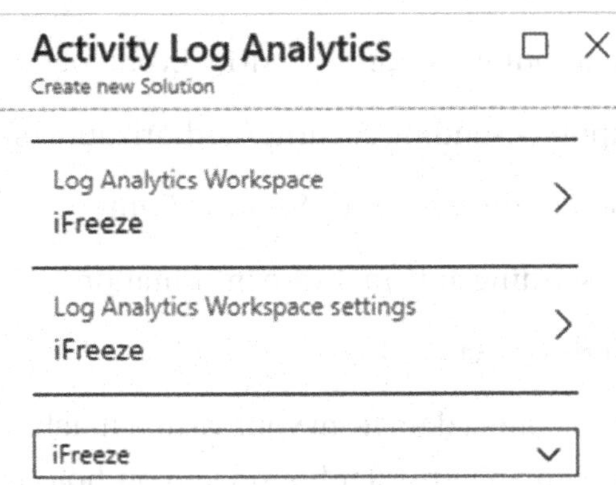

Note A node can be a virtual machine, a physical server, a network device, or other instance. You can buy additional nodes either upfront through a suite or by purchasing a pay-as-you-go plan.

Examples of nodes include the following.

- Insight and Analytics
  - Windows and Linux computers with one of the OMS agents installed
  - Azure classic cloud service web and worker role instances
  - Azure service fabric cluster nodes
  - Data sent through the data collector API with the Computer field populated
  - Each device sending logs via a syslog forwarder
- Automation and Control
  - Computers with the Configuration Management agent installed
  - Computers with an OMS agent collecting Change Tracking data

- Computers with an OMS agent collecting Update Management data
- Computers with Automation Hybrid Worker installed

- Security and Compliance
  - Windows computers sending Security Event logs
  - Linux computers sending security/authorization syslog events
  - Azure resources monitored by Security Center
  - Computers sending anti-malware information
  - Devices sending security logs

Azure Monitor can also collect data from your virtual machines and the networking dependencies so that you can analyze all inbound and outbound traffic.

5. When the workspace is ready, return to the Monitor blade and click **Activity log**. Select **iFreeze Azure Subscription**, then in the Resource Group field select **iFreeze.** For this case, select **All resources.** Save this query by clicking the **Save** icon.

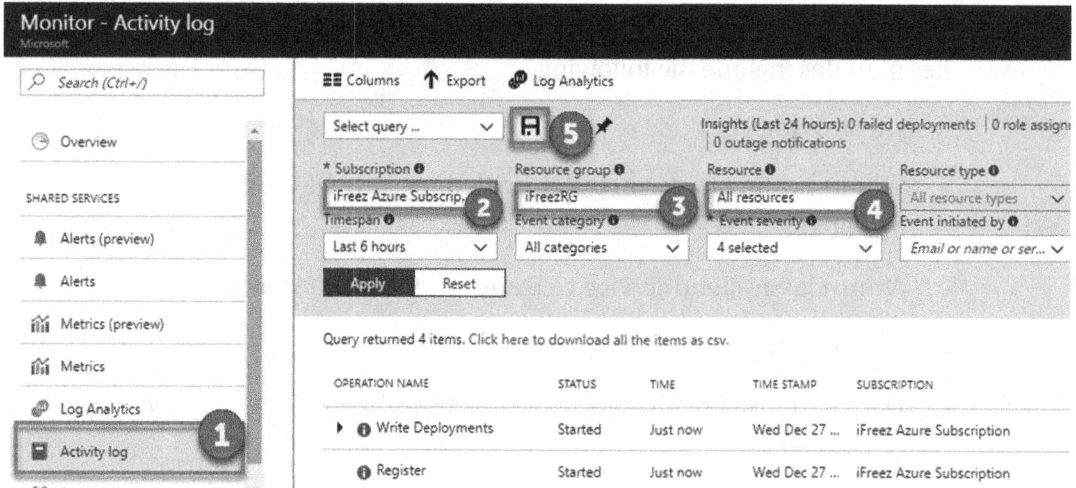

6. Name the current query **iFreeze-Logs** and click **OK**.

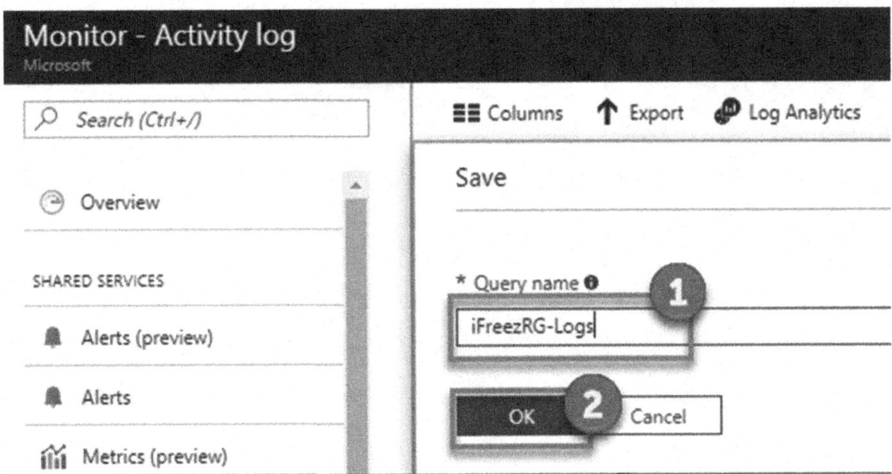

The activity log describes all operations performed on resources in your subscription. Now you can determine the what, who, and when for any create, update, or delete operations on resources in your subscription; for example, when a VM stopped and who stopped it. Activity log events are stored in the platform and are available to query for 90 days.

Now let's review Azure Metrics.

1. Return to the Monitor tile and click the **Metrics** section. You first need to select a resource by filtering and selecting using the drop-down options at the top of the blade.

2. Ensure that your resource has enabled diagnostic settings. To achieve this configuration, you have two options.

Option 1

a. Go to your resource, in this case, a VM called iFreezeWebserver.

b. Select **Diagnostic Settings** from the configuration blade.

c. Select **Logs**.

d. Click the **IIS Logs** checkbox. Azure provides the storage account name to store the logs.

e. Click **Save**.

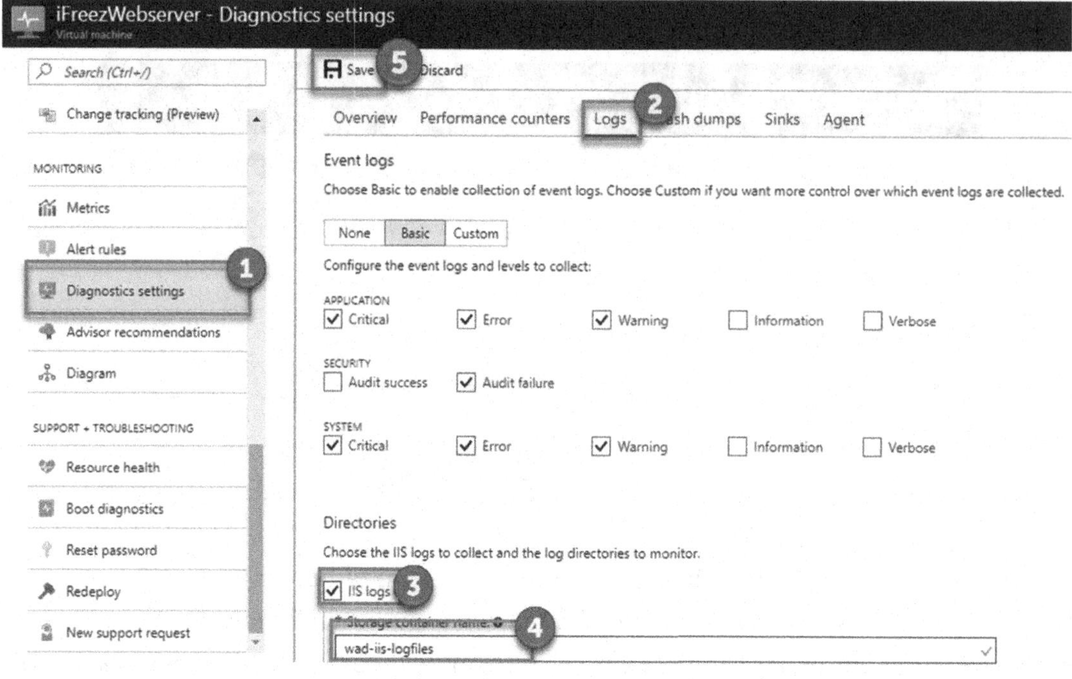

Option 2

a. Go to the Monitor tile and click the **Metrics** section. Select a resource by filtering and selecting using the drop-down options at the top of the blade.

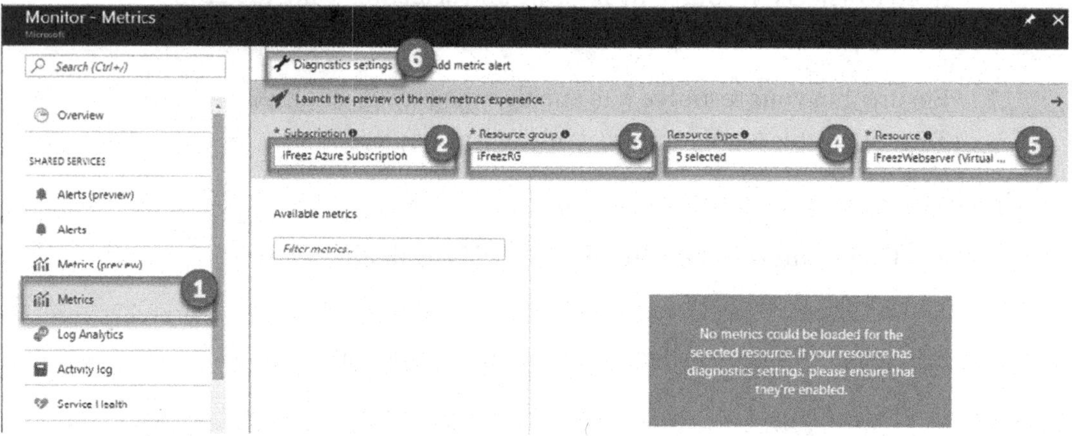

b. Click **Logs**. Select the metrics that you are interested in monitoring; in this case, we are collecting the basic logs.

c. Click **Save**.

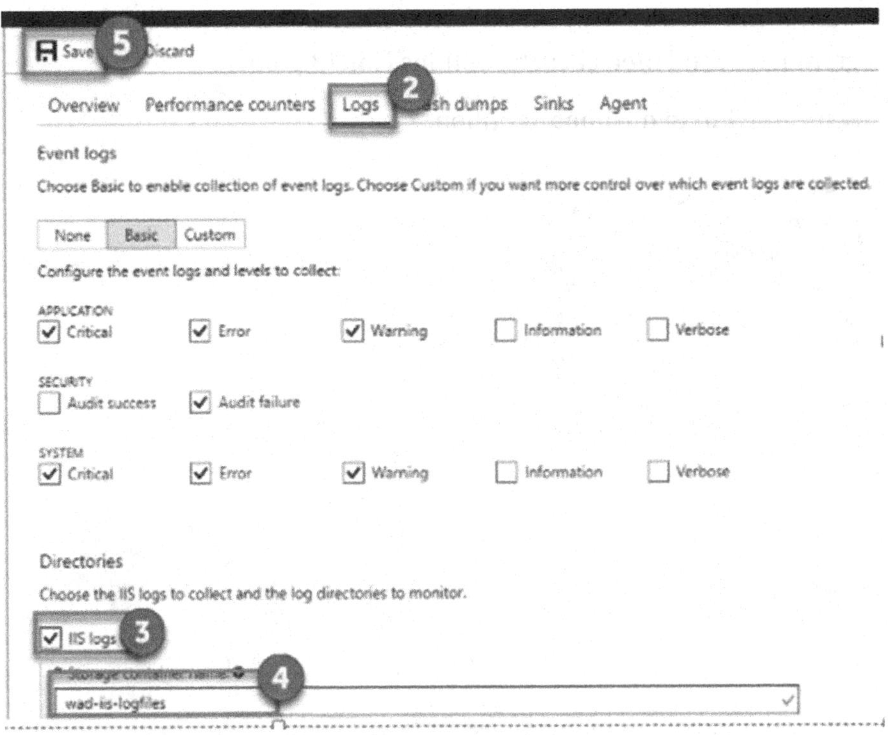

Note As of time of writing there is available a Metrics(Preview) option: Select **Metrics(Preview)** and then select the resource that you want to monitor.

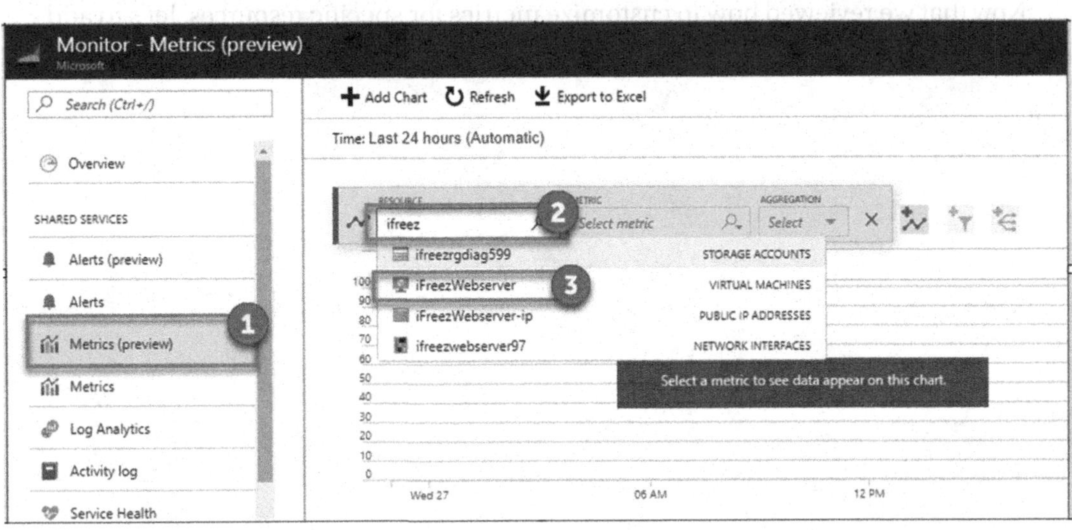

3. With Metrics(Preview) you can easily select the resource that you want to monitor. Select your preferred chart and a custom time granularity, and then click the options icon (3 points).

4. Select the **Pin to dashboard** option.

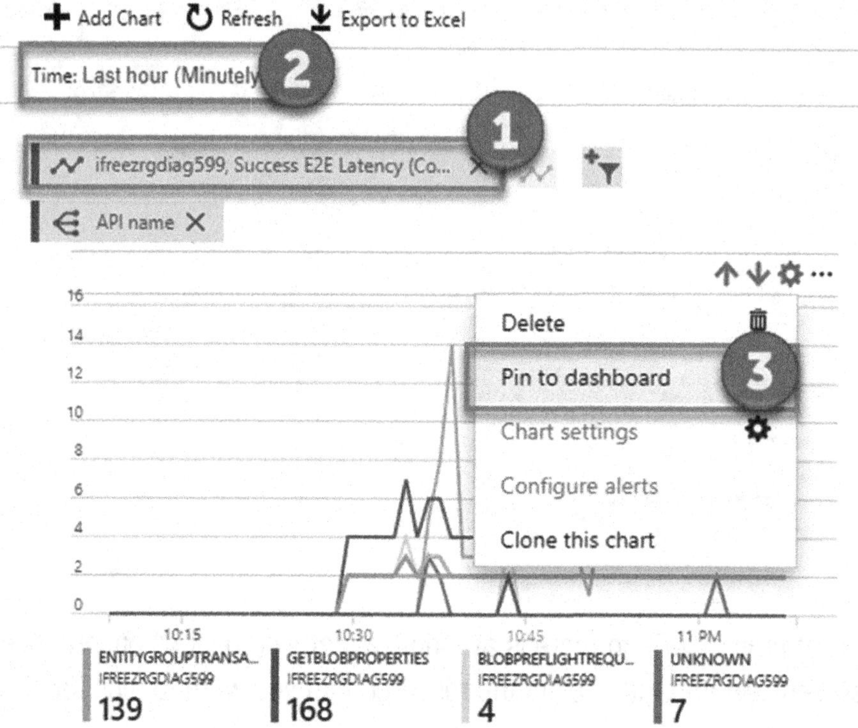

Now that we reviewed how to customize metrics for specific resources, let's to add Alerts.

1. Click the Monitor blade, select **Alerts**, and click **Configure**.

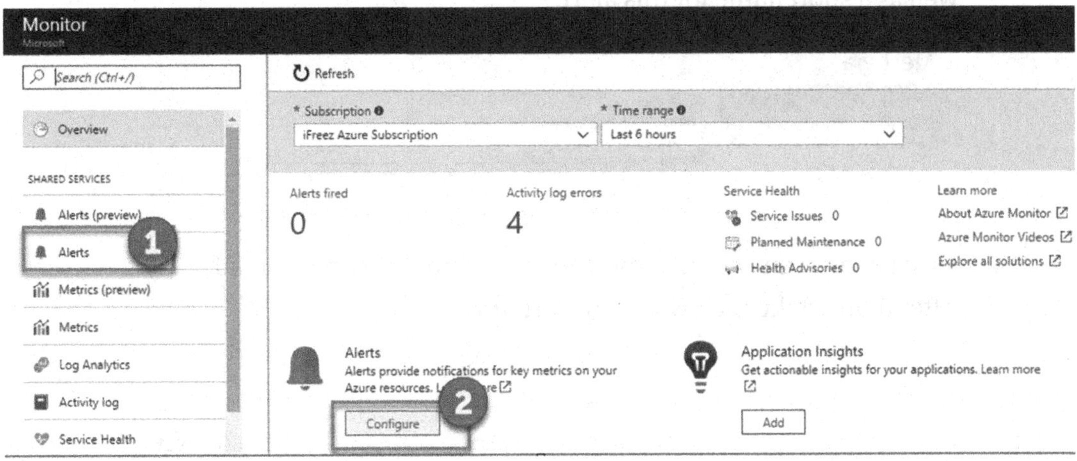

In this blade, we are going to configure an alert. The objective is to send a warning to the IT administrator when the web server has a high CPU % usage.

2. Configure the parameters as shown in the image below:

Add activity log alert
* Activity log alert name: webserverAlert
Description: Alert on high CPU %
* Subscription: iFreeze
* Resource group: iFreeze
Source
Input: Activity log
Criteria
* Event category: Autoscale
Resource type: Virtual machines (Microsoft.Compute/VirtualMachines)
Resource group: iFreeze
Resource: iFreezWebserver
Operation name: Create or Update Virtual Machine (virtualMachines)
Level: Warning
Status: Started
Event initiated by

3. Set up a new action group and provide an action group name as well as a short name for this alert.

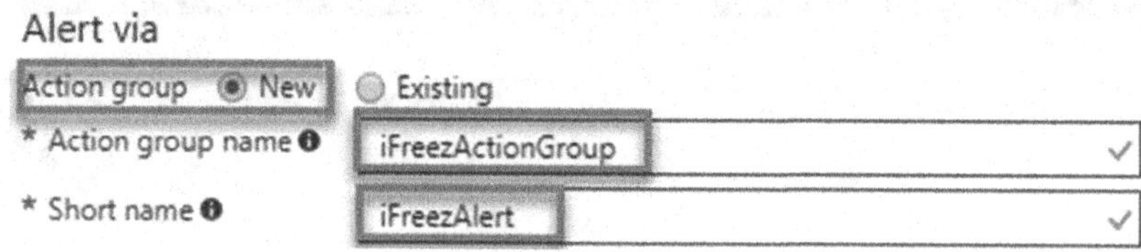

4. Give the alert an action name and set up the action type email. After that, set the mail when an alert fires.

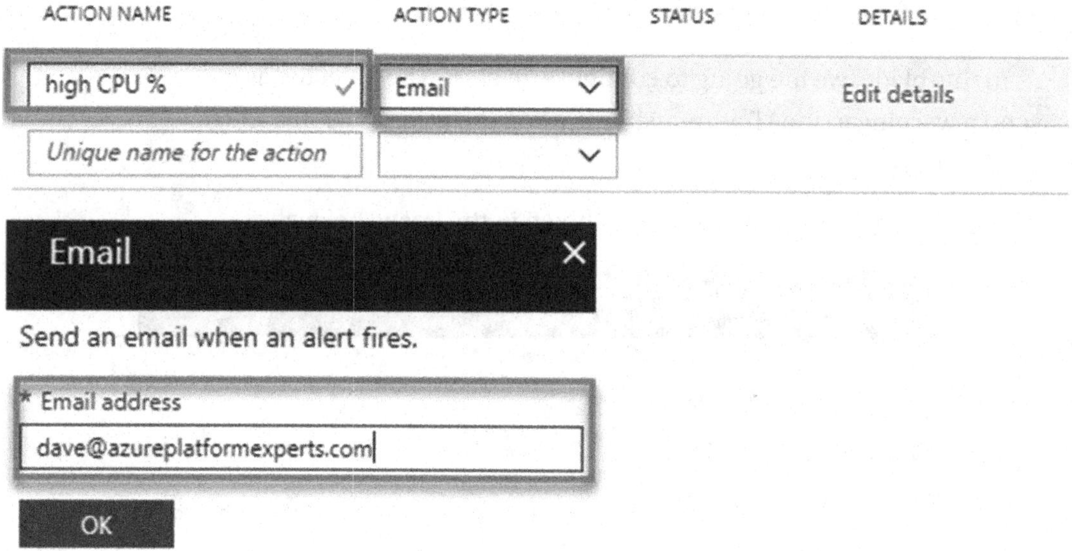

Now let's take a deep dive into Log Analytics.

1. Go to the Monitor blade and select **Log Analytics**.

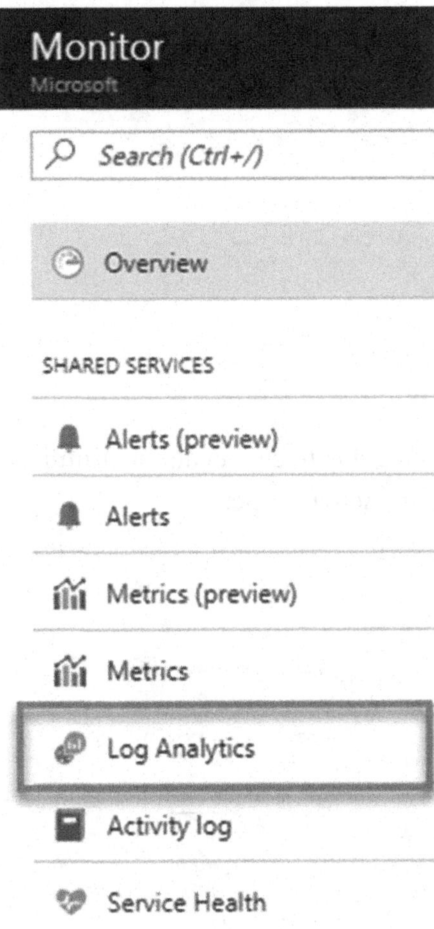

2. Once you select your workspace, type your custom query, or use a recommendation from the language converter.

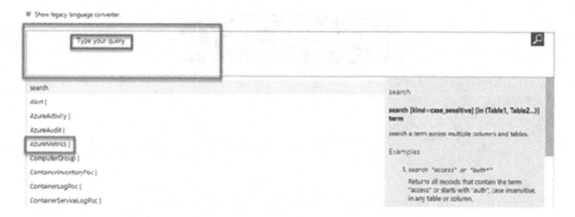

3. For this case, we are going to collect all the Administrative Category from Azure Activity type.

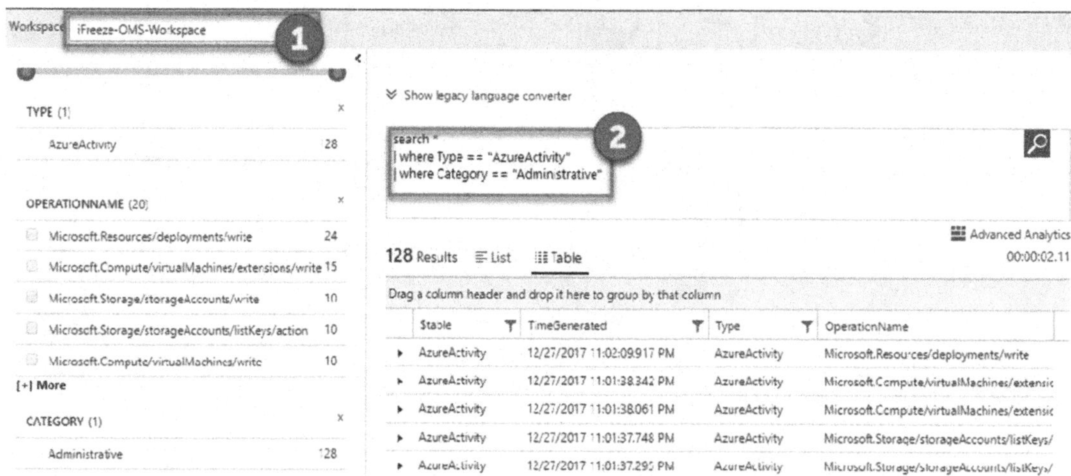

If you want to get started on Log Analytics queries, check out `https://docs.microsoft.com/en-gb/azure/azure-monitor/log-query/get-started-queries`.

Monitoring and Troubleshooting Azure Networking Using Network Watcher

1. Go to **More services** and search for **network watcher**. Click **Network Watcher**.

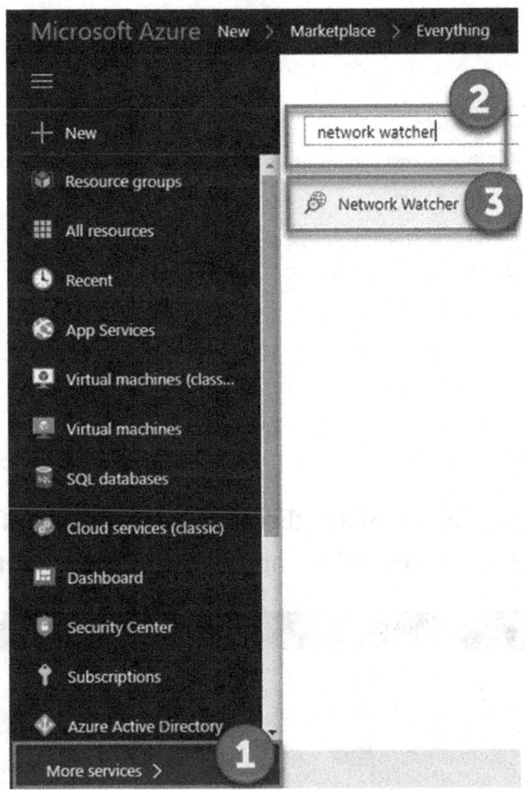

2. Select **iFreeze Azure Subscription**. You will see all the regions where Network Watcher is available. If you click the right options, you see two options. Select **Enable network watcher in all regions.**

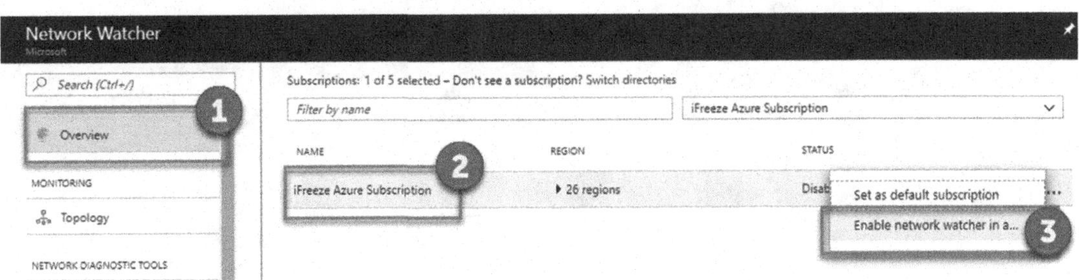

3. Go to the left blade and select **Topology**.

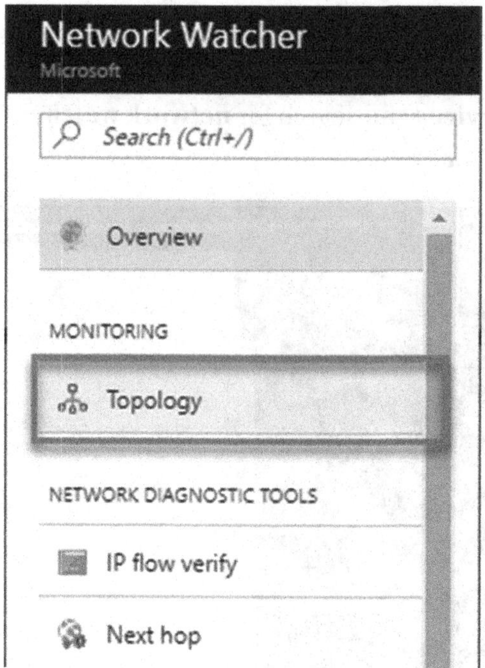

4. You will see a new blade. Select **iFreeze Azure Subscription** and the resource group, **iFreezeRG**. Then select **iFreeze-Vnet**.

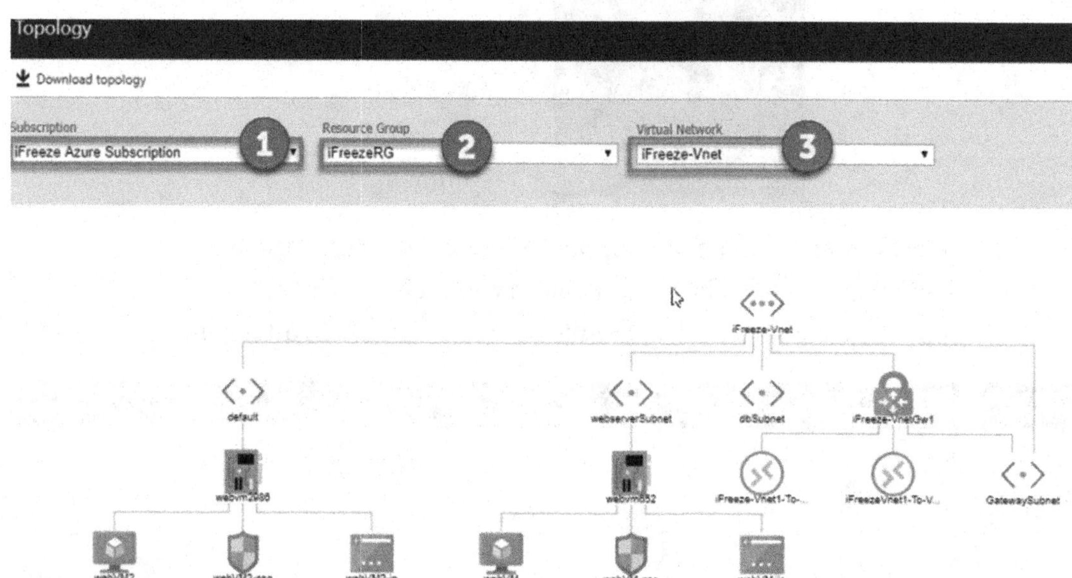

In the Topology blade, you are able to analyze the resources that you previously deployed, including compute and networking components. As you can see, network watchers provide an easy way to see what is happening across your entire network with diagnostic tools, which includes IP flow verification, security group views, VPN diagnostics, packet capture, and connection troubleshooting. Network Watcher also provides metrics and you can configure alerts to take specific actions.

Let's review how to troubleshoot your networking components.

1. Go to the Network Watcher blade and select **IP Flow Verify**. Check the inbound traffic for our webserver. Select **iFreeze Azure Subscription** and the **iFreezeRG** resource group. Then select the **webVM** VM. Select the network interface **webvm652**. The packet details are through protocol TCP and the direction is inbound. Finally, select the local IP address and port, as well as the remote IP address, as shown in the following image.

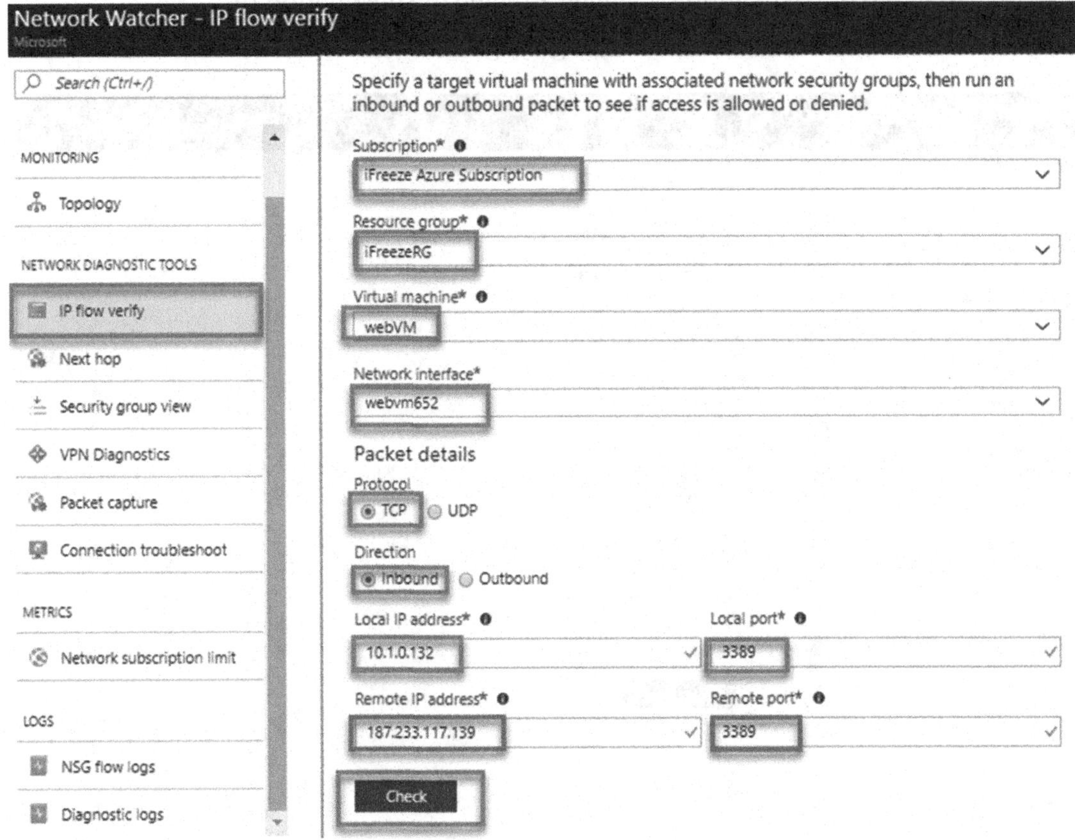

2. After you run the inbound check, you see the result in the same blade.

3. Now return to the Network Watcher blade and select **Next hop**. This service helps diagnose connectivity issues; for example, if VM traffic is sent to a destination successfully or if there is any block. Select **iFreeze Azure Subscription**, the **iFreezeRG** resource group, and then **webVM**. Select the network interface **webvm652** and the source IP address. Finally, provide the destination IP address, as shown in the following image.

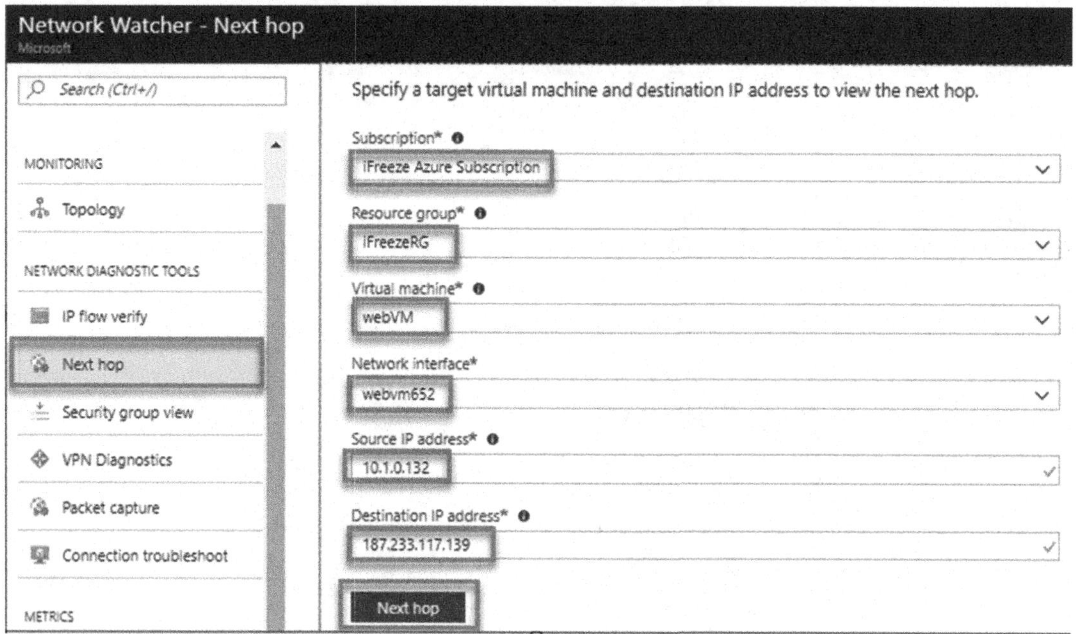

What result should you expect? Azure provides the following parameters as results, depending on the source IP address and the destination IP address: Internet, virtualAppliance, VirtualNetworkGateway, VnetLocal, HyperNetGateway, VnetPeering, and None.

In this case, the result should be Next Hop Type = Internet and Route table ID = System Route, as shown in the following image.

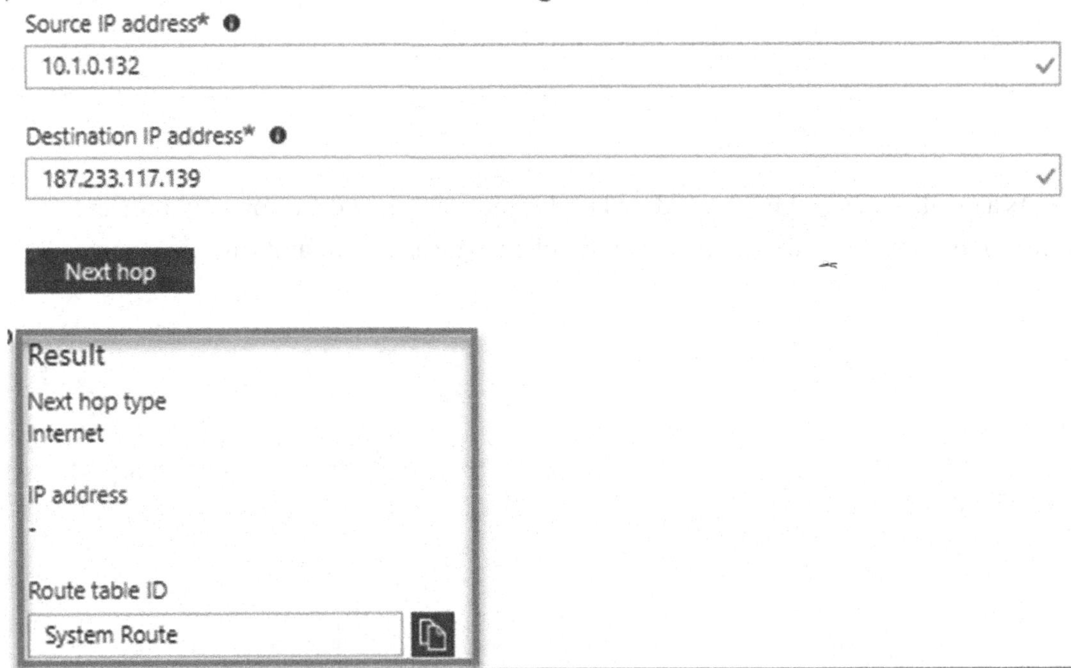

4. Now return to the Network Watcher blade and select the **security group view**. This service allows you to visualize the properties and details of your specific resource; for instance, in this case you are going review the iFreeze web server inbound and outbound effective rules by selecting **iFreeze Azure Subscription**, the **iFreezeRG** resource group, and then **webVM**. The network interface is **webvm652** , as shown in the image below.

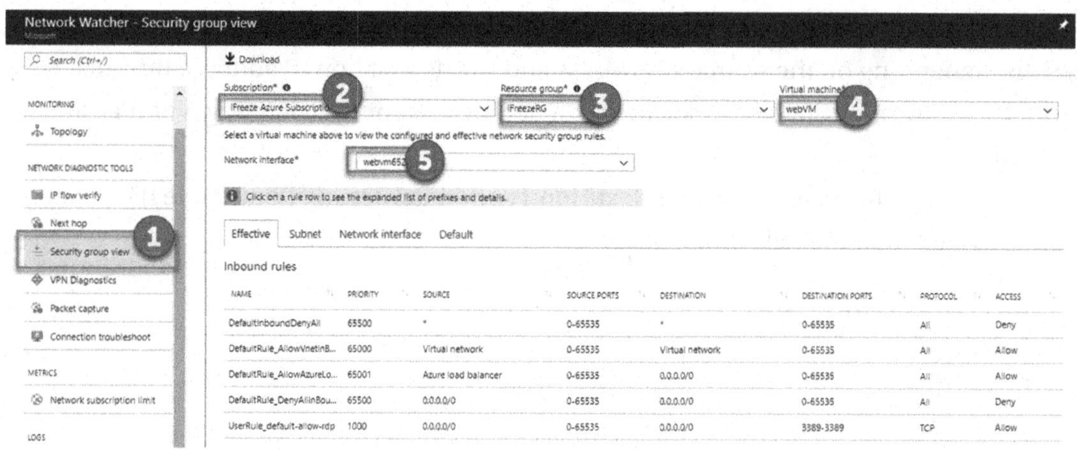

As a result, you see the inbound and outbound rules; however, you could review more parameters, such as the subnet, network interface, and default rules.

Effective | Subnet | Network interface | Default

Inbound rules

NAME	PRIORITY	SOURCE	SOURCE PORTS	DESTINATION	DESTINATION PORTS	PROTOCOL	ACCESS
DefaultInboundDenyAll	65500	*	0-65535	*	0-65535	All	Deny
DefaultRule_AllowVnetInB...	65000	Virtual network	0-65535	Virtual network	0-65535	All	Allow
DefaultRule_AllowAzureLo...	65001	Azure load balancer	0-65535	0.0.0.0/0	0-65535	All	Allow
DefaultRule_DenyAllInBou...	65500	0.0.0.0/0	0-65535	0.0.0.0/0	0-65535	All	Deny
UserRule_default-allow-rdp	1000	0.0.0.0/0	0-65535	0.0.0.0/0	3389-3389	TCP	Allow

Outbound rules

NAME	PRIORITY	SOURCE	SOURCE PORTS	DESTINATION	DESTINATION PORTS	PROTOCOL	ACCESS
DefaultOutboundDenyAll	65500	*	0-65535	*	0-65535	All	Deny
DefaultRule_AllowVnetOut...	65000	Virtual network	0-65535	Virtual network	0-65535	All	Allow
DefaultRule_AllowInternet...	65001	0.0.0.0/0	0-65535	Internet	0-65535	All	Allow
DefaultRule_DenyAllOutBo...	65500	0.0.0.0/0	0-65535	0.0.0.0/0	0-65535	All	Deny

An important objective for iFreeze is to be able to proactively monitor their global branches and connectivity, so we will make use of the VPN diagnostics and packet capture.

VPN Diagnostics enables us to troubleshoot our VPN connectivity in a granular way.

1. Select **VPN Diagnostics** from the Network Watcher blade, and then select **iFreeze Azure Subscription** and the **iFreezeRG** resource group. Select a specific location; in this case, **East US**.

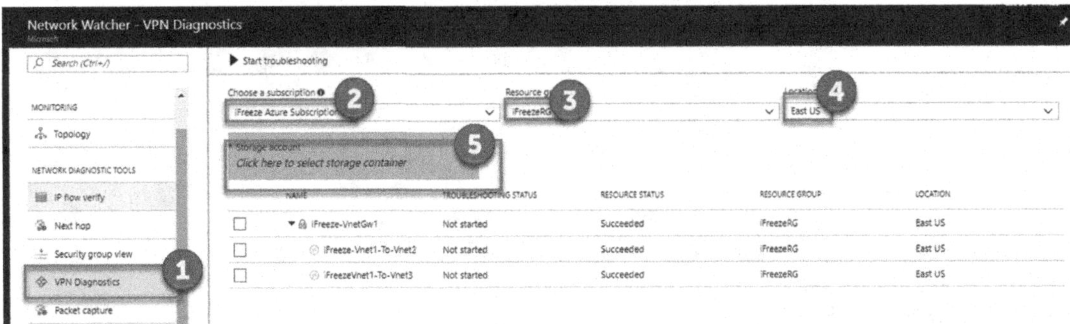

Before you can start the troubleshooting, you need to select an Azure storage account to store the logs generated. In this case, you create a new container called **ifreezevpndiagnostics**, as shown in the below image.

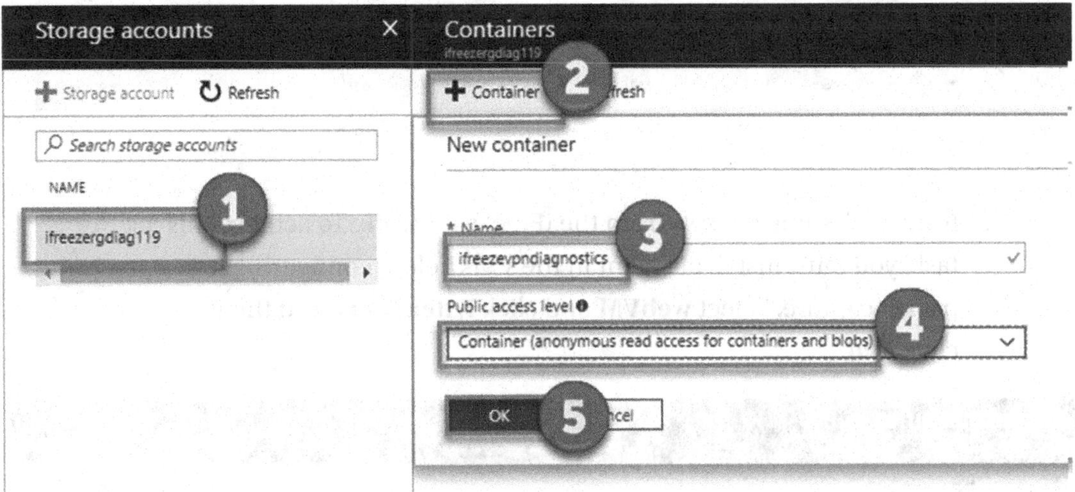

2. Select the resources from the networking components that you want to troubleshoot; in this case, select the two VNet gateways and click **Start troubleshooting**.

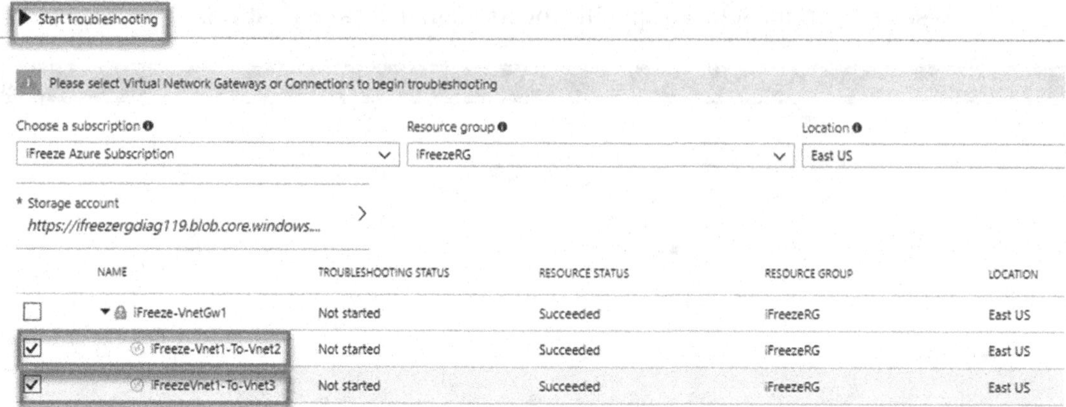

Once the troubleshooting has completed, you see an output similar to the shown in the image below:

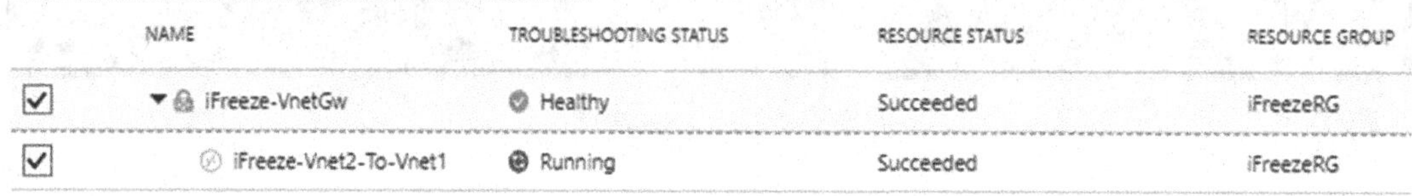

3. Now track some packets from the iFreeze network. To achieve this task, you must install an agent in the VMs before configuring the packet capture. Select **webVM** and click **Extensions**, and then click **Add**.

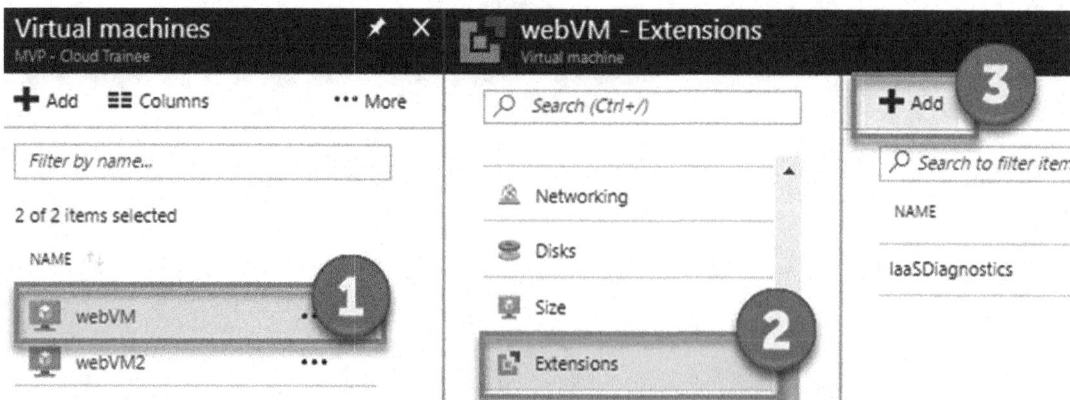

4. Look for the Network Watcher extension. Click **Create** and then **OK**.

Note This could take a few minutes to complete.

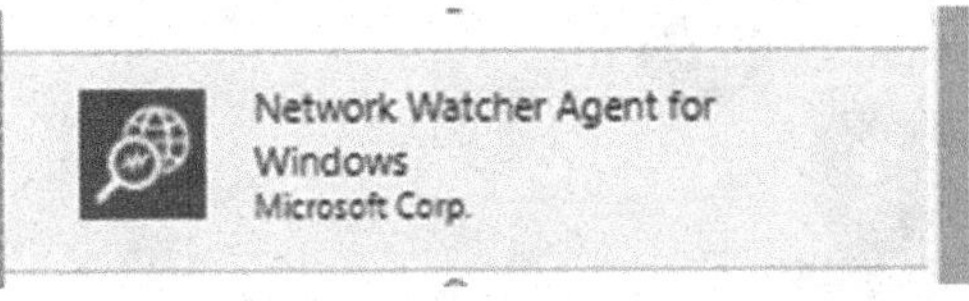

5. Return to the Network Watcher blade to start tracking packets from iFreeze VMs through the Azure network. Select **Packet capture** and then click **Add**.

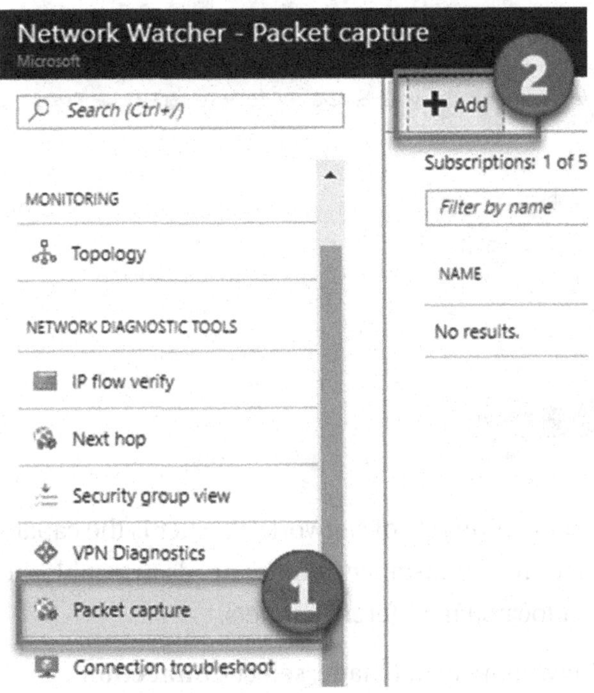

6. In this blade, select **iFreeze Azure Subscription**, resource group **iFreeze**, and target virtual machine **webVM2.** Specify a name for the packet capture: **packetwebVM2.** Choose the storage account where you want to collect the data, as shown in the following image.

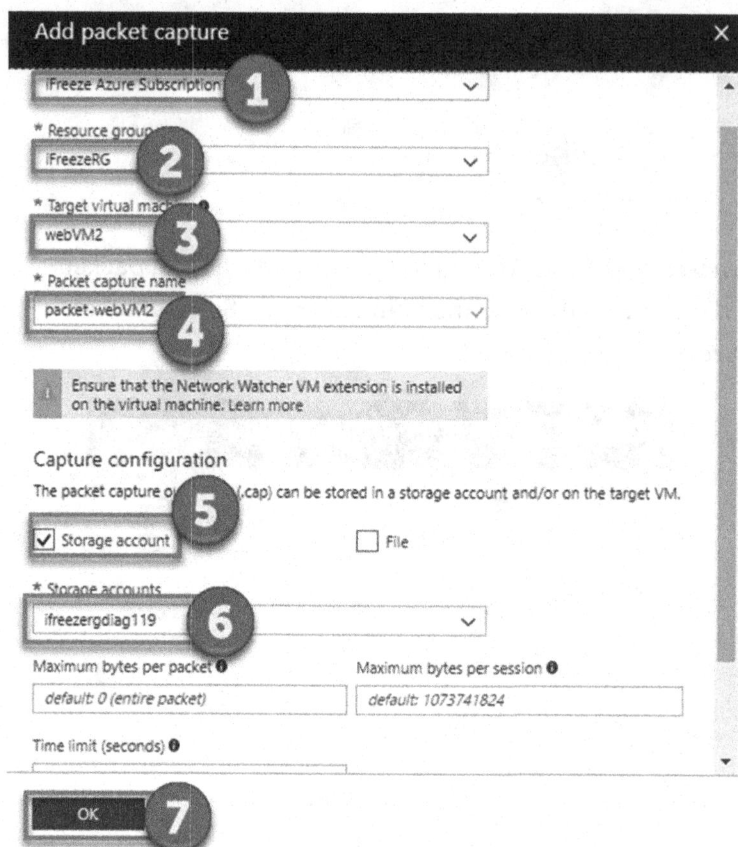

Another important functionality of Network Watcher is the capability to provide connection troubleshooting; for instance, iFreeze needs to troubleshoot the connection between resources in allocated in different subnets.

1. From the Network Watcher blade, select **Connection troubleshooting**, and then configure the source. Select **iFreeze Azure Subscription**, choose the **iFreezeRG** resource group, select your resource **dbVM**, and optionally set the specific **port**. In the Destination fields, choose **Select a virtual machine**. Choose the **iFreezeRG** resource group. Choose the **webVM2.** Set the port to **3389**, and then click **OK**.

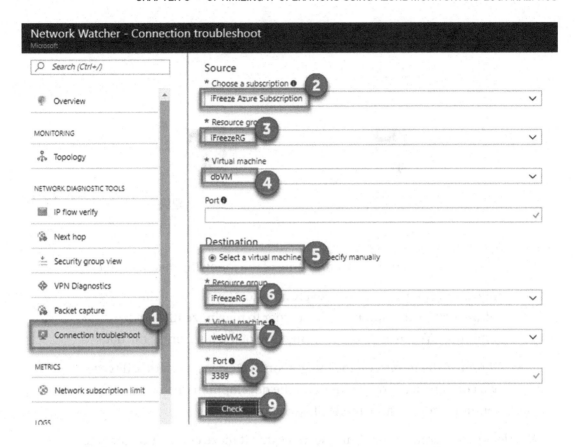

As a result, you see two views: Grid view and Graph view, as shown in the images below

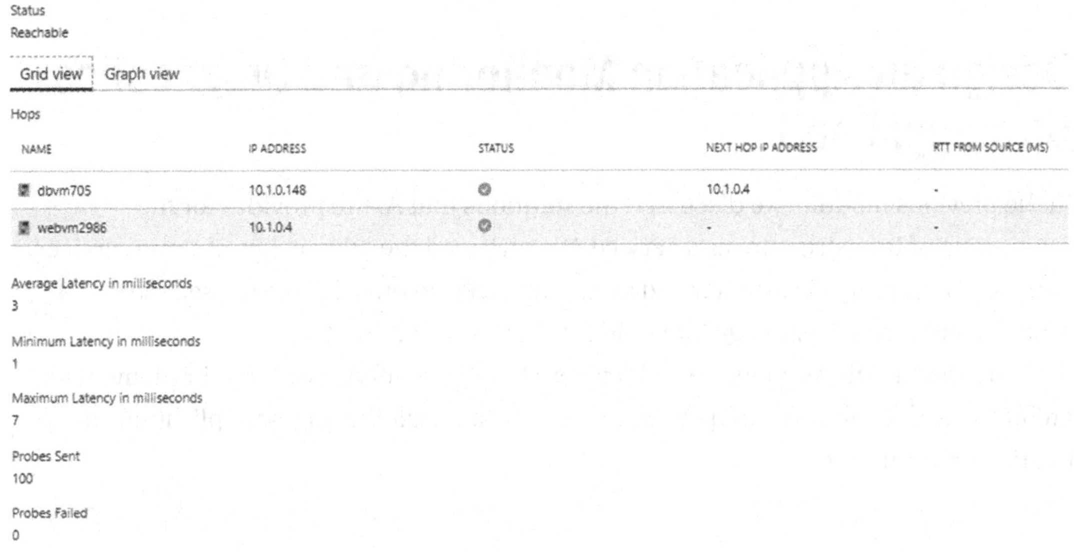

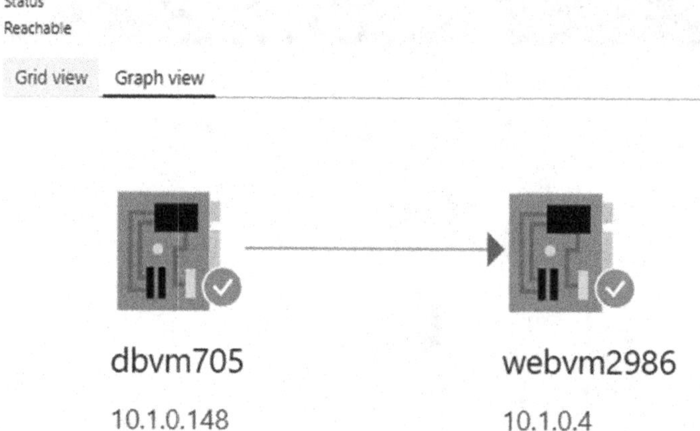

Across this hands-on-lab, we covered some of the following business objectives.

- iFreeze must be able to proactively monitor any status of the infrastructure and applications in order to maximize RPO and minimize RTO, in addition to taking care of the integrity of the data.
- Minimize the impact on the integration of DevOps scenarios. iFreeze will continue its IT operations and the development teams will continue their existing mode of operations.

Now let's review some of the Azure services that iFreeze could implement to maintain and provide monitoring capabilities at the platform level.

Design an Application Monitoring and Diagnostics Strategy: PaaS

In the previous module, we discussed the solutions that Azure provides for the monitoring of Infrastructure as a Service. We reviewed the advantages of some services and some best practices, and looked at examples based on the iFreeze use case to establish an adequate strategy for cloud infrastructure monitoring.

Throughout this module, we will review what Azure services offer to implement an architecture that allows us to have better control and visibility of our applications in hybrid environments.

Understanding the Different Azure Components Providing Monitoring of Applications and Azure Platform Services

Let's use the diagram as a reference for the monitoring components that we talked about in Chapter 5.

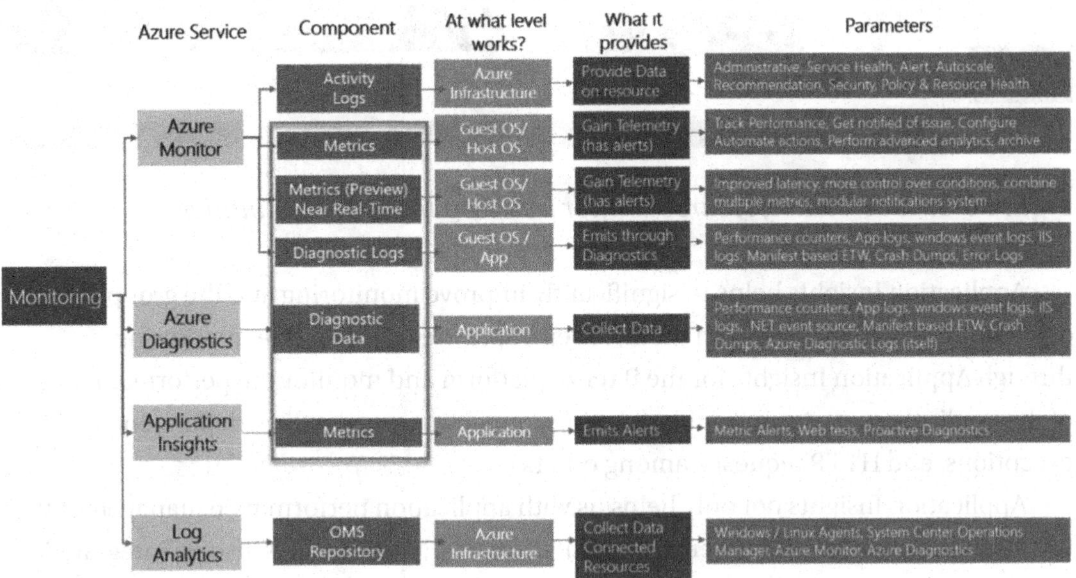

***Figure 6-3.** Overview of different Azure Monitoring services*

Within the application monitoring scheme, you can see that there are Azure services within two main categories.

- Those services that provide monitoring capabilities for our applications
- Those services that provide log and diagnostic logging capabilities

Within Azure Monitor, there are components such as Metrics and Application Insights that help us achieve a proactive monitoring strategy for our application, as shown in the image below.

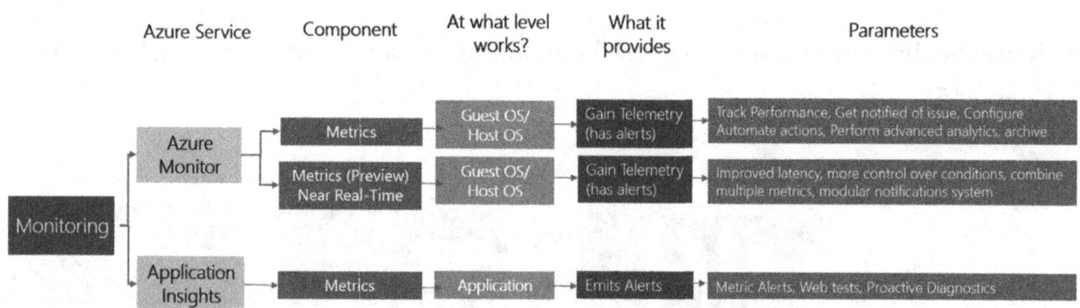

Figure 6-4. *Overview of Azure Monitor and App Insights capabilities*

Application Insights helps to significantly improve monitoring and the group of actions that we can take from them; for example, we could enable monitoring through Application Insights for the iFreeze platform and monitor the performance of the application, perform troubleshooting connections, and review dependencies, exceptions, and HTTP requests, among others.

Application Insights not only helps us with application performance management but also integrates a variety of environments, from .NET to Java. It is also an integrated component in each of the Azure services, which you can enable through your SDK or by adding the appropriate tracking code in your application.

Understanding the Different Azure Components Providing Diagnostics and Logging of Applications and Azure Platform Services

Let's take a look at the services that provide log and diagnostic logging capabilities for our application monitoring.

The following figure shows, in a granular way, the Azure components that provide diagnostic and logging capabilities for a PaaS scenario.

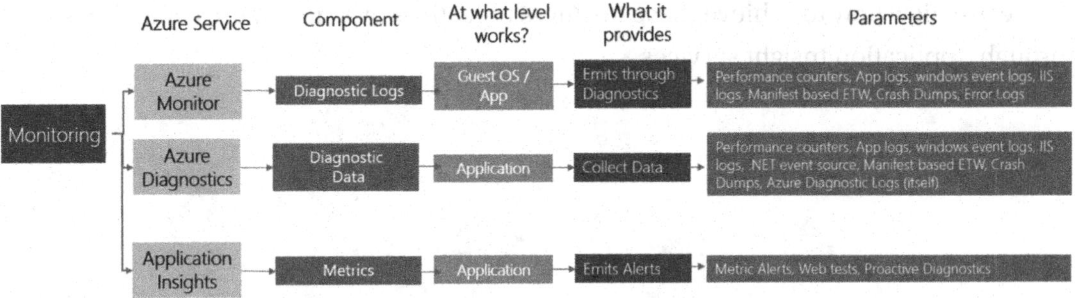

Figure 6-5. *Overview of Azure Diagnostics capabilities*

Architecting Applications Monitoring and Alerts Using Application Insights

As per iFreeze business objectives, they need to do the following.

- Adapt, as much as possible, existing development and testing platforms in IaaS or preferably PaaS/SaaS environments in order to have a reduction and optimization of costs.
- While IT operations are pretty well standardized in their operating systems, iFreeze must reduce the provisioning and maintenance time of its infrastructure in a simple and agile way.
- iFreeze must implement a solution to obtain better visibility on SaaS and PaaS applications to speed up productivity and have better integrity using corporate credentials.

Let's review how to achieve these business objectives by using Azure capabilities through Application Insight services.

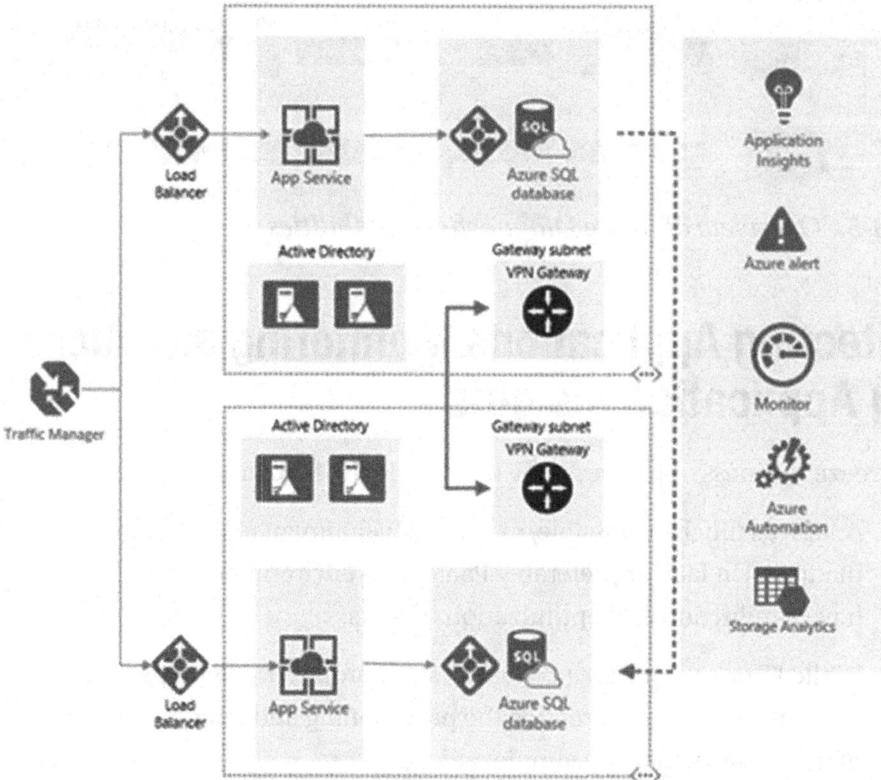

Figure 6-6. *Azure Monitoring Solution design sample diagram*

We will use the above diagram as a reference for the following steps. We assume that you deployed the resources before going through these steps.

Note This ARM template at `https://github.com/Azure/azure-quickstart-templates/tree/master/201-asev2-ilb-with-web-app` might help you to quickly follow the steps, in case you don't want to deploy all the previous resources from the diagram.

---

1. Go to the web app from your App Service environment (named iFreeze in this case), and then select the **Application Insights** option in the configuration blade.

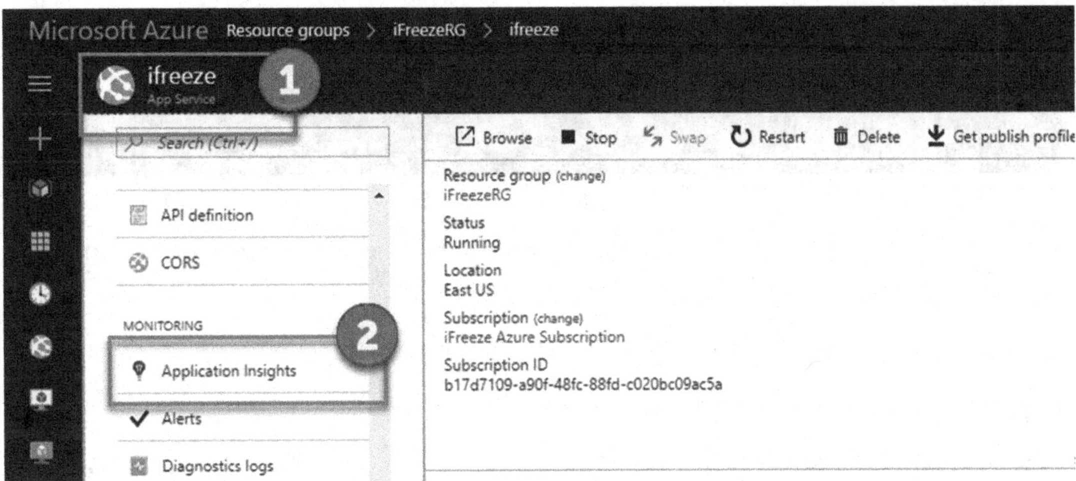

2. You will see a blade with couple of graphics that Application Insights provides by default. Click **View More Application Insights**.

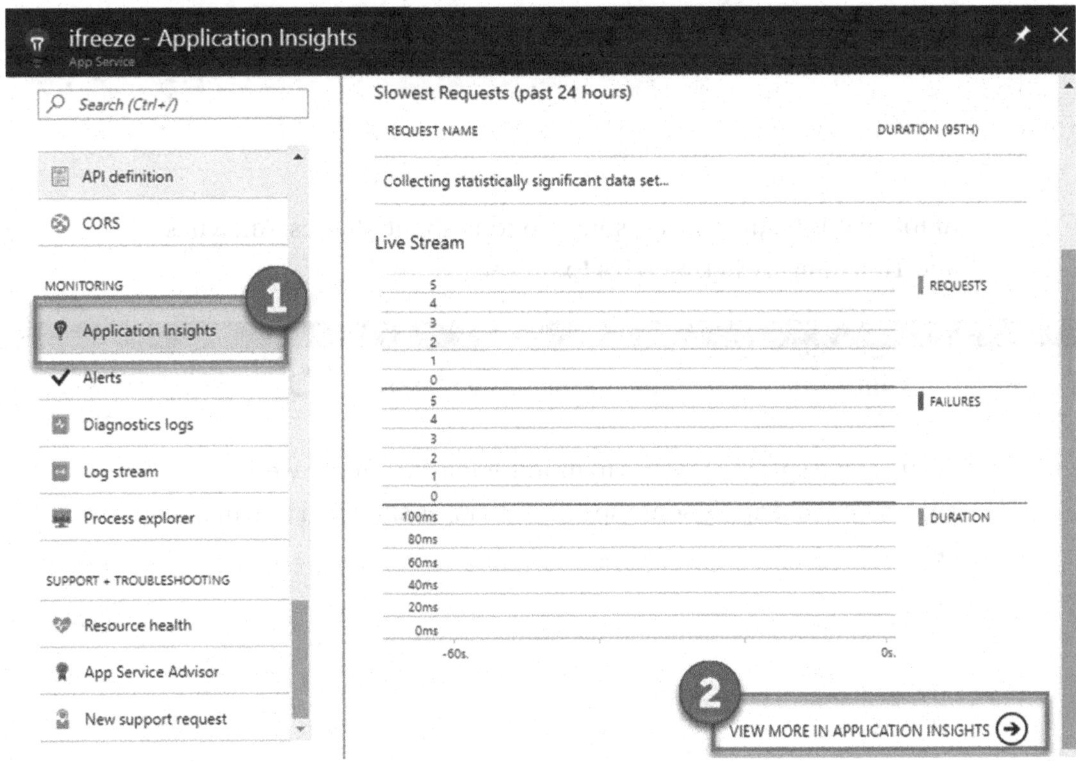

3. This blade contains a default graphics related to the iFreeze web app's health and some performance metrics.

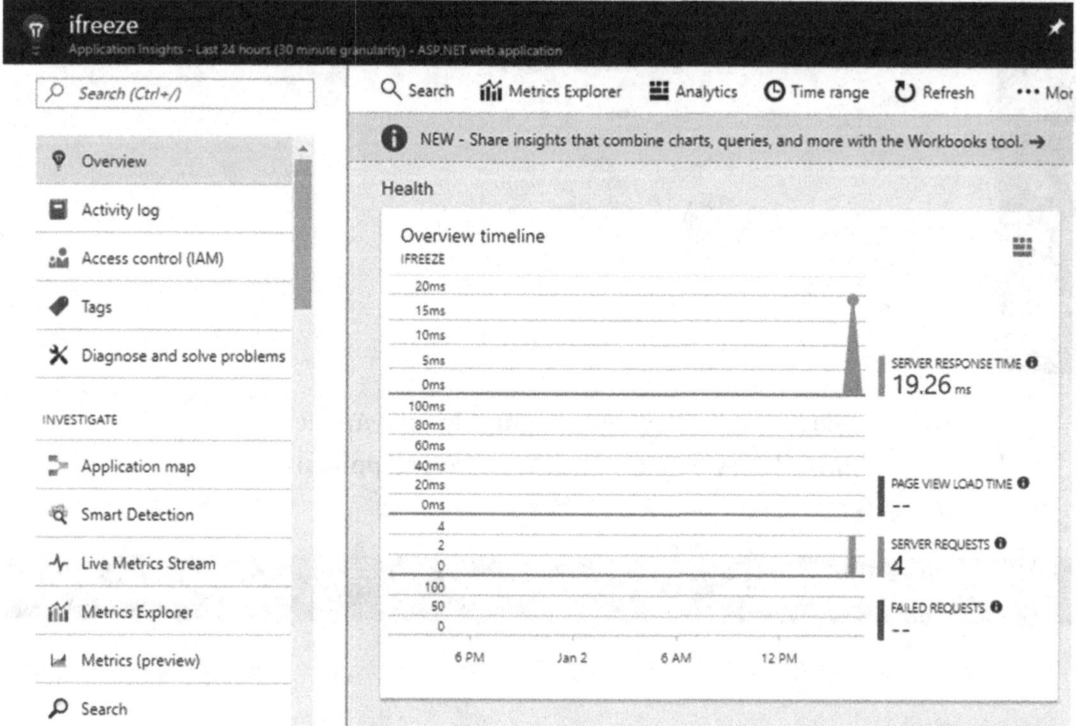

4. At top of this blade, you see some options about Metrics, Analytics and Time range. Click **Metrics Explorer**.

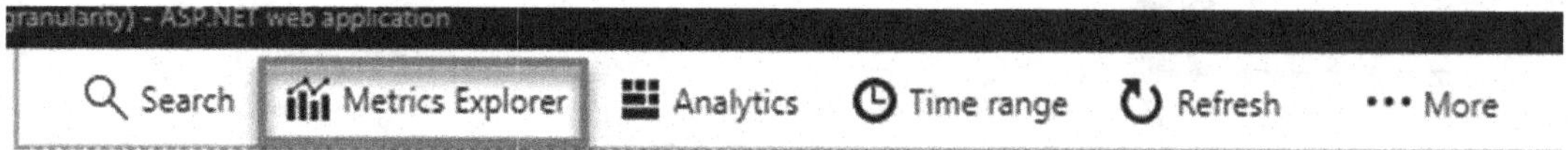

5. Set up some specific metrics to monitor for the iFreeze web application and apply some specific filters, as shown in the image below.

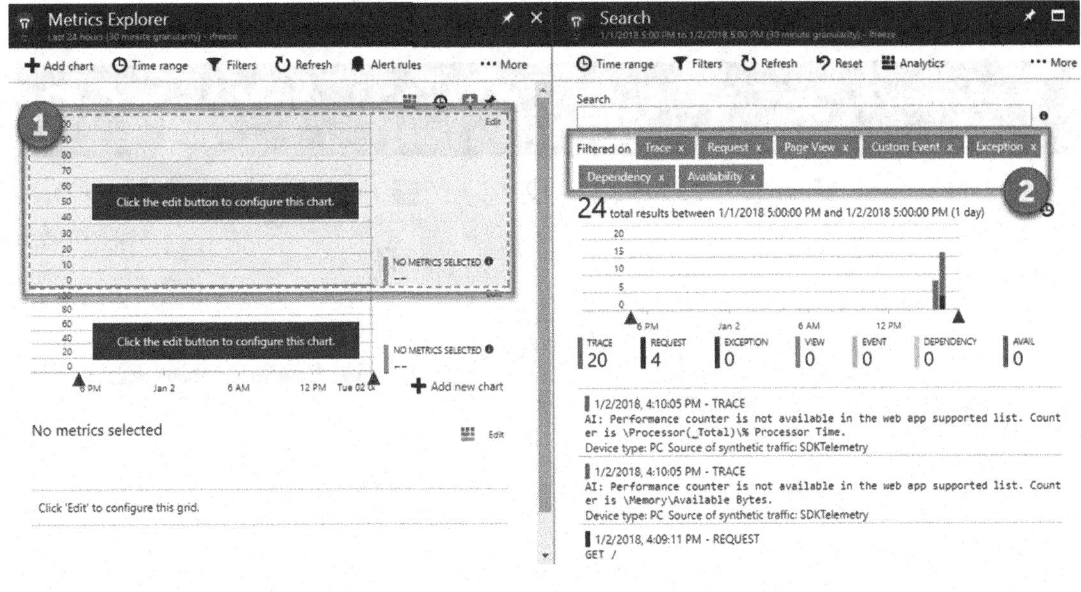

Note In most cases, Azure Metrics Explorer provides the capability to pin the graphic to the current dashboard. We will assume that you want to pin all the graphics we are reviewing from now on to the current dashboard, as shown in the image below:

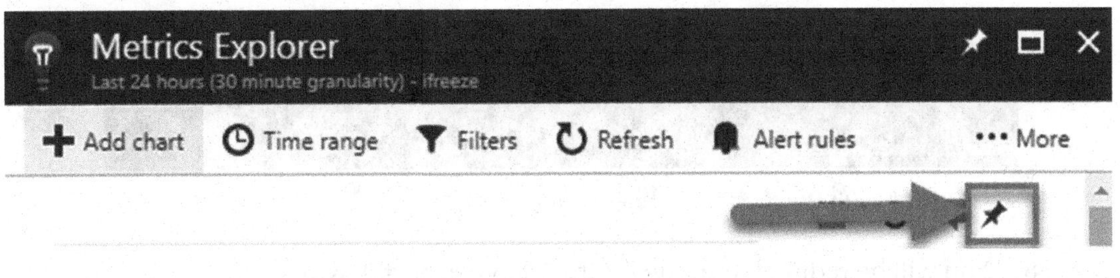

---

6. Click **More**, and then **Save favorite**.

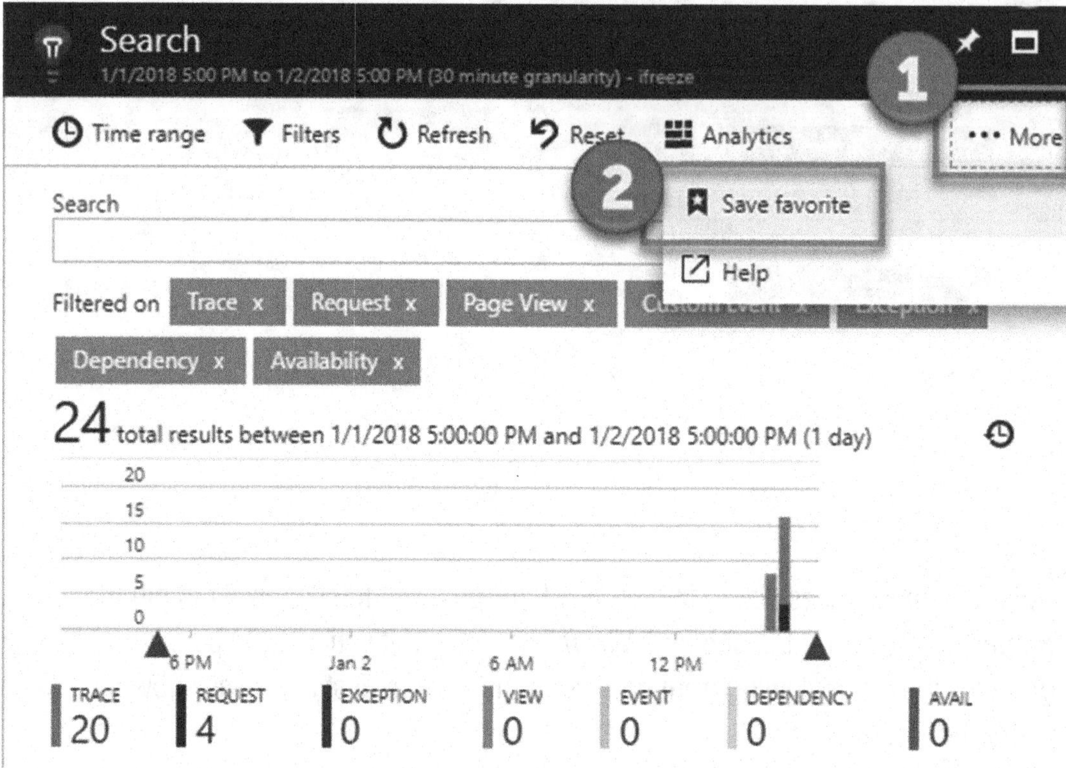

7. Now return to the Metrics Explorer blade and select **Analytics**.

8. You will be redirected to the Azure Analytics portal, with a URL similar to this one: `https://analytics.applicationinsights.io/subscriptions/b17d7109-a90f`. This is the main portal, where you can manage your Application Performance Metrics. Your screen should look similar to this one.

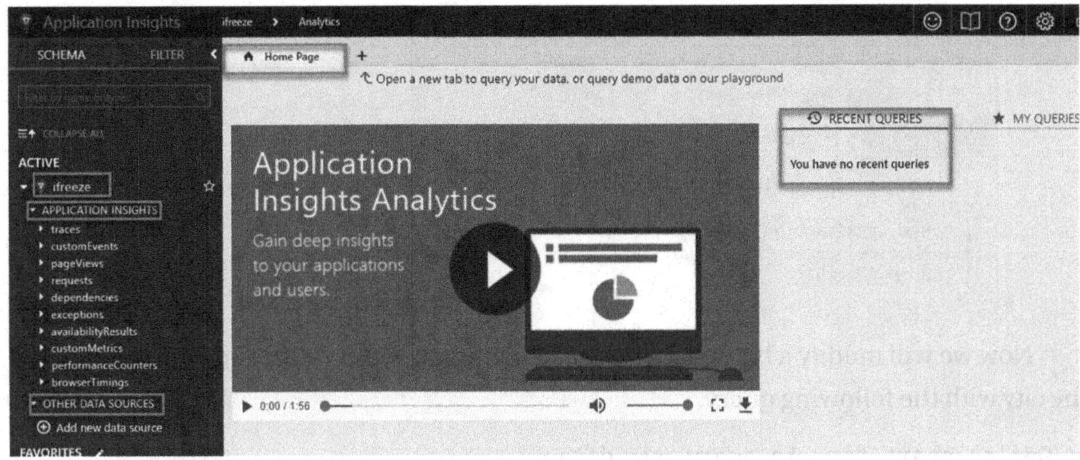

Application Insights enables you to track your application performance in a seamless way. You are able to specify queries on your resources and add other data sources in real time.

Let's look at a performance query example and review the 50th and 90th percentile of request durations in the past hour.

1. Go to the top bar and click the + icon.

2. Write the query as follows.

```
//Start our request
requests
//Define our time interval
| where timestamp >= ago(1h)
//Calculates the 50th  percentile
| summarize percentiles(duration, 50) by bin(timestamp, 2h)
//Render results
| render timechart
```

Tip With queries, you usually want to start with a filter to clean your data; this saves time.

Click **Go.**

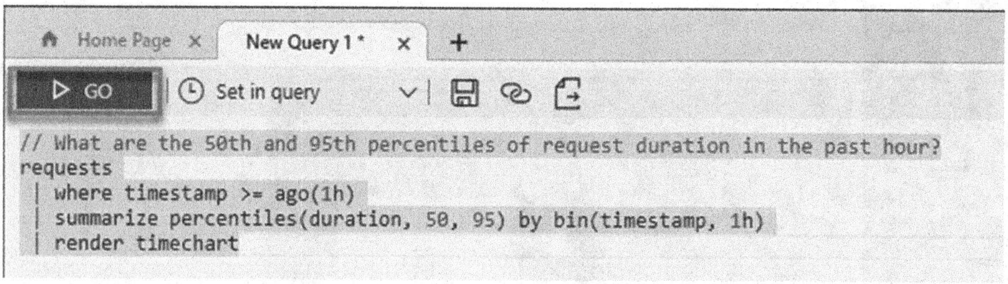

Home Page × New Query 1 * × +

GO | Set in query

```
// What are the 50th and 95th percentiles of request duration in the past hour?
requests
 | where timestamp >= ago(1h)
 | summarize percentiles(duration, 50, 95) by bin(timestamp, 1h)
 | render timechart
```

Now we will modify a bit the query by calculating the 50th, 75th, and 90th percentiles by city with the following query.

```
//Define start time to query our data
let startDate = datetime(2017-01-01T12:22:00);
//Define end time to query our data
let endDate = datetime(2018-01-30T15:18:00);
//Start our request
requests
//Define our time interval
| where timestamp between(startDate .. endDate)
//Calculates the 50th , 75th , and 90th  percentiles by city
| summarize percentiles(duration, 50, 75, 90) by client_City
//Render results
| render timechart
```

Click the Save icon.

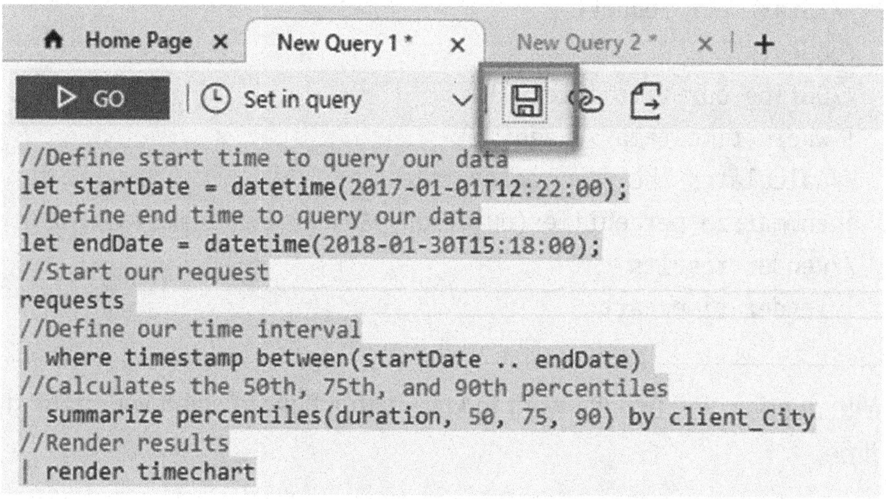

Home Page × New Query 1 * × New Query 2 * × +

GO | Set in query

```
//Define start time to query our data
let startDate = datetime(2017-01-01T12:22:00);
//Define end time to query our data
let endDate = datetime(2018-01-30T15:18:00);
//Start our request
requests
//Define our time interval
| where timestamp between(startDate .. endDate)
//Calculates the 50th, 75th, and 90th percentiles
| summarize percentiles(duration, 50, 75, 90) by client_City
//Render results
| render timechart
```

3. Name the query **Percentiles by City** and click **Save**.

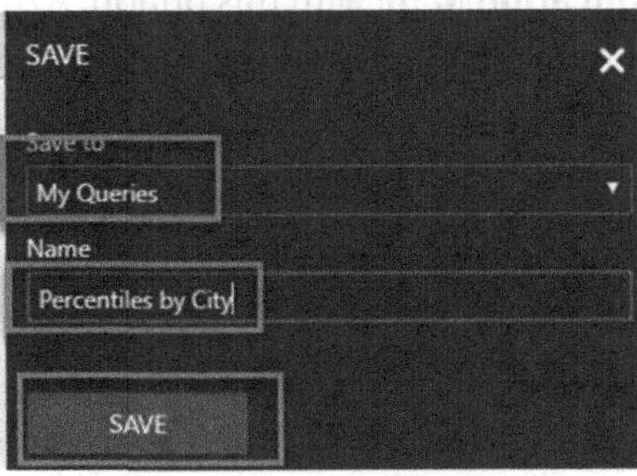

Azure also provides you an option within the Analytics portal to review your **favorites**, **saved** and **Shared** queries,

4. Go to the Analytics portal and click the top-right button. You will see this screen.

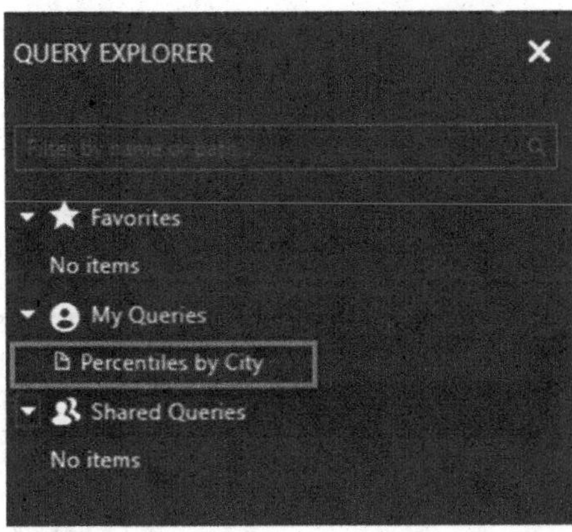

5. Return to the Azure portal and go to the Application Insights blade. Select **Application Map**; with this option, Azure provides a visual component to analyze the performance of your resource and its dependencies. Select a time range and the resource that you want to analyze, as shown in the image below.

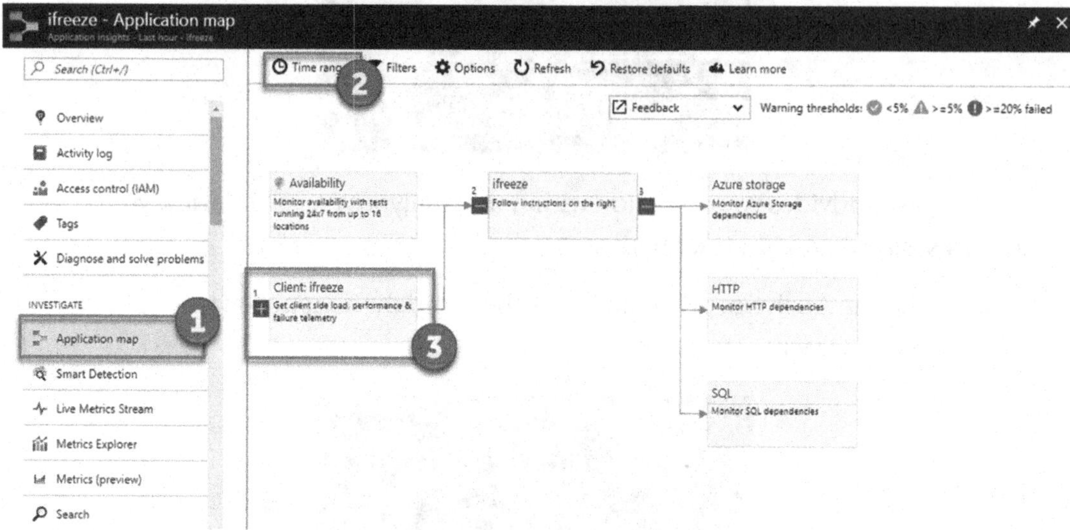

6. Select the **HTTP** dependencies and click **Start monitoring**.

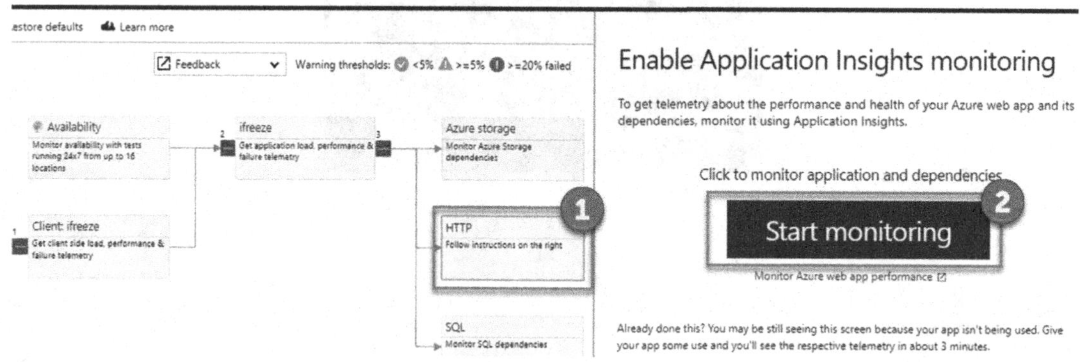

7. Enable an availability test.

Enable Application Insights monitoring

To get telemetry about the performance and health of your Azure web app and its dependencies, monitor it using Application Insights.

Application Insights extension installation is complete!

If you have traffic to your web app, or have added an availability test, then the data will light up in approximately 3 minutes.

Monitor Azure web app performance

While we're getting you set up...

Add an Availability test

Monitor your web application 24/7 from up to 16 locations worldwide

8. Now let's create the availability test. Select **Add test**. Provide a test name, type, and URL. You will also want to parse dependent requests and enable retries for availability test failures. Choose the time frequency at which this test will be executed periodically and the locations where you want to run this test. Finally, select the conditions to test if it is a failure or success, as shown in the image below.

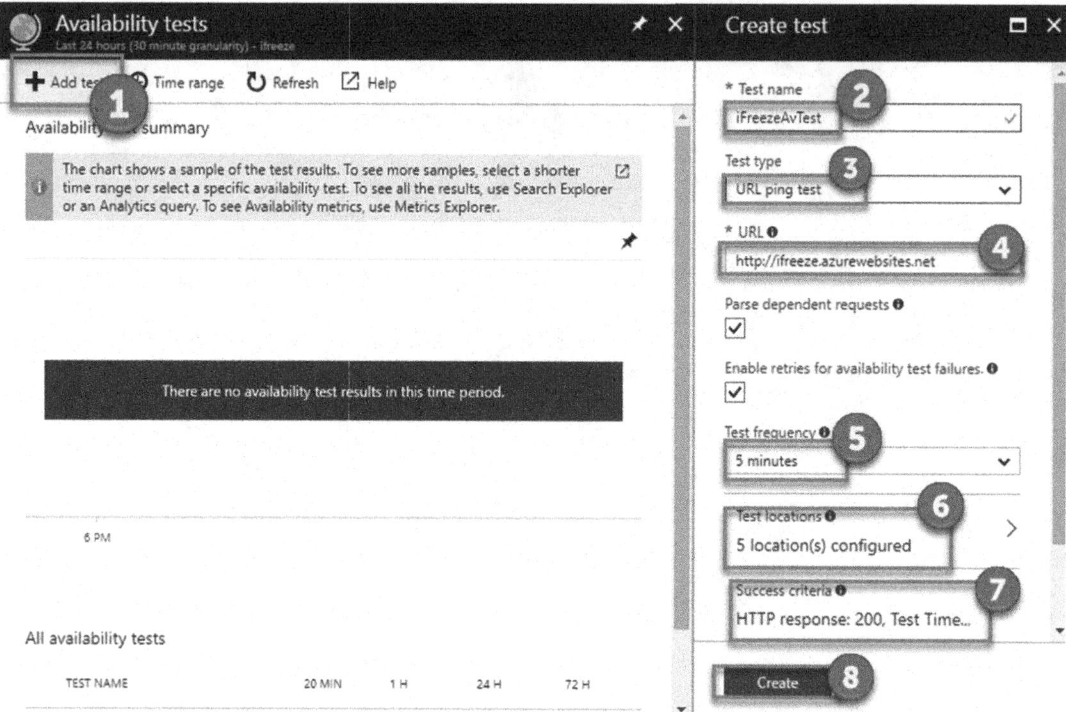

9. In order to provide scope to the iFreeze infrastructure and dev team, we could enable smart detection. Go to the Application Insight blade. Select **Smart Detection**. Click **Settings** and select the smart detection rule that you want to enable to provide detailed email notifications. Then provide the mail address and click **Save**.

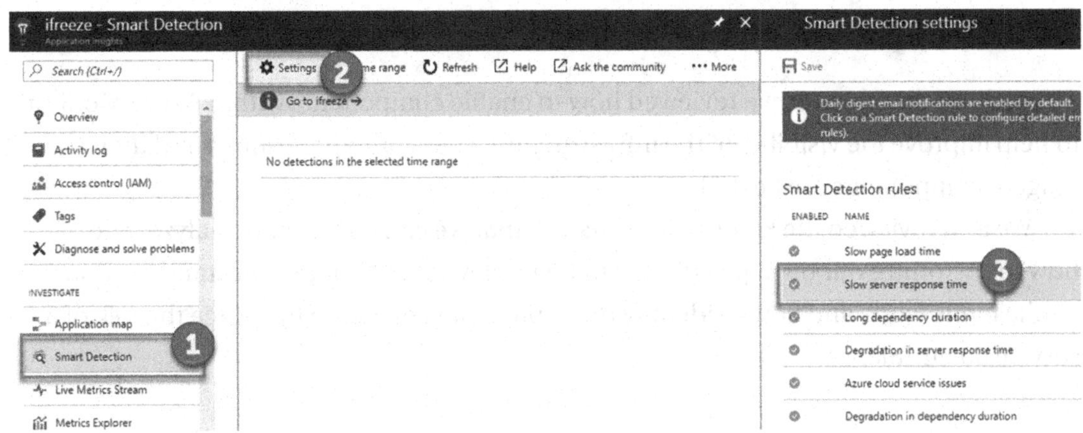

At the end of these steps, you are able to go back to your dashboard and review the key performance metrics that you added for the iFreeze environment, including errors, response time averages, availability tests, application maps, and data in and data out, as per the image below.

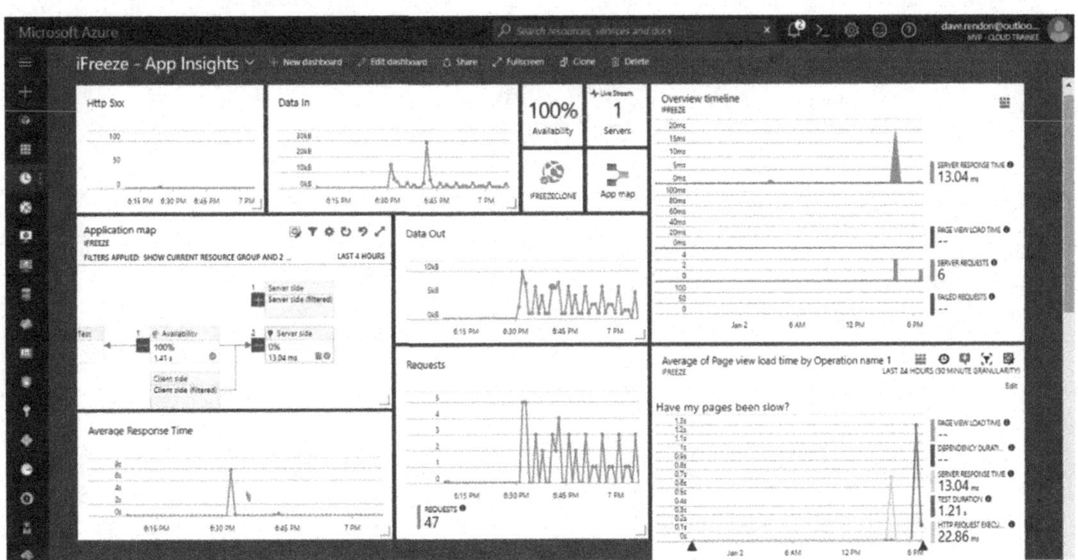

Summary

Throughout this chapter, we reviewed how to enable components within Azure Monitor to help improve the visibility of the infrastructure where our applications and their tangent components are hosted.

We also reviewed the kinds of information that we can collect and analyze, and how to customize our own queries within Log Analytics to better understand how our applications work, and how to identify potential points of failure to reduce the risk of a service downtime.

CHAPTER 7

Introduction to Azure Governance at Scale for the Enterprise

One of the core attributes of the cloud is the ability to operate at scale with speed and agility. Enabling and managing governance in Microsoft Azure for enterprise environments of all sizes also has scale and agility options. We have discussed and provided examples of using policies and initiatives to implement and maintain an organization's governance objective in Azure. In this chapter, we introduce scale options for governance management using automation and Azure blueprints.

This chapter is split into the following sections.

- Policy and Initiative Management Using Automation
- Introduction to Azure Blueprints
- Blueprints for Greenfield Environments
- Blueprints Life-Cycle Management

Policy and Initiative Management Using Automation

This section recaps the objectives shared in Chapter 4 and introduces the automation options available to you when managing at scale. It is important to note that when we mention scale, we do not mean large environments only. Scale, in our case, is better described as what happens in a restaurant. In a restaurant when you order a dish, it does not matter if it is for one or many. What matters is the ability to provide the same dish consistently regardless of how many. The same principles of consistency and

P. De Tender et al., *Pro Azure Governance and Security*, https://doi.org/10.1007/978-1-4842-4910-9_7

repeatability applies to a chain of restaurants, regardless of which location you go to, you expect to get the same dish.

Your Azure or on-premise environment shares the same principles as used at a chain of restaurants. Azure Policy is part of the toolkit to ensure that the environment is well-governed, complies with compliance and organizational objectives, and scales with consistency. There are other options in your toolkit to complete these objectives, as illustrated in Figure 7-1. These areas include migrating to the cloud, securing the cloud environment, IT continuity (backup and recovery), configuration management, and cost management.

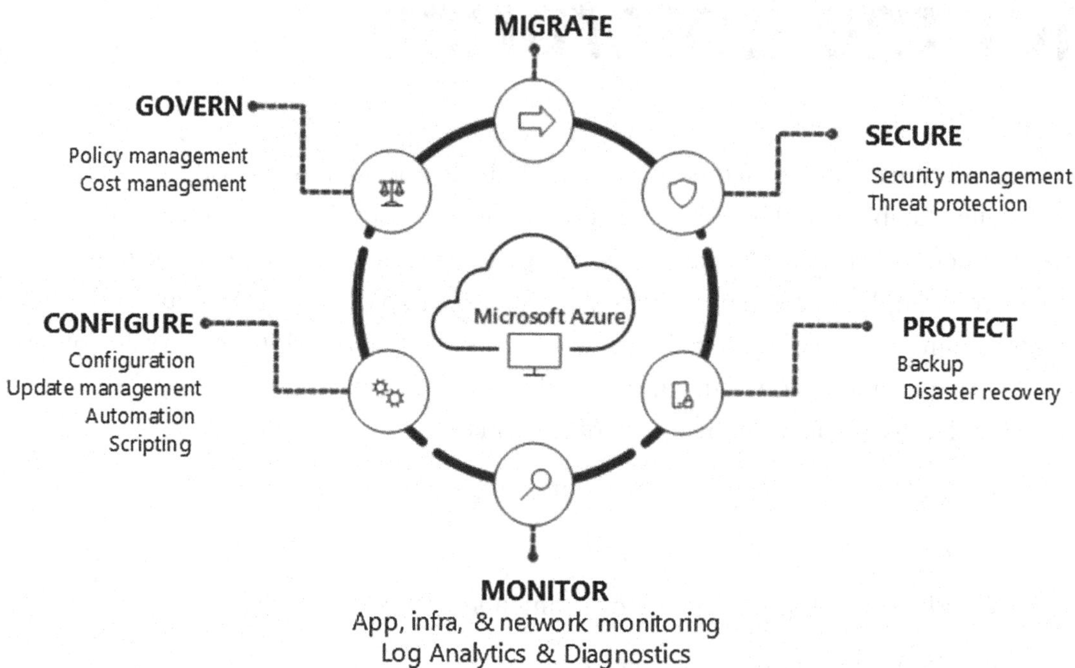

Figure 7-1. *https://docs.microsoft.com/en-us/azure/governance/azure-management*

Azure Resource Manager (ARM) Templates

The basic component in scope of your Azure governance and compliance management is a resource. All objects in Azure are fundamentally either a single resource or a collection of resources that are related and depend on each other to create a solution or service.

Azure Resource Manager (ARM) templates are the definitions of these resources or collections of related resources. When you use the Azure portal to create a resource, ARM creates this template in the background, and then invokes a deployment to create the resource on your behalf. ARM templates, when used in deployments, give you the ability to do scale deployments as well as document the settings used for the deployments. As an example, you can use the portal to create one virtual machine; but to create multiple virtual machines automatically, you use an ARM template that has multiple parameters, including the number of virtual machines, the naming prefix/suffix, and other unique properties. The portal wizard tabs are shown in Figure 7-2. Table 7-1 provides information about the tab requirements (some mandatory and others optional).

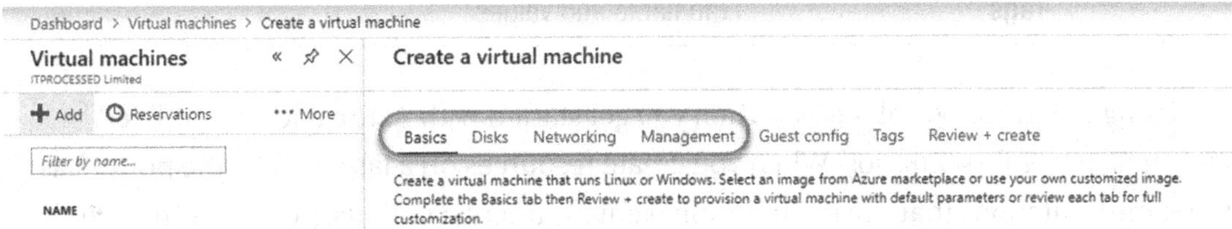

Figure 7-2. *Azure virtual machine wizard tabs*

Table 7-1. *Summary of Create VM Required Details in the Azure Portal*

Wizard Tab	Details
Basics	Subscription Resource group Virtual machine name Region Availability options Image Size Administrator account and authentication Inbound rules
Disks	OS disk type Data disks

(continued)

Table 7-1. (*continued*)

Wizard Tab	Details
Networking	Virtual network Public IP Load balancing
Management	Monitoring Identity Auto-Shutdown Backup
Guest config	Extensions
Tags	Tag name and values

Using the Azure portal is great when you get started with Azure and in simplified and small lab scale scenarios. When you create resources on a larger scale, the portal has the same limitations that exist in traditional environments: tedious, prone to errors, and human-scalable only. This is where ARM templates come into play. Using the Create VM feature as our example, you can use the following ARM template definition to deploy a VM.

```
{
  "$schema": "https://schema.management.azure.com/schemas/2015-01-01/
  deploymentTemplate.json#",
  "contentVersion": "1.0.0.0",
  "parameters": {
    "adminUsername": { "type": "string" },
    "adminPassword": { "type": "securestring" }
  },
  "variables": {
    "vnetID": "[resourceId('Microsoft.Network/virtualNetworks','myVNet')]",
    "subnetRef": "[concat(variables('vnetID'),'/subnets/mySubnet')]"
  },
  "resources": [
    {
      "apiVersion": "2016-03-30",
      "type": "Microsoft.Network/publicIPAddresses",
```

```
    "name": "myPublicIPAddress",
    "location": "[resourceGroup().location]",
    "properties": {
      "publicIPAllocationMethod": "Dynamic",
      "dnsSettings": {
        "domainNameLabel": "myresourcegroupdns1"
      }
    }
  },
  {
    "apiVersion": "2016-03-30",
    "type": "Microsoft.Network/virtualNetworks",
    "name": "myVNet",
    "location": "[resourceGroup().location]",
    "properties": {
      "addressSpace": { "addressPrefixes": [ "10.0.0.0/16" ] },
      "subnets": [
        {
          "name": "mySubnet",
          "properties": { "addressPrefix": "10.0.0.0/24" }
        }
      ]
    }
  },
  {
    "apiVersion": "2016-03-30",
    "type": "Microsoft.Network/networkInterfaces",
    "name": "myNic",
    "location": "[resourceGroup().location]",
    "dependsOn": [
      "[resourceId('Microsoft.Network/publicIPAddresses/',
      'myPublicIPAddress')]",
      "[resourceId('Microsoft.Network/virtualNetworks/', 'myVNet')]"
    ],
```

```
    "properties": {
      "ipConfigurations": [
        {
          "name": "ipconfig1",
          "properties": {
            "privateIPAllocationMethod": "Dynamic",
            "publicIPAddress": { "id": "[resourceId('Microsoft.Network/
            publicIPAddresses','myPublicIPAddress')]" },
            "subnet": { "id": "[variables('subnetRef')]" }
          }
        }
      ]
    }
  },
  {
    "apiVersion": "2016-04-30-preview",
    "type": "Microsoft.Compute/virtualMachines",
    "name": "myVM",
    "location": "[resourceGroup().location]",
    "dependsOn": [
      "[resourceId('Microsoft.Network/networkInterfaces/', 'myNic')]"
    ],
    "properties": {
      "hardwareProfile": { "vmSize": "Standard_DS1" },
      "osProfile": {
        "computerName": "myVM",
        "adminUsername": "[parameters('adminUsername')]",
        "adminPassword": "[parameters('adminPassword')]"
      },
      "storageProfile": {
        "imageReference": {
          "publisher": "MicrosoftWindowsServer",
          "offer": "WindowsServer",
          "sku": "2012-R2-Datacenter",
          "version": "latest"
        },
```

```
          "osDisk": {
            "name": "myManagedOSDisk",
            "caching": "ReadWrite",
            "createOption": "FromImage"
          }
        },
        "networkProfile": {
          "networkInterfaces": [
            {
              "id": "[resourceId('Microsoft.Network/
              networkInterfaces','myNic')]"
            }
          ]
        }
      }
    }
  ]
}
```

(Code reference `https://docs.microsoft.com/en-us/azure/virtual-machines/windows/ps-template`.)

In the example template, the required values are hardcoded. The recommended and common approach is to compliment the main ARM template JSON with a parameter template that takes input at the time of deployment. An example is a parameter file that gives you the option to specify the number of virtual machines to create. You can get additional information on using ARM, including creating and deploying templates, at `https://docs.microsoft.com/en-us/azure/azure-resource-manager/resource-manager-quickstart-create-templates-use-the-portal`.

Infrastructure as Code

In the previous section, we discussed and shared an example of using an ARM template to create a single or multiple virtual machines. However, like traditional environments, the virtual machines or resulting applications depend on the underlying resources. In the Azure, this would be resources like the network (VNets and subnets), storage accounts, key vaults, network security groups (NSG), and availability sets.

Deploying an environment as code is typically known as *infrastructure as code* (IaC). This approach requires an investment in the skills required to create, edit, and maintain ARM templates. Additionally, you cannot skip the planning and validation requirements for this level of automation. The Azure documentation and the various examples in the GitHub repositories allow you start with scale ARM deployments by leveraging sample templates that you can edit to suit your specific scenarios. The following two examples take you through two scenarios using the deploy template service in the Azure portal.

- Deploy multiple virtual machines using a template
- Deploy secure web applications using Windows virtual machines

Deploy Multiple Virtual Machines Using a Template

1. Connect to the Azure portal at `https://portal.azure.com`.
2. Click **+Create a resource**, and then click **See all** in the right-hand blade. Select **Compute**.
3. Click **More** and select **Template deployment** under Recommended in the far right-hand blade.

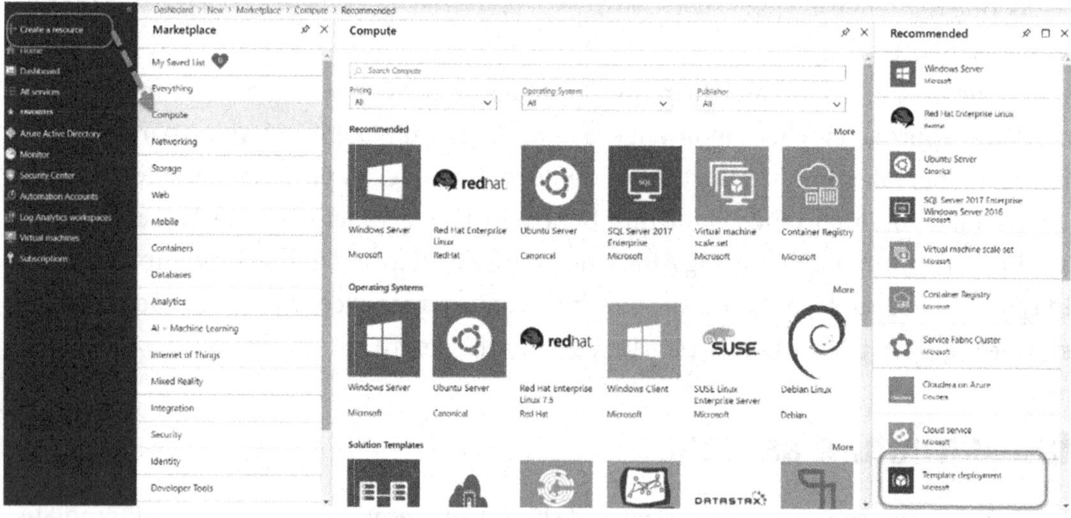

4. In the Template deployment blade, click **Create** to navigate to the Custom deployment blade. Note the options available to you.

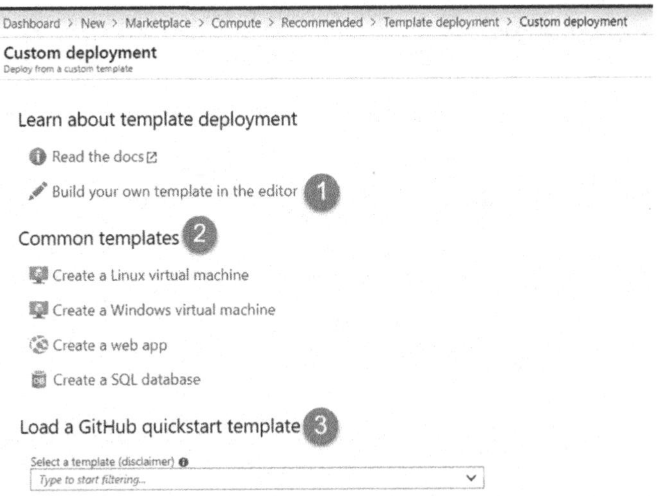

5. Under the **Load a GitHub quickstart template**, type **vm** in the filter field and select **201-vm-copy-managed-disks**.

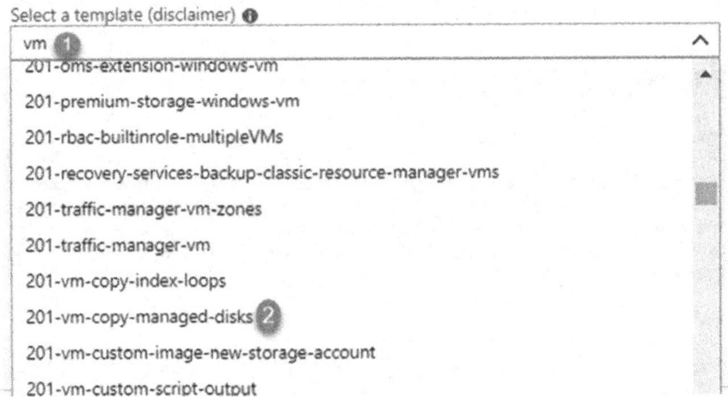

6. Click **Select template**, which opens the Multi VM Template with Managed Disk page with the option to fill in the parameters. You also have the option to edit the template or the template parameters.

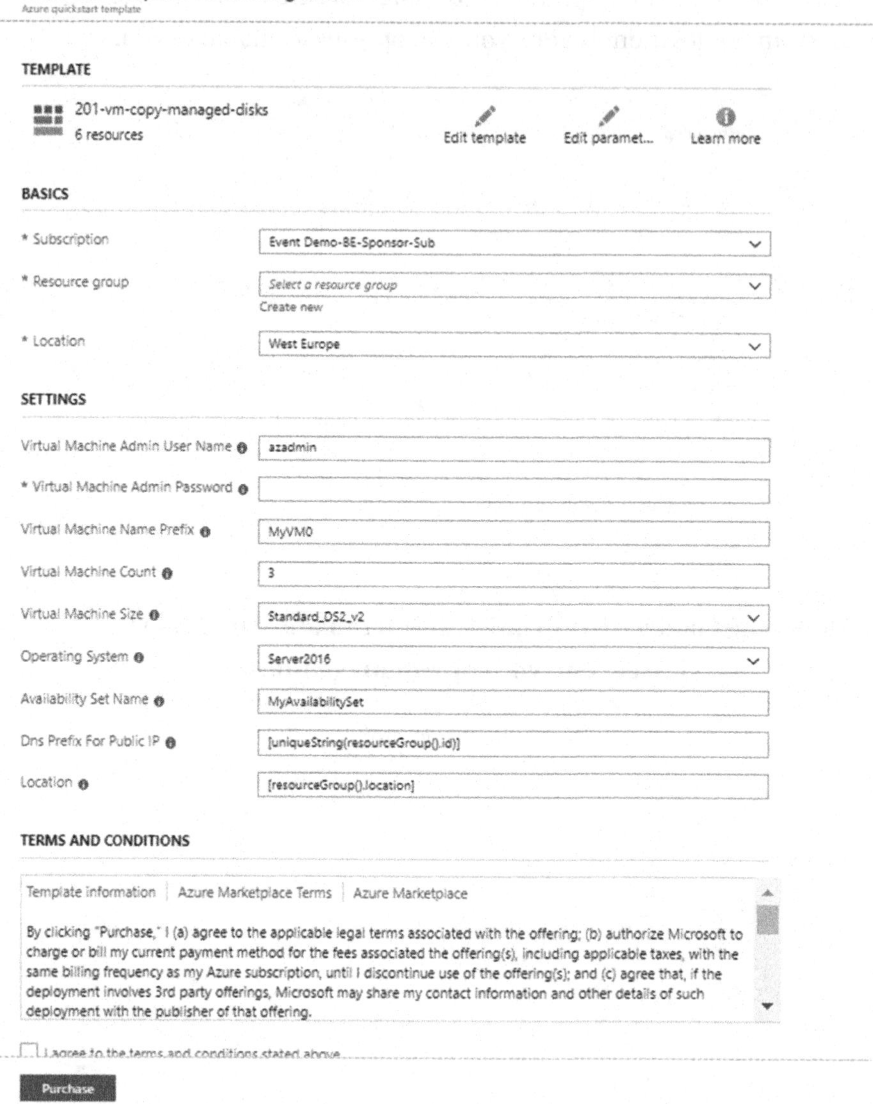

7. You can use the template as is by filling in the required information. Check the box to agree to the terms and conditions. Click **Purchase** to initiate the deployment of the multiple VMs (the default value is 3 but you can change this to suit your needs).

8. The result is a set of new virtual machines with the required resources created in a resource group under the subscription and resource group that you either selected or created in the front-end page.

Deploy Secure Web Applications Using Windows Virtual Machines

The second example is from the Microsoft documentation site at `https://docs.microsoft.com/en-us/azure/architecture/example-scenario/infrastructure/regulated-multitier-app`. Figure 7-3 is a copy of the architecture that is deployed when you use the template.

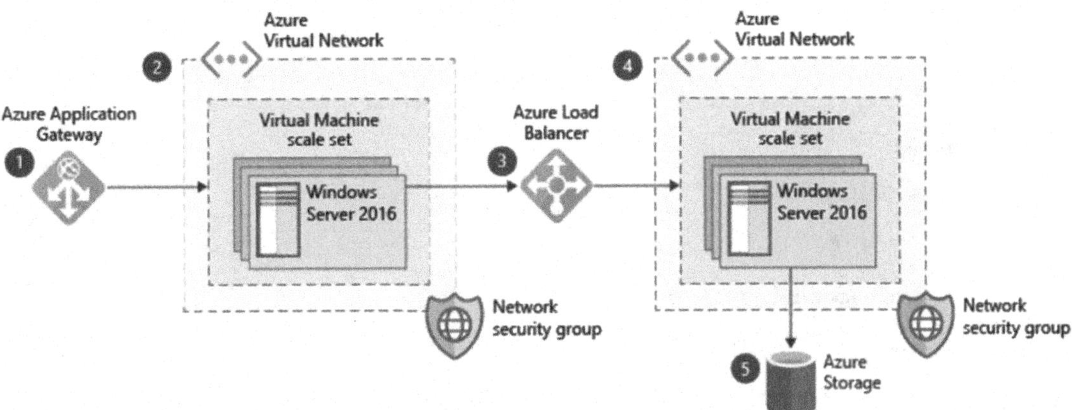

***Figure 7-3.** Secure web application deployment architecture*

The page details the components deployed with this template and gives you the option to deploy to Azure under the **Deploy the scenario** section. When you click **Deploy to Azure**, it connects to your Azure portal and the Custom deployment blade, as shown in Figures 7-4 and 7-5.

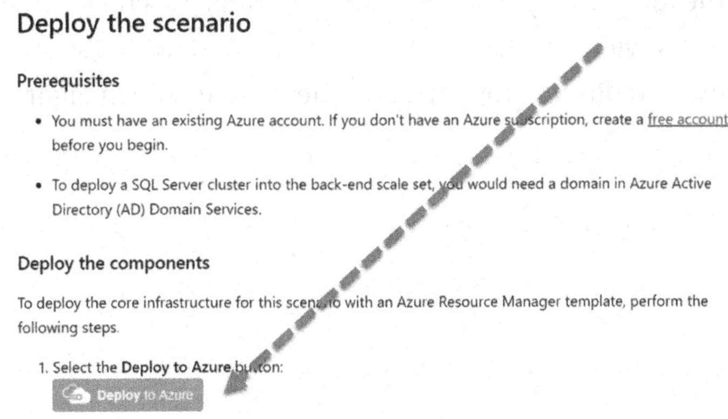

***Figure 7-4.** Invoking the Azure deployment*

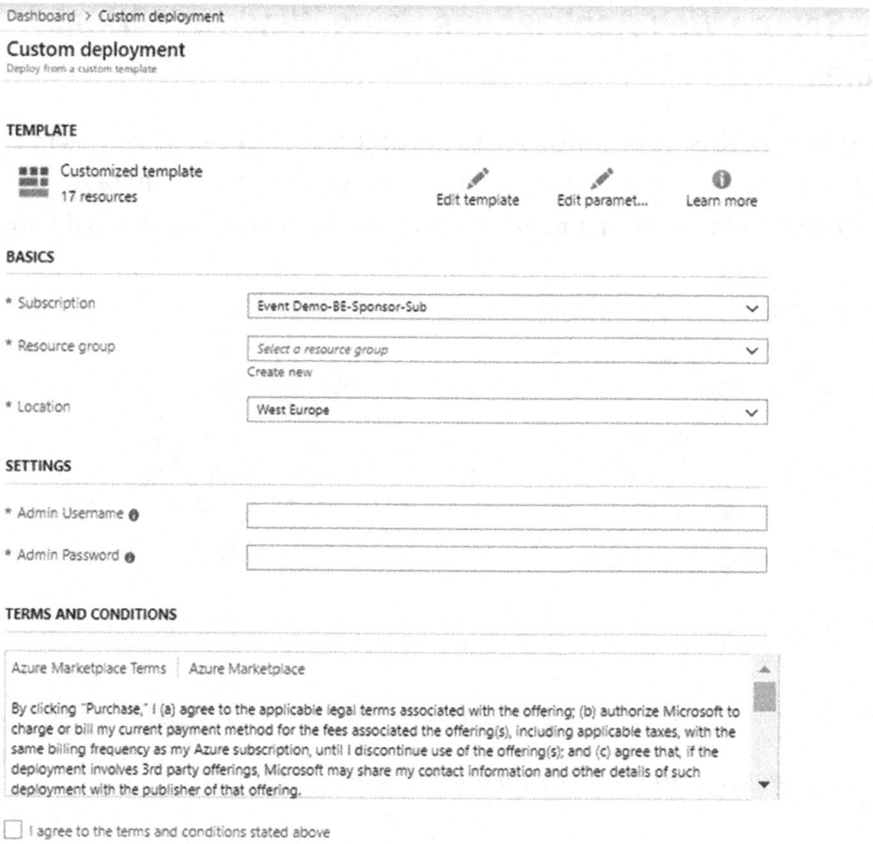

Figure 7-5. *Custom deployment page in Azure*

You can view the template by selecting **Edit template**, which opens the page shown in Figure 7-5. You can review the definition (see Figure 7-6), which shows the parameters, variables, and resource definition that matches the architecture in Figure 7-3.

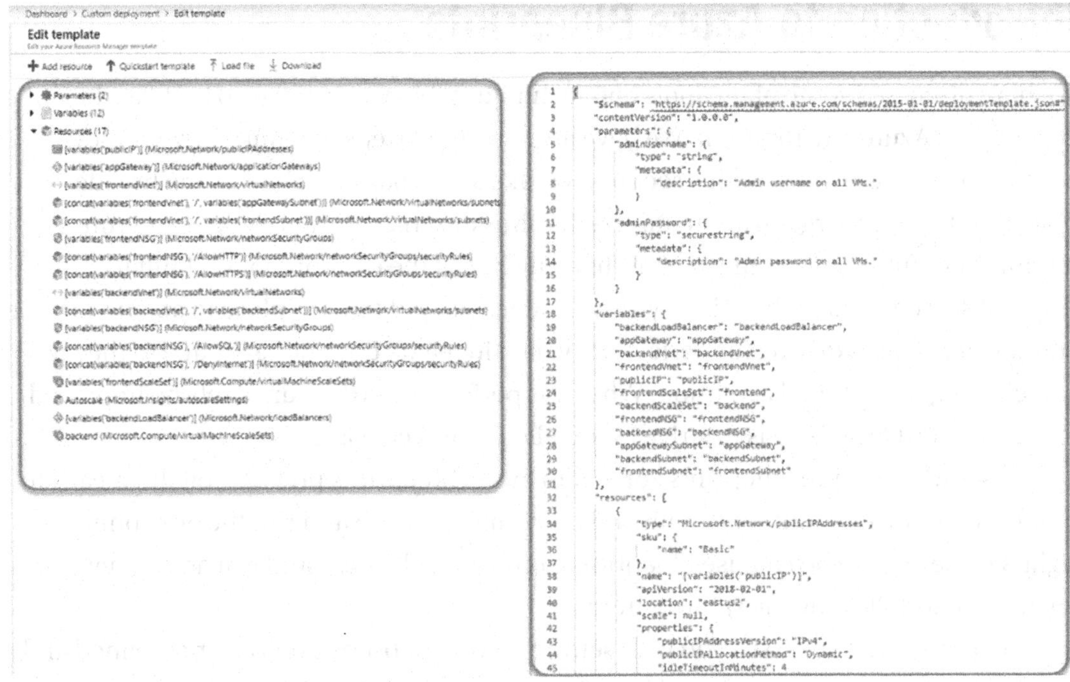

***Figure 7-6.** Template detail view*

You follow the same steps in the previous example to deploy this template. It is recommended that you perform these exercises in a test subscription. Publicly available free templates are great for getting started and learning, but in a live environment, you must ensure that you have performed the necessary planning and only allow authorized personnel the option to create resources in your subscription(s).

The preceding examples of IaC deployments are great but require you to manage these templates and their versions manually. You have the option to use tools like Visual Studio to control your template life cycle. Once your infrastructure is deployed, you will have to follow the steps in Chapter 4 to apply your governance objectives to the resources. Refer to Chapter 3 for steps on how to apply policies and initiatives to your Azure environments.

The next section discusses how you can simplify this process and add your governance artifacts to your scaled deployments.

Introduction to Azure Blueprints

We have discussed some of the tools and techniques that you can use to build and govern your Azure environment. We have also provided steps and links to resources on how to use these tools. In this section, we take a step back and look at the broader objective that every organization universally aims to achieve: "Built it right and run it right." Let's unpack what this means. In a nutshell, if the environment is built to the right standards and objectives, you do not need to put tools in place to adhere to compliance. This is driving for perfection, which in reality does not exist due to the laws of technology's continual evolution. What was perfect yesterday can surely be improved today. The next best thing is to strive for excellence and consistency.

This is where Azure blueprints come into focus. Blueprints provide you the means to build your Azure environments right and continually update and run the environment right. Furthermore, you can use blueprints to consistently build and run additional environments following the same patterns.

Blueprints in Azure assist you with setting up your subscriptions in a predefined and consistent manner.

The following is the official definition of blueprints from Microsoft (`https://docs.microsoft.com/en-us/azure/governance/blueprints/overview`).

> *Just as a blueprint allows an engineer or an architect to sketch a project's design parameters, Azure Blueprints enables cloud architects and central information technology groups to define a repeatable set of Azure resources that implements and adheres to an organization's standards, patterns, and requirements. Azure Blueprints makes it possible for development teams to rapidly build and stand up new environments with trust they're building within organizational compliance with a set of built-in components—such as networking—to speed up development and delivery.*

Explanations of the terminology used in Azure Blueprints, and how to define and use them, are briefly covered in the next sections.

Azure Blueprint Terminology

An Azure blueprint is a container that allows you to store one or more artifacts that you can assign to a subscription to build a consistent governed environment. The artifacts that you can store in a blueprint at the time of writing are

- Resource groups
- Azure Resource Manager templates
- Policy/Initiative assignments
- Role assignments

Figure 7-7 provides a pictorial representation of an Azure blueprint.

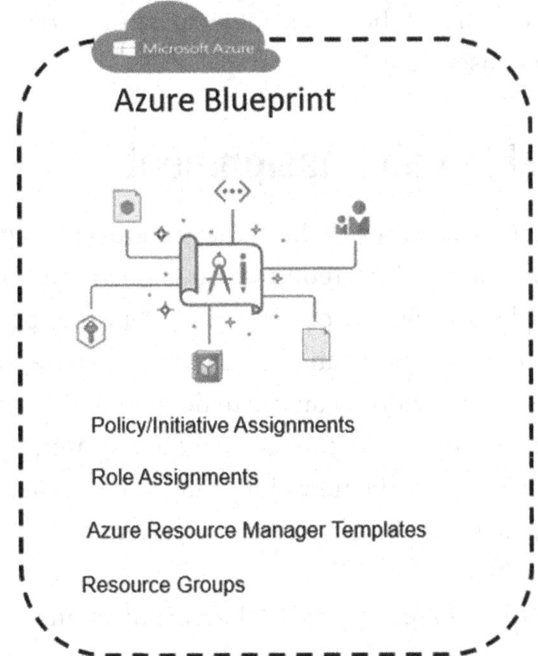

Figure 7-7. *Blueprint artifacts*

The simplest way to create and manage blueprints is through the Azure portal. The artifacts that you can use in a blueprint can be defined at the subscription or the resource group level of the definition.

Subscription level:

- Resource groups
- Azure Resource Manage templates
- Policy/Initiative assignments
- Role assignments

Resource group level:

- Azure Resource Manage templates
- Policy/Initiative assignments
- Role assignments

The blueprints that you define can be saved (location) either at a management group level or a subscription level. The policy/initiative assignment within the blueprint must be scoped at a level either at the blueprint location or below the blueprint location (management group or subscription).

Blueprint Publishing and Assignment

All new blueprints you create are set as a draft; they cannot be assigned in that state. You must first publish the blueprint, which requires you to provide a version and (optionally) notes. The version must be a string that can contain letters, numbers, and hyphens with a maximum length of 20 characters. Changes to a published blueprint require a new version and (optionally) notes that you can use to document the changes.

You can assign different versions of the blueprint to a subscription. If a subscription has a previous blueprint assigned, the new blueprint changes will be applied but the existing assignment artifacts remain. Given the assignment behavior, you must plan accordingly to avoid conflicts.

The following permissions are required for blueprint actions.

- **Create a blueprint definition:** `Microsoft.Blueprint/blueprints/write`
- **Create artifacts:** `Microsoft.Blueprint/blueprints/artifacts/write`
- **Publish a blueprint:** `Microsoft.Blueprint/blueprints/versions/write`
- **Delete a blueprint action:**
    - `Microsoft.Blueprint/blueprints/delete`
    - `Microsoft.Blueprint/blueprints/artifacts/delete`
    - `Microsoft.Blueprint/blueprints/versions/delete`

- **Blueprint assignment permissions:**
    - **Assign a blueprint:** `Microsoft.Blueprint/blueprintAssignments/write`
    - **Unassign a blueprint:** `Microsoft.Blueprint/blueprintAssignments/delete`

All the required permissions are part of the owner role. The contributor role has create and delete permissions but cannot assign or unassign blueprints. You can create a custom role for the purpose of blueprint role-based access control (RBAC).

Planning for Azure Blueprints

The use of blueprints requires some upfront planning and considerations. The following are the areas to consider in planning for your blueprints.

Location: Where you save the blueprint is key to your assignment capabilities. It is recommended that you save the blueprint as high as necessary in your management group hierarchy. This is covered in Chapter 4 of this book. It is important to note that you can only change the location by deleting and re-creating the blueprint.

Naming convention: The naming of a blueprint is up to you. You cannot have spaces in the name. Use an agreed upon naming convention for your organization and be consistent. A good naming convention facilitates your ease of management and reporting.

Version names: The version names that are typically used are like version standards for software; for example, use 1.0, 2.0, and so forth, to denote major versions, and use 1.1, 2.1 to denote changes that are minor to the major versions. Though the notes section is optional, plan to use this to document changes made to a previous version of the blueprint.

Artifacts: Plan to test the artifacts you use in a blueprint prior to adding to the definition; for example, ensure that you have validated the policy or initiatives work as expected prior to using in a blueprint definition and assignment.

Plan to review the online documentation on blueprints at `https://docs.microsoft.com/en-us/azure/governance/blueprints/overview`, where you will find information on blueprints and multiple samples of blueprints.

Blueprints for Greenfield Environments

In the previous section, we introduced Azure blueprints. In this section and throughout the rest of the chapter, we delve into creating and managing the life cycle of blueprints in greenfield and brownfield environments.

When you access the blueprints node in the Azure portal, you are presented with the Getting Started page, as shown in Figure 7-8.

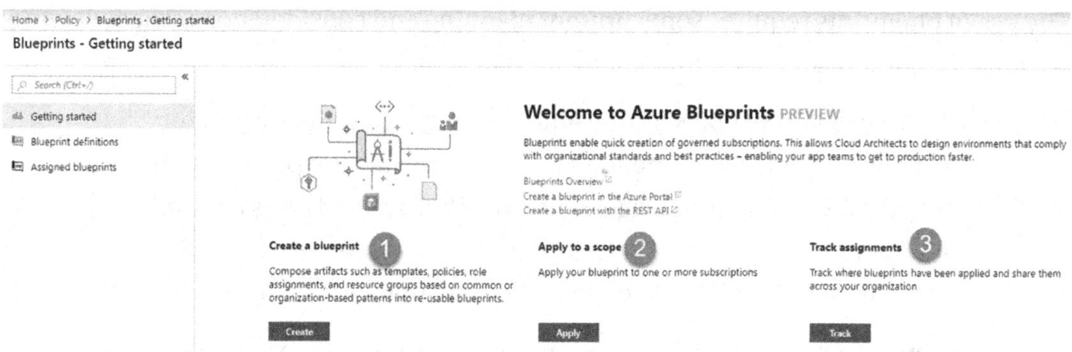

Figure 7-8. *Blueprints Getting Started node*

There are three top stages of a blueprint.

- **Create:** You create a new blueprint, starting with a definition that has no artifacts, or you start with one of the samples provided.
- **Apply:** The process of applying to a scope is effectively the assignment of a blueprint. At the time of writing, you can only assign a blueprint to a subscription.
- **Track:** This is the life-cycle management of assigned blueprints. View and update assigned blueprints.

Creating Blueprint Definitions

We will use two scenarios to illustrate the creation of a new blueprint definition.

- **Scenario 1:** The blueprint for POC and Sandbox subscriptions.
- **Scenario 2:** The blueprint to set up subscriptions with three resource group environments, with a resource group dedicated to automation accounts and log analytic workspaces.

The scenario 1 planning details are listed in Table 7-2.

Table 7-2. *Scenario One Planning Details*

Artifact	Artifact Details	Notes
Blueprint name	bp-poc-environments	Blueprint used for POC subscriptions
Version format	1.0	Starting version number sequence. Subsequent versions will be incremented
Role access	N/A	This blueprint does not assign roles
Resource Groups	Specified but not static	Resource group information at blueprint assignment
ARM Resource template	N/A	Will not use an ARM resource template
Policy/Initiatives	Allowed VM SKUs, Patch Settings Tag and Environment Tag	Default policies deployed by this subscription

It is important to note that you must create the artifacts you need in the blueprint beforehand. In our example, we created two initiatives: one to be used at the subscription level and one to be used at the resource group level. Additionally, we have Azure AD groups with members. You can create your equivalent policies/initiatives and Azure AD groups or users for the steps.

Create Blueprint Definition (Scenario 1)

1. Connect to the Azure portal at `https://portal.azure.com`.
2. Navigate to blueprints. Click **All services**. Type **blue** in **All services** filter and click **Blueprints**.

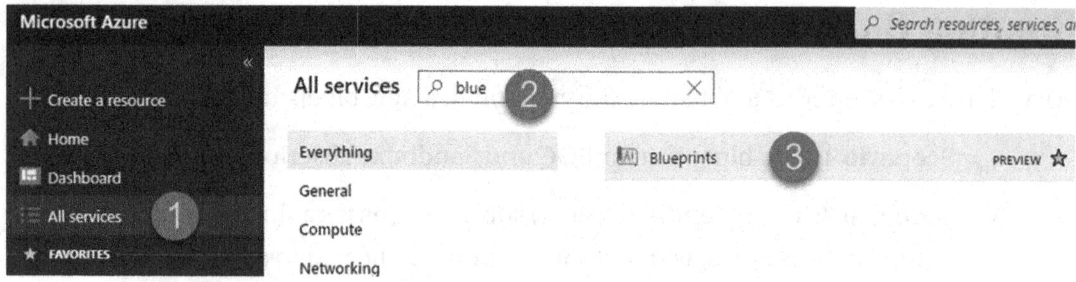

3. In the Getting Started node, click **Create**. This opens the Create Blueprint node and requires you to choose a blueprint sample.

Dashboard > Blueprints - Getting started > Create blueprint

Create blueprint

Choose a blueprint sample

You can start with a blank blueprint or pick one of our pre-defined samples to help you get started quickly

Blank Blueprint

An empty blueprint with no initial properties or artifacts.

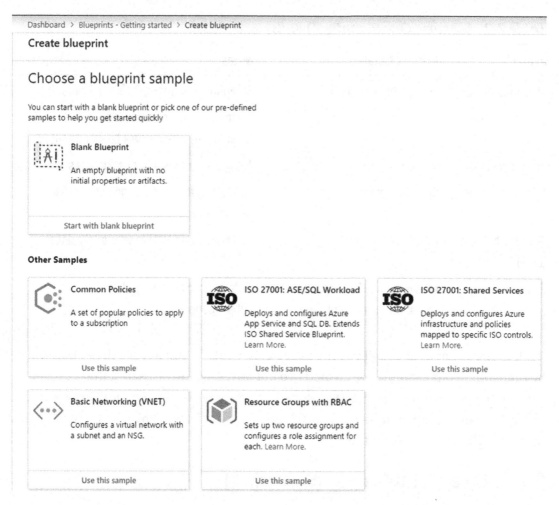

Start with blank blueprint

Other Samples

Common Policies

A set of popular policies to apply to a subscription

Use this sample

ISO 27001: ASE/SQL Workload

Deploys and configures Azure App Service and SQL DB. Extends ISO Shared Service Blueprint. Learn More.

Use this sample

ISO 27001: Shared Services

Deploys and configures Azure infrastructure and policies mapped to specific ISO controls. Learn More.

Use this sample

Basic Networking (VNET)

Configures a virtual network with a subnet and an NSG.

Use this sample

Resource Groups with RBAC

Sets up two resource groups and configures a role assignment for each. Learn More.

Use this sample

4. Select **Start with blank blueprint.**

5. Type a name for the blueprint—remember no spaces allowed. We use **bp-poc-environments** in our example.

6. Optionally, but recommended, provide a description. Select a location. In our example, this is our agreed management group location.

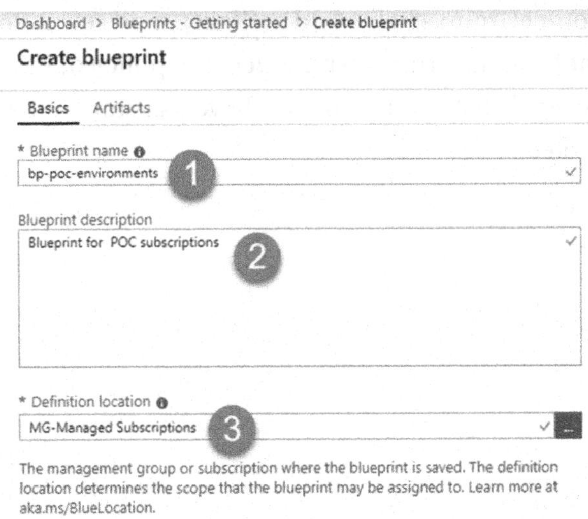

7. Click **Next: Artifacts**. Under Subscription, click + **Add artifact...** and select **Policy assignment** from the artifact type.

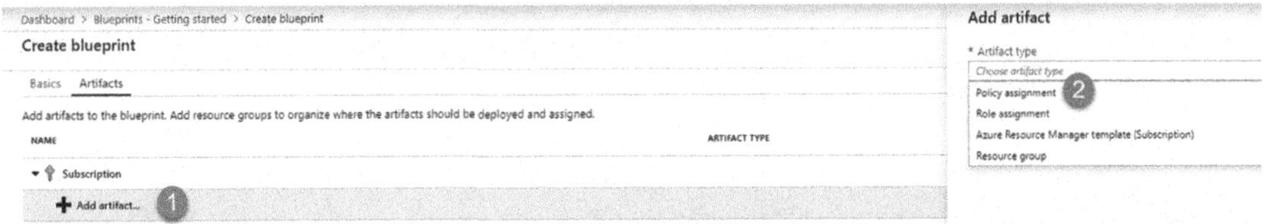

8. In our case, we select an initiative called BP-INI-Default Subscription Policies. (This initiative has three policies configured to be used for all default subscriptions.)

9. Under Subscription, click + **Add artifact...** and select **Resource Group** from the artifact type. Leave the default check boxes in place for **This value should be specified when the blueprint is assigned**, and click **Add**.

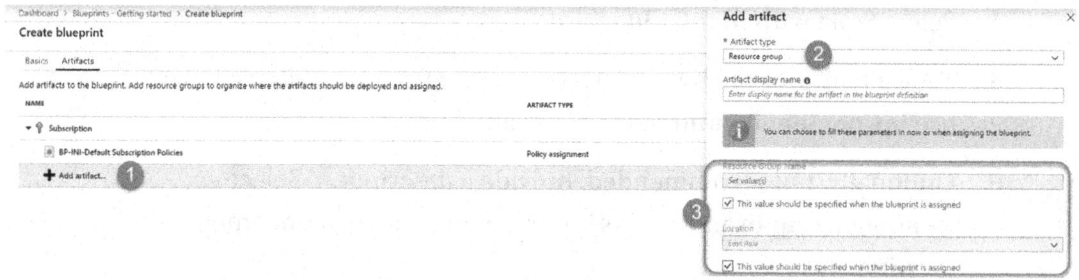

10. Under ResourceGroup, click **+Add artifact...** and select **Policy assignment** from the artifact type. Select the policy or initiative from the available list. In our case, we have a custom initiative created to select.

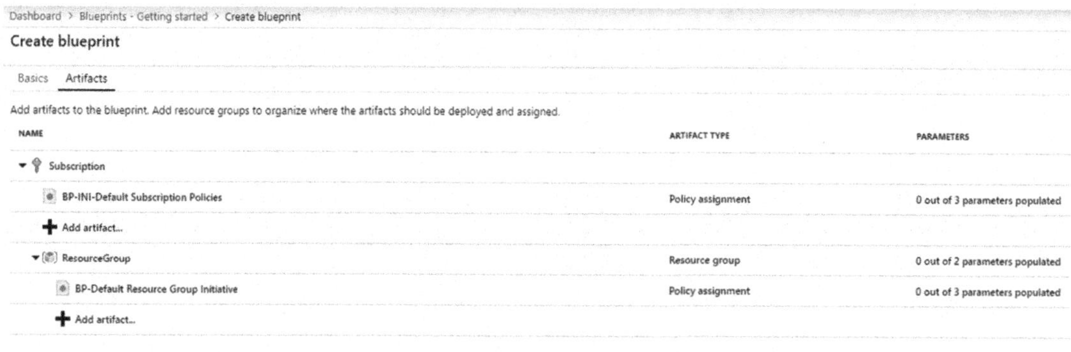

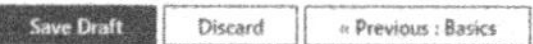

11. Review the blueprint definition and click **Save Draft** to complete the process.

12. Click the Blueprints Definitions node to verify that the blueprint has been created and is showing as a draft.

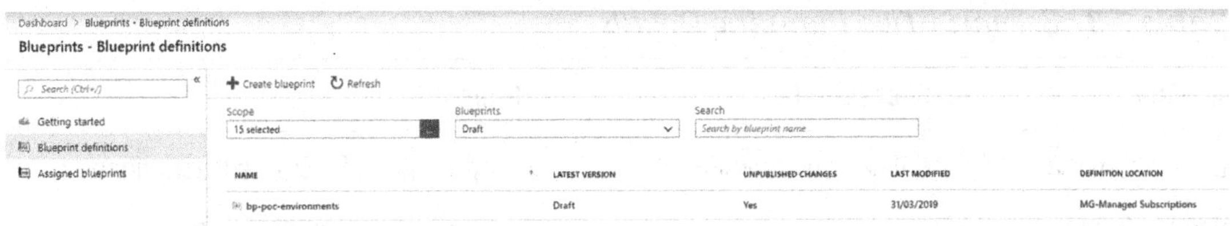

a. Note the name and the latest version (draft on first creation).

b. The Unpublished Changes field should show a value of Yes.

c. The date when you created it and the location will be the management group location where you saved the blueprint.

13. Click the draft blueprint and select **Publish blueprint**. Type a version value (for example, 1.0) and optionally type the details into the Change Notes field. Click **Publish**.

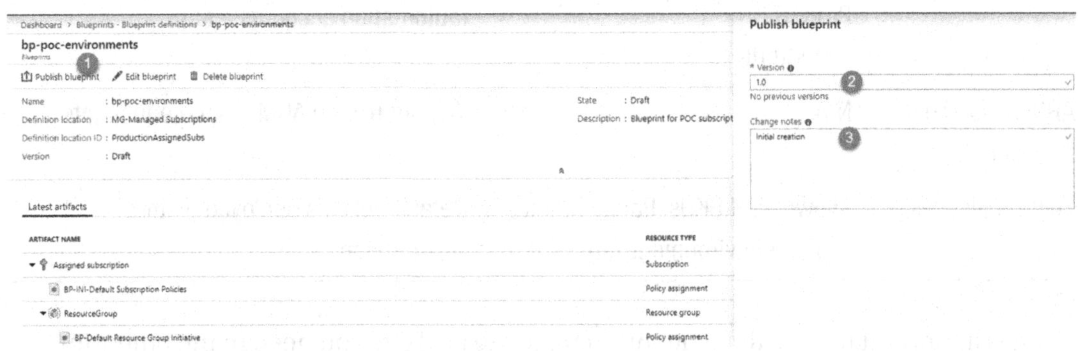

The blueprint is now ready to be used in assignments. We discuss assigning blueprints in the next section, but before moving on, let's look at scenario 2 using the planning details in Table 7-3.

***Table 7-3.** Scenario Two Planning Details*

Artifact	Artifact Details	Notes
Blueprint name	bp-default-environments	Blueprint used for POC subscriptions
Version format	1.0	Starting version number sequence. Subsequent versions will be incremented
Role access	Global Sub Admins – Owner Update Management Admins – Contributor User with reader rights to all resource groups	Custom global admins group have owner rights at the subscription level. Update management admins have contributor role on resource groups deployed by this blueprint.
Resource Groups	DevRG Pre-ProdRG ProdRG IaaSMgtRG	Resource group for IaaS and resource group for management of IaaS VMs (automation accounts, etc.)
ARM Resource template	N/A	Will not use an ARM resource template
Policy/Initiatives	Allowed VM SKUs, Patch Settings Tag and Environment Tag	Default policies deployed by this subscription

It is important to note that you must create the artifacts you need in the blueprint beforehand. In our example, we have created two initiatives: one to be used at the subscription level and one to be used at the resource group level. Additionally, we have the Azure AD groups with members. You can create your equivalent policies/initiatives and Azure AD groups or users for the steps.

Create Blueprint Definition (Scenario 2)

1. In the Getting Started node of Blueprints, click **Create**, which opens the Create Blueprint node and requires you to choose a blueprint sample.

2. Click **Use this sample** on the Resource Groups with RBAC sample.

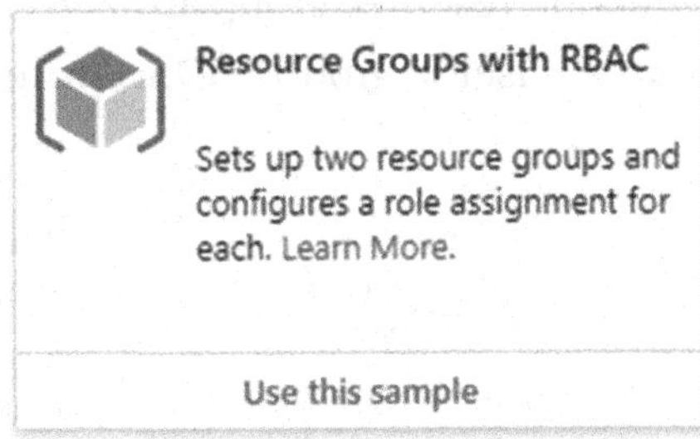

Resource Groups with RBAC
Sets up two resource groups and configures a role assignment for each. Learn More.
Use this sample

3. Type a name for the blueprint—remember no spaces allowed. We use **bp-default-environments** in our example.

4. Optionally, but recommended, provide a description. Select a location. In our example, this is our agreed upon management group location.

5. Click **Next: Artifacts.** Note that this sample has preconfigured artifacts that can be edited or removed. You can also add your own artifacts.

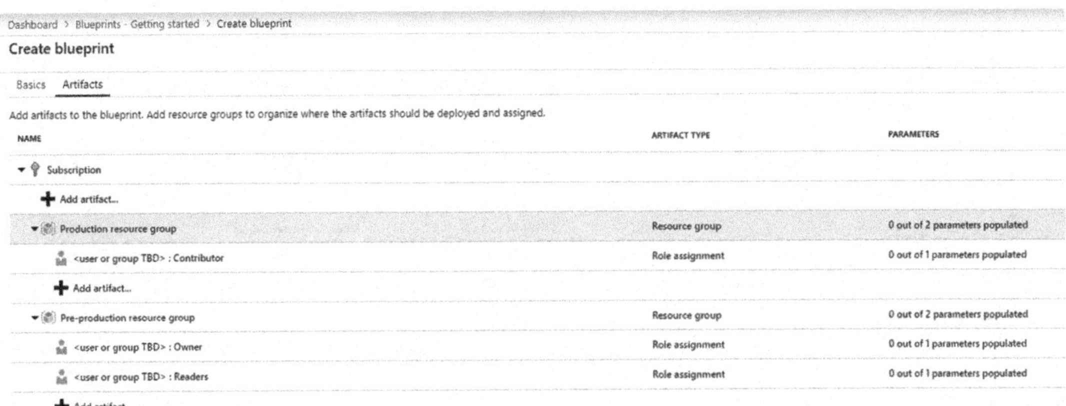

6. Under Subscription, click + **Add artifact...** and select **Resource group** from the artifact type. Type **Development resource group** in the Artifact Display Name field, and click **Add.**

7. Under the new resource group name (development resource group), click + **Add artifact....** Select **Role assignment**. Select the **Owner role** and click **Add.**

8. Repeat the previous step and an additional role by selecting **Reader.**

9. Under the Pre-Production resource group artifact, click the **...** button at the end of the <user or group TBD>: Owner and click **Edit artifact**.

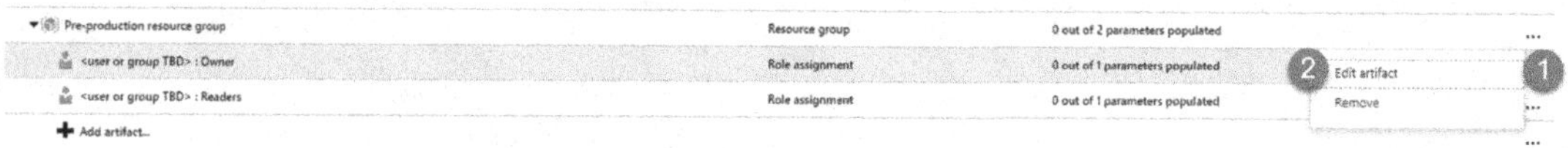

10. Change the value to **Contributor** and click **Save**.

11. In our example, we also added an initiative to the subscription level and an initiative to each of the resource group levels. Perform this step by selecting + **Add artifact** and selecting **Policy assignment** for the artifact type.

12. Finally, click **Save draft** to complete the definition.

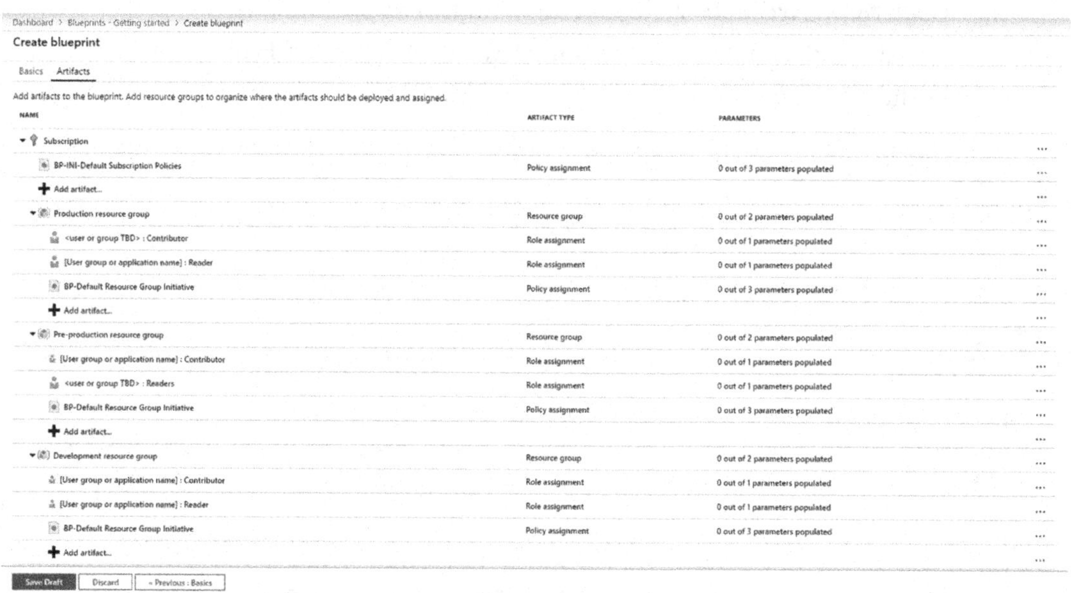

13. Under Blueprint Definitions, select the draft blueprint. Follow the steps used in scenario 1 to publish it.

Assigning Blueprints

The previous section followed the steps to create two blueprint definitions. The next step is to assign the definition to a subscription. In our next example, we assign the scenario 2 blueprint to a new subscription. Note that at the time of writing, blueprints can only be assigned to a subscription, and not at the management group level.

1. In the Azure portal, navigate to Blueprints.
2. Under Blueprint definitions, select the scenario 2 blueprint you created by clicking it.
3. Click **Assign blueprint**.

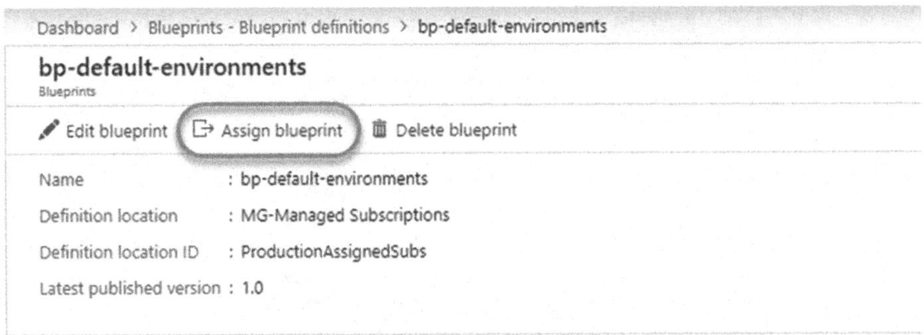

4. Select the applicable subscription. Optionally, change the assignment name. Optionally, change the location (Azure Region). Set the lock assignment to **Read Only**.

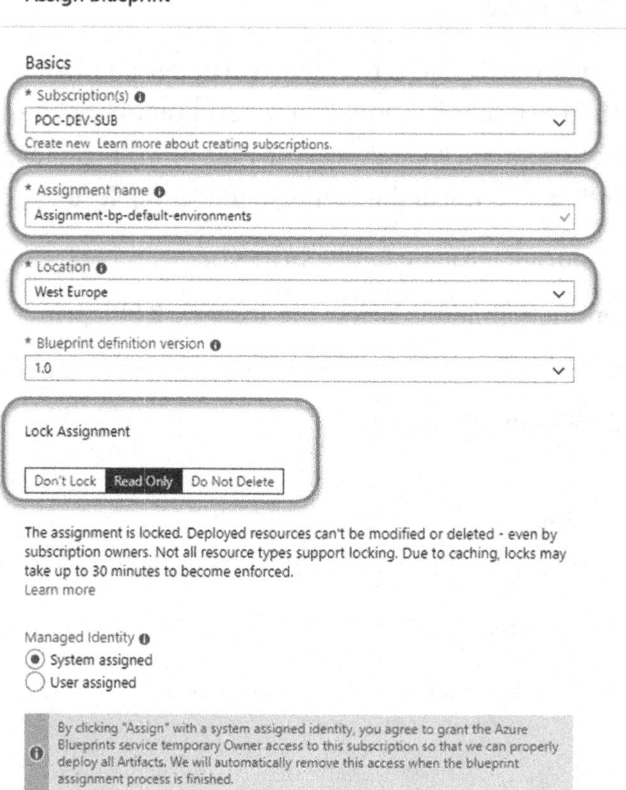

5. Under the artifact section, configure the parameter values for each artifact type that was set to request this information at assignment time. In our example,

   a. The subscription initiative requires an owner, which you pick from a list of values, an environment value, and a cost center value.

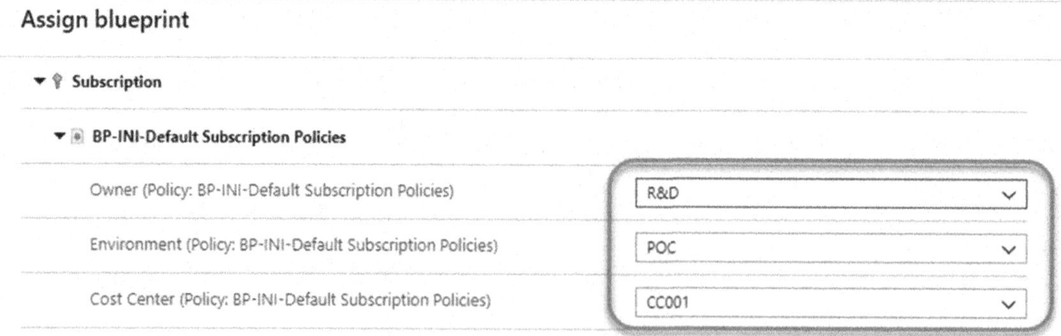

b. Under each resource group artifact level, the artifacts also require values: resource group name, the group or user to be granted contributor role access, and the reader role access user/group. The initiative requires the allowed SKUs values, as well as tag values to support update management.

Production resource group

Resource Group: Name — ProdRG

Resource Group: Location — West Europe

[User group or application name] : Reader

[User group or application name] ([User group or application name] : Reader) — rstar (rstar@itprocessed.com)

<user or group TBD> : Contributor

Prod contributors - User or Group — Update Management Admins (null)

BP-Default Resource Group Initiative

Allowed SKUs (Policy: BP-Default Resource Group Initiative) — ["Standard_D1_v2","Standard_D2_v2"]

Patch Phase (Policy: BP-Default Resource Group Initiative) — 3

Reboot Allowed (Policy: BP-Default Resource Group Initiative) — No

Pre-production resource group

Resource Group: Name — Pre-ProdRG

Resource Group: Location — West Europe

[User group or application name] : Contributor

[User group or application name] ([User group or application name] : Contributor) — Update Management Admins (null)

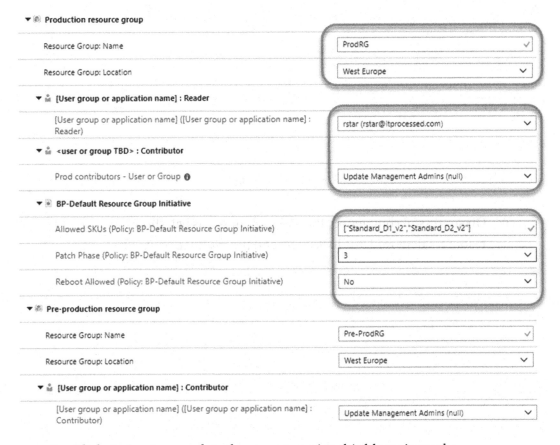

6. Click **Assign** to complete the steps to assign this blueprint to the selected subscription.

7. Navigate to the Assigned Blueprints node. This will initially show a provisioning state of waiting.

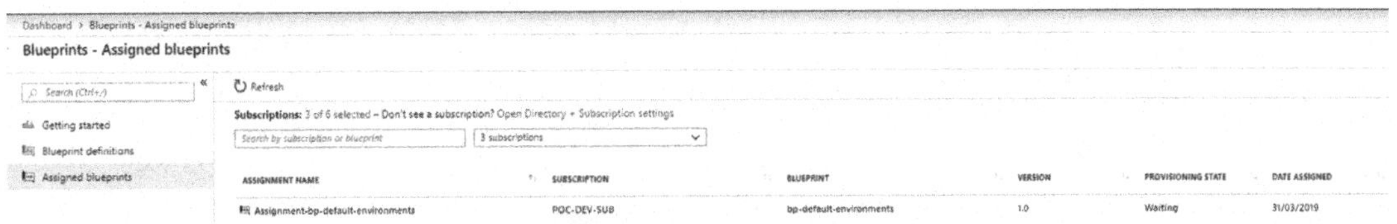

8. Click the blueprint assignment to view the current status. It should show the progress of the artifact deployments.

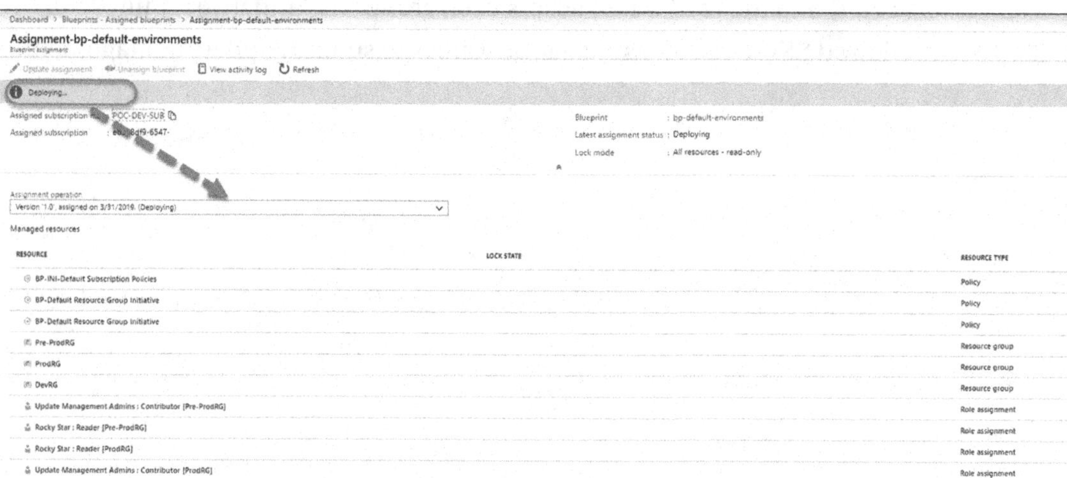

9. On successful completion, the assignment status will show the resources deployed, the lock state, and the resource type.

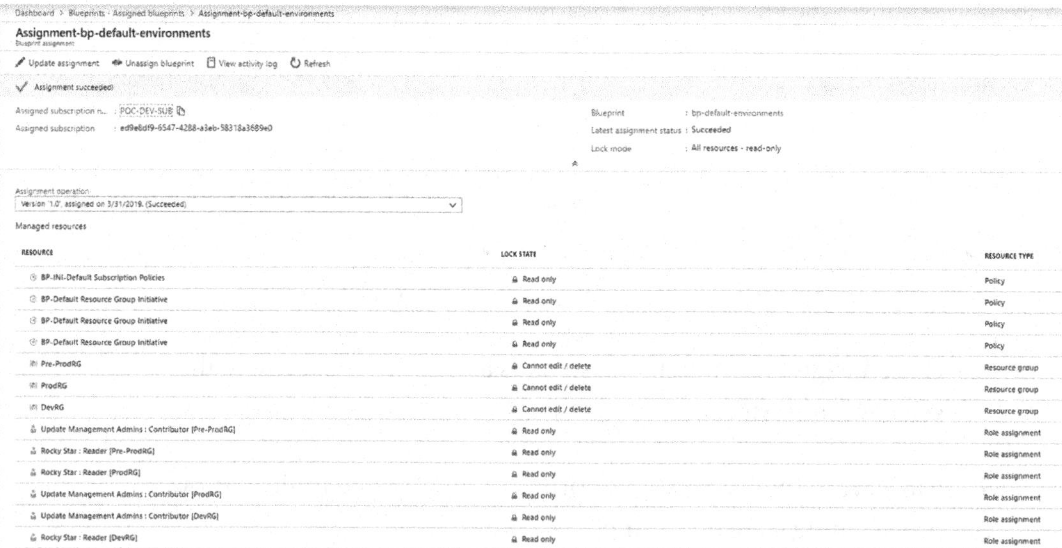

10. Review the target subscription to verify the assignment. In our case, the specified resource groups are shown as successfully created.

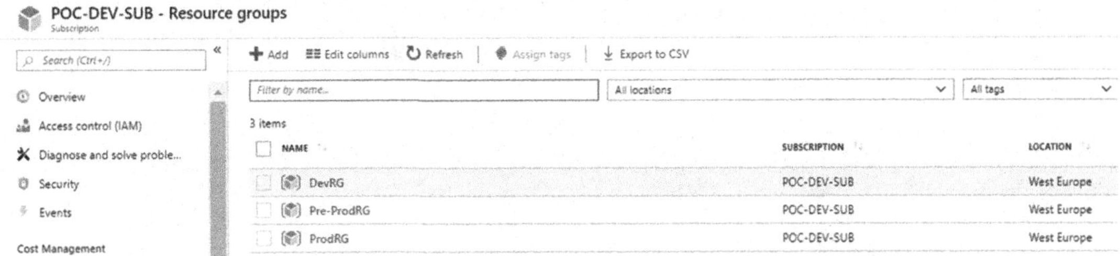

The respective policies are assigned to the resource groups.

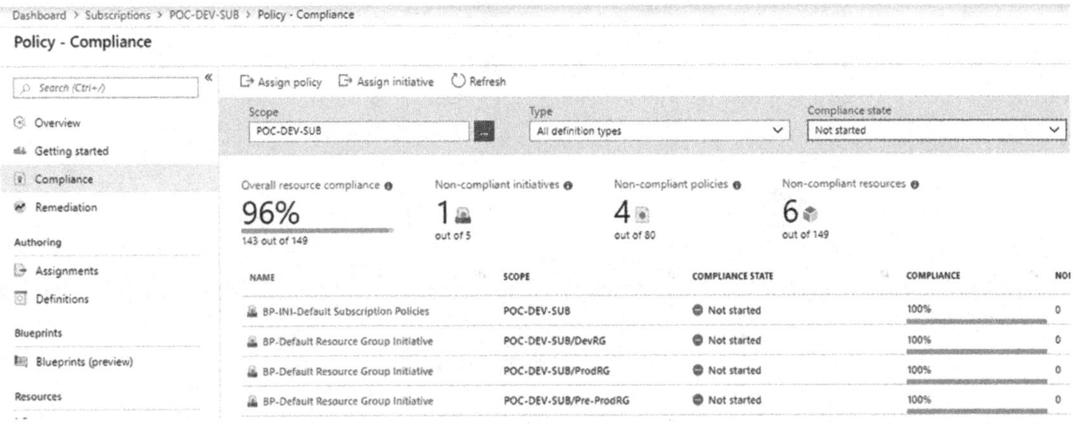

Using blueprints, you have a consistent process to ensure that your environment is deployed with the necessary artifacts and guardrails. The sample blueprints provided are a great resource to get you started. Microsoft continues to add samples. The ISO 270001 sample is the most comprehensive blueprint definition available to you.

You can get additional information from the samples at `https://docs.microsoft.com/en-us/azure/governance/blueprints/samples/`.

Figure 7-9 is the architecture of the ISO 27001 Share Services blueprint from the Microsoft documentation site. This is one of the samples that you can use when you create your own blueprints. All the resources shown in the diagram are deployed when you assign the blueprint.

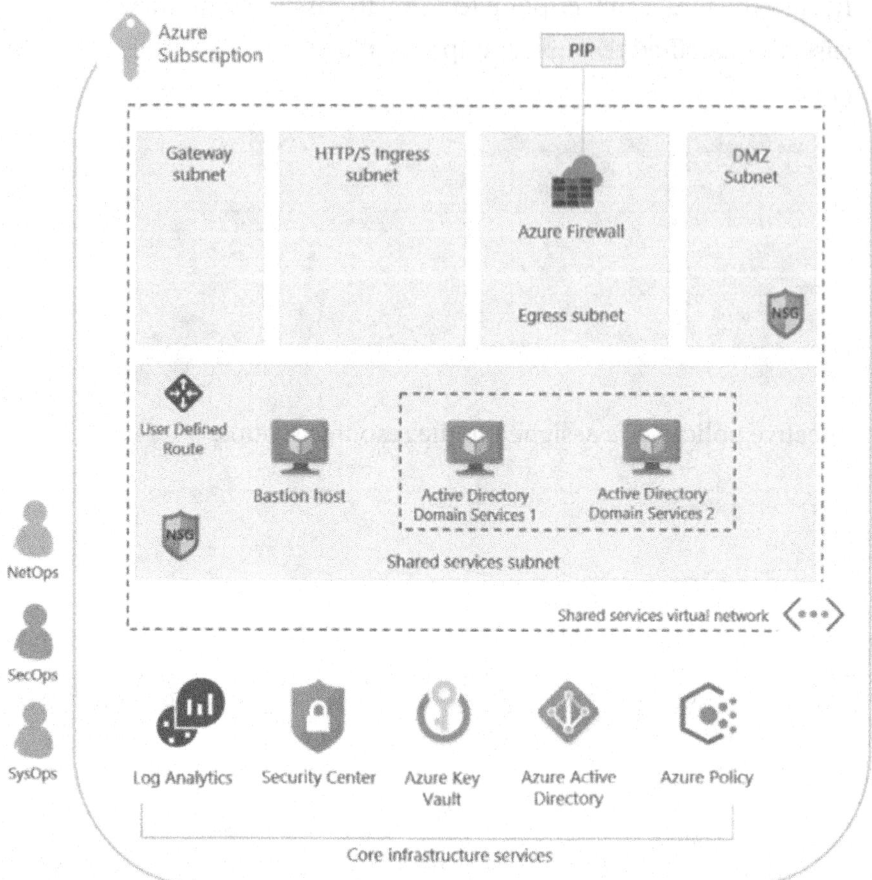

Figure 7-9. *Architecture of ISO270001 Shared Services blueprint*

Blueprint Life-Cycle Management

Blueprints are very much like all other Azure features and services that have rules that you must consider when you create, publish, and assign to configure and maintain your Azure environments.

Blueprint Life-Cycle Stages

A blueprint goes through the following stages. Each stage has its behavioral rules. The following are the blueprint creation and editing stages.

- **Draft:** This is the state of a blueprint when you first create and save it. In this state, the blueprint cannot be assigned.
- **Published:** This is the state in which you publish a draft blueprint or make changes to an existing blueprint and publish it as a new version.
- **New Version:** Once published, the version of a blueprint cannot be edited and saved as the same version. Instead, you republish and save it as a new version. This allows you to have multiple versions of the blueprint, which you can assign independently. When a blueprint has multiple versions, only the current version is displayed in the definition node. You can see the different versions of a blueprint by selecting the Published Versions tab, as shown in Figure 7-10.

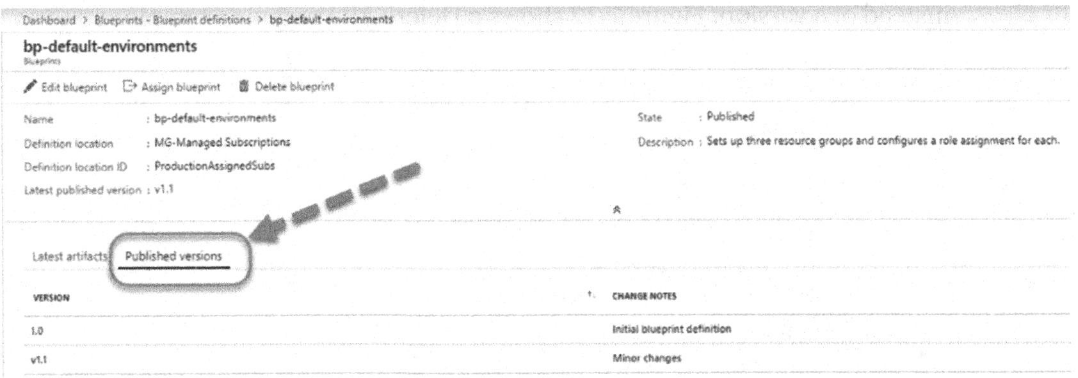

Figure 7-10. *Published Versions tab*

- **Delete Version:** You can delete specific versions of a blueprint. You must ensure that the target version is not assigned, however. Use the Published Versions tab to select the blueprint version that you want to delete. Take note of the version in the delete dialog, as shown in Figure 7-11, before confirming the deletion.

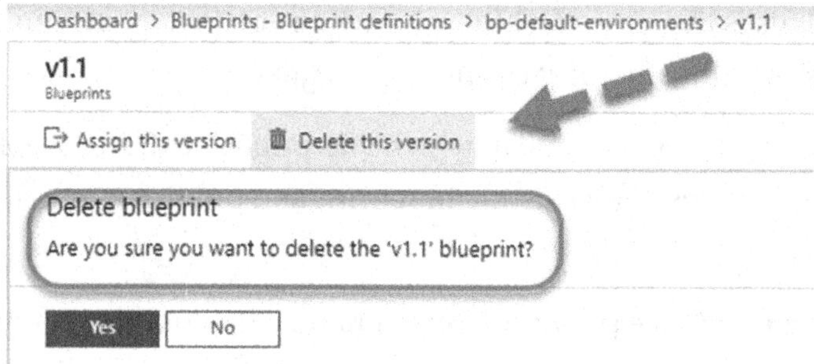

***Figure 7-11.** Deleting a version of a blueprint*

- **Delete All Versions**: You can delete all versions of the blueprint in one operation. You perform the delete action from the main blueprint when you select it. There is a subtle difference in the delete dialog in that it shows the blueprint name for the confirmation, instead of a version. Figure 7-12 shows a Delete All Versions example.

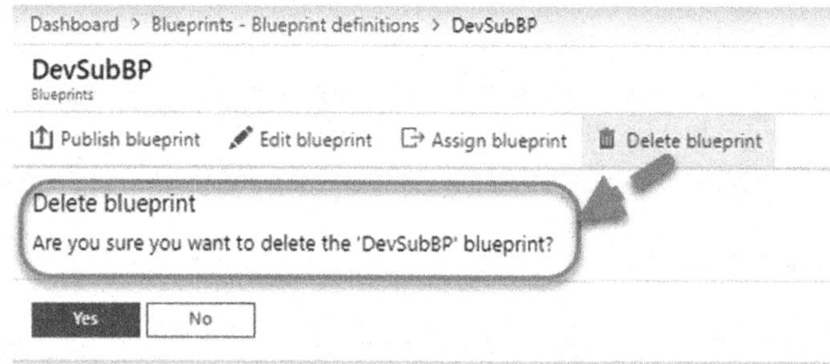

***Figure 7-12.** Delete all versions of a blueprint*

Note that you must ensure that all assignments are removed from all versions of the blueprint before you can delete it.

Blueprint Unassignment and Locks

Azure Blueprints can create update resources within a subscription, once assigned. The reverse (unassign) is not true. When you unassign a blueprint, it leaves all resources in place. You must perform a manual clean up if you need to remove any of the artifacts. This is by design because resources created by the blueprint may be in use. The blueprint lays down the resources and uses blueprint locks to protect the resources from unauthorized edits.

Blueprint Locks

Blueprint resource locking is different from the normal Azure resource locks. An Azure resource lock can typically be managed by users with the right level of RBAC access. Blueprints, however, use a lock that is enforced by the managed identity that is used to create the blueprint.

Table 7-4 is from Microsoft documentation at `https://docs.microsoft.com/en-us/azure/governance/blueprints/concepts/resource-locking`.

Table 7-4. *How Blueprint Locks Work*

Lock Mode	Artifact Resource Type	State	Description
Don't Lock	*	Not Locked	Resources aren't protected by Blueprints. This state is also used for resources added to a **Read Only** or **Do Not Delete** resource group artifact from outside a blueprint assignment.
Read Only	Resource group	Cannot Edit / Delete	The resource group is read only and tags on the resource group can't be modified. **Not Locked** resources can be added, moved, changed, or deleted from this resource group.
Read Only	Non-resource group	Read Only	The resource can't be altered in any way—no changes and it can't be deleted.
Do Not Delete	*	Cannot Delete	The resources can be altered, but can't be deleted. **Not Locked** resources can be added, moved, changed, or deleted from this resource group.

It provides information on how the four states of blueprint locks—Not Locked, Read Only, Cannot Edit/Delete, and Cannot Delete—work.

The default option when you create a blueprint assignment is Don't Lock. In this state, the artifacts deployed by the blueprint through assignment can be altered.

You can change the lock type by updating assignments in the assigned blueprints node when using the Azure portal. Note that the resource lock effect is impacted by Azure Resource Manager role caching, so the effect can mean that a deny action can take up to 30 minutes before taking effect.

An attempt to perform an edit or delete action on a resource deployed by a blueprint that is in a locked state will result in an error similar to that shown in Figure 7-13.

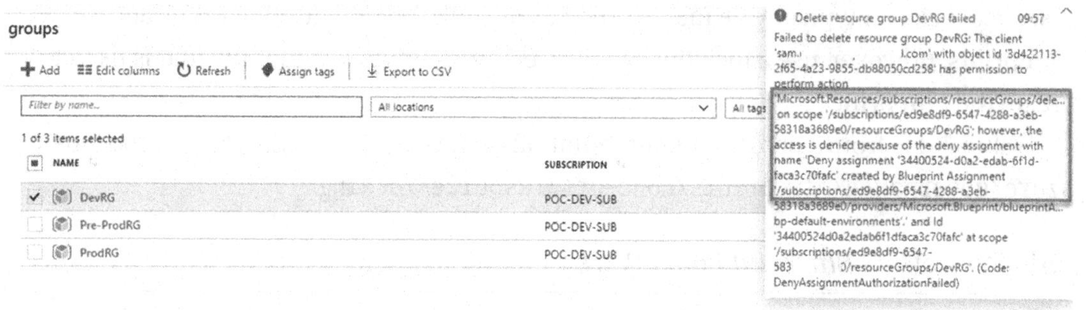

Figure 7-13. *Effect of a lock updating blueprint assignments*

Updating Blueprint Assignments vs. Version Update

You can update blueprints using two options.

- **Assignment Update**: Make changes to the same blueprint version, select a different version to apply, change the lock states, or change artifact parameters.
- **Create a new version of the blueprint**: This is when you want a new independent version of a blueprint and still maintain a relationship to your original blueprint.

Exporting and Importing Blueprints

Once you have invested time in creating and testing blueprints, you can export the definition as a means of backup and also as a means to import into a different Azure subscription. Export and import are not native to the Azure portal. Microsoft has published a solution in the PowerShell gallery called Manage-AzureRMBlueprint to allow you to perform the blueprint export and import actions using Azure CLI. You can access this solution at `www.powershellgallery.com/packages/Manage-AzureRMBlueprint/2.2`.

Summary

In this chapter, we started with an introduction to governance at scale with deployments through ARM templates. ARM templates are great and effectively the way that almost every action in Azure is executed. However, using ARM templates can be challenging and require a very high degree of skill, as well as the time to be able to use it effectively. Blueprints, introduced in the second section of this chapter, simplify the scale challenge and add enterprise scale controls that support life-cycle management.

The blueprint feature is still in preview at the time of writing but is ready for use. The use of management groups and blueprints form the bedrock of a well-organized and managed Azure environment. Explore these features and the many that are released and updated—in some cases, on a daily cadence. Remember that you now have the option to build it right and run it right.

CHAPTER 8

Azure Sentinel (Preview)

Honestly, it took us some time to decide if we would include a preview service and dedicate a full chapter to it in this book. But with what we have seen and experienced so far, what Azure Sentinel does (and promises to do once General Availability (GA)), we could not do else but talk about it. After all, this book has a clear focus on Azure security and governance—where Sentinel definitely has a place!

All the information written here is based on preview features and release. Although its feature set already looks pretty solid and complete, know that things might change along the way.

For now, this is what we will cover in this chapter.

- What Azure Sentinel is
- How to onboard and use Azure Sentinel
- How to get started with Azure Sentinel
- Using Azure Sentinel to get clear views on your security alerts

What Is Azure Sentinel?

In Chapter 5, we heavily discussed Azure Security Center as a centralized dashboard informing you about the overall security state of your Azure environment. The key strengths of Azure Security Center are the dashboarding, the integration with machine learning, and real-time feedback on security risks and what can be improved in your environment to optimize overall security.

Azure Security Center is great at reporting and alerting about security risks, but it is only half of the solution. It is missing integration with the day-to-day operations within an organization. What we often see in the field is IT admins exporting the list of recommendations on a weekly basis, turning them in to action items in their operations tool (SIEM solution). This is doable, but probably not the most efficient solution.

P. De Tender et al., *Pro Azure Governance and Security*, https://doi.org/10.1007/978-1-4842-4910-9_8

And that is exactly where Azure Sentinel comes in.

The following is the definition put forward on the official Microsoft Sentinel product page.

> *Azure Sentinel Preview is a cloud-native SIEM that provides intelligent security analytics for your entire enterprise at cloud scale. Get limitless cloud speed and scale to help focus on what really matters. Easily collect data from all your cloud or on-premises assets, Office 365, Azure resources, and other clouds. Effectively detect threats with built-in machine learning from Microsoft's security analytics experts. Automate threat response, using built-in orchestration and automation playbooks.*

Before moving on to the technical details, let us explain SIEM.

What Is SIEM?

SIEM stands for *security information and event management.* It refers to a collection of security alerts and how to respond to them with relevant events or by taking action, if you want. The management is centralized in a so-called SIEM solution, which is software that collects and responds to security events occurring in your IT landscape, and provides alerts, filters data, and more. Not all SIEM solutions are identical, but most of them have these capabilities on board. However, other solutions take it one step further and help you analyze security events and "learn" from them—providing richer detection mechanisms, better reporting features, and more to-the-point information; filtering out the noise and focusing on what really matters.

No matter the differences between third-party SIEM solutions, they all have one thing in common: a centralized log. Often, this is an audit log from a device in your environment that captures logging information like diagnostics or security alerts, using the syslog protocol. All the devices, appliances, servers, and software applications that you have in your IT landscape should be able to report to the SIEM solution. The main difference is how they handle the received information.

Within the specific domain of security handling, this mechanism is known as Security Orchestration Automation Response (SOAR). It specifically points at the "learning" aspect. The more intelligent your SIEM solution is, the more powerful it is for your environment. Honestly, if we were selecting a SIEM solution for our organization, we would mainly focus on the SOAR aspect of the tool, rather than what it's reporting and its dashboarding capabilities. As that is where the true power and intelligence of such tool comes from, and resulting in the biggest benefit for you as the customer.

Why Azure Sentinel?

Now that you have a basic understanding of what a SIEM solution is and does, and where the focus points of Azure Sentinel come in, let's drill down a bit more in detail about specific Azure Sentinel characteristics and capabilities.

Azure Sentinel is active in four different domains.

- **COLLECT**: The core capability of any SIEM solution is receiving and collecting data from different sources in your environment. This includes appliances, servers, network devices, compute devices, and end-user activities. While running in an Azure public cloud, Azure Sentinel can collect information from different sources, whether running in a public cloud, private cloud, or an on-premises infrastructure.
- **DETECT**: One of the key strengths of Azure Sentinel is that it is backed by Microsoft Security Graph and machine learning for data analytics. It is capable of detecting threats that were never detected before. From the information and intelligence received from all Microsoft cloud systems (Azure, Office 365, Windows 10, Dynamics365, Xbox, Outlook.com, and more), Microsoft has a rather good view on what is going on, and going wrong, on the Internet. Any detected threat is reported to Azure Security Center and Azure Sentinel within seconds or minutes.
- **ANALYZE**: Based on all received information and logging, a powerful cloud-based analysis engine kicks in real time, assisting in analyzing and investigating all sources of information. Together with the detection engine, it provides near real-time security feedback about your cloud and hybrid infrastructure.
- **ORCHESTRATION**: Azure Sentinel is capable of responding to threats using built-in orchestration and automation, which optimizes the overall security handling of detected and reported issues—often without any IT admin's involvement.

Azure Security Center vs. Azure Sentinel

Assuming that you read Chapter 5 and deployed it in your environment as part of your learning journey, an obvious question comes up. What makes Azure Sentinel different from Azure Security Center? Honestly, most of the four aforementioned topics can be achieved with Azure Security Center. Not immediately out of the box, but the baseline is at least provided.

In a few short words to emphasize the comparison, Azure Security Center offers a full overview of your security posture, and stays compliant with security policies out of specific industries (PCI, ISO, etc.). It assists with minimizing vulnerabilities, and provides a standard and complete security offering across your IT landscape, both cloud and on-premises. It mainly could be used as a *reactive tool*, providing reports and dashboards about "what happened," as well as the "as-is state."

Azure Sentinel could be described as a *proactive tool*. First, it gathers log information from different sources directly into Sentinel. (ASC relies on Log Analytics, which technically allows you to import data from external sources). Next, Sentinel provides features like hunting, machine learning, and case management for security events (described in detail later in this chapter). Most of these capabilities are just not available in Azure Security Center.

It is more a situation of having both tools deployed, instead of having one or the other. (And we honestly hope the bundled strengths will be reflected in the pricing too, once Sentinel becomes GA).

Summary

In this section, we introduced you to Azure Sentinel, a new service in Azure that helps organizations optimize their security. It relies on powerful alerts, detection mechanisms, and hunting capabilities.

Enabling Azure Sentinel

With the overview and introduction behind us, it is time to dig into the technology and show you what it is capable of delivering. This section focuses on how to enable Azure Sentinel in your Azure subscription. Know that things might change in the future, once Sentinel is in GA. It will also likely require some kind of licensing or consumption plan once it is out of preview.

Deploying Azure Sentinel

Deploying Azure Sentinel is rather straightforward and similar to deploying almost any other Azure resource.

1. From the Azure portal (`https://portal.azure.com`), authenticate with a user account. Have enough administrative rights to deploy new services and resources.
2. Browse to **All services**.
3. Search for **Azure Sentinel**.

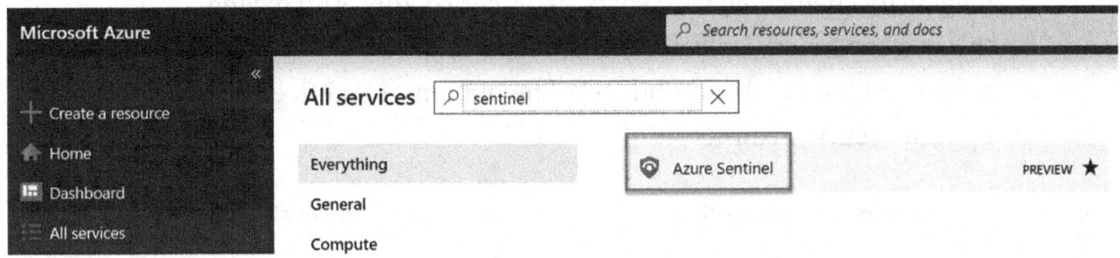

4. Select **Azure Sentinel** to open its blade.

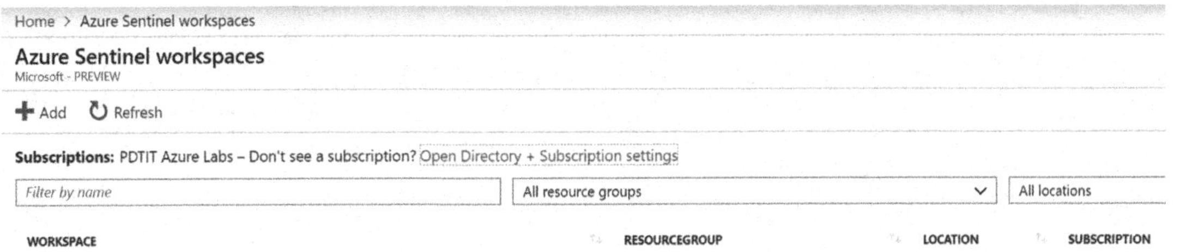

No Azure Sentinel workspaces to display
Use Azure Sentinel to easily aggregate security data generated by end point devices, network infrastructure, and other security systems, then leverage it to detect and respond to threats in your environment.
To get started, connect a workspace to Azure Sentinel. Learn more
Connect workspace

5. Click **Connect workspace**. This opens a list of the Log Analytics workspaces that it detects within your Azure subscription. You also have the option to create a new one specifically for Azure Sentinel.

6. For our test scenario, create a new one. This allows you to easily remove it later, once the GA-version becomes available, as well as to not have any interaction or dependency with your existing workspaces. Since Sentinel is exposing a lot of security information about your setup, you don't want to expose all the information it gathers to your IT administrators. Separating the logging to a dedicated workspace takes care of this. And having this in a separated/isolated configuration might be a requirement to be compliant with your business' regulations, like PII, enforced by your security teams.

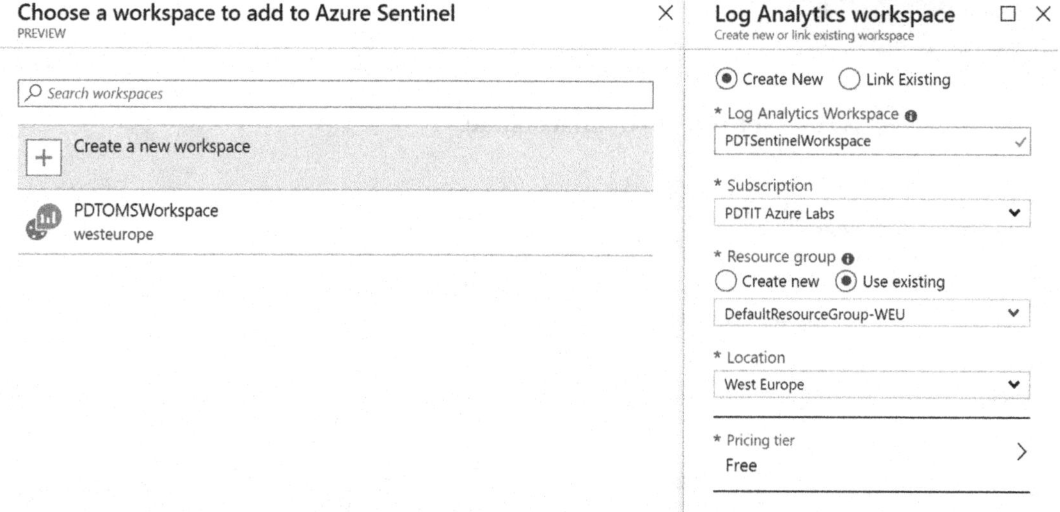

7. Wait for the new workspace to be created; select it and confirm the creation of your Sentinel environment.

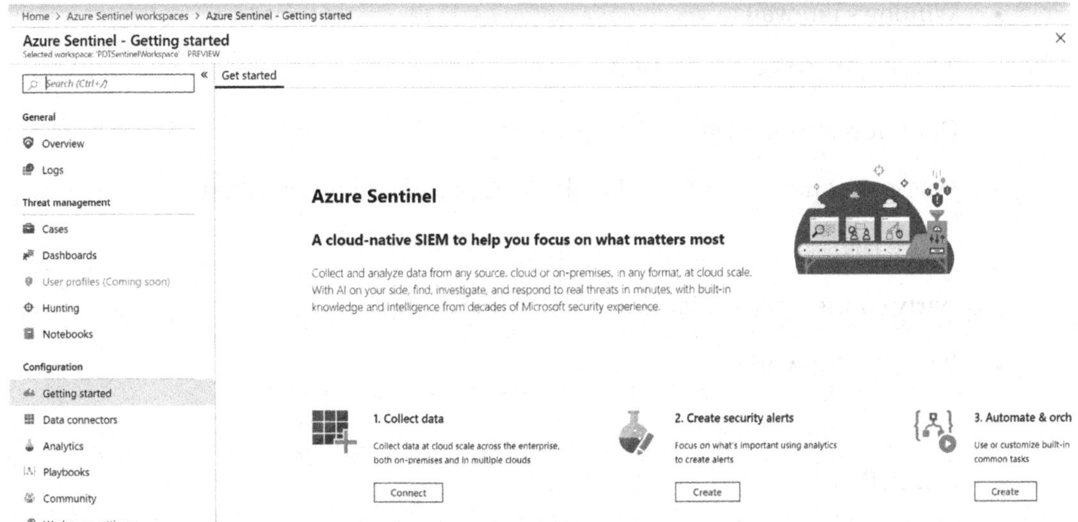

8. You are now at the welcome screen, ready to continue with the configuration and fine-tuning.

Collecting Data

The main functionality and intelligence of Azure Sentinel comes from the information it receives. So obviously, the first step in enabling Sentinel is collecting data.

Sentinel uses connectors to receive data. Several connectors are provided by Microsoft for most of its solutions; third-party vendors provide their connectors.

Microsoft Connectors available at the time of writing:

- Azure Active Directory
- Azure Active Directory Identity Protection
- Office 365
- Microsoft Cloud App Security
- Azure Advanced Threat Protection
- Microsoft Security Events
- Azure Security Center
- Azure Information Protection
- Azure Web Application Firewall

- Windows Firewall
- Amazon Web Services (AWS)
- Common Event Format
- Syslog (Requires a Linux VM with Management Agent installed)
- Azure DNS

Third-party connectors available at the time of writing:

- Palo Alto Networks
- Cisco ASA
- Check Point
- Fortinet
- F5
- Barracuda

1. From the Sentinel workspace, press **Connect**.

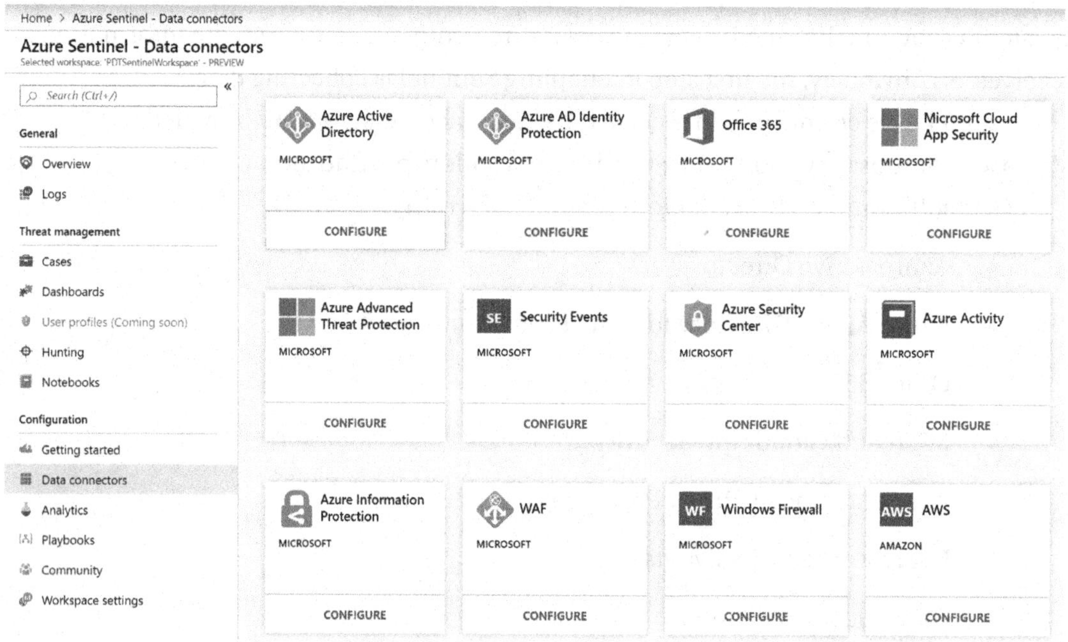

2. This opens the list of current data connectors. (We are pretty sure that this list will include more vendors by the time Sentinel becomes generally available).

3. Let's start with Azure Active Directory. From the Azure Active Directory box, click **Configure**.

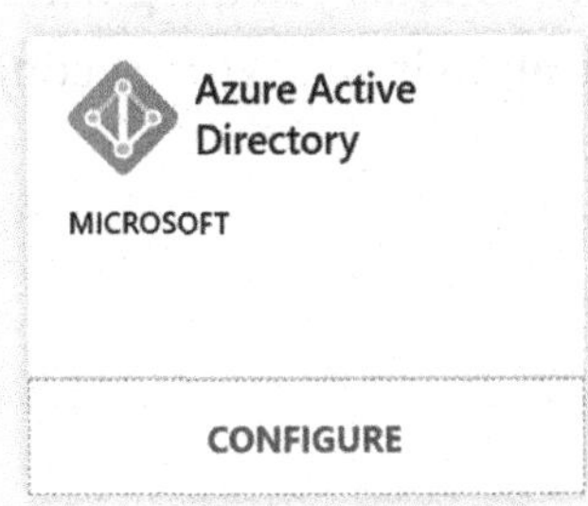

4. This opens the Azure Active Directory connector configuration blade. Press the **Connect** button for Azure AD Sign-on Logs.

Home > Azure Sentinel - Data connectors >

PREVIEW

Description

Gain insights into Azure Active Directory by connecting Audit and Sign-in logs to Azure Sentinel to gather insights around Azure AD scenarios. You can learn about app usage, conditional access policies, legacy auth relate details using our Sign-in logs. You can get information on your SSPR usage, Azure AD Management activities like user, group, role, app management using our Audit logs table.

 Disconnected

Connection

^ Connect Azure Active Directory logs to Azure Sentinel

Select Azure AD log types

Azure AD Sign-in logs Connect

Azure AD Audit logs Connect

Note: To integrate with Azure AD alerts:

- Your organization needs an Azure Active Directory Premium **P2** license.
- You must have **global administrator**, or **security administrator** permission in Azure AD.

Note You also need an Azure Active Directory Premium P2 license to make this process work.

---

5. Assuming that your account has Azure AD Global administrator or security administrator permissions, you are greeted with a successful connection notification in just a few seconds.

Notifications

More events in the activity log → Dismiss all ...

Connected successfully

Azure AD sign in logs was connected successfully at 6:35:45 PM

a few seconds ago

6. Do the same for the Azure AD audit logs.
7. Select **Next steps** in the configuration blade.

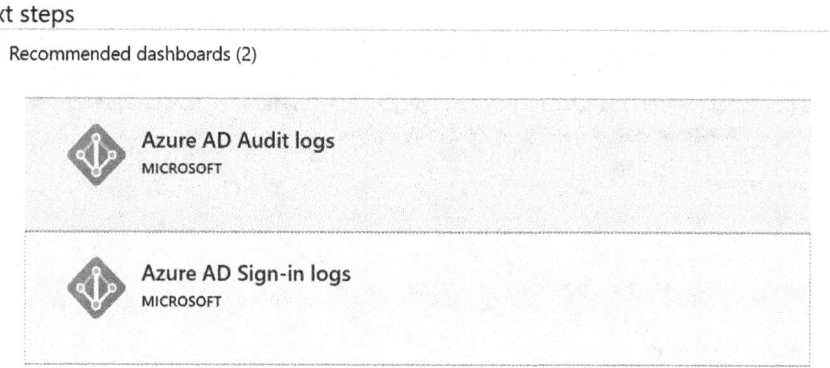

8. Select **Azure AD Sign-in logs**, and confirm the installation of that solution by pressing the **Install** button in the blade.

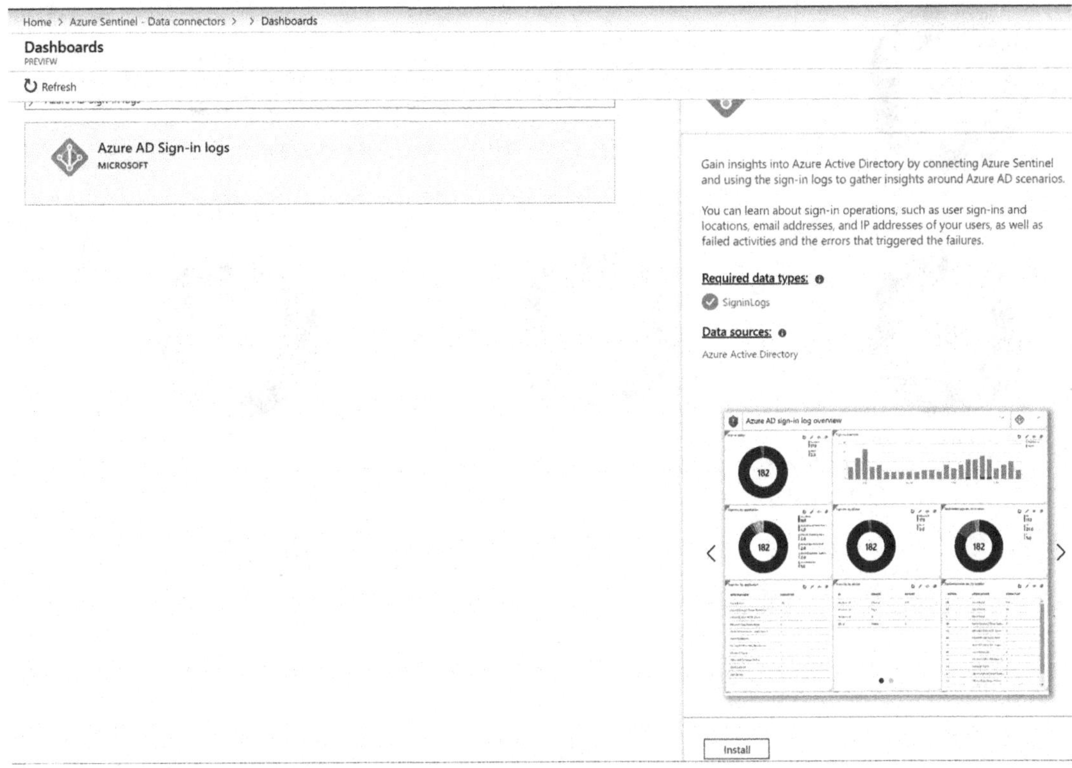

9. Repeat this process for the Azure AD audit logs.

10. Once installed, check out the dashboards for each of them.

Azure AD sign-in log overview
Sign-in status
182
Successful 179
Failed 3.0
Sign-ins overtime
SUCCESSFUL
FAILED
Sign-ins, by application
182
165
4.0
3.0
2.0
2.0
1.0
Sign-ins, by device
182
179
3.0
Application sign-ins, by location
182
GB 153
US 24.0
5.0
Sign-ins, by application
APPDISPLAYNAME SIGNINCOUNT
Azure Portal 165
Azure Advanced Threat Protection 4
Office365 Shell WCSS-Client 3
Microsoft App Access Panel 2
Azure AD Connector - Logic Apps 2 2
Azure Notebooks 1
Microsoft Office Web Apps Service 1
Microsoft Teams 1
Office 365 Exchange Online 1
O365 Suite UX 1
App Service 1
Sign-ins, by device
OS BROWSER AMOUNT
Windows 10 Chrome 171
Windows 10 Edge 7
Windows 10 IE 1
iOS 12 Mobile 3
Application sign-ins, by location
LOCATION APPDISPLAYNAME SIGNINCOUNT
GB Azure Portal 148
US Azure Portal 13
Azure Portal 4
GB Azure Advanced Threat Prote... 3
US Office365 Shell WCSS-Client 3
GB Microsoft App Access Panel 2
US Azure AD Connector - Logic ... 2
US Azure Notebooks 1
US Microsoft Office Web Apps S... 1
US Microsoft Teams 1
Azure Advanced Threat Prote... 1
US Office 365 Exchange Online 1
Audit logs
46
245
186
30.0
20.0
5.0
3.0
1.0
245
155
49.0
41.0
245

This completes the installation of the Azure identity connectors to the Azure Sentinel dashboard.

Since we also covered Azure Security Center in this book, why not add that connector to your dashboard as well?

1. From the Azure Sentinel workspace, select **Get data**.
2. From the list of connectors, select **Azure Security Center**.

3. From the Azure Security Center pane, make sure that you select Connected.

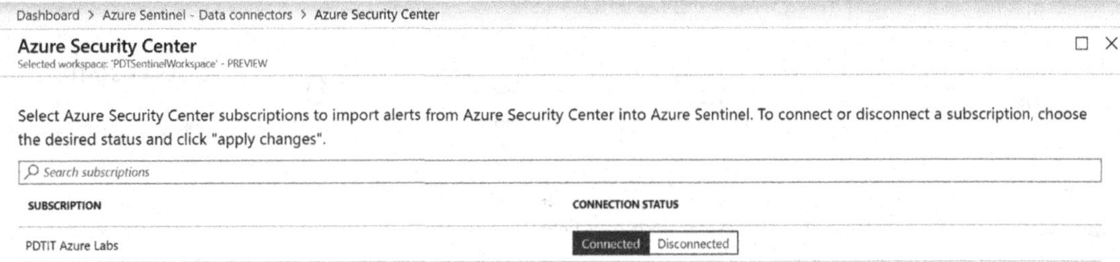

4. Confirm the changes by clicking the Apply **changes** button.
5. Wait for the notification informing you this connector was set up successfully.

The Azure identity connector immediately offered to install the necessary dashboards, but this option is not (yet) available for Azure Security Center. Let's see what this looks like in the overall Sentinel Overview dashboard later.

Feel free to add several other connectors and dashboards.

Note Several of the available connectors are similar to the Azure solutions that are used in the former OMS and current Log Analytics. These allow only a single connection to a workspace. This could mean that you first need to disconnect a solution before you connect it to the Azure Sentinel workspace. Azure Security Center is an example.

Azure Sentinel allows integration with logging information from several network appliances, like F5, Cisco, Fortinet, and others. All of them rely on the syslog protocol to ingest data into Sentinel; however, Sentinel does not understand this protocol. You should deploy a Linux VM as a collection server for them, on which you install the Microsoft Monitoring Agent. This server will act as a gateway for injecting data into Log Analytics.

With the three connectors enabled in the demo setup, the overall Azure Sentinel - Overview dashboard starts to look like Figure 8-1 after 24 hours (you don't have to wait that long to start seeing data).

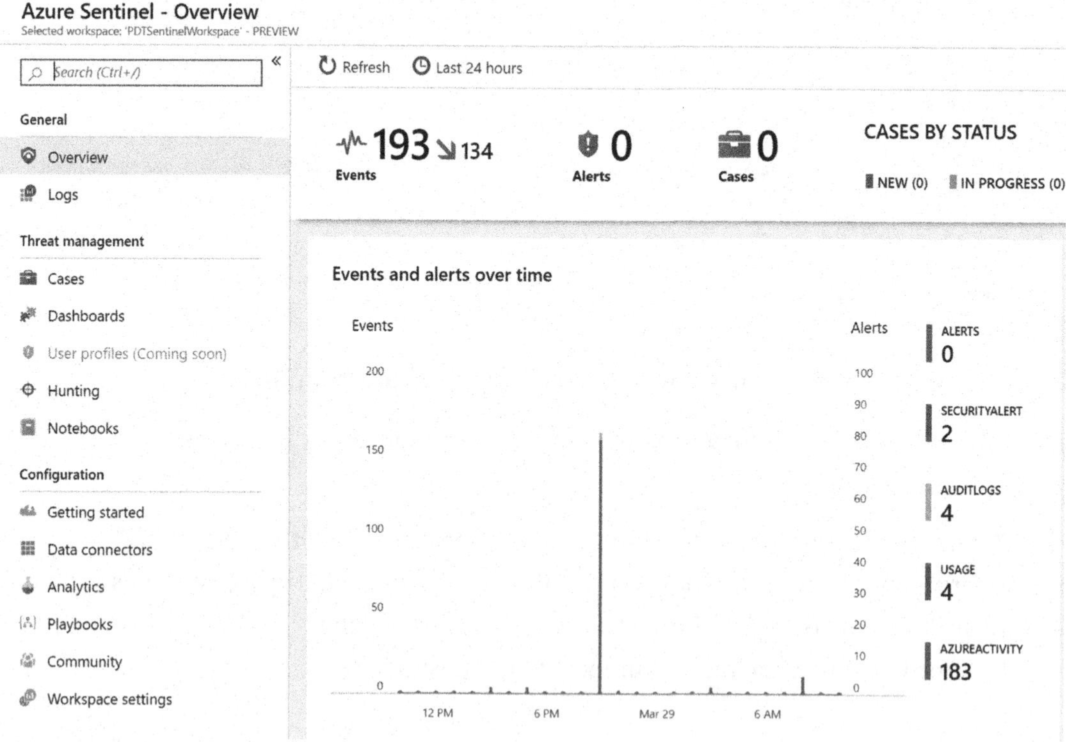

Figure 8-1.

6. This dashboard already tells a lot of information, just by quickly looking at.
   - Events went down from 193 to 134 in 24 hours; this could point at a stabilization of security attacks, for example.
   - There are two security alerts; this is based on information ported from Azure Security Center.
   - There are four audit log items coming from the Azure audit activity connector.
   - There are 183 Azure activity events, based on the Azure Activity connector.
7. Click the **SECURITYALERT** icon ion the dashboard.

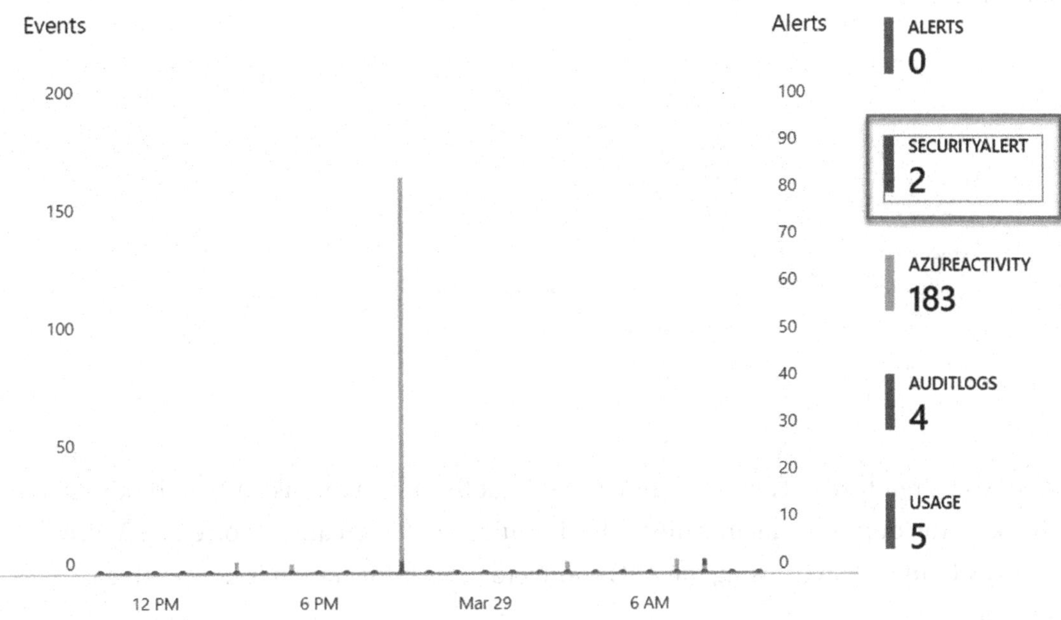

This redirects to Log Analytics and runs a specific query for security alerts with specific filter criteria.

```
SecurityAlert
| where ProviderName != 'ASI Scheduled Alerts'
| where ProviderName != 'CustomAlertRule'
```

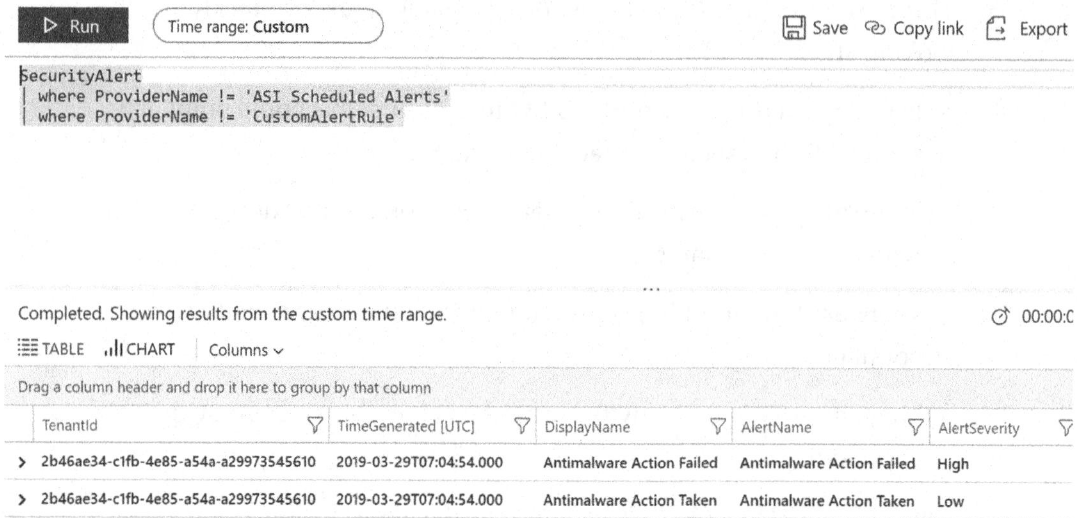

Selecting the Antimalware Action Taken item shows more details about this specific event.

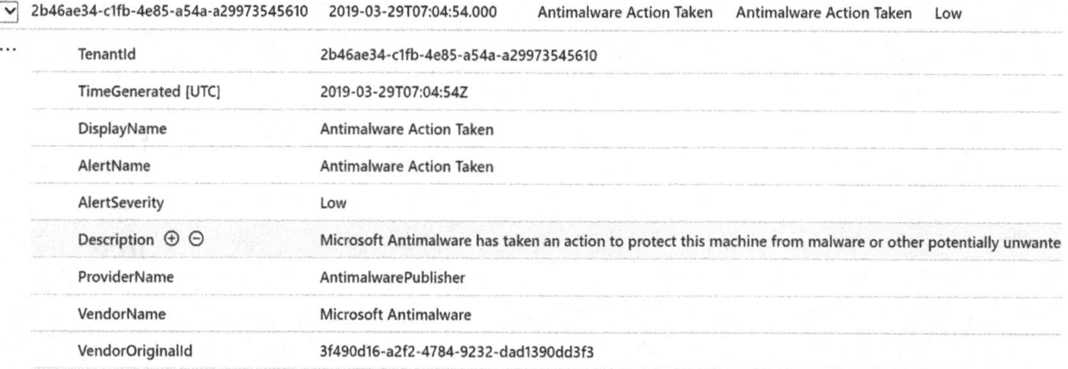

If you already read Chapter 5, remember that this event points back at the simulated attack on the demo virtual machine. This is initially detected and reported by Azure Security Center. And by using the ASC connector, this information is now visible in Sentinel.

We can do the same for some other pointers in the Overview dashboard.

1. Select **AUDITLOGS**.

2. This redirects to Log Analytics, running the AuditLogs query.

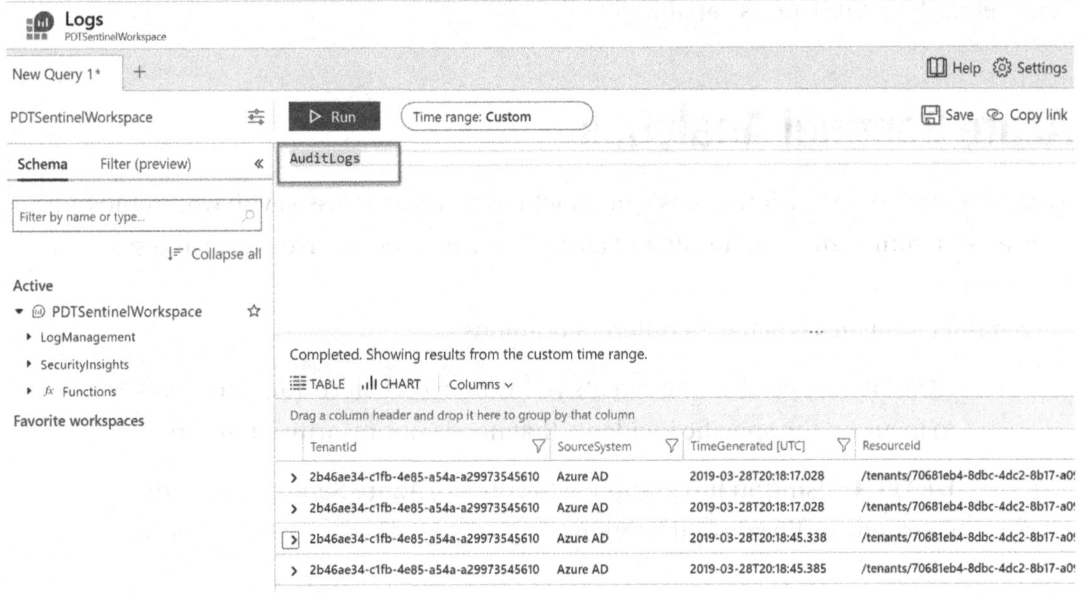

Notice another section in the Overview dashboard called Data Source Anomalies.

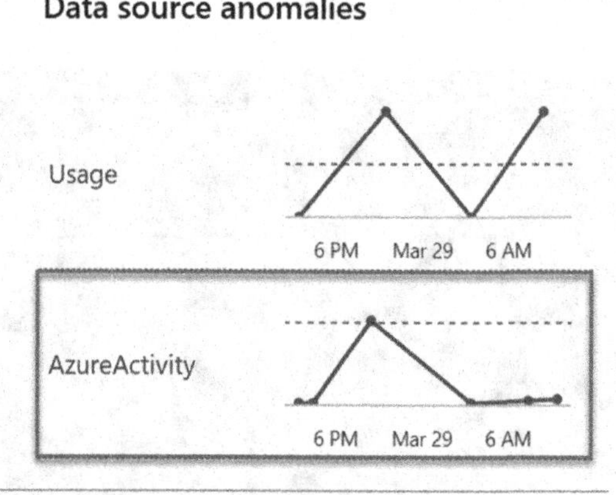

This pane is used to highlight any major differences in source information. While this is all acceptable in our demo scenario, in a full production environment, this could mean an attack is ongoing (e.g., when your firewall is generating a massive number of logs in a short period of time).

Summary

In this section, you learned how to enable Azure Sentinel and deploy connectors as data sources. You became familiar with the dashboards. In the next section, we will cover Sentinel analytics and alerts capabilities.

Azure Sentinel Analytics

Azure Sentinel Analytics integrates with machine learning to assist you with removing "noise" and minimizing the number of alerts that you need to investigate as a sysadmin or security officer.

Sentinel Analytics is active in different domains.

- **CONTROL**: Specifies the threats you want to get alerts for. Allows you to focus on the specific incidents that need your priority attention.
- **DETECT**: Using an integration with GitHub, Azure Sentinel relies on an extensive library of detections.

- **PLAYBOOK:** Similar to Azure Security Center, Sentinel uses playbooks (integration with Azure Log Apps), a step-by-step scenario that is activated whenever an alert is generated.

Create Analytics Alerts

To use analytics, you need to create alert rules. This is done as follows.

1. From the Azure Sentinel blade, select **Analytics**.

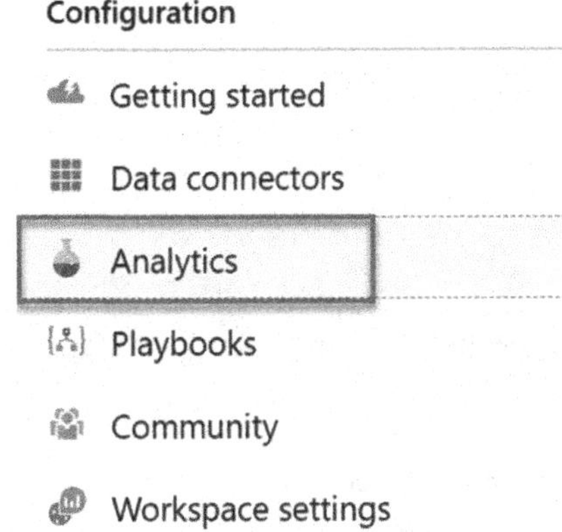

2. Select + **Add** to create a new rule.

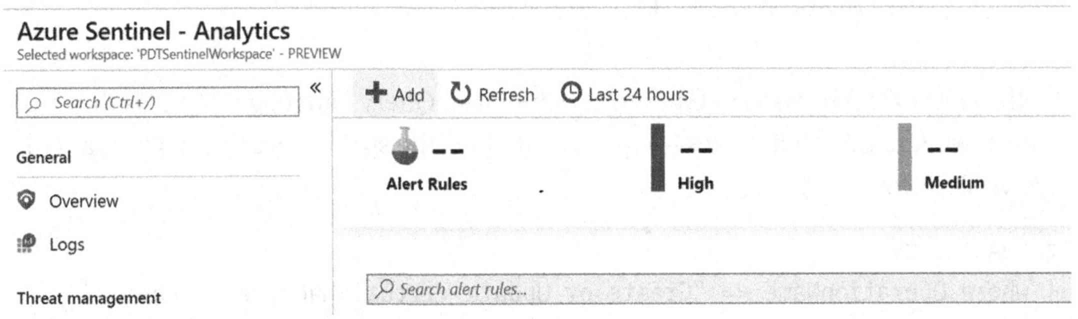

For this demo, we use the scenario of being alerted whenever a new Azure virtual machine extension is created or updated. (The security integration here could be in your environment. VM extensions can only be deployed out of an ARM template or a DevOps process, so whenever this alert comes up, being initiated by an admin user, your security teams are notified about it.)

3. In the Name and Description fields, provide a descriptive title for the alert (e.g., New VM Extensions Loaded). Also, set the severity to your level of choice. Medium would be OK for now.

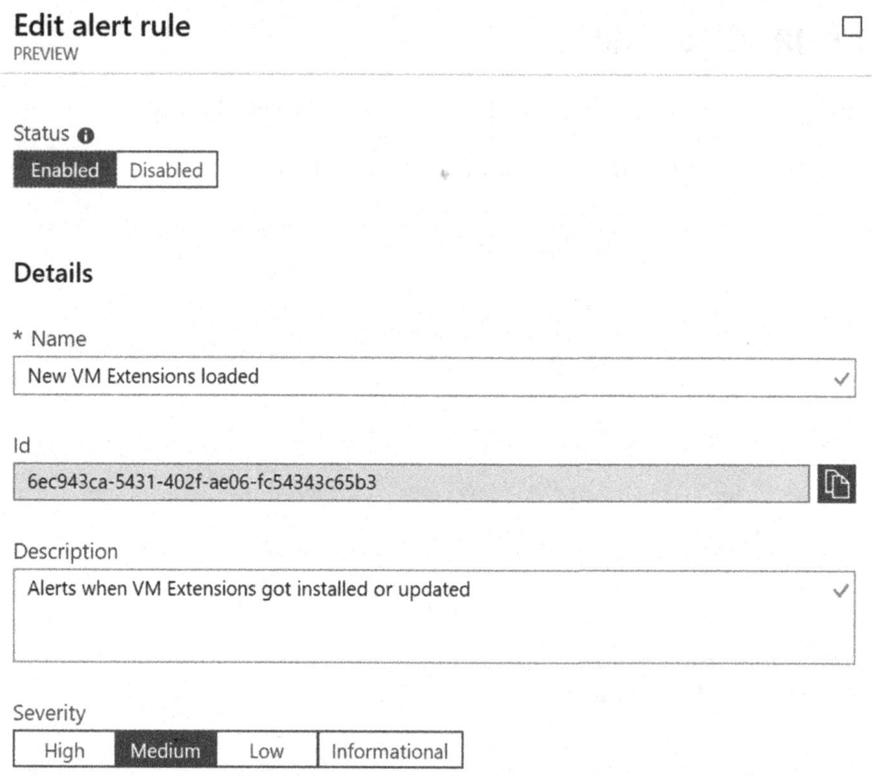

In Set Alert Query, you need to provide the Kusto Query Language (KQL); is the same as what Log Analytics uses—a query that filters the specific event that you want to receive alerts for.

```
AzureActivity
 | where OperationName == "Create or Update Virtual Machine Extension"
 | where ActivityStatus == "Succeeded"
 | where TimeGenerated > ago (24h)
```

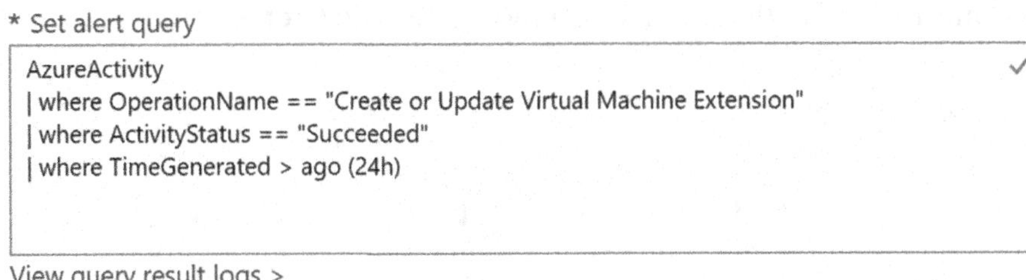

4. In the Alert Trigger settings, define the threshold and the scheduling that you want to use for this alert. Threshold is **1**. Frequency is **5 minutes** to speed up the demo a little bit. Period is set to 24 hours, as that is the maximum timeframe we want checked.

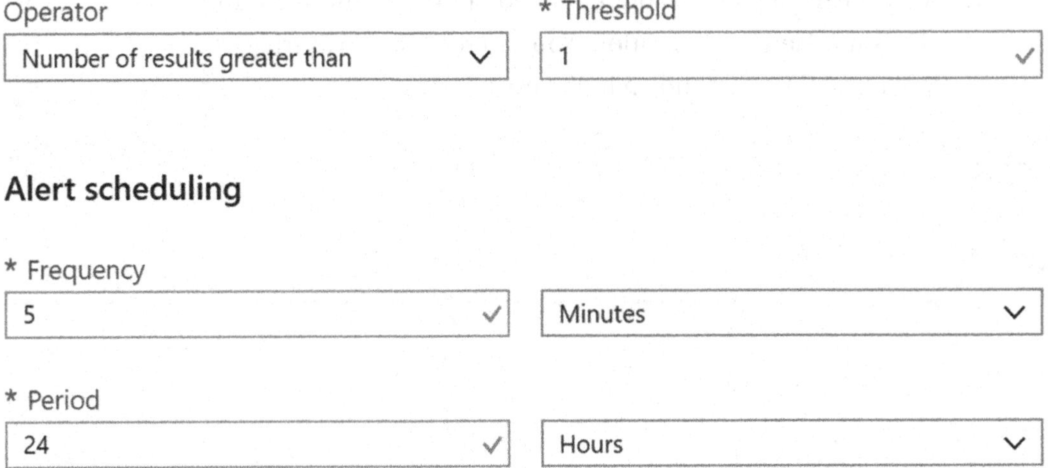

5. Confirm the creation of this alert by clicking the **Create** button.

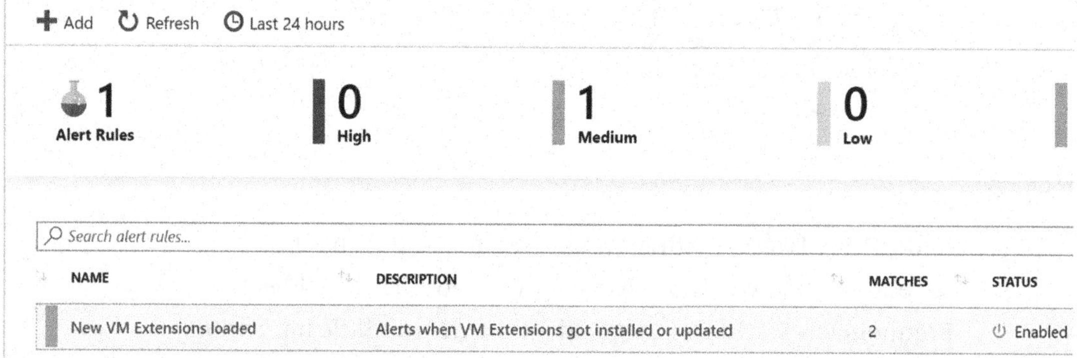

6. To test this alert, deploy at least one new Azure virtual machine. If you deployed VMs within the last 24 hours, that information will be recognized too.

7. After the deployment is done, wait for another 5 minutes, and check the Alert configuration. You can see that it was triggered by looking at the chart shown in Figure 8-2.

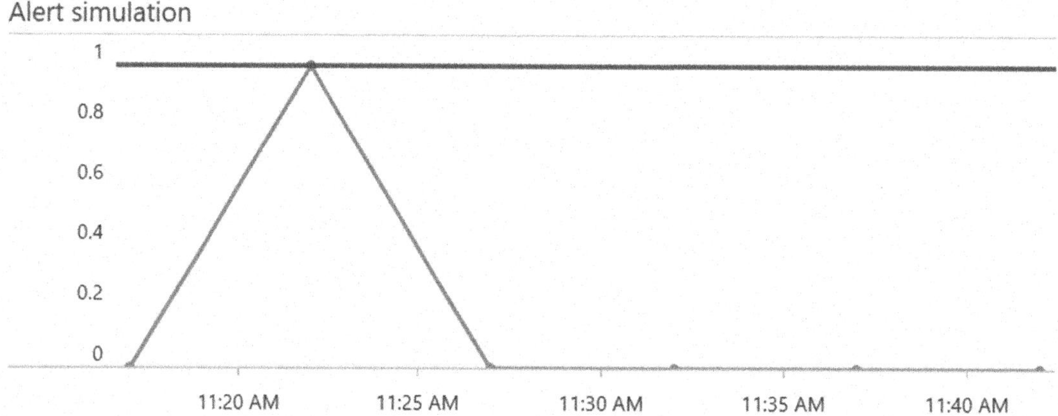

Figure 8-2.

For now, this works as expected. But what happens if 200 Azure resources were created in a short period of time? Do we want 200 alerts for this similar event? Obviously not. That's where the Suppression setting in the alert configuration becomes useful. When turned on, the analysis mechanism blocks duplicate alerts from showing up. At the same time, it looks at your interval threshold timings. Imagine you have a threshold of one day, and similar alerts come up over several days. Each day, it presents one alert item. If you define a threshold of 60 minutes, and similar events happen every 5 minutes during 4 hours, it shows a single alert every 60 minutes (in reality, without suppression, there would be 48 alerts for this scenario).

Summary

This section introduced you to enabling Sentinel Analytics and explained how to create alerts based on custom queries.

Handling Cases

We are now at the stage where we receive alerts for incidents. Great! From here, your system administrators or security officer would go out and start investigating the incident.

But Azure Sentinel can help with this, relying on a concept called *cases*. Cases are mainly a collection of individual alerts, displayed as an aggregation of information as defined in the alert (severity, status, etc.). Overall, these would be similar to incidents in your SIEM solution or your operations tool. For each case, you can see the time it was created and its status (in progress, closed).

1. From the Azure Sentinel blade, select **Cases**. This shows a list of all cases in your Sentinel workspace and the base status information (open cases, new cases, in progress cases, etc.).

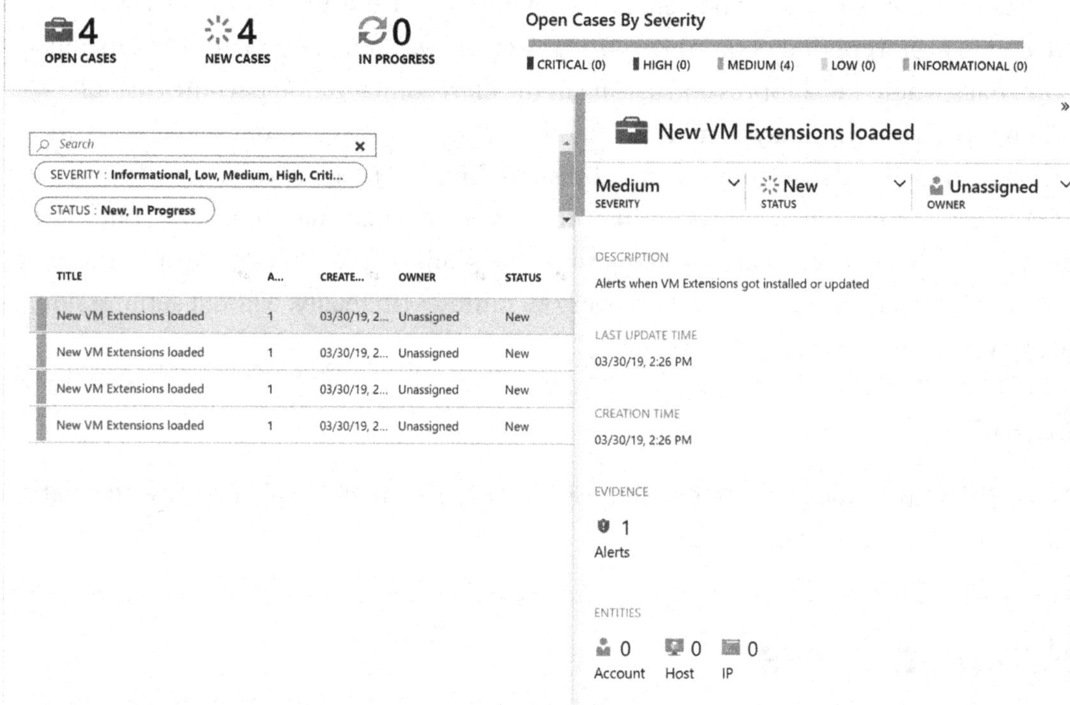

Assigning Cases

Probably one of the first actions that you want to take for a case is allocating a responsible person to start investigating it. This is easily done, as follows.

1. From a specific case item, click **OWNER** (default = **Unassigned**).
2. From the list of accounts, select the account that you want to assign as the owner of the case item.

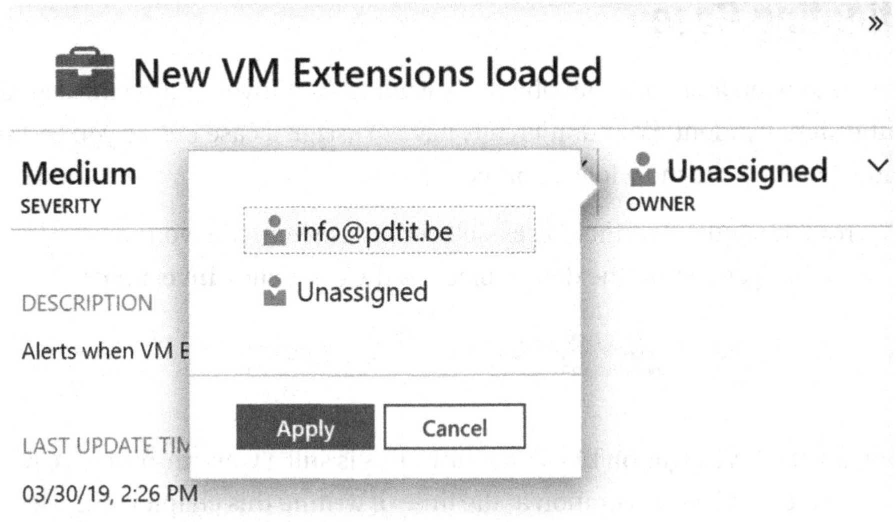

3. Confirm the assignment by clicking **Apply**.
4. You also want to update the status of this case from new to in progress. To do this, click **STATUS** (default = **New**) and change it to **In Progress**.

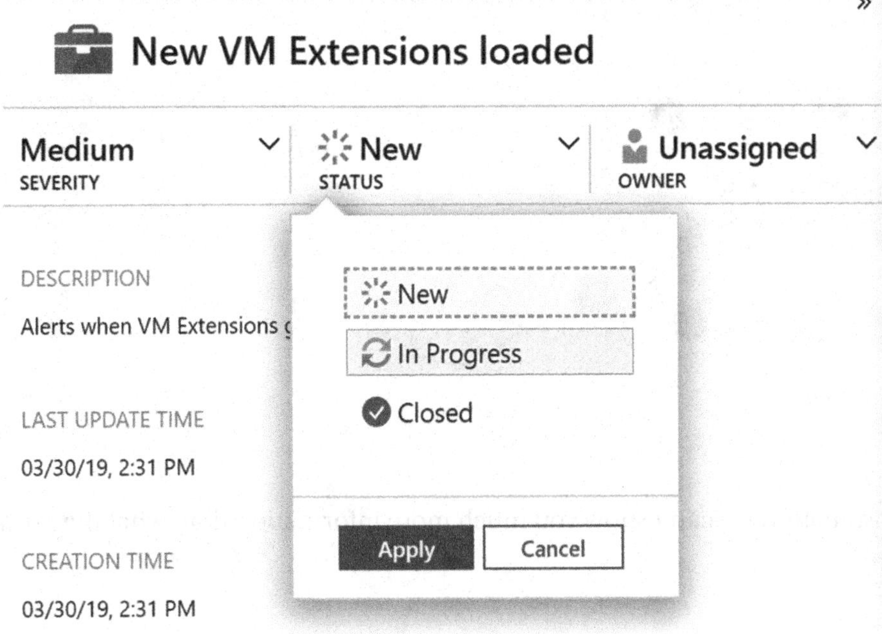

5. Confirm by clicking **Apply**.

Investigating Cases

Once a case has been assigned, you obviously want to start investigating the actual root cause of the alert/incident. (You don't really have to assign a case before you can start investigating, but it is the most logical process.)

1. From the Azure Sentinel Cases, select the case item that you want to investigate. From the details blade of the case, click **Investigate**.

This opens the Investigation blade. For now, this is still a work-in-progress, which requires a private preview registration at the time of writing this chapter. The idea, however, is pretty neat. An *investigation graph* is displayed to help you understand the scope and pinpoint the root cause of the incident and potential security threat by correlating relevant data together.

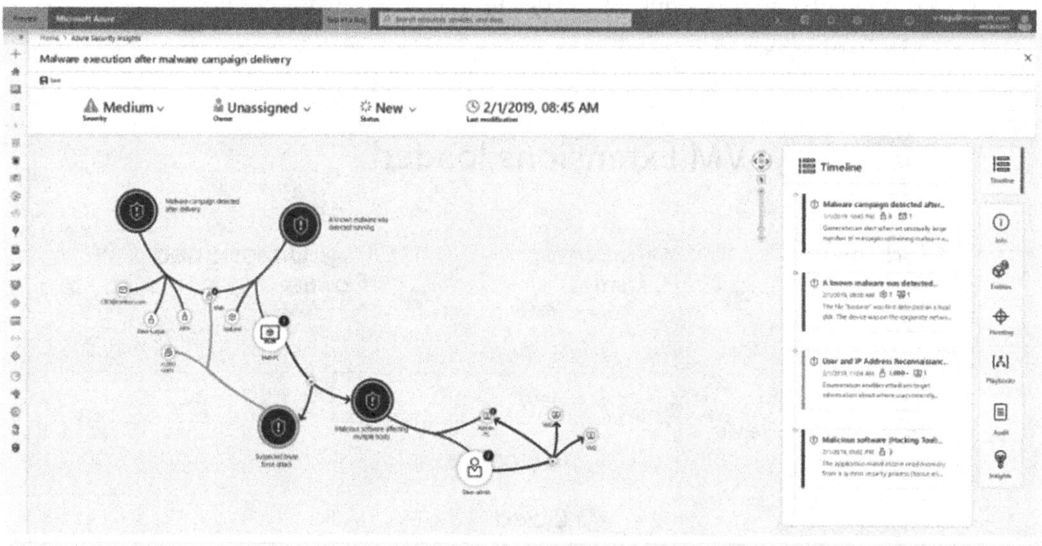

Unfortunately, we can't show you much more information than what the portal is displaying.

Closing a Case

Imagine that you worked on a case and you now want to close it. Azure Sentinel offers two options.

- **Closed: Resolved.** The incident was investigated and fixed.
- **Closed: Dismissed.** The incident was closed without needing further fixes or investigation.

Closing is a case is done using the following steps.

1. From an open case item, select **STATUS**. Then, select **CLOSED**.

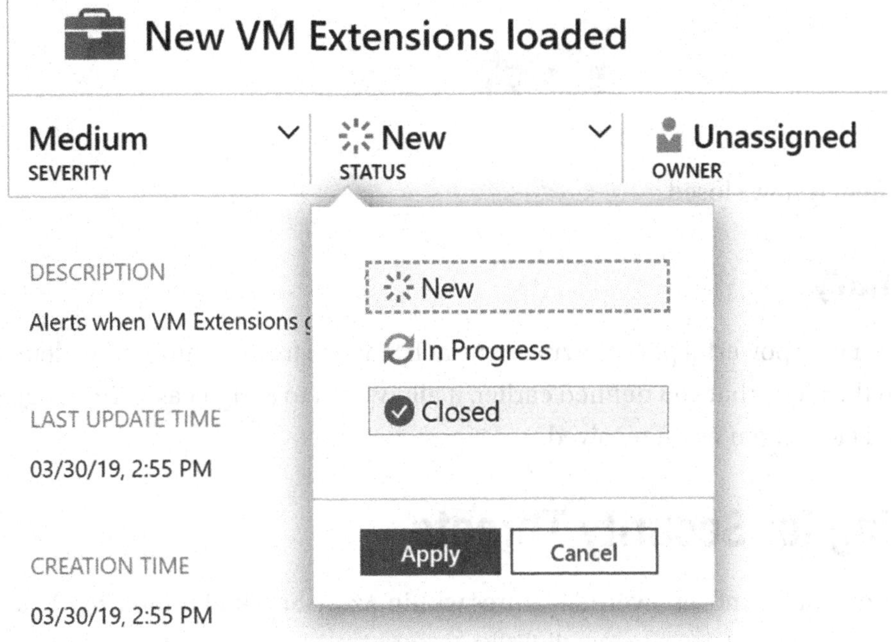

2. Describe the reason for closing the case item.

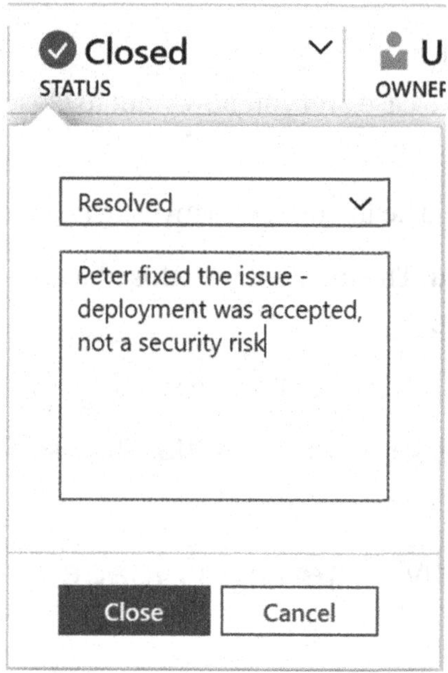

The item is now closed.

Summary

Cases are a very powerful part of Azure Sentinel. Starting from an automatic detection, based on the alerts that you defined earlier, it allows you to assign cases, investigate them, and close them when resolved.

Hunting for Security Threats

Probably one of the most powerful features within Azure Sentinel is *hunting*. As a security officer, one of your responsibilities is investigating threats and trying to avoid them in the future. Acting on alerts is mainly a *reactive response*. Azure Security Center is recommended for this, primarily. However, if you want to *proactively* investigate threats and security risks, then you want to use the *hunting* feature in Azure Sentinel.

Azure Sentinel already has a lot of hunting queries built into the product, as well as integration with a public GitHub repository, where you can reuse the community and product group-created hunting snippets (technically, these could be JSON or Kusto Query Language scripts).

From an overview perspective, Azure Sentinel's hunting feature offers

- **Built-in queries**. Developed by Microsoft Security researchers and offered as an example library to start using hunting.
- **Kusto Query Language**. Similar to Log Analytics, Azure Sentinel hunting allows you to build powerful KQL-queries to find the information that you are looking for.
- **Bookmarks**. From Log Analytics directly, or from Azure Activity Log, you can create your own bookmarks, which are saved in for you to reuse.
- **GitHub**. Start from a full library of examples on the Azure Sentinel hunting repository at `https://github.com/Azure/Azure-Sentinel`.
- **Notebooks**. Jupyter interactive Notebooks, which are workflows with a specific use case to check for.

Let's dive into several of these options and learn how to use them.

Hunting Using Built-in Queries

As a starting point, this is probably the easiest. It helps you become familiar with the process of *hunting*.

1. From Azure Sentinel, go to **hunting**. This shows a list of built-in queries for you to use. Some examples are
   - Anomalous Azure AD Apps
   - Processes executed in Base64 encoded files
   - User and Group enumeration
   - Summary of failed user logons

- Azure AD sign-ins from new locations
- Masquerading files as malware
- PowerShell downloads

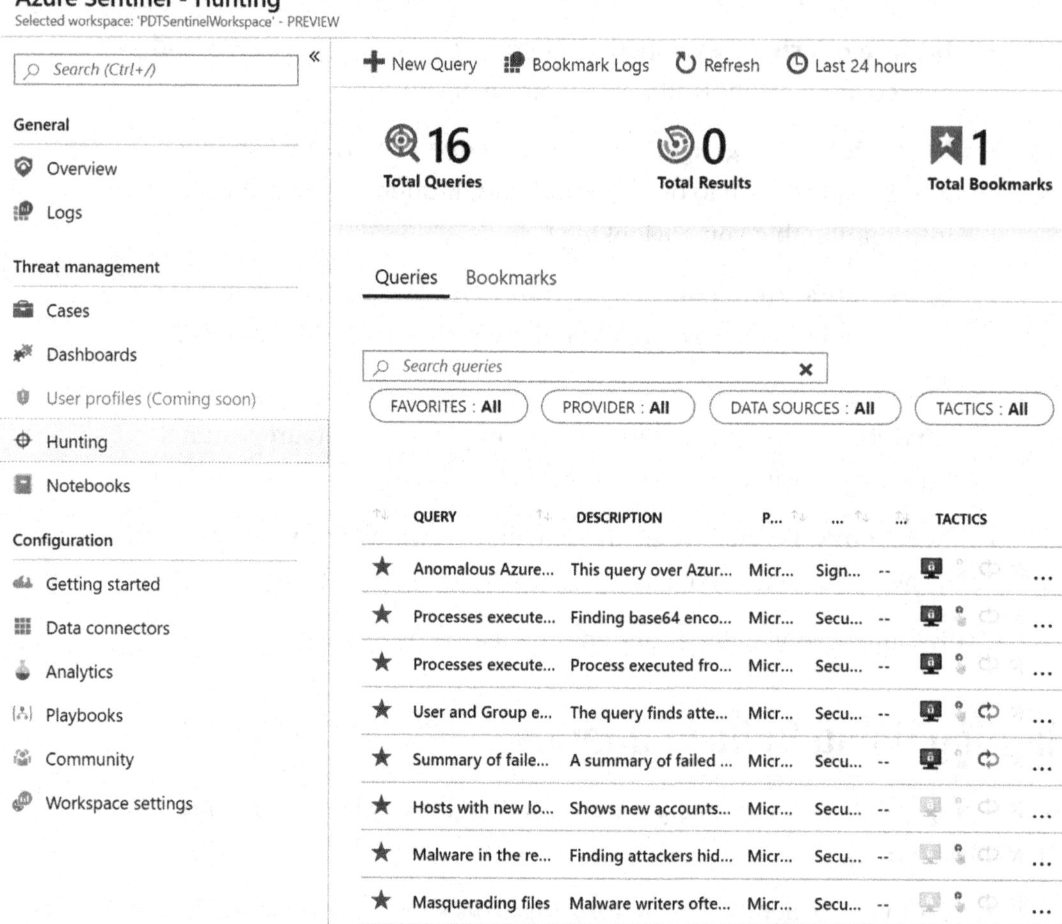

2. Select a query, for example, **Azure AD signins from new locations**.

Azure AD signins from new locations

Microsoft	1	SigninLogs
Provider	Results	Data Source

DESCRIPTION

New AzureAD signin locations today versus historical Azure AD signin data. In the case of password spraying or brute force attacks, one might see authentication attempts for many accounts from a new location.

QUERY

```
let start=datetime("2019-03-29T18:59:26.066Z");
let end=datetime("2019-03-30T18:59:26.066Z");
SigninLogs
|where TimeGenerated > start and TimeGenerated < end
| where TimeGenerated >= ago(1d)
| summarize perIdentityAuthCount=count() by Identity,
```

View query results >

TACTICS

Initial Access The initial access tactic represents the vectors adversaries use to gain an initial foothold within a network.
read more on mitre.com

Run Query View Results

3. Go through the Kusto Query to become familiar with what the query is looking for. Specifically, it is checking the Azure AD logs from the past day. From a security perspective, this query could identify password spraying or brute force attacks when showing multiple logons from the same or different locations.

4. Press the **Run Query** button. This runs the query in the back end, and shows the result in the top icon row.

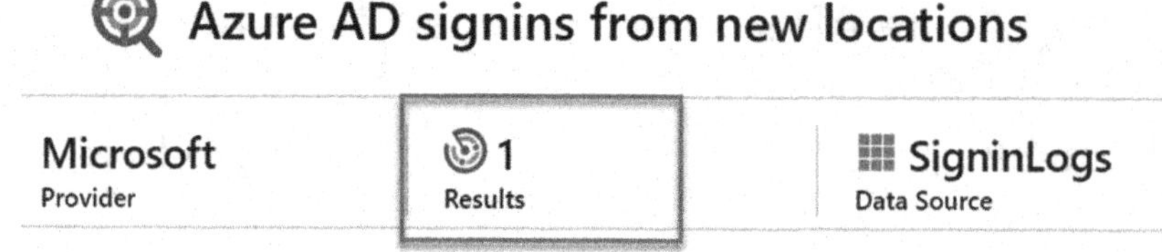

5. From the same area, press the **View Results** button. This redirects you to Log Analytics, and runs the specific query related to this object. It also shows the actual result as output.

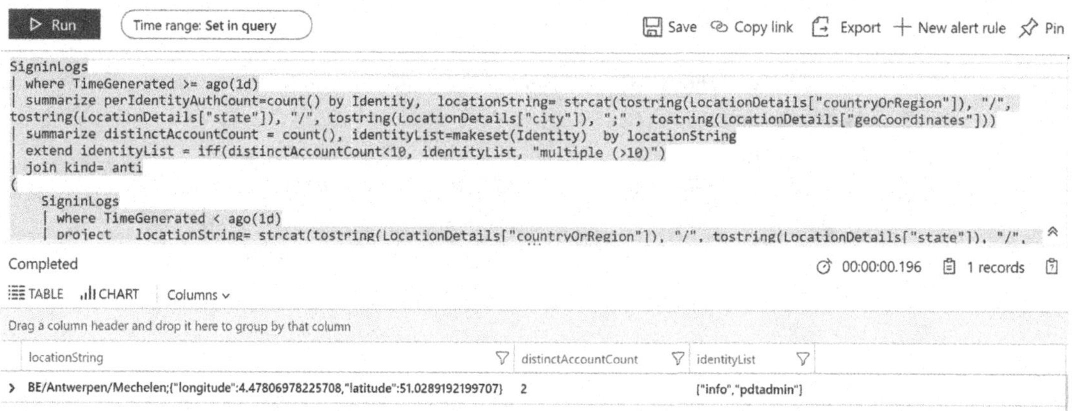

That's about all it takes to use the built-in hunting queries.

Hunting Using Kusto Query Language

Besides using the prebuilt queries, nothing stops you from running your own custom queries as a hunting process. To do this, go through the following steps.

1. From Azure Sentinel – Hunting, select **+ New Query**.

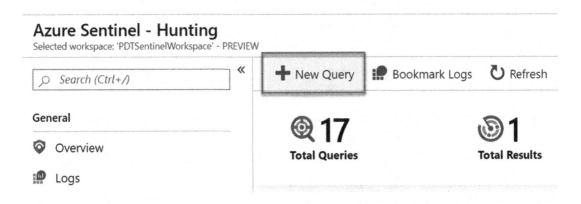

2. In the **Create custom query** window, complete the required fields (Name, description, custom query). For this example, we reuse the same query as the one that we used earlier for testing the alerts (but you can use any custom query you want.)

3. Optionally, you can define a category of tactics.

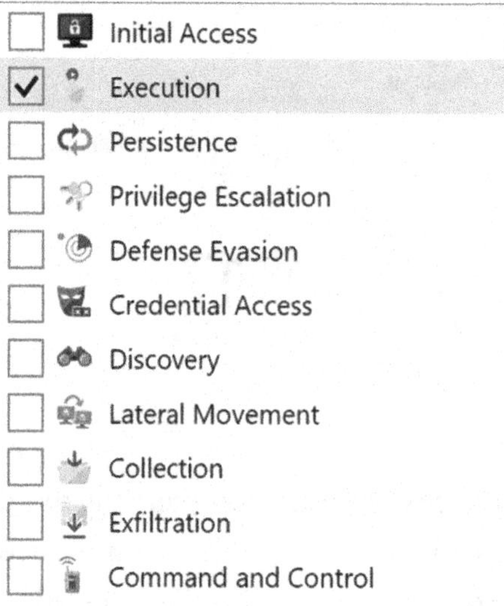

Note Tactics is based on a global list of known tactics and techniques of systems attacks, as known within the security world. A good source of information is the ATT&CK knowledge base from MITRE (attack.mitre.org), which provides an overview of common surface attacks, including the category and a description of the attack.

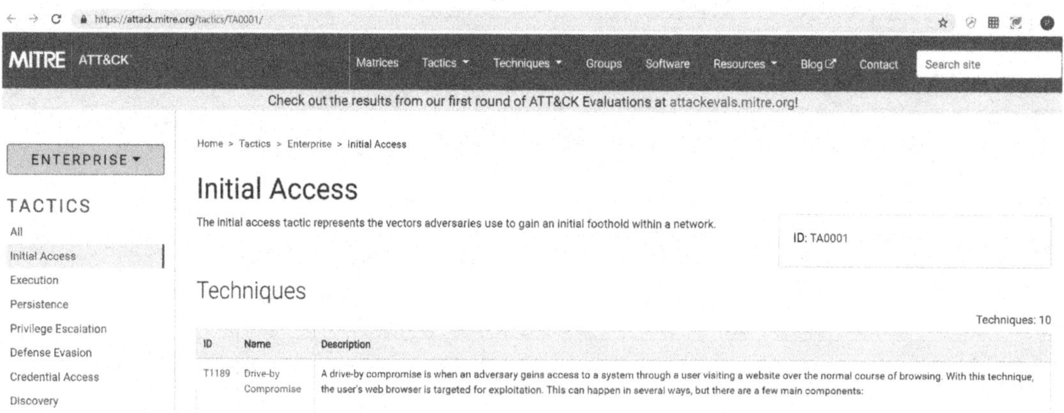

4. Confirm by clicking the **Create** button.

5. Notice that your item is added to the list of queries.

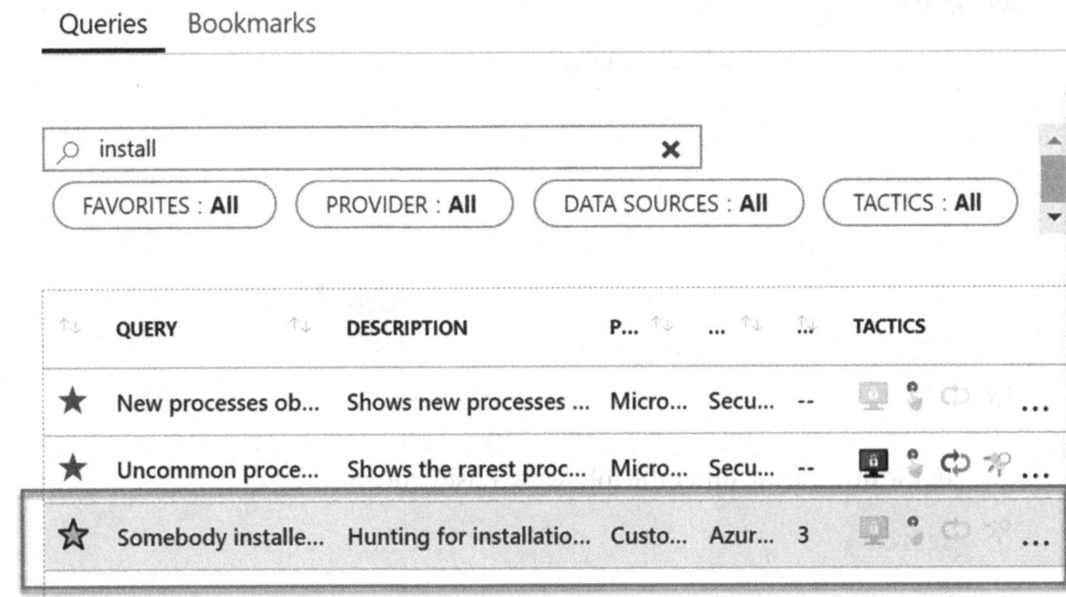

6. From here, you could run the query or view results.

Hunting Using Bookmarks

Imagine you are querying the overall Azure Sentinel Log Analytics based on a certain query you built from scratch. Or maybe you started from a "search *" query in Sentinel Log Analytics and filtered out the information you needed by clicking and selecting the involved items.

With the custom query option, you could copy/paste the Kusto Query Language query to a new custom query item, and run it whenever needed. This works fine, as you learned a few minutes back. But wouldn't it be cool if you could have this created automatically? Well, that's exactly what bookmarks do. Much like favorites in a browser, by using the integration with hunting bookmarks, you can immediately save custom queries.

Let's give it a try.

1. From Azure Sentinel, select **Logs**.

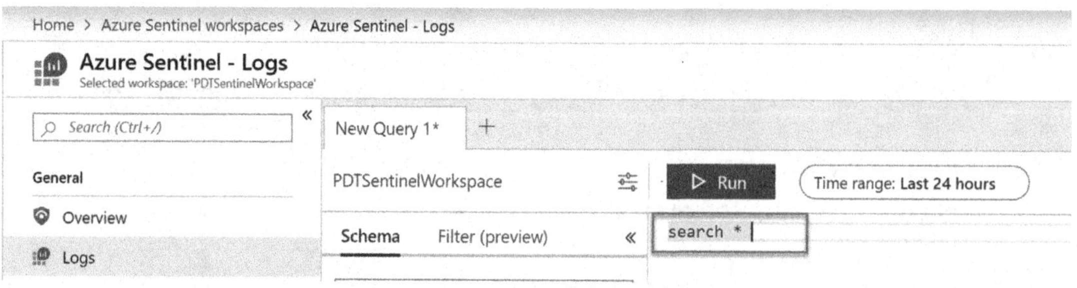

2. In the query field, enter the following Kusto query.

```
search *
```

3. Press the **Run** button to execute the query. It shows you a list of results from Azure activities from the last 24 hours. Open any item by clicking the arrow in front of the line.

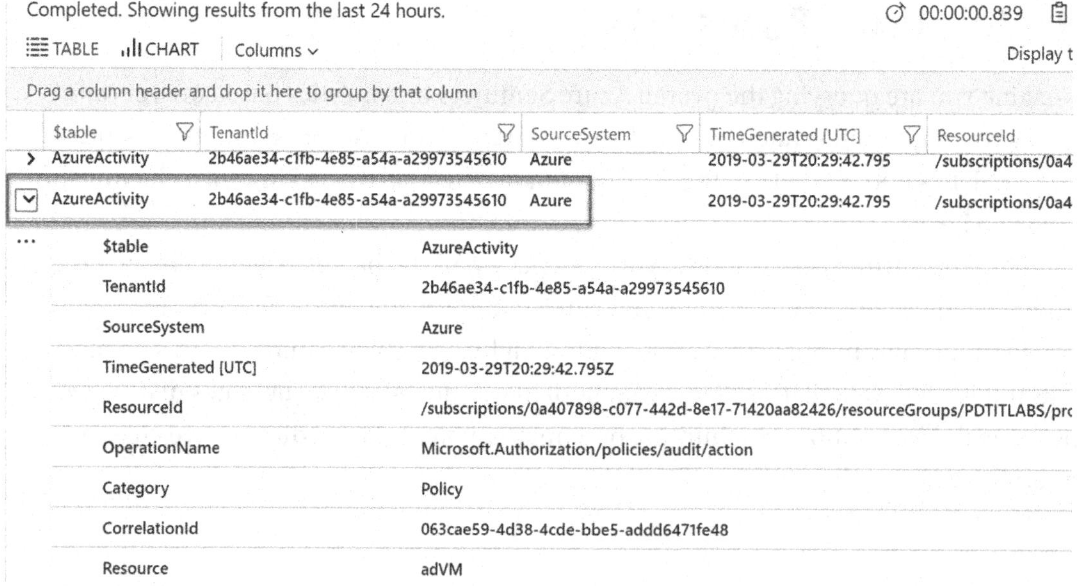

4. If you want to filter this output and reuse it for hunting, click the **...** button of the result item to open the context item.

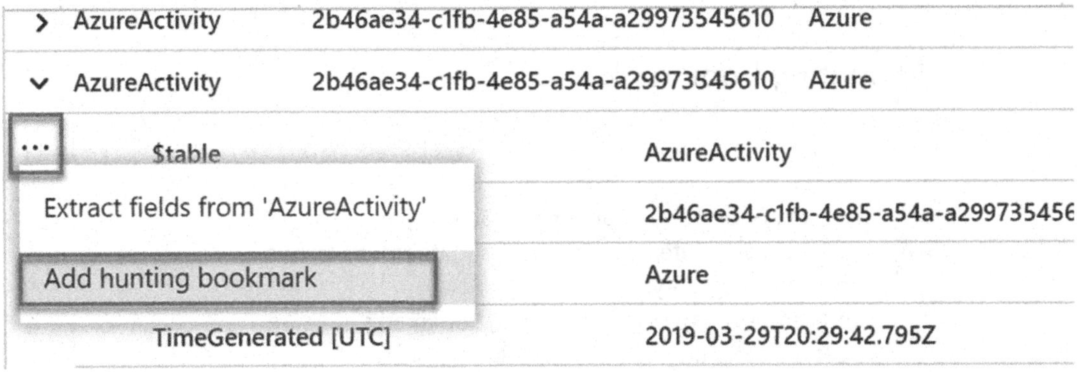

> AzureActivity 2b46ae34-c1fb-4e85-a54a-a29973545610 Azure

⌄ AzureActivity 2b46ae34-c1fb-4e85-a54a-a29973545610 Azure

... $table AzureActivity

Extract fields from 'AzureActivity' 2b46ae34-c1fb-4e85-a54a-a2997354561

Add hunting bookmark Azure

TimeGenerated [UTC] 2019-03-29T20:29:42.795Z

5. Click **Add hunting bookmark.** This opens the Add Bookmark blade, where you can provide a name, description, tags, and notes for this bookmark item.

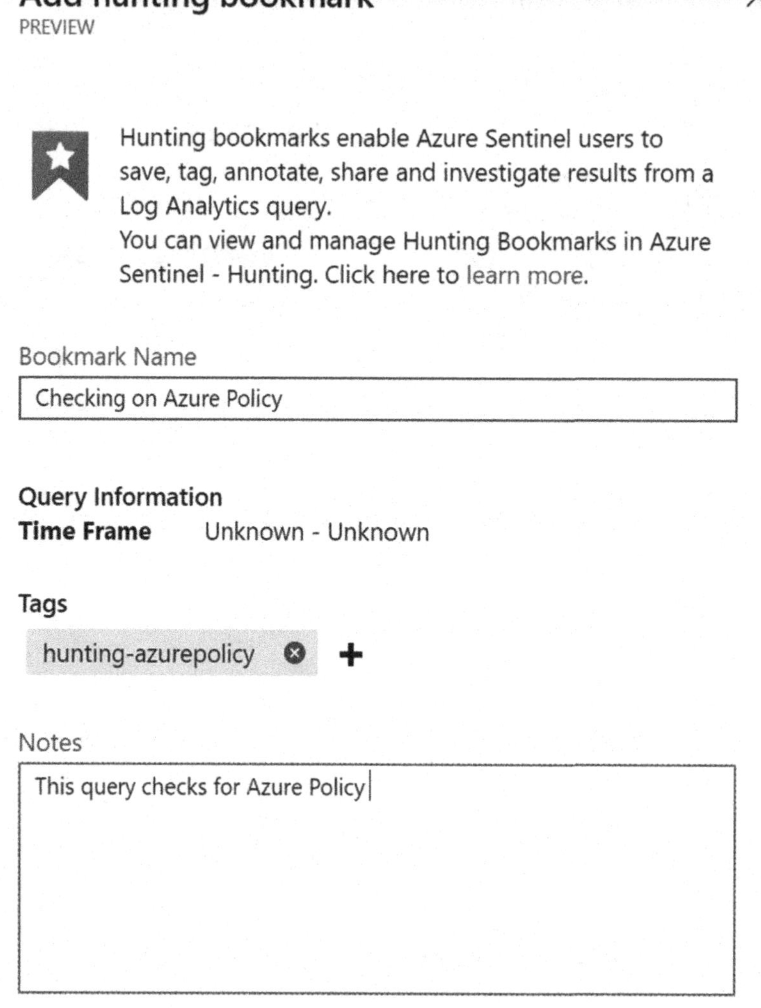

6. Confirm by clicking the **Add** button.

7. From the Azure Sentinel blade, select **Hunting**.

8. Select **Bookmarks.** This shows you the list of custom hunting bookmarks that you saved earlier.

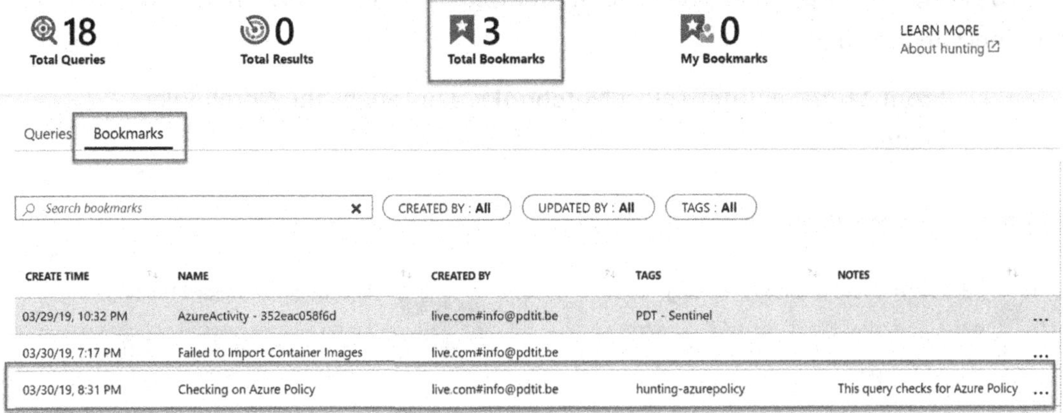

9. By selecting the bookmarked item, you can run an investigation, similar to what we described earlier in this section.

That's all it takes to run a custom query, and save it as a hunting bookmark.

Summary

Hunting is a feature of Azure Sentinel that differentiates it from Azure Security Center. By using several hunting configuration options, it allows any organization and its security teams to take a proactive approach in fighting security threats.

Azure Sentinel Notebooks

Besides the prebuilt or custom Log Analytics queries, Azure Sentinel brings another instrument to the table—Azure Notebooks, which helps security teams by providing insights and actions to investigate on anomalies or attacks.

Azure Notebooks are based on the open source project Jupyter, which provides a combination of Python code, Markdown documentation, graphics, data, and visualizations—all from within the same environment.

To get started, you can import several examples of Notebooks from the Azure Sentinel GitHub page.

1. From Azure Sentinel, select **Notebooks**. This opens the Notebooks blade.

Azure Sentinel Notebooks Include:

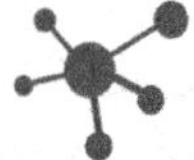

Alert Investigation and Hunting

Quickly triage different classes of alerts by enriching them with related activity and events from multiple data sources.

Endpoint Host Guided Hunting

Hunt for signs of a compromise by drilling down into the security relevant activities related to specific endpoint hosts.

Office Logon Anomalies Guided Hunting

Investigate suspicious logons in Office365 data by visualizing geographic data and displaying unusual logon patterns.

Clone Azure Sentinel Notebooks | Go to your Notebooks

2. Click the **Clone Azure Sentinel Notebooks** button. This redirects you to `https://notebooks.azure.com`, which is currently in preview.

Microsoft Azure Notebooks Preview | My Projects | Help

(i) This site uses cookies for analytics, personalized content and ads. By continuing to browse this site, you agree to this use.

Import from GitHub

Welcome to Azure Notebooks!

To import this GitHub repository (https://github.com/Azure/Azure-Sentinel) click import below.

Import | Return to GitHub

3. Click **Import**.

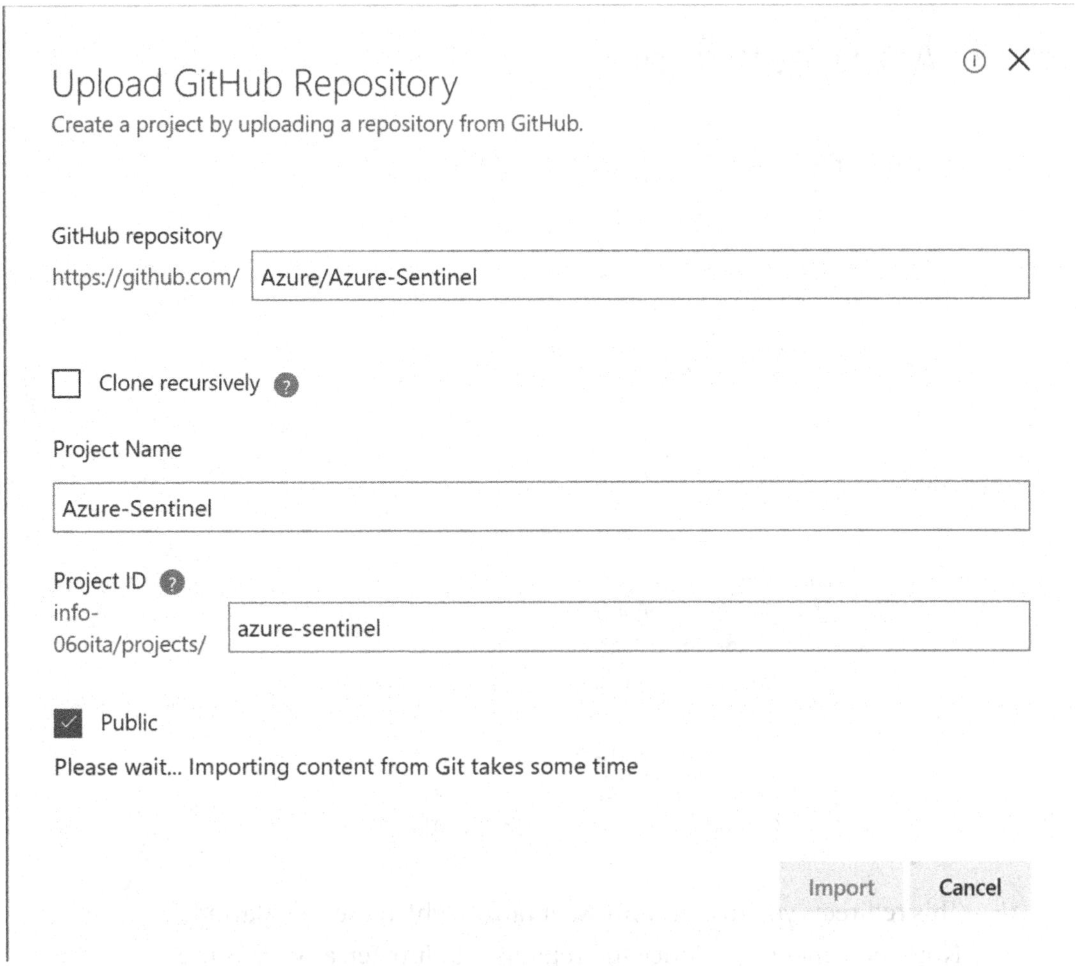

Upload GitHub Repository

Create a project by uploading a repository from GitHub.

GitHub repository

https://github.com/ Azure/Azure-Sentinel

Clone recursively

Project Name

Azure-Sentinel

Project ID

info-06oita/projects/ azure-sentinel

Public

Please wait... Importing content from Git takes some time

Import Cancel

4. In the Upload GitHub Repository window, click **Import** once more. It takes a few minutes to get all the provided examples uploaded to your Notebooks environment.
5. Once cloned, select **Notebooks / Sample-Notebooks** to open the examples. The Get-Started example is shown in Figure 8-1.

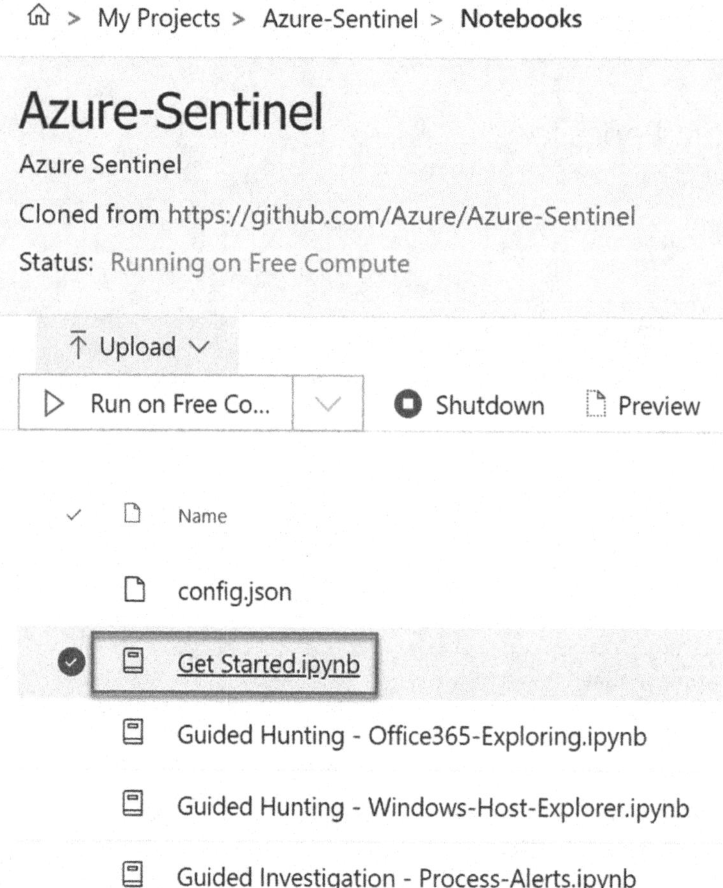

6. This redirects you to a new browser tab, in which the Get Started Notebook opens up. Notice the reference to Jupyter, as well as the actual context of the Notebook, based on different sections.
   - Get Started (Markdown format)
   - Prerequisite Check (what needs to be completed on your machine in order to use this Notebook)
   - Actual scripts (this could be Python, C#, or F# code)

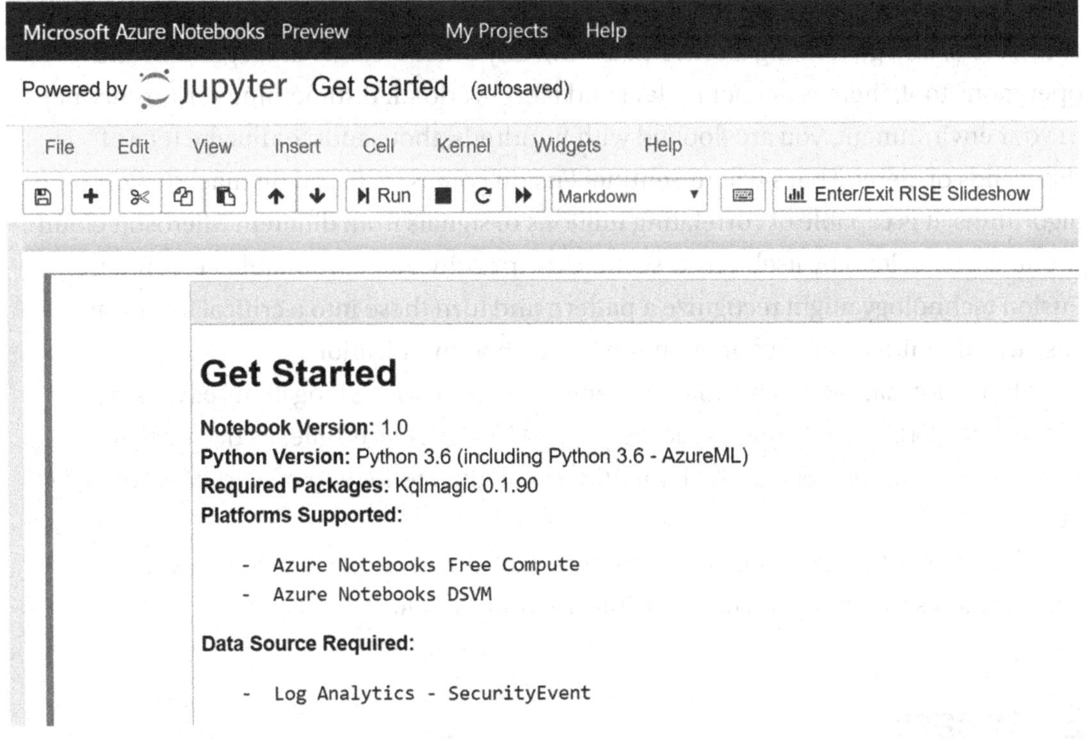

7. This completes the steps on how to use Azure Notebooks to complement hunting in Azure Sentinel.

Summary

Azure Notebooks are an adaptation of the open source Project Jupyter. Notebooks allow you to define full workflows based on Python, C#, or F# code, with Markdown documentation, graphics, and more. Although Project Jupyter was initially used for data analytics that were not security specific, it nicely integrates with Azure Sentinel for optimizing security analytics.

Azure Sentinel Fusion

Although it's not available yet, let's close this chapter on Azure Sentinel by talking about another cool feature-in-the-making—Fusion.

It should be clear by now that Azure Sentinel focuses on log analytics, data connectors, and generating alerts. But as with any other systems management and operations tool, there is danger in data and alert overload. If something serious happens in your environment, you are flooded with hundreds, thousands, or maybe tens of thousands of alerts. That's where Sentinel Fusion comes in. Based on machine learning algorithms, it is capable of correlating millions of signals from different Microsoft cloud products. Each item by itself might seem a low-priority, non-actionable item, but the Fusion technology might recognize a pattern and turn these into a critical important case that definitely needs your attention for further investigation.

More information on Fusion is available on the Microsoft blog at `https://azure.microsoft.com/en-us/blog/reducing-security-alert-fatigue-using-machine-learning-in-azure-sentinel/`. It mentions a median reduction of alert noise up to 90 percent.

The power of Fusion comes from built-in machine learning, which will allow an organization's own machine learning information as well.

Summary

This chapter covered as much as we could describe about the currently in-preview service Azure Sentinel. You should now have a good understanding what the service does, how it maps, and how it differs from Azure Security Center and Azure Log Analytics. We guided you through the initial deployment and showed you how to enable several data source connectors to feed the engine. You learned how to configure alerts, which resulted in cases. We also discussed the scenarios around hunting, which helps you to proactively scan your environment and search for security issues before they become a serious threat. Finally, we introduced Fusion, a promising machine learning engine to be added to Azure Sentinel.

Index

P. De Tender et al., *Pro Azure Governance and Security*, https://doi.org/10.1007/978-1-4842-4910-9

B

C

M

N

O

P, Q

R

S

T, U, V, W, X, Y, Z